STEELY DAN
Reelin' in the Years
BY BRIAN SWEET

D1589444

OMNIBUS PRESS

LONDON · NEW YORK · SYDNEY

First published 1994 © Omnibus Press
This edition, copyright © 2000 Omnibus Press
(A Division of Book Sales Limited)

Edited by Chris Charlesworth
Cover designed by Phil Gambrill
Picture research by Brian Sweet & David Brolan

ISBN: 0.7119.8279.1
Order No: OP48185

Exclusive Distributors:
Book Sales Limited,
8/9 Frith Street,
London W1V 5TZ, UK.

Music Sales Corporation,
257 Park Avenue South,
New York, NY 10010, USA.

Macmillan Distrubution Services,
53 Park West Drive,
Derrimut, Vic 3030
Australia

To the Music Trade only:
Music Sales Limited,
8/9 Frith Street,
London W1V 5TZ, UK.

Every effort has been made to trace the copyright holders of the photographs in this book but
one or two were unreachable. We would be grateful if the photographers concerned would
contact us.

Printed by Creative Print and Design (Wales), Ebbw Vale

A catalogue record for this book is available from the British Library.

www.omnibuspress.com

Contents

INTRODUCTION 4

ACKNOWLEDGEMENTS 6

CHAPTER I .... *My Old School* 7

CHAPTER II .... *Shuffling Up Your Downs* 17

CHAPTER III .... *Proud To Be Your Slave* 37

CHAPTER IV .... *Thirty-Five Sweet Goodbyes* 53

CHAPTER V .... *Slow Hand Row* 64

CHAPTER VI .... *Laughing At The Frozen Rain* 85

CHAPTER VII .... *Luckless Pedestrians* 98

CHAPTER VIII .... *The Crimson Tide* 114

CHAPTER IX .... *Bodacious Cowboys* 133

CHAPTER X .... *New Frontier* 157

CHAPTER XI .... *Big Noise, New York* 169

CHAPTER XII .... *C'mon Snakehips* 194

CHAPTER XIII .... *Sizzling Like An Isotope* 207

DISCOGRAPHY 219

INDEX 235

Reelin' In The Years

Ironically, the idea that there were evidently other people in this world who craved information about Steely Dan as much as I did came to me in 1987 – at a time when Becker and Fagen had been divorced for more than six years and when they were conspicuous by their absence. The Steely Dan fan magazine, *Metal Leg*, was founded that year but when in 1994 that idea had expanded into a full band biography, Becker and Fagen had at least emerged from their respective musical hidey-holes and were gigging again. Having got married and been reintroduced to the fun of local live gigs by his wife Libby Titus, Donald Fagen had slowly but surely regained his musical appetite after a desolate decade of depression and creative block and unfurled a relative blaze of activity: the New York Rock and Soul Revue album and mini-tour, a second solo album, 'Kamakiriad' and two consecutive US summer tours in which Becker and Fagen actually sanctioned being billed as Steely Dan again. And the revival continued: Walter Becker released his first solo album, 'Eleven Tracks Of Whack', then came Steely Dan's first official live album, 'Alive In America', and Steely Dan's Art Crimes Orchestra traversed three continents on a mini world tour in 1996.

But all of those events pale into insignificance when compared to the release of the first Steely Dan studio album, 'Two Against Nature', in almost twenty years. Now that really is an event worthy of celebration. Despite all their recent peripheral musical activities, Becker and Fagen have been and always will be most at home in the recording studio and Steely Dan's incredible reputation hangs on those impossibly long hours spent writing the songs in the first place and then fretting ceaselessly over the execution of those compositions in luxurious recording studios. No group or artist can ever be presumptuous enough to live up to the impossible expectation of such a lengthy recording hiatus, and it speaks volumes for the integrity of their re-formed partnership that Becker and Fagen have emerged from that self-imposed recess with another fine record and with their heads held high. I'm sure Becker and Fagen would be the first to admit that they cannot be described as prolific, but then quality is always preferable to quantity.

Speaking early on in the round of promotional interviews for the new album, Donald Fagen asserted that he felt he had "plenty of juice left" and so optimism predominates; 'Two Against Nature' heralds a new beginning. Becker and Fagen might be using the same name, but Steely Dan 2000 bears virtually no resemblance to the one that recorded 'Aja' and 'Gaucho' or any of those which preceded them. With the advent of the internet and to a lesser extent their rapturous receptions on recent tours, Becker and Fagen have at last realised that they have a vast ready-made audience for this new career of theirs and that the "loyal fandom" have merely been in long-term hibernation with them, waiting patiently for the buds of spring to bloom again.

At this point, it seems that Becker and Fagen's band-that-never-was is back on the music industry's lips as never before and with a top ten album, sure-fire touring triumphs this summer and perhaps most importantly of all doing everything explicitly on their own terms, all looks set fair for the ever-burgeoning second career of Steely Dan.

Brian Sweet, March 2000

Acknowledgements

I would like to thank everyone who agreed to be interviewed for this book: Gary Katz, Roger Nichols, Denny Dias, Kenny Vance, Chuck Rainey, Michael Omartian, Daniel Lazerus, Elliot Scheiner, Keith Thomas, Jimmy Vivino, Bernard Purdie, Terence Boylan, Warren Wallace, Steve Barri, Royce Jones, Paul Griffin, Peter Locke, Ed Caraeff, Ed Lambert, Lonnie Yongue, Richie Lifschutz, Peter Aaron, Jane Aaron, Elliott Randall, Mary Kupersmith, Sandy Yaguda, Wayne Robins, Randy California and Mrs Elinor Fagen.

Unfortunately, for reasons best known only to themselves, Walter Becker and Donald Fagen declined to be interviewed despite several earnest requests. There were others whom I was keen on speaking to but was unable to locate, including Joel Cohen and Gloria "Porky" Granola and Jenny "Bucky" Soule. If any of these people read this, I would still be interested to hear from them.

My thanks also to the following people: Dave Edney, Trevor Johnson, Martin Stone, James Harris, John Sakamoto, Robert Colledge, Steve Coram, Katie Bayliss, Sue Cox, Pete Fogel, Shari Kamburoff and Joe "The Big Man" Schmitz in Cincinnati. For information on *Metal Leg*, the Steely Dan fanzine, please write to Metal Leg, PO Box 244, Bridgwater, Somerset TA6 3ZE, England or visit www.metalleg.com

CHAPTER I

My Old School

The Steely Dan story opens on January 10, 1948, when Donald Jay Fagen, its senior partner, was born in Passaic, a town of around 55,000 inhabitants in North Eastern New Jersey on America's East Coast. Donald was the first child and only son of Joseph 'Jerry' Fagen, a Jewish accountant, and his wife, Elinor. Six years later they had a daughter called Susan.

If Donald Fagen inherited any of his musical talent, it probably came from his mother who, between the ages of twelve and seventeen, sang with a band at a small hotel in Parksville in what was popularly known as the Borscht Belt, a predominantly Jewish resort area among the Catskill Mountains in upstate New York. Elinor loved singing and each summer performed popular songs of the era with a small group of musicians until increasingly serious attacks of stage fright forced her to discontinue. "I have a bit of that myself," her son would later admit.

A lover of all types of music, particularly Broadway musicals, Elinor Fagen sang almost constantly around the house while Donald was growing up and he attributes his own peculiar vocal phrasing to his mother's influence. She had a large record collection and would sing along to records by singers who were popular in the early Fifties, among them Tommy Dorsey, Helen O'Connell and Sylvia Sims. "I can't ever remember when there was silence around the house," Donald has recalled. "She was either playing records or singing. She was an excellent phraser and I think just listening to her sing all my life gave me a natural swing type of feel."

When Donald was ten and in sixth grade the family moved from Passaic to Fair Lawn, New Jersey, and soon afterwards moved again to a ranch-style home in Kendall Park, also in New Jersey, which was close to Princeton University. Donald disliked the neighbourhood; it was true suburbia. Writing about this period of his life in 'The Nightfly' he described it as... "One of the worst suburbs I've ever seen. It was a brand new development with houses that were all exactly identical, mounds of dirt instead of lawns and those little twigs instead of trees. It was very desolate and totally stultifying. To me it was like a prison. I was very upset about it. I think after that I had a different attitude towards my parents. I think I lost faith in their judgement. What I mainly realised was their judgement wasn't the same as mine, their view of life was different. In fact, it was probably the first time I realised I had my own view of life."

From a very young age, Donald would fall asleep listening to music. His first love was rock'n'roll, especially Chuck Berry whose 'Reelin' And Rockin'' was the first record he bought. He liked the lyrics and "that nasty strident sound", as he would later describe it. But rock'n'roll was rapidly superseded by a precocious preference for jazz. "It was very fashionable at the time for kids to go to the Newport Jazz Festival," Fagen has said. "For some it was probably for the social thing – probably for the majority. My cousin told me what radio station to listen to, I heard some of their records and was knocked out. My sister started taking piano lessons and I started learning to play off those records. I became a real jazz snob. I lost interest in rock'n' roll and started developing an anti-social personality."

By the time Donald was eleven he was listening to Symphony Sid's jazz radio show from Manhattan and he can recall finding a record in a shop – pianist Red Garland's 'Jazz Junction' – that he had heard played on Symphony Sid's show. "I went down to E. J. Korvette's and there it was right in this bin, along with a lot of other albums with unfamiliar names. I bought it and ever since I've tried to imitate his style in the privacy of my own home."

With jazz now his preferred choice of music, Donald developed a strong prejudice against rock'n'roll. Part of the reason was the dearth of authentic rock'n'roll that swept America after the first wave of rockers disappeared in the late Fifties. Elvis was in the army, Chuck Berry was in jail, Jerry Lee Lewis was ostracised for marrying his 13-year-old cousin and Buddy Holly was dead. Others, by dint of circumstance or action by conservative forces, had been temporarily silenced. "In the early Sixties you started having a lot of cover records, white copies, white rock'n'roll records and Frankie Avalon, and they stopped playing a lot of black music for a couple of years there, and I lost interest in it," Donald explained. His prejudice against rock'n'roll would last until 1966 after America had been invaded by British groups, spearheaded by The Beatles and The Rolling Stones.

When he was twelve years old, his parents bought Donald a piano and it was evident from his early efforts that he had a talent for the instrument. The first song he played was 'Exodus', the theme from the Otto Preminger film that was a hit for Ferrante and Teicher in 1960. Although it was Donald's younger sister, Susan, who studied piano first, the Fagens took Donald to the Princeton New School of Music where they assumed he would probably want to take lessons in order to make the most of his talent. Donald played 'Exodus' for the teacher, who noted that he played good chords, but said that she couldn't teach him unless he was prepared to learn to sight read. On the way home in the car Donald told his parents that he had no interest in learning to sight read, he just wanted to play. In the end he continued with his constant practise but took no formal lessons. As soon as he arrived home from school each day, he would sit down at the piano and play his favourite songs for hours on end. He also started composing his own material: "Little songs about mythological subjects and stuff we learned in school."

The only real tuition he received came from a family friend who visited the Fagen home and showed Donald some jazz chords. Later, when Donald was fifteen, his father drove him into Princeton to attend a music theory course run by a *New York Times* music critic named Wilson. Donald loved it, although he didn't fully appreciate all the theory. Most of his tuition came from listening to jazz records and emulating the chords he heard.

When a couple of jazz loving elder cousins befriended Donald, he became something of a jazz élitist and, in the 'cool' fashion of the times, took to wearing black turtleneck sweaters. More importantly, he spent so much time playing the piano, he didn't have many neighbourhood or school friends. Most weekends, he and his cousins took the bus into Manhattan to visit jazz clubs and watch performers like Sonny Rollins, Thelonious Monk, Miles Davis and Charlie Mingus. Donald has recalled how on one occasion at a

Charlie Mingus gig at the Village Vanguard, a club in Greenwich Village, he sat in the "kiddies' section" – the banquettes along the wall right next to the drum kit – and the power of Dannie Richmond's drumming caused his glass of Coke to keep sliding towards the edge of the table. He had to continually push it back to the centre of his table to stop it falling on to the floor. Donald was most impressed. A measure of his dedication to attending these gigs can be gleaned from the fact that if he missed his last bus home he was stranded. On one occasion he did miss the last bus home and was forced to spend the night in the Port Authority bus terminal sleeping on a bench. His parents were blissfully unaware of this but Midtown Manhattan was a considerably safer place in those days than it is now.

Donald attended South Brunswick High School in New Jersey where he shunned most of his fellow students in a typical display of cultural superiority. However, he did participate in some of the school activities, playing a baritone horn in the school marching band. In his High School Yearbook he is described as a "jazz enthusiast (he formed a jazz trio there), an individualist and a thinker". He harboured journalistic ambitions and contributed to the school magazine, and there is evidence to suggest that his cynical, acerbic personality was already past the development stage. It was the custom at South Brunswick for each pupil to make a "will" on leaving and in his Fagen left "seven barrels of steaming, fetid boredom". One of the few sporting interests he developed was a fondness for table tennis – a pastime which has continued to this day.

When the Fagens acquired a black and white cabinet TV in the late Fifties Donald enjoyed detective shows, particularly *Peter Gunn*, and grew to love Henry Mancini's jazz-based theme music. He even bought a number of *Peter Gunn* soundtrack albums and Mancini records, and often mentioned "TV-style arrangements" when discussing Steely Dan's music in later years. He would write about his love for Henry Mancini in an article in *Première* magazine in 1987.

A fan of the Beat Poets, Jack Kerouac in particular, Donald went to Bard College in 1965 to study English Literature. His first room-mate was an art student named Lonnie Yongue who had already been at Bard for two years when Fagen arrived, so he took on the responsibility for showing the newcomer around. Like Donald, Yongue was trying to teach himself to work the saxophone but unlike Donald he kept unusual hours, staying up all night painting and sleeping during the day. He was also a heavy drinker who experimented with a variety of drugs and, in his own words, "blacked out almost every night". Yongue and Donald lived like Cox and Box, with Yongue getting up as Donald prepared for bed and going to bed when Donald was getting up. When their paths occasionally crossed, Yongue would say, "Good morning, Fagen", and Donald would respond with, "Jesus, Lonnie, you've turned it all around".

Some students, including Donald, made sandwiches to sell in the dormitories after ten o'clock to make a little much needed extra money. Yongue's studio was adjacent to their kitchen and Fagen listened while he read aloud passages from William Burroughs' *The Naked Lunch* as the sandwiches were being prepared. Tuna salad was their biggest seller and Yongue positively hated tuna. Cleaning up after the caterers was not one of Yongue's most treasured Bard memories.

Yongue soon recognised Donald's true vocation and questioned why he was studying English Literature and not music. Eventually he helped persuade Fagen to switch to music but "he was miserable", Yongue has said. Despite this, in the summer of 1966 Donald went to Berklee College of Music in Boston for the summer, but his heart wasn't really in it and he admitted later that he spent most of his time "goofing around on the street" and smoking pot with his friends.

While he was at Boston his music teacher apparently landed a job he couldn't possibly afford to pass up, so he gave Donald three months' worth of tuition in one lesson. Fittingly, Donald lived on Symphony Road and remembers... "It was a foul summer. I had almost no money and was eating a lot of brown rice. But I picked up a lot of good stuff from the Berklee course. I remember the practice rooms were always being used at Berklee, so I'd take the bus up to MIT and use their practice rooms. Amazingly, MIT had these great practice rooms with little pianos in them. You'd go to this huge vault-like door and open it up and go in. I'm sure I could have survived a nuclear holocaust in one of those rooms. But it was great; the pianos were tuned up really nicely and I'd just play scales all day. And eat brown rice. But I never had the patience to be a professional musician. There are great gaps in my musical knowledge. I'm mostly self taught."

Disillusioned with the teaching methods and lacking the discipline needed for a serious music course, Fagen returned to Bard after his summer at Berklee and resumed his English Literature course. They were no longer room-mates but when Lonnie Yongue bought Traffic's 1967 album 'Mr. Fantasy' Fagen borrowed a copy and hung on to it for a long time and was heavily influenced by the album. When Yongue did a painting of Fagen and himself, with Fagen on one side of a big room and Yongue on the other side, Yongue's art teacher told him it was a classic study in alienation. Both parties fit the bill. Unfortunately, the painting was destroyed in a fire in 1967. In his final year Donald wrote an extensive Senior Class Project on the novels of Hermann Hesse, including *Siddhartha, Narziss und Goldmund* and *Peter Camenzind*. He eventually graduated in 1969.

During his time at Bard Donald did take some formal music lessons: "I learned music theory and harmony at college, but didn't get as far as harsh discipline in music," he has recalled. "I studied some orchestration and composition and definitely knew I was going for a career in music of some kind, even though I ended up with a degree in literature." He often speculated that if he hadn't made it in the music business, he would have probably ended up as an English teacher.

But the real turning point in Fagen's life occurred two years before graduation, on an autumn day in 1967 when he was walking past the college music club at Bard. Most days he would have bypassed the building without so much as a second thought, but the music flowing from the room that day stopped him in his tracks. He went inside to investigate and found a baby-faced, bespectacled blond kid sitting on the stage, cradling a red Epiphone guitar and playing what sounded to Donald like very authentic blues licks.

Fagen would remember the encounter clearly years later. "(He had) a little amplifier turned up all the way, bending notes and getting sustain. He'd been listening to all these

Howlin' Wolf and B. B. King records. Well, I'd never really heard anything like that."

So he approached the guitarist and introduced himself. The guitar player was called Walter Becker.

❧

The other half of the duo who would become Steely Dan was a couple of years younger than Donald Fagen. Walter Becker was born on Monday, February 20, 1950, in the Forest Hills area of Queens in New York. Like Donald, he has one sister, Wendy, who is three years his junior.

The first music Walter Becker remembers hearing was Fifties pop music. "Rosemary Clooney comes to mind," he recalls. "I remember (hearing her) in the back of my father's car driving down the West Side Highway in New York City." Like Fagen, Becker developed a similarly precocious love of jazz, but failed to learn to work the saxophone and in 1966 took up the guitar instead. "I was a self-taught player. I learned mostly from other players," he says.

Walter's ambition to become a saxophone player was inspired by Charlie Parker, but as a budding guitarist, he'd taken some guitar lessons from a young neighbourhood kid who called himself Randy California who'd moved to New York from his native Los Angeles in 1966 to do session work. California shared the same birthday as Becker except he was a year younger, and he taught Becker some blues guitar tricks and techniques. California himself had been taught to play by his drum playing step-father, Ed Cassidy. Originally called Randy Wolfe, he changed his name to California and later went on to form Spirit with Cassidy and two ex-members of The Red Roosters.

Becker and California lived close to each other in Forest Hills and Becker owned a Gibson Les Paul guitar which he kept at California's apartment and which he tried to sell to him for $50. California, who was still only 15, thought the instrument was too heavy and resisted the deal. Becker played bass when he and California played with some other local musicians.

California lived a penurious existence in a rough neighbourhood with his mother, three sisters and Ed Cassidy in a basement flat. His mother taught him his first chords when he was eight years old, so he was able to give the eternally keen Becker some basic instruction. But Walter's initial attraction to the guitar was frustrated by his inability to get beyond the technique he had devised for himself and he switched to bass guitar which he found easier. "I was attracted to the idea of only four strings," he said. "This would simplify matters considerably."

Becker attended Stuyvesant High School in New York and started at Bard College in 1967. He enjoyed hanging out there, but neglected his studies and later admitted..."I wasn't very impressed with the programme. They were asking me to read stupid books and get up early in the morning. I couldn't relate to that at all. I did meet some interesting people there. It was basically a good scene for my disasters." Becker only stayed for three semesters studying languages before flunking out.

Becker was 17-years-old and had only been at Bard for one semester when Donald

Fagen chanced on his playing in the college music club. In fact, he had already approached Fagen once about joining one of his groups on guitar but at that point Fagen already had three occasional guitar players, although none of them were particularly skilled on the instrument. Now Donald had good reason to reassess Becker's worth.

"He had a three man guitar section," Walter has said. "One guy who played badly and offensively, one guy who played very crudely and one guy who just wore the guitar in an interesting way." At the time Donald was trying to incorporate jazz ideas into the band against considerable resistance from the other members.

The band went under the name of The Leather Canary but at various other times Donald would change the personnel – and name – to suit the gig. The Bad Rock Group might play the Hallowe'en party, while The Don Fagen Jazz Trio might play wherever a gig was available or at charity benefits such as NAACP nights. Bard College wasn't blessed with too many competent musicians, but Fagen was the piano-playing jack-of-all trades who could at short notice assemble whichever type of group was needed for whatever kind of dance or party.

Now, by a stroke of good fortune, Donald had heard what Walter Becker could play. That he was considerably more talented than any of the other guitarists in Donald's groups was obvious, but equally important was their discovery that they both listened to the same jazz radio stations and disc jockeys which broadcast from Manhattan, liked the same genre of Beat writers – William Burroughs, Gregory Corso, Jack Kerouac, Allen Ginsberg and Lawrence Ferlinghetti – and, perhaps more significant in the long term, shared a similar dry sense of humour. They had so much in common that an immediate and lasting friendship was formed.

"We were writing songs together within a day of meeting each other," Donald said. "We had both been jazz fans since we were nine or 10 years old, listened to the same jazz shows and radio and we both got into soul and pop in the mid-Sixties." The songs they began to write reflected their caustic sense of humour, their depth of academic knowledge and their taste in arcane lyrics.

The rapidly established bond between Becker and Fagen convinced the latter to find a place for his younger partner in one of his groups. Donald was excited by the encounter and reckoned that he had made a significant breakthrough in his long running quest for a partner who shared his own idealistic musical aspirations.

"We were jazz fans," he said. "We were writing tunes where some of the chords weren't triads and you couldn't use your capo that much. It was very bizarre. The bands that we came up with sounded like The Kingsmen performing Frank Zappa material."

"Donald was the dean of the pick-up band syndrome at Bard," said Walter. "At the beginning of every term someone would re-open the club and they'd need a band for two nights. There were about eight musicians on the whole campus, and most of them were poor. Most of our bands were made up of guys who hadn't mastered your basic Dave Van Ronk techniques. They had a limited exposure to the things that we were trying to emulate. There were never enough people to put together a band where everybody was a strong player."

Although they started working together, they had no real plan as to how to proceed, other than that they wanted to form a band good enough to warrant a recording contract. Their main problem was finding singers. Donald had never sung before. "Walter had done a few gigs at the Night Owl in the Village before he got to college so I was sort of hoping he would sing, but neither of us wanted to do it," he said. Additionally, Becker had aspirations towards becoming a bass player but nobody seemed to need one so he reverted to the guitar for the time being and, in a poker game at Bard, won a huge JBL Malibu speaker with 1000lb of sand in the bottom. Walter liked nothing better than cranking up his Telecaster through the JBL and blasting Jimi Hendrix solos all over Ward Manor.

Donald Fagen was as meticulous then as he became later in his life when it came to auditioning musicians. Several of his friends tried out for his band at Bard but he wouldn't lower his standards, even for close pals. Almost all of them were given the thumbs down. Some of them understood; others didn't. "In the early days we were going to put together a band that was modelled on The Velvet Underground," said Donald. "We auditioned a few girls to have the Nico role." At the time, of course, the Velvets had yet to acquire the Bohemian chic they would attain long after their demise, and as another Bard student commented, "auditioning" girls was a full time occupation anyway.

In fact, rehearsal space at Bard was difficult to find until one entrepreneurial student hit on the idea of using an abandoned chicken coop. He stuck egg crates to the walls to act as soundproofing and various Bard bands used the room. There were several drawbacks: in the summer the overpowering heat often led to the hippest characters on campus being reduced to stripping down to their underpants in order to survive conditions and then there was a very low ceiling which bruised many a skull when players stood upright without due care.

A requirement of the music department at Bard was the equivalent of an oral examination which took the form of a performance. The student had to select a piece and then perform it in front of the lecturers and any guests invited by the student. Most of the students chose a classical piece, but Fagen got a very large band of musicians together and performed a nine-minute reading of Dylan's 'Like A Rolling Stone'. The band consisted of two acoustic pianos, an electric piano, bass, drums, three guitars, percussion and organ and sounded like Phil Spector's Wall of Sound. The examiners had never before heard anything like it and were aghast.

A fellow student of Becker and Fagen's at Bard College was Terence Boylan, affectionately known as "Boona", one time member of The Appletree Theatre and writer on the *Buffalo Broadside*. Through their mutual interest in music, Boylan had got to know Becker and Fagen well and had struck up a friendship with them. They played occasional gigs together and a particularly memorable one was at a dance in Blithewood where their set featured The Temptations' 'Ain't Too Proud To Beg', Martha and The Vandellas' 'Dancin' In The Streets', Chuck Berry's 'Route 66', several Dylan tunes including 'Just Like Tom Thumb's Blues' and 'Outlaw Blues', and Little Richard's 'Lucille'. They had only managed two rehearsals and were therefore reduced to repeating the set and jamming to fill in time. They even played Becker and Fagen's own composition 'Who Got the Credit?' and Walter Becker later admitted that they played 'Route 66' no less than five times.

Terence Boylan maintains that Becker and Fagen's personalities were already well developed at Bard; while most other students were at emotional and intellectual sixes and sevens, Becker and Fagen were already in the process of cultivating the acute sense of irony that would become the basis of Steely Dan. They seemed to know exactly what they wanted in any given situation.

On one occasion they sat Boylan down to explain to him their version of the history of the world. First came the formation of the planet, the cooling of the earth, the discovery of fire, the invention of the wheel, then Charlie Parker and "it's been downhill ever since". Becker and Fagen firmly believed that all musical innovation ceased after "Bird"; all who followed had merely found ways to blow his riffs in slower or slightly different forms.

Boylan was very much influenced by Van Morrison, The Band, and early Bob Dylan. When he secured a recording deal with MGM, he enlisted Becker and Fagen's assistance with the album and they helped him arrange all his own compositions before they went into the studio. The album was recorded at the Hit Factory (owned by songwriter/producer Jerry Ragavoy) and was the first time that Becker and Fagen had been into a real recording studio. Walter Becker especially was impressed by the potential of multitrack recording and the array of studio gimmickry and kept asking questions; Fagen, on the other hand, was much more concerned with getting the parts right. Both were amazed that they were getting paid for doing something that they loved doing and had been doing for free anyway at Bard. They were also impressed by the timing of session drummers Herb Lovelle, Jimmy Johnson and Darius Davenport.

Jerry Ragavoy suggested that Boylan might like to hire session bass player Chuck Rainey for a couple of the songs and he did play on one but it didn't make the final cut. Boylan had written all the songs himself – including his own arrangement of Bob Dylan's 'Subterranean Homesick Blues' which he retitled 'Pillow' – and produced the album himself. Boylan attempted a Becker and Fagen composition called 'Stone Piano' but it was in Fagen's key and he dropped the song – a decision he later regretted. Boylan admitted steering Fagen into playing piano parts that *he* wanted to hear though Fagen could probably have come up with something better.

Becker overdubbed the guitar parts and the album was recorded in less than two weeks, and that included some marathon 10-12 hour sessions. 'Alias Boona' was recorded and mixed for $21,000, which was slightly over budget. Boylan moved to another studio to mix the record and admitted that with all the technical problems, he blew it. "The only interesting thing about that record was the fact that it was our first real experience of a modern recording studio," said Fagen later.

Boylan had met photographer Eliot Landy at Bob Dylan's house in Woodstock when he called to show Dylan some photos he had taken for 'Nashville Skyline' and Boylan hired him to take the cover photo of 'Alias Boona' which showed him with his parents' Old English Sheepdog.

Boylan and his elder brother John were staff writers/producers and he took Becker and Fagen to see his publishers, Koppleman and Rubin, who had been responsible for signing Tim Hardin and The Lovin' Spoonful. They had recently signed Petula Clark and were looking for material for her, and Becker and Fagen played them two songs, 'Who Got The Credit?' and 'Bus Driver Is A Fruitcake'. Not surprisingly, Koppleman and Rubin scratched their heads and had no idea what the songs were about... they certainly weren't suitable for Petula Clark.

After the release of 'Alias Boona', Boylan and his band, including Becker and Fagen and Herb Lovelle, rehearsed for a twelve date tour to promote it. In the end, because they had to go back to college, they managed to squeeze in only one solitary gig to a crowd of undergraduates at the Alexander Hall in Princeton, New Jersey. Boylan said they were more organised in regard to the transport and equipment than the actual set and had only rehearsed a couple of times, but at each rehearsal they ran through some Becker and Fagen tunes with Boylan singing lead and Becker and Fagen joining in on harmony vocals. Becker and Fagen asked him to write out the set list and the keys of the songs before the gig and although on many of the numbers they were figuring it out as they went along, they were very cool about the whole thing. The band was well received but it was to be Becker and Fagen's first and last gig with Terence Boylan.

Bard had been subjected to regular drug busts throughout the Sixties and on May 8, 1969 at 4.45 am at least two dozen cars belonging to state troopers descended on the college. At the same time, Sachs Annexe was ransacked by the Dutchess County Sheriff's (Lawrence Quinlan) men. Quinlan, in tandem with the state troopers and a number of informants, searched two dormitories, several off-campus houses and arrested 44 people, among them Donald Fagen, Walter Becker and Fagen's girlfriend, Dorothy White. Walter had already officially left Bard by this time but liked hanging out there and was sleeping on another student's floor. Consequently the sheriff had warrants for everyone except him. Ironically, Gordon Liddy of subsequent Watergate fame was the assistant district attorney that year and they typed one up for Walter anyway for fourth degree possession of marijuana. Walter called him "The Wild Bill Hickok of the Judiciary".

Fagen was dragged off to Poughkeepsie jail with the others, and the most traumatic part of the ordeal was having his treasured long hair shorn. Sitting in the cell in his standard issue prisoner's uniform with cropped hair, Fagen looked very sorry for himself.

Bob Dylan had earlier made his comment on the predictability of the Bard drugs raids ("Must bust in early May/Orders from the DA") in his song 'Subterranean Homesick Blues'. In the same song the couplet "The pump don't work/Cos the vandals took the handles" also purportedly refers to an incident at Bard.

The college freed the thirty-six students (eight were non-students) arrested by providing bail bonds totalling $141,000. Their legal fees alone came to some $1,800, but the bail bonds and legal fees would eventually be billed to the students.

At a hastily convened meeting of those arrested, lawyers advised everyone to keep their experiences confidential. They pointed out that an officer is supposed to announce his purpose and state that he has a warrant for whatever purpose; if the suspect requests to see the warrant, the officer must show it. But even if the suspect doesn't request to see the warrant, it does not vitiate the lawfulness of the arrest. Also, physical force could be used to enter a room if there is the possibility that evidence could be destroyed between the time of the knock and the answer. The President of the college, Reamer Kline, assured the students that the college would stand behind them.

Force had indeed been used on several of the doors in Ward Manor and students were ordered to do different things: some to stay in bed, others to get out of bed so that it could be searched, while others were body-searched. The officers' biggest mistake proved to be in not identifying themselves to the students.

According to the students, officers were hooting and laughing as they searched rooms and they even played a Beatles' album in one room. Posters were ripped down, beds were torn apart, curtains were pulled down and fireplaces inspected. Almost all their rooms were left in total chaos and as quickly as the police had descended, a crowd of students gathered and began chanting "Pigs!" One wag began playing 'Gee, Officer Krupke' from *West Side Story* very loudly on his record deck.

"Every spring they used to have a bust on campus," Becker said some years later. "You know, just to raise a little hell in town and a little revenue for the local lawyers." But after all the fuss, all charges were later dropped. One month later, in June, Donald graduated and moved back to New York with his girlfriend.

Having graduated, Donald Fagen could now devote all his concentration to what had by now become his obsession – writing songs with Walter Becker. They had even settled on a suitable adjective to describe their material: "Cheesy".

❧

Shuffling Up
Your Downs

Towards the end of 1969 Donald Fagen was holed up in a house on President Street in Brooklyn with his girlfriend, Dorothy White, and a medical student called Richard Ransohoff. Walter Becker lived out in Queens with his sister and grandmother. Together, they began trying to sell these "cheesy" compositions to publishing companies in New York. Little did they realise how frustrating and arduous this would be.

Fresh out of college, Becker and Fagen knew next to nothing about the way the music business worked. Naïvely, they decided to hawk material around music publishing offices in Manhattan without realising that this was antiquated and, indeed, legally unwise. But with the flush of youth and an optimism of which Mister Micawber would have been proud, they set out with their black and white songbook under their arms intent on impressing their worth upon some unsuspecting music publisher.

They didn't even have a tape of their songs. They couldn't afford the studio time to record even remotely proficient demos and even if they had been able to afford it, they lacked the necessary expertise to know how to approach a studio recording session. Without a demo tape – perhaps the single most essential ingredient needed to sell popular songs – they boldly opted for an old-fashioned personal performance.

More often than not they would be turned away at the door, but if the scrawny composers succeeded in bluffing their way past a succession of receptionists and secretaries, Fagen would take a seat at the omnipresent piano, Becker would stand alongside, they'd open their exercise book of lyrics and proceed to actually sing a selection of their songs for the startled publisher.

The limitations of the manner in which they imposed themselves upon world weary publishers were soon evident. After only a couple of songs they would be told with ominous regularity and in no uncertain terms to leave forthwith, the words "no commercial potential!" resounding loudly in their ears. On other occasions, a telephone would ring during their performance or other trivial interruptions would break the listener's concentration and their continuity. Even when they did manage to complete a song, the obscurity of their lyrics and the unusual structure of their melodies generally presaged an end to their hopes of a breakthrough for yet another day. "When you're stepped on there, you're done for good," Walter Becker would reflect on the finality of their frustration and depression in New York.

This depression was compounded because they had no escape from failure. Obsessed as they were with their quest, they had hardly any social life to speak of and what there was had to involve little cash outlay. Occasionally they visited the home of a neighbourhood friend in Brooklyn called Richie Lifschutz and played chess for hours on end, and when the weather permitted they rode their bikes in Prospect Park. Most of the time, though, they were at each others' houses writing songs or brooding over their misfortune. Fagen would later recall that his mother used to tell him that "misfortune builds character". Sometimes just for a change of scenery they would head downtown to Lonnie Yongue's loft apartment in Washington Market and compose on a piano in the loft below Yongue's. It was commonly known as the cheese factory, but Yongue didn't see much of them and was apprehensive about interrupting their songwriting sessions.

Richie Lifschutz had his own artistic ambitions and he was so knocked out by Becker and Fagen's material that he wrote a play based around their work, calling it *Ego, The Making Of A Musical*. Its plot followed the making of a rock musical (The Who's 'Tommy' had only just been premièred) and included Becker-Fagen songs with titles like 'Let George Do It', 'Mock Turtle Song', 'Soul Ram', 'Brooklyn', 'Stone Piano' and 'Brain Tap Shuffle', all of them sounding not that far removed from the kind of titles that would later appear on Steely Dan albums. Lifschutz also created a character called 'Charlie Freak' after their song and featured a group called 'Parker's Band'. Although he was a few years younger than Lifschutz, Walter Becker gave him tips on how to write songs and suggested he listen closely to Bob Dylan. Lifschutz took piano lessons and spent hours every day practising his scales and even co-wrote a song (with Kenny Vance of The Americans) which was recorded by Jay and The Americans. Becker and Fagen professed indifference to Lifschutz's play but whenever they approached a publisher they would make sure they mentioned that someone was writing a play based on their material. Somewhat inevitably, Lifschutz never succeeded in getting his play performed. Becker and Fagen trudged on regardless.

Their luck changed – ironically enough – on a day when most of the Brill Building publishers and music copyists were away at a weekend convention. As usual they had taken the elevator to the top floor and were circling their way down the stairs, calling at each occupied office as they descended. They had already endured their usual quota of rejections and accompanying humiliation when they reached the fourth floor and knocked on the door of JATA Enterprises.

JATA was the acronym for Jay and The Americans, a vocal group from Brooklyn who had been signed by top flight songwriters Leiber and Stoller in the early Sixties. Originally known as Binky Jones and The Americans, they became Jay and The Americans on the suggestion of lead singer John 'Jay' Traynor, but Traynor left in 1962 after their first hit 'She Cried' and was replaced by David Blatt who used the stage name Jay Black. It was customary in those days for singers to change their ethnic names to exotic-sounding stage names and the other members of the band followed suit. Becker subsequently claimed that the group used to refer to themselves as Jay and The Jews and when challenged about it, happily admitted that he "fit right in along there".

With Jay Black out front, Jay and The Americans enjoyed no small measure of success during the Sixties. After 'She Cried', they had several other Top Twenty hits, including 'Come A Little Bit Closer' (No 3), 'Cara Mia' (No 4) and a cover of The Drifters' hit 'This Magic Moment' (No 6), and their hit 'Sunday And Me' (No 18) provided Neil Diamond with his first big success as a songwriter at the tail end of 1965. They lost their momentum during 1966, scoring just one minor hit that year, and during 1967 and 1968 their career took a dive with the onset of the summer of love and psychedelic music. As a direct consequence of this dry spell, Jay and The Americans formed a publishing and production company, which was located in the Brill Building on 49th Street and Broadway.

What Becker and Fagen didn't know about JATA that fateful afternoon was that it had been financed largely by Mafia money. Often described as a 'very forceful' character, Jay Black had plenty of supporters and friends in the world of organised crime. He was a compulsive gambler, and over the years had frittered away a large proportion of both his and the group's earnings. Much as the other members wanted to put a stop to the squandering of the group's profits, they were dissuaded from impetuous action by the 'muscle' behind Black. On the other hand, there was a positive angle to the relationship – Black's shadowy supporters had financed the setting up of their Brill Building operation.

JATA's office manager, Eddie Chorane, answered Becker and Fagen's knock. He was confronted by two scruffy, long-haired "derelicts" who gave him their practised sales patter. He went back inside and spoke to another employee who in turn referred him to someone else before Chorane confronted one of the actual band with Fagen and Becker's request.

"There's two guys outside," Chorane told Kenny Vance. "They say they're songwriters, do you feel like listening to them?" Vance was grateful for a chance to interrupt his own workaday routine. Wearing an outfit he had purchased on Sunset Boulevard in Los Angeles, polka dot shirt, brown thick-ribbed corduroy pants and a giant thick hippie belt, he invited them inside. He was unprepared for the sight that greeted him. These two weren't typical of the song-peddlers who usually came calling; in their trenchcoats and scarves these two pallid would-be songwriters looked dishevelled and wasted, as if they had spent the last month living on the street. "They looked like insects, with no vibe coming from them," Vance said later. In fact, they were so introverted that he really didn't have a frame of reference at all. "Librarians on acid," was another term he used to describe them from this first encounter.

Becker and Fagen stepped inside the cramped inner office, as ever bemoaning the fact that no one would listen to their songs. There was an upright piano against one wall. Fagen opened their song book and, singing together, they performed a series of songs: 'Shuffling Up Your Downs', 'The Caves Of Altamira', 'Tell It To The Fat Man', 'The Roaring Of The Lamb' and 'Charlie Freak'.

Vance was impressed. He thought that 'Charlie Freak' stood out among the material and asked what they intended doing with these songs. They told him that they wanted to form a group of their own. Vance asked them to return on an appointed day and suggested that they go upstairs to a company called Peer Southern who rented the entire seventh floor. There was a two-track studio up there (which had occasionally been used by Lionel Hampton) and if Vance slipped Charlie Mack, the engineer, a few dollars he would let him use the facilities. At long last Fagen and Becker had cause for a little optimism.

Vance had never heard anything like these songs and didn't even pretend to understand them, but some sixth sense told him that there was something about the pair that was worth following up. When Becker and Fagen returned to the Brill Building a few days later Vance proposed that he should manage them and produce some piano/voice demos in the studio upstairs. JATA's production company funded the operation and over a period of time about twelve songs were cut, including 'The Roaring Of The Lamb', 'Oh Wow, It's You Again', 'Android Warehouse', 'Take It Out On Me', 'Parker's Band', 'A Little With Sugar', 'More To Come' and 'Charlie Freak'. Talking about these demos some years later, Becker dismissed them completely. "We were wiseass college kids writing bizarre, somewhat grotesque things and gradually we moved away from that," he said.

Their demo tape complete, Vance was faced with the same problem that Becker and Fagen had faced: to find a record company that didn't reject the material out-of-hand because their songs were far removed from the teen romance style of most, if not all, Top Forty hits.

Becker and Fagen's delight at having at last made some progress towards their goal was hardly unqualified. They were well aware of Jay and The Americans' reputation in the music business, but with no other offers forthcoming they had little alternative but to place all their faith in Vance and hope for the best. Even with Vance's knowledge of the internal workings of the music business and all his contacts, Becker and Fagen were amused by the incongruity of the tall American trying to market their weird compositions.

In 1969 Jay and The Americans were pretty much regarded with derision. Their act, complete with cute choreographed dance steps, was pure showbiz and they had been reduced to playing at progressively smaller and considerably less prestigious venues. But any lingering doubt in Becker and Fagen's minds was finally dispelled one night when Donald was visiting his parents in Cleveland. (They had moved there in 1968 when Jerry Fagen went into partnership with his brother.) They were watching TV when Jay and The Americans appeared on *The Tonight Show*. Fagen's parents were sufficiently impressed by their son's link with a member of this famous and once successful group to advise him and his partner to actively pursue their relationship with Kenny Vance. Back in Brooklyn, Fagen discussed it with Becker and they decided that there really was no alternative. They were under contract and had to stick it out.

It might also have occurred to them that, if they had broken the contract, unpleasant men with bulging shoulders and concealed weapons might have come looking for them sooner rather than later.

❧

Becker and Fagen's intention had always been to form a band based exclusively around their songs and they were always on the lookout for alternative outlets for their material. In the summer of 1970 they noticed an ad in the *Village Voice* which read: "Bass and keyboard player required, must have jazz chops. No assholes need apply". The phone number listed belonged to a guitar player called Dennis Dias who lived out in Hicksville on Long Island.

Walter Becker called Dias at his home. During their conversation, Dias told Becker that the group weren't sure if they really wanted a piano player after all. Becker told Dias that he would bring along his partner anyway. "When you hear the piano player, you'll change your mind," Becker assured him.

Denny Dias was born in Philadelphia in December 1946. His parents moved to Brooklyn when he was still a baby and moved on again to Hicksville when he was eight. His parents were both music fans, invariably tuning into the *Colgate Palmolive Hour* to watch Louis Armstrong and other popular artists of the day. Denny got his first guitar, a $5 model with only three strings, when he was twelve, but he wasn't interested in it and the guitar stood in a corner until one day a cousin started studying guitar and this inspired Dias to start teaching himself to play. Once he had attained a certain level of proficiency, he sought professional tuition and went through several tutors until he found Billy Bauer, the Metronome Poll winner of 1946, who not only taught the guitar but music theory as well, and eventually Dias majored in music at college. He was uncertain as to which course to take and changed to engineering, switched again to maths and, when he graduated junior college, attended downstate medical school studying computer science as related to medicine. But by now, music had become his chief interest and he only lasted one term at college before deciding to take a year off from studying academically to "see what happened". He figured that the opportunity to study would still be there next year and he desperately wanted to try his hand as a full time musician.

Dias played in the Hicksville High School dance band but his first real group was called The Saints – whose theme tune was rather unimaginatively 'When The Saints Go Marching In' – and he had been in various groups throughout the years, including one called The Grapevine. By 1969 he was the guitar player in Demian, a band named after a Hermann Hesse novel. Demian's Italian-bred bass player, Jimmy Signorelli, had quit the group to return to college, which is why Dias placed the ad in the *Village Voice*. Before Signorelli's departure Demian had been gigging as a four-piece at night-clubs in and around Long Island, playing Top Forty covers, some older Top Forty songs and material which really interested the band – soul tunes such as James Brown's 'Cold Sweat', The Four Tops' 'Reach Out, I'll Be There', Sam and Dave's 'Hold On, I'm Coming' and, inevitably, a couple of Otis Redding numbers.

Demian's lead vocalist was an ex-lifeguard and cab driver called Keith Thomas, who had been friends with Dias since their grade school days. "We were bored to shit," Thomas said of their enforced live chart covers. Dias and Thomas were both writing their own songs but audiences generally wouldn't allow them to play their own material during their shows. They were itching to do something more creative and fulfilling, and hoped that recruiting a keyboard player would add another dimension to the band.

Neither Fagen nor Becker could afford a car, so the first problem to overcome was how to hook up with the guys on Long Island. With Fagen toting his Fender Rhodes piano and Becker his Dan Armstrong Plexiglass bass, they took the Long Island railroad out to Hicksville station where Dias and Thomas were waiting to pick them up. Then they drove to Dias's house, where the audition took place in a rather cramped kitchen.

Just as Kenny Vance had been shocked by his first meeting with Fagen and Becker, the experience stayed with Keith Thomas for a long time, too. "Fagen looked like Jean-Paul Belmondo on acid," he said. "He had shoulder length hair, he was real skinny and he had these Michelin tyre lips, with his head jammed into his shoulders; he had a real hipster persona. Walter Becker, with his long blond hair and sunglasses, looked like a Nazi youth camp!"

Dias didn't really have room for a band to rehearse so it became the norm for them to repair twice a week to Thomas's basement at 43 Ellwood Avenue in Hicksville. At that time Thomas was working in the physiotherapy department of the local hospital, but working long hours at the hospital and rehearsing and gigging with Demian was taking its toll on him, both mentally and physically. He was dropping pills to maintain the pace.

By the time Becker and Fagen auditioned, Dias and Thomas had tried out about a dozen different bass players. "Each one was worse than the last," said Thomas. "Although the ad had warned that no assholes need apply, just about *every* asshole applied. Guys would show up and play variations on Question Mark and The Mysterians' '96 Tears' for about an hour and a half." Becker and Fagen plugged their instruments in. "I remember thinking either these guys are gonna suck horribly or they are gonna be fuckin' geniuses," said Thomas. "And they proceeded to play twenty of the most original songs I'd ever heard in my life."

As ever, the songs were taken from their black and white exercise book, the same list of demos they had already recorded with Kenny Vance: 'Android Warehouse', 'Finah Mynah From China' (later to become 'Yellow Peril'), 'Parker's Band', 'Soul Ram', 'I Can't Function' and a song sometimes referred to as 'Stand By The Seawall', which would much later be adapted to become the middle section of 'Aja'. Even at this early stage of their career, they had the chord structures and some of the lyrics to what would eventually become one of their best known compositions.

The longer the performance went on, the more Keith Thomas was impressed. "I was looking at Denny and my fuckin' eyes were rolling in my head. Where the hell did these guys come from? And it wasn't like they were playing variations on three chords; this was dense, interesting stuff, particularly at that time." Once Fagen and Becker had finished running through their own compositions, they jammed with Demian for two or three hours.

Despite their apparent aloofness and introspection, Becker and Fagen were invited to join the band for their sensational songwriting skills. They had a discussion with Dias and Thomas as to what should be their battle plan. The pair may have had outstanding musical talent, but they were still surprisingly naïve about the machinations of the music business and had no idea what to do with the songs, only that they wanted a recording contract. Certainly, Becker and Fagen were desperate for a break, but not desperate enough to consider playing live. They wanted absolutely no part of it; the thought hadn't even occurred to them and if it had it would have horrified them. Becker admitted this naïveté quite openly in an interview years later. "They (Demian) worked in clubs and stuff, which was something we'd never heard of."

The reasons for Becker and Fagen's reluctance were firstly because they were unfamiliar with, and dismissive of, the chart hits of the day, secondly because they were looking for an outlet for their own compositions, and thirdly because the prospect of playing in bars and clubs where there were regular outbreaks of violence intimidated them no end. They believed their strength lay in the songs which they had so painstakingly composed. They bluntly told Dias and Thomas: "What do you want to play night-clubs for? If you need money, get a job. Otherwise you're just wasting your talent and you'll never get to do what you really want to do."

Dias and Thomas were frustrated for an entirely different reason. Whereas before they weren't able to play their own material live, now they had what they considered great and innovative songs at their disposal but the composers wouldn't play ball.

Dias and Thomas didn't need much persuading to learn to play and sing Becker and Fagen's tunes. In fact, another result of Becker and Fagen joining the band was that Dias and Thomas completely abandoned their own attempts at songwriting. Denny Dias had only been writing for a year or so and although he had no trouble with writing music, he was dissatisfied with his lyrics and neither did he have much faith in any of his erstwhile songwriting partners' lyrical abilities.

While they had a full band to play their songs, they also had personnel problems. The other member of Demian, drummer Mark Leon, took an instant dislike to Becker and Fagen and made no secret of it. Becker and Fagen preferred a simple, straightforward rock and roll backbeat which did not detract from the subtleties of their compositions; a player who was 'neat' – heavy with his left hand and right foot. Leon's drumming was too busy for them.

Denny Dias was a bebop-influenced guitarist, which Fagen and Becker loved and which they could accommodate, and Keith Thomas had noticed how Mark Leon's jazz leanings had been frowned upon during Demian's live performances. "Sometimes, during our version of 'Cold Sweat', he would announce, 'In the middle of the fatback drum solo I'm gonna do Buddy Rich from *West Side Story*', and he'd go into that with all kinds of fuckin' drum sounds and clear the room."

Soon after joining Demian but before they actually recorded their demos with the band, Fagen and Becker demanded that Dias and Thomas fire Mark Leon. They were never ones to do their own dirty work if they could get someone else to do it for them. When Leon was confronted with their decision he, in Thomas's words, "went bananas, berserko". He caused quite a scene, but Dias and Thomas had half-expected it, since sudden rages formed a normal part of Leon's personality anyway. Eventually Leon's rage subsided and he left peacefully.

A few years later Fagen recalled the general dismemberment of Demian somewhat differently. "We used to chastise and abuse them, so they all quit. And so there was Denny and we'd ruined his band. So he had no place else to go."

Becker and Fagen already had a drummer in mind to replace Mark Leon – John Discepolo, whom they had already encountered as Jay and The Americans' road drummer, and they introduced him to Dias and Thomas. Fagen and Becker felt some sort of kinship with Discepolo which Becker later confirmed. "When we joined Jay and The Americans we had access once more to a drummer who didn't find us totally repugnant," he said. For his part, Discepolo also knew how to handle Becker and Fagen.

But regular commuting on the Long Island Railroad to Hicksville for rehearsals soon eroded Becker and Fagen's enthusiasm. It was a busy commuter railroad, uncomfortable and expensive for such cash-starved individuals, so they persuaded Denny Dias to pick them up in New York. The usual arrangement was for either Fagen to make his way to Becker's house in Queens, or for Becker to get himself over to Brooklyn from where Dias would chauffeur them to and from their rehearsal room at Ellwood Avenue. Many less tractable individuals would not have undertaken such extensive and constant running around, but the generous, mild-mannered and quietly spoken Dias was delighted to oblige them. He certainly didn't want to hand his two songwriting buddies the opportunity to bail out over the issue.

Initially, rehearsals took the form of Becker and Fagen teaching the others their compositions, perfecting them and then for some fun at the end, jamming around with various soul and pop standards. With the former, Donald Fagen would normally sing the melody line which Keith Thomas then tried to recreate with plenty of coaching from Fagen. Fagen disliked the sound of his own voice and was a very reluctant singer, but was very keen on Thomas's first tenor. "Boy, that voice has a lot of personality," Fagen told him.

But, according to Keith Thomas, Fagen's ideal voice at that time would have incorporated a mixture of Van Morrison, Steve Winwood and Marvin Gaye. "I think he used to fantasise about having that kind of voice," said Thomas. "They wanted a soulful voice with a lot of blues feeling and with a lot of personality, too – they wanted a fuckin' impossible voice!"

Although Becker and Fagen had joined Demian, it quickly became their group, with them calling all the shots. They wrote the music and the lyrics, they worked out the arrangements, they decided on the production and they flatly refused to play live. Keith Thomas remembers Fagen being terrified of live performances. His excuse was that his voice wasn't strong enough to withstand the constant pounding.

In consultation with Vance, the quartet decided their next step should be to cut some masters. They booked time in Vinnie Odo's Manhattan studio, which would later become the site for the infamous Seventies night-club, Studio 54. It was an eight-track studio and Odo engineered the sessions himself.

Prior to their association with Demian, Becker and Fagen's demos had been simple piano and voice arrangements. But now Denny Dias, Keith Thomas and John Discepolo were familiar enough with the material to assist on the recording of the demos and with the benefit of a band, Becker and Fagen were able to record much fuller arrangements. Among the songs they recorded during those sessions were 'Brain Tap Shuffle', 'Mock Turtle Song', 'Old Régime' and 'Let George Do It'.

Walter Becker co-sang on a number of the demos and Denny Dias really liked his co-vocal interpretation of 'Mock Turtle Song', the Charles Dodgson poem from *Alice Through The Looking Glass*, which Becker and Fagen had adapted to music. Dias admitted he was looking forward to hearing Becker sing more frequently. Obviously Becker didn't feel the same way.

Vance took the demo tape to all his contacts in the business, but he was met with the same negative reaction; people were shocked or bemused by the nature of the material and it was a struggle to get even a modicum of interest let alone some kind of deal. "I remember when we made those four demos," Walter Becker said. "People would get to the song 'Let George Do It' and they would get visibly discomforted. Jeff Barry was discomforted. This was the kind of person who seemed to be having the first bad thought of his life. That was bad for us. People thought of us as a non-commercial thing.

"Our big thing was going into the studio 'on spec,' you know, which means that not only are you not getting paid, but you have no hope of ever getting paid, and not only that, but no record company has shown the least interest in the project you're about to embark on. That's what 'on spec' meant to me."

While they were recording 'Brain Tap Shuffle', which was based on – or written while under the influence of – an LSD trip, Becker and Fagen toyed with the idea of trying to incorporate an example of their arcane sense of humour into the background lyric of the song. It went:

> Piz wah piz wah
> Do the brain tap
> Watch your mind snap
> Mash your kneecap
> Rock and roll crap

Fagen obviously spoke from experience when he remarked to Keith Thomas: "LSD's a lot of hard work." They eventually thought better of the idea and omitted the extra lyrics. Keith Thomas has said that much of their studio work at this time was pure experimentation around the structure of the tune. "Becker and Fagen wanted what they heard and heard what they wanted," he said.

In fact, in their mounting frustration and quest for some encouragement, Becker and Fagen wrote and recorded at least one unashamed attempt at commerciality entitled 'Undecided'. Still as yet unreleased, 'Undecided' was a sub-three-minute acoustic pop ditty about as far removed from 'Android Warehouse' as it was possible to get. It featured Keith Thomas on lead vocals, but even with a repetitive singalong chorus still failed to inspire anybody to sign them.

Becker and Fagen often discussed with the others why they had so far failed to get anywhere. Keith Thomas felt the reason why they had failed to sell their songs was that they lacked the ability to schmooze with record company executives. They were too shy to make good salesmen, even when they were selling their own material. It was a vicious circle: the more they were rejected, the more they retreated into themselves, becoming even more sullen and uncommunicative than usual. Thomas said: "They were sort of in a dark period at this point and I think that the dark period was as a result of not being able to sell the material." Becker and Fagen weren't in the habit of going out for a beer with the rest of the group either.

After spending a considerable amount of time recording the Vance demos without success and without any worthwhile income, Vance realised that they needed some regular work and invited Becker and Fagen out on the road with Jay and The Americans as backing musicians. If nothing else, it would also help take their minds off their other difficulties.

Becker and Fagen discussed the offer and, loathe as they were, decided to accept. By now the golden days of Jay and The Americans playing to large packed arenas had long since passed, and they were relegated to playing small night-clubs and bars, mainly on the east coast, for peanuts. Becker and Fagen were usually only called upon two or three weekends a month.

Although the prospect daunted them, once they got into it, the gigs became great fun, with all manner of antics taking place to stave off boredom. Becker played bass and Fagen played an RMI electronic piano. The contrast between the monkey-suited and flower-shirted Americans and the shabbily dressed backing musicians could hardly have been more pronounced. "It was like being part of The Four Tops," Becker said.

In between their stints backing Jay and The Americans they continued to write songs relentlessly, although they still had no outlet for them and Jay himself certainly wasn't interested. "He thought we were amusing," Becker said. The feeling was mutual.

On one occasion Becker and Fagen made a trip south to Fort Lauderdale in Florida with the Americans for a gig at a club called The Bachelors Three. A number of Jay Black's 'fans' also went along, ostensibly as security on the trip. All the hoods were immaculate dressers and one of them in particular took exceptional care over his appearance, always wearing a very expensive suit, tie and studded cufflinks. Unfortunately for Walter Becker, his suitcase was exactly the same model as this hood's and their cases somehow got mixed up. When the mobster arrived at their hotel and opened his case a week's worth of sweaty, dirty laundry rolled into a ragged ball fell out onto his lap. Becker escaped any physical retribution.

On stage Jay and The Americans would run through their repertoire of past hits complete with formation dancing and all the while Becker and Fagen would sit behind them furtively mocking the band, the songs and their ridiculous dance routines. Various members of the group were also regularly subjected to Becker and Fagen's cynical, caustic humour, though generally not to their faces. With their security guys in tow, discretion was the better part of valour. Walter Becker used to refer to the Americans' guitarist, Marty Kupersmith, as a guitar *owner*, a few years later in a radio interview Becker simply said he was "very bad" then apologised for his bluntness. They regularly shared private jokes which did nothing for the band members' self-consciousness, since each one would be wondering whether he was the current target for ridicule.

Occasionally, when they became bored with playing 'Cara Mia' and 'Only In America' night after night, Becker and Fagen would deliberately modulate the songs up a half tone to make them more fun to play and watch bemused as the other musicians failed to notice. Becker has said they even began writing "little Motown bridges" for some of the songs. "Our bridge for 'Cara Mia' took off like a 747," he told one interviewer years later.

In time Becker and Fagen would look back nostalgically and admit to enjoying backing "four guys in suits". It provided them with a constant source of amusing material for Steely Dan interviews but even this depended on their mood. On another occasion Walter Becker might describe darker, painful memories. "It was a long, horrible period, more or less images of toilets interspersed with arenas," was how he occasionally recalled his Jay and The Americans experience. "We played some awful places. Jay's basically a right-winger, but he has left-wing attitudes towards some things like long hair and drugs."

The Jay and The Americans gigs invariably provided Becker and Fagen with some respite from their very serious and demanding quest and offered them an opportunity for some laughs. "We ended up backing Jay and The Americans in one of their later phases – playing community gardens in Queens, that kind of scene," said Fagen. "I wish we had a recording of those gigs. It was fun. We'd change chords to the songs, wonder if he was gonna make that long note on 'Cara Mia' ..."

Marty Kupersmith had a Gretsch Country Gentleman guitar which Becker and Fagen hated because it kept going out of tune in the middle of gigs. On one occasion Kupersmith was given some particularly nasty looks by Jay Black when his guitar was playing up, but what Jay didn't realise was that Becker and Fagen had modulated 'Let's Lock The Door' and 'Come A Little Bit Closer' up half a tone and Kupersmith's guitar hadn't in fact gone flat at all. Eventually, after much persuasion from Becker and Fagen, Kupersmith traded in his Gretsch for a classic 1961 Fender Stratocaster.

After one Jay and The Americans' gig in New Jersey Kupersmith was driving a brand new rented car back to New York with Becker and Fagen in the rear. The car kept overheating and after several stops at gas stations to top up the radiator, Kupersmith's patience ran out and he rammed the accelerator pedal to the floor. Becker and Fagen found it hard to suppress their laughter when a piston blew straight up through the bonnet.

In January of 1969 Jay and The Americans scored another hit with a cover of the Doc Pomus/Mort Schuman song 'This Magic Moment', which had originally been a hit for The Drifters in 1960. That Top Ten hit put them back in business and enabled them to play much larger halls again. They also began playing oldies shows, which were often lucrative engagements, including one at the 20,000 seater Madison Square Garden with The Four Seasons. Other groups with whom they shared bills included The Angels and The Shirelles.

When Becker and Fagen backed The Americans at Madison Square Garden, Vance hoped the experience of playing in front of thousands of people would prove invaluable to them later on. But Becker and Fagen could hardly have cared less; they were only interested in getting through the current run of gigs. They sought studio experience not performing expertise.

Jay and The Americans' last ever released single was another remake of a Drifters' hit, 'There Goes My Baby'. Becker and Fagen arranged and played on both the 'A' side and the 'B' side, another Neil Diamond song, 'Solitary Man'. They also worked on a version of Martha and The Vandellas' 'Heatwave' with The Americans, but the record was never released.

By now Jay Black's gambling habits had spun out of control. He was so compulsive he would gamble on anything, and when his losses became too severe his 'bookmakers' would look in the newspaper to find where Jay and The Americans were playing and try to collect the debt by putting a lien on the show's takings. Hence the band would sometimes play a show and then not be paid, or would collect only a small portion of the agreed sum at the end of the evening.

Black was subpoenaed several times backstage at Jay and The Americans' gigs. Fagen remembered one such an incident in Queens with customary humour and candour: "Yeah, the guy with the gun and everything. We don't want to get into that if you wanna know the truth, 'cause we could wake up with a horse's head in our bed." His reluctance to go into detail can be put down to an occasion when members of the Gambino family were in the next room to the band at a Jay and The Americans' gig. For a while that night, Becker and Fagen's jokes and wisecracks dried up; they were scared shitless.

With Jay and The Americans facing imminent bankruptcy, a promoter called Ken Roberts, at that time also the manager of Sly Stone (no stranger to financial imprudence himself), devised a strategy whereby they would play a set number of 'Solid Gold' shows a year. Each member of the group could draw a modest set salary for a certain period of time, thus allowing the band to pay off their debts and hopefully move towards a more viable position. The rest of the band were securely under Jay Black's thumb and no one, it seemed, dared to tell him to curtail his gambling.

Another condition of Roberts' strategy was that the backing musicians should take a fifty percent cut in wages. Becker and Fagen were earning $100 a show then, so their wages dropped to $50 a show, or $200 a weekend, whichever was more. They told one interviewer that the offending individual – "Whom I fear to defame publicly," Becker said – was jokingly known as 'gimme a receipt'. This only hardened their resolve to escape from the embarrassment of playing with the struggling Americans.

To compensate for their reduction in road earnings, Becker and Fagen started "composing" songs for JATA's publishing company; making up titles and receiving cheques in exchange. "We got $50 for every song," Becker said. "We'd make up the titles and get the cheques. And that was what we lived on."

☙

As time passed and the remotest glimmer of progress eluded them, the atmosphere between Becker and Fagen and Kenny Vance was exhausted and became very tense. Often Keith Thomas dropped pills to get himself together which annoyed Becker and Fagen, as did Kenny Vance wanting to sing and play on some of the songs. The atmosphere degenerated into one of awkward tension and barely concealed hostility. It was obvious to everyone that Becker and Fagen's frustration could boil over at any moment.

Vance feared the deterioration in their relationship would lead to Fagen and Becker rescinding their contracts and was desperately trying to keep them interested. He asked them to do some horn and string arrangements on Jay and The Americans' 1969 album 'Sands Of Time'. They confessed they didn't know how to go about voicing chords for horns and strings – and weren't inclined to find out. Vance told them to get off their asses and go and find out how to do it, so they went to a library, read some music theory books and taught themselves the basics. When the album came out, though, they weren't actually credited – the album notes cited horn and string arrangements as: "You know who you are... thanks."

This was probably due to Jay Black's reluctance to give any credit whatsoever to the two cocky young upstarts whom he would later dub "the Manson and Starkweather of rock". Using their new-found knowledge, Fagen took the book into one of their own sessions and sat with it on his lap while writing a string arrangement for 'Shuffling Up Your Downs'. They then experimented with different versions of the song, Walter Becker singing it alone, then Kenny Vance trying it himself.

Vance continued hawking the demos around New York. Some of those he saw included Jerry Leiber, Richard Perry and Aaron Schroeder. Leiber and Stoller's office was on the tenth floor of the Brill Building, and Leiber was already semi-retired by then. Mike Stoller wasn't present when Vance, Becker and Fagen went in and, with Becker acting as front man, performed 'Number One', 'Parker's Band' and 'Charlie Freak'. By now Vance had manipulated himself into a position where he assisted in singing the tunes and he stayed behind afterwards to hear the verdict: "It's too Germanic," Leiber said. Fagen later recalled that Leiber did show some interest in their material, comparing it to German art songs in the style of Bertolt Brecht and Kurt Weill. But, more significantly, Leiber also said that he wouldn't know what to do with it anyway.

In 1983 Kenny Vance would release ten of the more complete demos on Aero Records as 'Becker and Fagen – The Early Years'. It included 'I Can't Function', 'Yellow Peril', 'Soul Ram' and 'Come Back Baby'. Other intriguingly titled demos which didn't make the album or subsequent demo releases included 'Take A Dip With Dinah', 'Footprints On The Moon', 'Surreal', 'Mr Lyle', 'Any Way You Want It' and 'One Ticket to LA'.

Personal differences between Kenny Vance on the one hand and Becker and Fagen on the other seemed to extend into everything they did. Vance admitted he was intimidated by their knowledge of literature and jazz and, swallowing his pride, asked them to recommend any records that he should listen to or books to read. They mentioned a particular Charlie Parker album called 'Swedish Schnapps' and musicians such as Charles Mingus, Bill Evans and Art Blakey. The reading matter would probably have included Nabokov, Corso, Snyder, some science fiction writers and Samuel Beckett. Vance has said that Becker and Fagen could evaluate a person's vocabulary in no time at all and then rib them mercilessly about their linguistic failings or any characteristic faults. Becker once accused Vance of having the "soul of a kreplach" (a fish popular with Jewish families and rich in nitrates).

Kenny Vance was then also working to fulfil a production deal with United Artists for a group called The Kings County Carnival. This was actually The Americans minus Jay Black under a different name, and they recorded several of the same Becker and Fagen tunes which formed the basis of their own demos. The Kings County Carnival went into a studio with Fagen and Becker and recorded eighteen rhythm tracks in one day. Among them were 'Shuffling Up Your Downs', 'Tell It To The Fat Man' and 'Number One'. Becker and Fagen also played on all the songs.

For some unknown reason all these rhythm tracks seem to have disappeared, probably much to Becker and Fagen's relief. United Artists had actually agreed to buy the publishing rights to the Becker and Fagen tunes, and by sending UA the work in progress, the indigent composers were more able to afford their rent each month.

Vance's next project for his two protégés was to score a movie on which a close friend, David Finfer, was an associate producer and editor. The film was written, produced and directed by a young film maker called Peter Locke (whom Vance occasionally and jokingly referred to as Federico Loche). Locke and Vance had known each other since they were twelve years old, having grown up together in a small community called Bell Harbour in Rockaway Beach in Queens. The movie was entitled *You've Gotta Walk It Like You Talk It Or You'll Lose That Beat* and featured Richard Pryor in one of his earliest roles, Robert Downey, Liz Torres, and Zalman King, fresh from his role in TV's *The Young Lawyers*. The project was a real family affair: Locke's own mother and grandmother appeared on screen playing cameo roles (his grandmother played Daisy who gets "mooned" at by a pervert in the park) and Locke eventually wound up marrying Liz Torres. Torres was at the time playing clubs in New York and Billy Cunningham and a piano player by the name of Barry Manilow often accompanied her in shows at the predominantly gay Continental Baths.

Peter Locke was first introduced to Becker and Fagen in the editing room which he rented from Norman Mailer on West 45th St. He recalls they were quiet, shy and obviously talented and they told him that they wanted to be jazz musicians. Locke was impressed by Kenny Vance's enthusiasm and Fagen and Becker's lack of it; it was manifestly obvious that they were being dragged into doing something in which they had no interest.

Fagen, Becker and Vance watched the film together while the director outlined the scenes where he needed music, gave them guidance as to the length and effect of each piece and handed them his own lyrics for the title song. All the other songs in the film and on the subsequent soundtrack album reflected Becker and Fagen's own ideas and taste.

Locke had attended the only film course at Syracuse University, where he made a three-minute movie, before moving on to San Francisco State to study English Literature. It was there that he shot his second and third student films. He began shooting *You've Gotta Walk It Like You Talk It* in 1968 and continued into 1969 on a $50,000 budget, but had been unable to find a distributor so the film had temporarily been put on hold. He later admitted that in hindsight he really didn't know what he was aiming for with the movie. It ended up as a social, satirical comedy.

In 1970/71 Locke's persistence paid off when he secured another $17,000 from Jerry Balsam of JER Releasing – who saw some merit in the film – to reshoot it. Locke went on to add scenes with Pryor, Steve Landisberg, Liz Torres, Billy Cunningham and others. Although his script was complete, he allowed a considerable amount of ad-libbing in the reshoots, and extra scenes for the film were shot at a Brooklyn hotel and in Prospect Park.

The film opens with the main character, Carter Fields, despondent and suicidal – as the main film's narrator puts it "he doesn't know his ass from a hole in the ground." He bungles a few attempts at suicide, jacks in his job on Wall Street and goes off in search of a meaningful existence; along the way he gets his girlfriend pregnant, gets mixed up with a group of revolutionaries, marries his girlfriend and finds a job in advertising. He photographs the birth in close up for a commercial, but Carter is such a big time loser that it's only a matter of time before he is fired for incompetence, deserted by his wife and left to bring up his child alone.

Fagen, Becker and Vance leased Peer Southern's recording studio in the Brill Building to record the material. They dubbed themselves The Original Soundtrack for the project and enlisted the help of Denny Dias and John Discepolo, while Vance was credited as producer. The engineer there at the time was a guy called Mallory Earl and he went crazy when he accidentally ripped the tape on 'If It Rains'.

Becker and Fagen's compositions included some throwaway instrumentals and, astonishingly for someone as shy and introverted as Donald Fagen, he was coerced into appearing in a scene playing an angry young man by the name of Fellestrio (presumably a pun on fellatio) who is the son of a character played by the late Stan Gottlieb. In a scene shot near a New York City pier, Fagen wore a hat with a long-haired wig cascading down beneath it and when he took off the hat all his hair fell out. Fagen and Becker later ridiculed the scene in a radio re-enactment of it, while appearing as guests of KPFK in Los Angeles. Becker did the voice over and Fagen acted out the part to complete silence from the three interviewers. Fagen asked pointedly, "Was it funny? Did you laugh?" No-one did and Becker said that was why the scene was cut from the film, adding acidly "It was the best scene in the film, of course." Fagen heaved a sigh of relief when his acting début ended up on the cutting room floor. The music was credited to Becker, Fagen and Billy Cunningham. The latter was a lounge piano player who composed some incidental piano music for the film and who also made a brief appearance in it as the fat lady!

On the soundtrack album the title song is sung by an unaccredited Marty Kupersmith and features some jaunty piano from Fagen; when the piano solo comes in Kupersmith urges Fagen on with the unlikely words "Rip it on me, Donald". Peter Locke was given a co-writing credit on the title song because he had supplied the words and Fagen's girlfriend, Dorothy White, was given a co-writing credit on the best song on the album, 'Roll Back The Meaning', because she also assisted with the lyrics. Kenny Vance sings the solo lead vocal and the lyrics hint at Becker and Fagen's musical predicament, but at least they found cause to mix some optimism with their dissatisfaction.

As ever Fagen was reluctant to sing these songs alone and so Kenny Vance was lumbered with doing the vocal on 'Dog Eat Dog'. He tried it a few times, but it was obvious his voice was much better suited to slower melodic material. Vance told Fagen that if anybody should sing 'Dog Eat Dog', he should. Bearing in mind the attitude and energy of the song and the fact that he was its co-writer, Fagen eventually agreed to sing it, and having heard his fine rendition it's difficult to imagine anyone else doing it better. As the song fades, Fagen injects some whoops and Apache war cries. Its lyrics feature a reference to Red Hook, a town near Bard College where Becker and Fagen spent some of their leisure time while at Bard.

Several examples of lyrics used in early Fagen/Becker demos would eventually be reprised in later Steely Dan songs. The lyrical colour contrast between 'Red Hook' and 'black book' can be heard in 'Black Friday' with "Gonna strike all the big red words/From my little black book". The "hooters and the hats" from 'Ida Lee' appear rearranged in 'Josie' and "drinking dinner from a paper sack" cropped up again in 'Daddy Don't Live In That New York City No More'.

Of the instrumentals – which are largely filler material – 'Flotsam And Jetsam' sounds as if it was composed around a studio jam with lashings of echo and resembles Robbie Robertson's 'Chest Fever' from The Band's début album, 'Music From Big Pink'. 'War And Peace' comprises a brief drum solo with random, dissonant piano chords from Fagen. Vance was again given a co-writing credit on the album's longest song, 'Red Giant/White Dwarf', with Denny Dias's guitar meandering through the tune like a Sunday afternoon stroller. The soundtrack album closes with a ballad called 'If It Rains', the introduction of which contains a snippet from the film, a desperate plea from Carter Fields' doting mother. Vance again sings accompanied only by Fagen's piano.

The record hardly sold at all until seven years later when Visa Records released it to capitalise on Becker and Fagen's success as Steely Dan. There was some wrangling over the fine print which explained that it was not an official Steely Dan album. It's worth mentioning, too, that the album ran to just over thirty minutes which was hardly value for money. Doubtless Fagen and Becker would have been much happier if the material had remained buried along with the film. Fagen later commented: "It's amazing how many people have managed to come across that horror. It's nothing to be proud of."

You've Gotta Walk It Like You Talk It Or You'll Lose That Beat came at one of the lowest points in Becker and Fagen's career. They were only marginally closer to reaching their goal than when they started. The music on this album comes across as the sort of thing they could have turned out in their sleep – even at this early stage in their career. Nevertheless it was a must for Steely Dan collectors. The sleeve took the same form as the poster for the movie designed by a cartoonist friend of Peter Locke's named Peter Bramley. It showed a caricature of Zalman King as the protagonist Carter Fields hanging by the neck from a rope. Surrounding the main picture were various other cartoon scenes from the film.

Years later Walter Becker told KPFK's listeners that the film was so under-budgeted that some of the exposures didn't match so that the new scenes could be distinguished from the original ones. Asked how they became involved in the creative process, Becker said: "I wouldn't call it a creative process. We became embroiled in it when the suggestion was made that if we went into a recording studio and recorded however many minutes' worth of dogmeat is on this album, we would each get a cheque for $250, or some similar amount to that." Becker freely admitted that they did it only for the money and when he was challenged about their lack of artistic integrity he refused to take the bait.

The film, which ran for about 85 minutes, was premièred in August/September 1971 at the Cinema Malibu and Cinema Village in New York and received savage reviews. One female critic wrote that the film was "low budget, sometimes technically amateurish, almost always crude" but was "sometimes viciously funny. Young women only seem to exist as alternatives to masturbation... old women are grotesque jokes." The *Daily News* critic was almost as savage: "Masquerading as satire, this comedy is sophomoric and absolutely dull. The dialogue is scattered with vulgarisms and the action is spiced up with quick pornographic shots. Not even the acting is inspired."

Other critics picked up on Locke's influences – Brian de Palma's *Hi, Mom!* and Robert Downey's *Putney Swope* – and the latter made a cameo appearance in the film as the head of an ad agency. *Variety* suggested that the film suffered from "a weak storyline, comic situations that are overdone and tasteless, sloppy editing and colour and camerawork that is often blurred and shaky." Despite its slim chance of box office success, the *New York Post* thought that it "may have some appeal for New Yorkers, youth audiences and devout followers of Robert Downey."

On a brighter note, Richard Pryor garnered some praise for his role as a gibbering lush in a men's room. And one critic did spot some "refreshingly hilarious scenes" in the film. One of the editors of the movie was Wes Craven who later went on to create Freddy Kreuger and the *Nightmare On Elm Street* series of splatter movies.

The movie débâcle was just about the last straw as far as Becker and Fagen were concerned. They may have been saddled with contracts they no longer wanted to be a part of, but their patience, which had held surprisingly firm for a few years, had now run out. With another unsatisfactory project behind them, the atmosphere between Vance and Becker and Fagen became virtually untenable. As the weeks passed they accused him of not understanding them or their songs, trying to persuade them to sell out and go commercial (which Vance denied) and of not knowing how to go about selling the songs. At one point, they told Vance they wanted to call Frank Zappa who they believed would "get" the material and, they believed, have the clout to provide them with a deal.

Vance defended his position and argued that with their latest group of demos, including 'I Can't Function', 'Don't Let Me In' and 'Come Back Baby' , a commercial for Trans Texas Airlines and the film score for *You've Gotta Walk It*, he was nearing the point where he would finally be able to crack it and get a deal. Meanwhile, John Discepolo had left both Jay and The Americans and Becker and Fagen's employ and had been replaced in both positions by another Eastsider, John Mazzi.

֍

Fagen and Becker had, through Kenny Vance, become friendly with an independent producer called Gary Kannon who lived near Fagen in Brooklyn. He'd been an insurance salesman, worked as Becker and Fagen's driver but, more crucially, been a partner with Richard Perry in a venture called Cloud Nine Productions, which was set up in 1966 and funded by a $2,000 donation from each of their respective parents. Together they produced some singles for the Kama Sutra label before the money ran out and the venture folded.

Kannon was also very friendly with Jay and The Americans and in particular Kenny Vance. When Leiber and Stoller produced Jay and The Americans, Kannon was allowed access to the studio to observe the recording process at first hand. An ex-physical education major and all-round sports fan, Kannon enjoyed "getting his feet wet" producing occasional projects and when Cloud Nine Productions folded in 1968, he got a job working for Bobby Darin's publishing company, TM Music. After running songs for Darin, Kannon was invited to go into production when Darin wanted to expand his operation into a production company.

Kannon eventually got a job at Avco Embassy records, which was owned by movie producer Joseph Levine and run by Hugo Peretti and Luigi Creatore, the producers responsible for most of Sam Cooke's records. The job involved a certain amount of A&R activity and in 1968 one of Kannon's first signings was a Boston-based progressive rock band called The Bead Game, another band named after a Hermann Hesse novel, in this case *The Glass Bead Game*. The album which Kannon produced was called 'Welcome' and the drummer and lead singer of the band, Jimmy Hodder, would figure prominently in the early years of Steely Dan.

At the time Kannon was also trying to carve a niche for himself in the music business and was writing songs and playing a little acoustic guitar. He had written a song entitled 'Long Way Down' which appeared on an Eric Mercury album called 'Electric Black Man' (another Kannon signing) which he produced in 1969. Kannon preferred to cite Mercury's album as the first production job for which he would like to be remembered.

Meanwhile Vance had persuaded Kannon's ex-partner, Richard Perry, that a Becker and Fagen song called 'I Mean To Shine' was suitable for none other than Barbra Streisand, who was still red hot from the film *Funny Girl*. This was quite a scoop for Vance; his charges were keeping exalted company – other songs on the album were written by John Lennon, Carole King and Burt Bacharach and Hal David.

This produced an abrupt and rather comical contrast in Donald Fagen's lifestyle: the night before the Streisand session, he was part of the backing band at a Jay and The Americans gig "in some Mafia toilet on Staten Island", and within hours he was ensconced in Columbia Studios teaching the song to Streisand and playing organ on the session, too. When asked about the session later, Becker claimed that Richard Perry destroyed the song: "He changed the lyrics and the melody and left out the bridge." Fagen simply said that it was "not a very good song", but still added that it was "altered beyond the point where we would have to take responsibility for it."

The next project which came Kannon's way was recording an album with a young singer/songwriter called Linda Hoover. Kannon was spending increasing amounts of time with Becker and Fagen and asked them if they had any suitable songs and eventually most of the songs for the record were Becker and Fagen compositions. They also played on the album, along with John Discepolo, offering her 'The Roaring Of The

Lamb', 'Jones' (a song based on jazz terminology for a drug habit and written by Walter Becker alone), 'Turn My Friend Away' and 'I Mean To Shine'. Vance wrote a song called 'City Mug', and Denny Dias contributed an instrumental arrangement of The Band's 'In A Station' featuring a five-piece woodwind section. Linda Hoover herself had written a few songs, but all agreed they were less than inspired. "She had three songs that she'd written in her whole life; one about her mother, one about her boyfriend and one about fall," Becker said later.

There was a considerable amount of expectation behind the record, but Denny Dias remembers being disappointed when they came to record Hoover's vocals – she wasn't the singer most people thought she was. "Before we had Steely Dan we wrote what we felt were very respectable pop tunes that your average B flat female vocalist might be honoured to do," said Becker. "But we could never find any average B flat female vocalist who felt that way about them. And it was obvious because there was always some element of this fatalistic mentality that crept into the lyrics of the tune."

In 1975 Fagen elaborated on their songwriting efforts on her behalf: "I think there were two songs that were more or less in the present style, which sounded very strange by the way, with a very naïve female vocalist singing them who didn't have the faintest idea what she was singing about."

Morris Levy, the owner of Roulette Records, loved Hoover's album and was keen to release it, but he had allegedly been promised half the publishing rights by someone who was in no position to promise that. Kannon suggested that Levy should call Vance – who did own the publishing – but they were unable to agree on a deal and so Levy declined to release the record. Levy told Kannon that he appreciated the hard work he'd put in on the record and paid for him to go to Florida for a two week vacation.

During the recording of the Linda Hoover album in New York, Kannon had introduced Becker and Fagen to a guitarist he had first encountered in Boston while working on The Bead Game's album. Jeff Baxter had once been a member of The Fugs, The Holy Modal Rounders and Ultimate Spinach though he didn't remember the latter with any fondness whatsoever: "We were a horrible band, but we had a great following". He was grateful when the opportunity arose to quit that band and graduate to session work. He had then moved up to Boston, working mainly with folk artists such as Eric Ericson and Paul McNeil.

Baxter, widely known as "Skunk" due to an adolescent indiscretion, impressed Becker and Fagen with his versatility and technique and he in turn was impressed with the sophistication and challenging nature of their compositions. "Their music was the only stuff I'd heard in the past ten years that made any sense to me and didn't make me nauseous," he said later. Baxter and Becker and Fagen became good buddies and made a pact to call each other if either succeeded in obtaining a recording contract and forming a band.

Becker and Fagen then gave Jay Black notice that they were quitting. At the same time Denny Dias and Keith Thomas' band Demian dissolved into a situation where the rehearsals grew fewer and fewer until they ceased completely.

There was consolation for Denny Dias in that he was still included in their future plans, but Keith Thomas wasn't. Neither was Kenny Vance. A few weeks later he telephoned Donald Fagen in Brooklyn on a Sunday morning, only to be told by his former room-mate Richard Ransohoff that he and Becker had that very day left for a job at ABC Dunhill Records in California.

℧

CHAPTER III

Proud To Be Your Slave

One Monday night in November 1971, Gary Kannon lay in bed watching a football game on TV and simultaneously writing a letter to a prospective employer. Kannon's long-time friend and associate Eddie Lambert had been working in Los Angeles for almost a year with ABC Dunhill's music publishing division and had already been lobbying heavily on his behalf. Lambert and Kannon had worked together running songs at Bobby Darin's publishing company in the late Sixties, and thanks to Lambert, Jay Lasker, president of ABC, and his head of A & R, Steve Barri, were already aware of Kannon's production credits and experience.

During the half time interval, Kannon finished drafting his letter to Lasker. He mailed it the following day and promptly forgot about it. A couple of days later Kannon received a call inviting him to fly out to California to meet the ABC president.

Under the stewardship of its owner, producer Lou Adler, the Dunhill label had of late enjoyed no little success with a number of Top 40 acts including The Mamas and Papas, Three Dog Night, Tommy Roe and The Grass Roots. Jay Lasker had been in charge at the label when Dunhill was bought by ABC and was installed as president of the merged corporation. By late 1971 they were looking to expand their limited horizons away from the Top 40 into the burgeoning underground album music market.

Eddie Lambert felt that his old Brooklyn buddy Gary Kannon would be ideal for the role of underground A & R man cum staff producer. Lambert realised that the existing A & R staff – himself included – didn't have the right sensibility to work with underground acts and as Kannon was "a little musically to the left of all of us", it was very likely he would be invited to come to Los Angeles as ABC's "house freak". Reflecting on Kannon's appointment in 1975, Walter Becker was typically facetious: "ABC wanted someone with a Fu Manchu moustache to produce underground records."

Kannon flew out, met with Lasker and Steve Barri and was promptly hired. During the course of his meetings he told Barri about two unique songwriters with whom he'd been working in New York and gave him a copy of Walter Becker and Donald Fagen's demo tape. Barri was impressed, and Kannon actually staked his reputation – and his new job – on the line by demanding that Becker and Fagen be hired in some capacity at ABC. Kannon told Barri bluntly that if this didn't happen he would quit.

Ironically enough, after all the rejection and humiliation Becker and Fagen had endured in New York, Barri thought the material was "really exceptional and different from anything else I'd heard in a long time". He discussed it with Lasker and told Kannon that ABC "definitely wanted him and definitely wanted them, too" – Kannon as a staff producer and Becker and Fagen as staff writers.

Arriving in Los Angeles, Kannon, his wife and two kids stayed with Eddie Lambert for about six weeks until they got settled and found somewhere of their own to live. Kannon soon called Becker and Fagen to ask them if they fancied a job as staff writers for ABC; needless to say they did, and within a month they had joined him in Los Angeles.

But before Becker and Fagen could sign, they had to extricate themselves from their contract with Kenny Vance. They had already gone a long way towards this by vilifying and belittling him at every opportunity. Vance could see what was coming and very nobly told them, "If you don't wanna be with me any more, I'll tear up the papers". True to his word, Vance *did* rip up the contract on the condition that Becker and Fagen gave him half the publishing of their first album by way of compensation. Red Giant Music, Vance's publishing company shared the royalties with Wingate Music.

Nevertheless, Vance was unhappy that Becker and Fagen treated him in this manner. Becker and Fagen's sudden departure to LA seemed premeditated and a certain bitterness remained etched on his memory for a long time. That Kannon, one of his closest and most trusted friends, seemed implicated in the conspiracy and now held the key to their future only made matters worse.

Vance wasn't the only one to lose contact with Becker and Fagen. Their contact with Denny Dias had dwindled and even he too was unaware they had left for California. When Becker did finally reach Dias, he expressed frustration at being bound by a contract to Kenny Vance in New York when ABC had offered them a far more promising opportunity in Los Angeles.

"He (Kannon) said he'd got us a job as staff songwriters and we should come at once," Fagen explained. "We went. We found places to live in Encino, this oasis of nothing in the desert, and every morning we'd hitch a ride to West Hollywood where we had an office and a piano. ABC was involved in commercial AM singles. They had The Grass Roots, Tommy Roe, stuff like that. But they wanted to get into the underground and sell albums too. So they hired Gary, who could certainly pass any criteria for being underground at that time. He neglected to tell them that with underground music you don't need staff writers."

Walter Becker had never been to California before, but he and Fagen had no qualms about flying out to LA to take up this exciting new challenge. Working as staff writers wasn't *exactly* what they were looking for: staff writing would be a difficult task to adapt to, but at least it was steady employment ($125 a week) and they were confident it was the first step towards manoeuvring ABC into a position which allowed them to get their own band together and release their own records on the label. On top of that, Los Angeles – and Hollywood in particular – was now the hub of the US rock industry, a sprawling, sun-kissed web of boulevards and canyons where laid-back rock stars nested in ranch-like homes during the day, and worked and played in studios and clubs at night. Going west was the right direction for any would-be US rock musician in 1971. Becker and Fagen said the move made no difference to them either artistically or personally. "If you never cross the threshold of your domicile, it doesn't matter where you live, now does it?" remarked Fagen. However, within a few years that perception had changed considerably.

The artist roster at ABC Dunhill at that time included many acts that did not write their own material so there was a need for a constant flow of songs. Becker and Fagen had been writing steadily for a number of years and although they had a backlog of material, they knew full well that they were going to have to start from scratch as far as coming up with anything remotely suitable for ABC's traditional Top 40 acts.

Once they established themselves in their office, it soon became apparent – if it wasn't beforehand– that they weren't cut out to be staff writers. If they'd had an ounce of staff writer muscle in their bodies they would surely have cracked it in New York. The main problem was their lyrics, as Becker recalled later. "We weren't too successful, because the lyrics always turned left in the middle of the song. It didn't take us too long to find out that it wasn't gonna work, because the 'hits' we were coming up with were really too weird or too cheesy for anyone to record. We really had to go out of our way to write a song for The Grass Roots. We did it. I mean, we wrote some of the cheesiest songs you ever heard. But, uh, they were so cheesy they were laughable."

Becker and Fagen did, in fact, write a song called 'Tell Me A Lie' for The Grass Roots but it was never recorded. "You could always tell we were laughing down our sleeves at the band," said Becker. "We were The Grateful Dead of Beverley Boulevard."

But after the hard times in New York, Los Angeles was a picnic. With a steady income and an easygoing California lifestyle, Walter Becker gained twenty pounds in his first year there though Fagen stayed as thin and weedy as he always had been. Becker later admitted that the whole staff writer period was one big dodge. "We had the idea in mind that we would organise a band as quickly as possible when we came out here because most of what we wrote was pretty unusual material and most acts that were looking for songs weren't going to be interested. So we had this notion in the back of our minds and we started to bring people out even while we were supposed to be staff writers at ABC. We announced that we were forming a band shortly after we signed our contracts."

Becker and Fagen were there under false pretences and the sooner they could form their own band and get their teeth into recording their own compositions the better. The songwriting job didn't provide either an aesthetic or an intellectual challenge. "A staff writer is supposed to be a researcher of radio as well as a creative person," Fagen said. "It's essentially imitating what you hear on the radio and putting it out eight or ten months later. We weren't doing so good 'cause we're sort of funny. When you're writing for other artists, it's difficult to get them to do songs if the lyrics aren't absolutely banal."

Despite their own disinterest and that of the ABC artists, they continued trying to write simple pop songs, all the while renting equipment for themselves at ABC's expense which would be used by their intended group. Becker and Fagen later maintained that all the members of the band were already selected in their own minds well *before* they went to California. Initially, ABC were unaware that their funds were being appropriated to hire and buy equipment for Becker and Fagen's band. When some senior staff got an inkling of what was going on Kannon admitted the truth to Steve Barri. Eventually Barri apprised Jay Lasker of the situation and they agreed to officially fund the would-be group.

At least one Becker-Fagen song impressed the top management at ABC. They thought 'Dirty Work' would be ideal for either The Grass Roots or Three Dog Night, and that it would make a certain hit single for Becker and Fagen's own band itself once it had been formed. Another title Becker and Fagen composed which did not fit their "cheesy" criteria was a tune called "Proud To Be Your Slave" which according to Fagen had "a Carole King-type feel". Publisher Eddie Lambert was also impressed. "It was probably the best song that they ever wrote that was not recorded by Steely Dan," he said. Lambert's concerted efforts to place the song with a major artist met with no success, however, and he was annoyed that he could not persuade anyone to record it. "Proud To Be Your Slave" was eventually consigned to the same fate as all their other attempts and to this day remains unrecorded.

Six months passed and none of their songs was recorded successfully. It was time for Becker and Fagen to abandon their staff writer pretence and assemble their own group. They needed no encouragement to call their cohorts back east and as Baxter, Hodder and Dias assembled in Los Angeles one by one, Becker and Fagen took them upstairs to Jay Lasker's office and introduced them to him and other ABC staff. They would say: "We just found this fantastic guy and you've gotta sign him for our band. After a while they stopped asking 'What band?'

First to get the call was Denny Dias, their old pal from Hicksville, whom they had promised would be first on their list. Dias had been waiting all this time for precisely such a call and in the meantime he'd been taking any job – including washing cars – to support himself. Dias's gamble of quitting school proved to be worthwhile after all; his immense faith in Becker and Fagen and their songs looked like being rewarded, although his resolve had wilted many times since Becker and Fagen left for the Golden State. He was very close to giving up on the notion when their call came.

As ever, Dias was short of funds and couldn't afford the flight to California, so he undertook the long drive across country from Hicksville to the West Coast. Arriving in Los Angeles, his first stop was Walter Becker's house and when Becker played him the demos of 'Midnite Cruiser' and 'Change Of The Guard', Dias was stunned. This was very different from the type of material that had first floored him two years ago back in Hicksville. "What's happened to the songs?" he asked. "Well, now that we're finally gonna get our shot, we wanna make sure that it sells," replied Becker.

It was understandable that Becker and Fagen should compromise their material somewhat, especially after all their years of frustration. In fact, Fagen tried to explain this compromise by admitting that... "We've simplified. The early material, aside from being more complex and sophisticated, was also a little more pretentious." He rather cryptically referred to their older songs as "classical and jazzical Third Stream".

Steve Barri and his ABC colleagues had by now admitted defeat on the staff writer front and allowed Becker and Fagen free rein to interpret the material as they saw fit. It was so unique that the only solution was for them to record the songs themselves and ABC generously decided put all their resources behind them.

Despite their refusal – or inability – to lower themselves to what they saw as the lyrical ineptitude of the Top 40, Becker and Fagen knew the key to success lay in the melody that surrounded the lyrics. If a song had a great hook and chorus they could get away with murder with the words. They also knew that their recording contract would be terminated if they didn't come up with the goods within a set period. They therefore planned to break the audience in slowly, intermingling simple pop with more and more complex material as time went by. On each successive album they gradually introduced more jazz phrasing and increasingly enigmatic lyrics and Fagen wasn't afraid to discuss their philosophy publicly. "I think it'll get better," he said even before Steely Dan was a reality. " I think we'll start working back toward more ambitious musical things."

The contract that Becker and Fagen signed – negotiated by ABC attorney Evan Medow – was slanted heavily in ABC's favour but they would have signed virtually anything for the opportunity to get their songs on record and demonstrate their songwriting talents to the world. "I got killed in there." Medow admitted candidly.

After recruiting Denny Dias, Becker and Fagen contacted moustachioed guitarist Jeff "Skunk" Baxter and asked if he knew of a likely candidate for the drumstool. Baxter recommended The Bead Game's Jim Hodder with whom Kannon was already familiar. Although the band seemed to be falling nicely into place, Fagen later remembered things quite differently. "We needed people who could negotiate the chord changes and stuff and at the same time we needed guys who'd work for nothing – and they're very difficult to find," he said. "I think we would've preferred to have grown up on the same block with five or seven guys who thought the same way we did and had a working unit all these years, but it didn't work out that way. We were all strangers and they were very nice about the whole thing and more or less abdicated their own musical conscience and listened to us."

One very serious drawback was Fagen's ongoing lack of confidence in his own ability as a vocalist. Previously he'd always had Walter Becker's vocals to fall back on. They now decided that Becker was a little flat which left Fagen exposed, and he didn't relish the prospect of singing, especially live. Indeed, Fagen didn't believe he could sing a note. Even Steve Barri and Eddie Lambert were drawn into the wrangle of trying to persuade Fagen that his voice should form the basis of the group's sound. To them the demos they had heard with Fagen singing solo were indisputable evidence that Donald should front the band.

While Becker and Fagen were involved with putting their band together in the summer of 1972, Kannon was assigned by ABC to co-produce an album by a group of long-haired, pot-bellied Texans called Navasota. Although Navasota wrote their own material, Kannon asked Becker and Fagen if they had a suitable song for the band and they came up with a hard-rocking number called 'Canyon Ladies'. It was a simple enough tune, but is probably the hardest edged song they ever wrote and it would never have fitted into Steely Dan's *oeuvre*. The lyrics were mostly indecipherable anyway and Kannon ensured they earned session fees by playing on the album. Becker and Fagen once again put to good use their experience arranging horns and strings for Jay and The Americans on five songs on the 'Rootin'' album. It was recorded at the Village Recorder and Jeff Baxter played pedal steel guitar on a couple tracks. Kannon co-produced with Dennis Collins under the banner of 12th Street Productions.

By chance, Becker and Fagen also ran into Mark Volman and Howard Kaylan (aka Flo and Eddie), former vocal leads with The Turtles, at these sessions and this led to their singing backgrounds on Steely Dan's early demos.

'Rootin'' was the first record Gary Kannon produced for ABC. "They were a really kick-ass rock 'n' roll band from Houston," he said. "They were much along the same lines, if not harder, than ZZ Top who were their rivals at the time." The five members of Navasota would have given their right arms to have achieved half the success that ZZ Top went on to enjoy.

Not long after the sessions for the Navasota album Gary Kannon decided to revert to his original surname of Katz, which is how he would be named on all the Steely Dan albums to come.

❧

With their musical allies all settled in Los Angeles, Becker and Fagen began rehearsing their group with no name outside normal office hours in a room in ABC's building which was occupied by an accountant between nine and five. They would arrive at six o'clock with sandwiches to sustain them through the night, move all the office paraphernalia to one side and rehearse until the early hours. Afterwards Fagen would always follow Baxter home because he liked the way his 1968 Ford Torino looked from the rear! During the day Jeff worked at repairing and customising guitars for liquid wages.

Eventually someone in the accounts department at ABC complained about their rehearsal routine and they were moved into more appropriate space in a half-built recording studio ABC were constructing behind their existing building. ABC even bought them a PA system with which to rehearse.

The group's début album was recorded at the Village Recorder in West Los Angeles, which was to be the studio for the first three Steely Dan albums and which laid the foundations of a lasting relationship between Becker and Fagen and the general manager of the Village, Dick LaPalm. He was to become as big a fan of their group as anyone they came into contact with.

When it came to choosing a name for the band, Becker and Fagen didn't know where to start. As avid fans of good literature they had a large reservoir of ideas to delve into and this may have made the decision even more difficult. They didn't want to be too clever but the pressure was on to come up with a name soon. They later claimed that if they had known how long the band would last, and how successful it would be, they would have taken more care over choosing a name.

Many suggestions were made, some patently less serious than others – including Big Nardo and The Eighth Grade – and they eventually settled on Steely Dan, the name given to a rubber dildo used by Mary in William Burroughs' controversial Swiftian novel *The Naked Lunch*, which had been a student favourite in the late Sixties when Becker and Fagen were at Bard. "Steely Dan wasn't entirely serious as it has something to do with the fact that we use a steel guitar," said Becker. "Well, you could say that, but you wouldn't be right. You could say that it comes from a chapter in *The Naked Lunch* by William Burroughs. If you said that, you'd be right. We were stuck for a name and we had used this particular name in a song that we had written a long time before ('Soul

Ram'), and now we had a steel guitar player in the band. It seemed like a good name to us at the time. In fact, it turned out the name had a certain zing to it and helped the band become popular at the beginning, I think."

Years later Fagen would admit he was actually deeply embarrassed by the name. Indeed, Becker and Fagen would often regret having chosen the name because critics and journalists were forever trying to find parallels between Burroughs' book and Steely Dan. In the February 1977 issue of the *New Times*, Arthur Lubow cornered 62-year-old William S. Burroughs in a hotel and played him Steely Dan's music. Although he admitted to previously being unfamiliar with their music, Burroughs decided that Steely Dan and their music were "... too fancy. They're too sophisticated, they're doing too many things at once. To write a bestseller, you can't have too much going on. You take *The Godfather*, the horse's head. That's great, but you can't have a horse's head on every page. These people tend to have too many horses' heads."

When he was shown the article Walter Becker retorted: "I thought that was an extremely verbose statement on the part of William Burroughs. His comments are usually quite a bit briefer than that. The connection (with Burroughs) has been overstretched almost to the limits of elasticity." Becker would soon have the opporuntity to take it up with Burroughs personally anyway. "I plan to have Thanksgiving dinner with William Burroughs; he's a friend of my girlfriend." Becker wound up his tirade with a typical joke: "*Naked Lunch* is a fairly difficult work. Put it this way, William Burroughs at one point claims that he doesn't remember writing it. I don't see why I should remember having read parts of it."

℃℈

In late August 1972 ABC president Jay Lasker hosted the company's quarterly promotion and product meeting at the Sportsmen's Lodge in North Hollywood and introduced the fall release schedule. Promotion and salesmen from all over America were present for the occasion and a new marketing campaign was launched. It was called "The championship season for the family of ABC/Dunhill Records" and among the artists and albums to be given the special treatment were bluesman John Lee Hooker and his LP 'Soledad On My Mind', former James Gang guitarist Joe Walsh with his 'Barnstorm', Lucille-wielding B. B. King's 'Guess Who' and the début album by Steely Dan, a group unfamiliar to most of those present. Their LP 'Can't Buy A Thrill' was supposed to be rush released in September 1972, but in the event ABC decided to hold on to the album until November.

In a press release issued the same month, Becker and Fagen said of their lyrics: "We have certain recurring themes but we don't have any particular fixations. Anything is grist for our mill. There's no real limitations to it. We can write about anything. Our lyrics contain certain associations which we hope will evoke in our listeners the sensation that they are remembering something they forgot a long time ago. Perhaps thousands of years ago! Before they were even born!"

Somewhat curiously, in the same press release Jeff Baxter was quoted as saying: "I truly think our forte is performing." Considering that the band had not yet played live, this was an optimistic judgement, and an early indication of the chasm that would open up between the studio perfectionist songwriters on the one hand and the live performers that made up the band on the other.

Around about the same time Becker and Fagen made the acquaintance of recording engineer Roger Nichols who would play a big role in the Steely Dan saga. They met him one night when they were in the studio laying down songwriting demos for other artists and since no-one else wanted to stay for the session, Nichols was elected to do it. He was a native of Oakland in Northern California, but had lived all over the United States because his father was in the Air Force flying B747s. One of three children, Nichols was the sort of kid who could build his own stereo system when he couldn't afford to buy one. "I just tore apart all these old radios, which was great 'cause I learned a lot that way," he said.

A physics nut, with a degree in nuclear engineering from Oregon State University, Nichols was employed at the San Onofre power station in Southern California during its construction between 1965 and 1968, and on his days off he worked in recording studios. His interest in music stemmed from an obsessional hatred of clicks, snaps and pops on records and his position in the studio meant that he could take home 15 ips two-track tape copies for near perfect sounding music. Nichols once lived in the same neighbourhood as Frank Zappa and attended the same high school, Cucamonga, and their friendship blossomed in the early sixties due to their mutual interest in music. Zappa would go over to Nichols' house where they recorded Zappa's guitar, bouncing tracks together and generally experimenting with overdubs.

From there Nichols' interest in music had driven him towards building his own studio with friends in a four-car garage in Torrance. They called it Quantum. In their spare time they recorded high school bands and worked on advertisements for such clients as Angel Stadium and a clothing store called Forman and Clark. The arrangements were done by a young guitarist called Larry Carlton who would later make significant contributions to Steely Dan albums. Also featured on some of the ads was a young brother and sister team, Richard and Karen Carpenter. The studio became a success and Nichols and his two partners built a larger studio in an old post office, again in Torrance, and started making records. They worked on an album with Kenny Rogers and The First Edition and eventually expanded from 4 to 16 track.

Gradually they diversified from studio ownership to dealing in hi-fi and audio equipment and this led to another lucrative sideline – supplying equipment to other studios. Nichols became so busy he had virtually no time to sleep, but his dedication eventually paid off when he was asked to supply all the equipment for ABC Dunhill's first studio. ABC recognised Nichols' talent and offered him a job which he accepted. Phil Kaye was in charge of the studios at ABC and Nichols became a jack-of-all-trades, doing maintenance, making tape copies, engineering and frequently sleeping at the studio. Among others, Nichols worked on records by The Grass Roots and Hamilton, Joe Frank and Reynolds.

Unknowingly, Fagen, Becker and Katz were on a collision course with Roger Nichols.

Not only were they concerned that their songs were as good as they could possibly make them, they were equally concerned that they should sound as good on record as was technologically possible. Nichols turned out to be the ideal man for the job. "I thought they were great because they cared about what stuff sounded like and wanted to take time to get things happening right," he said. "The other artists I was working with never wanted to do that. They were both hi-fi nuts, especially Walter with his quad electrostatic speakers at home and the latest cartridge and tone arm."

Working at night with ex-Mamas and Papas singer Denny Doherty, Nichols and Katz recorded demos of two Becker and Fagen songs, 'Sail The Waterway' and 'Giles Of The River', which Doherty hoped might secure a solo record deal for himself. He wasn't successful but 'Giles Of The River' would later be recorded by ex-Steppenwolf vocalist John Kay on his 1973 solo album 'My Sportin' Life'. Fagen later dismissed the song, saying: "You could tell there was something wrong with it just by the title."

While Steely Dan were recording what was to become their first single 'Dallas', drummer Jim Hodder was called on to sing an early vocal. He did a fine job. 'Dallas' was another old song from their New York days which had originally been sung by Fagen and had originally been called 'Bye, Bye, Dallas'. A fine example of an early commercial Fagen/Becker composition, it opens with Fagen's keyboards before expanding into a melodic chorus sung in multi-part by the whole band. Jeff Baxter played a lovely pedal steel accompaniment and the song climaxes with a bongos-based instrumental section. Denny Dias had yet to arrive in California when 'Dallas' was recorded but it was released as a single (backed by 'Sail The Waterway') in June of 1972. Steely Dan's contract required them to release a single prior to the LP, but soon afterwards ABC decided it wasn't truly representative of Steely Dan, that it was sending out the wrong signals and, more to the point perhaps, wasn't getting any positive reaction from radio stations, so it was quietly withdrawn.

Years later, Jeff Baxter claimed that the reason 'Dallas' had been so hastily withdrawn was because they feared that with its pedal steel instrumental break and almost country rock feel, Steely Dan would be seen as a country and western act. Nonetheless Baxter still loved the song and has often talked about recording a solo version.

'Dallas' was cut well before the rest of "Can't Buy A Thrill' and Probe Records, ABC's European outlet, released the single in the UK. It was "reviewed" in *Melody Maker* but the paper neglected to mention anything about the song, the band or its chances of success. When it was withdrawn, those already slim chances receded to zero. 'Dallas' failed to make any impact whatsoever in the charts on either side of the Atlantic.

This didn't stop Becker, Fagen and Katz from establishing a very healthy rapport with Roger Nichols. They wanted him and no one else to engineer their sessions and they actually deferred the start of recording what would become 'Can't Buy A Thrill' until Nichols returned from his summer vacation.

This postponement did nothing to appease Jay Lasker's waning patience. When Lasker had been in charge at Dunhill, the label's rapid rise to success meant that he had come to expect almost immediate results. He regularly spoke with Steve Barri and asked when they could expect to see some return on their investment in Steely Dan. By this time ABC had advanced them a considerable sum of money but the group were not yet even in the studio.

Fortunately for Becker and Fagen, Lasker had come to trust Barri's judgement and each time the subject came up Barri was able to placate him by stressing how special he thought Steely Dan were going to be. "It's not gonna be like Three Dog Night," Barri told Lasker, invoking the name of ABC's then most successful signing. He would reiterate the need for patience and plead for them to be allowed – within reason – as much time as they needed. Reluctantly Lasker conceded. Barri was certain that ABC were on to a winner and he didn't want to jeopardise the stability of the relationship by rushing them. Once in the Village Recorder, Steely Dan took a great deal of care over the album and in a harbinger of things to come pulled in outside musicians to complement the band. They had a wealth of material to pick from and were not averse to re-recording old songs like 'Brooklyn' which had been part of their demo tape back in New York.

All the while, they were looking for a singer to take over from Fagen. Some way into the project, with time running out, Fagen's discomfort with his own vocals – despite the protestations of the other members as well as producer Katz – led to them asking Jim Hodder if he knew of a likely singer. Hodder's first suggestion was ex-Middle Class, Jake and The Family Jewels vocalist David Palmer, and they promptly called him back in New Jersey to ask if he fancied joining them in California. Palmer was an old acquaintance of Jim Hodder and had been alternating between singing in bands and working in factories in Boston and New Jersey. His musical career was going nowhere fast and Becker and Fagen hired him sight unseen. Becker couldn't resist cracking a joke at Palmer's expense: "We saw his teeth and then we knew. Anyone with six eye teeth is alright with us." He signed with Steely Dan and was immediately put to use singing on a couple of the more straightforward pop tunes, 'Dirty Work' and 'Brooklyn'.

Gary Katz was convinced this was a retrograde step. Just as Kenny Vance had done before him, he berated Fagen daily about not singing his own compositions, but Fagen was resolute. "I think they had a conflict about it on the one hand, because Walter and I wrote them, we knew what they were about and understood best the attitude that was best to convey them – they realised I could do that," he said. "On the other hand I had a very small range and really hardly any experience and they sort of looked at it two ways – on the one hand they wanted somebody with a bigger voice, a kind of thrilling rock and roll vocalist, but I think we knew we weren't gonna find anybody who could convey the attitude, which was really the most important thing, so they wanted me to do it."

Becker and Fagen later admitted that they had to narrow down the melodies somewhat in order to bring the songs within Fagen's vocal range. While writing songs for others they had included some ambitious musical ideas which weren't appropriate with Fagen at the helm.

Roger Nichols was quick to realise what he had let himself in for. "We finished it in less than six months, which was quick for them. But even then their acceptance level was way above everyone else's. They never had the attitude of 'It's getting late that's good enough', or 'No-one else will notice'. Everything had to be as near perfect as technically and humanly possible."

Quite where they took the title of the album from is still a mystery. Fagen once said it was because Becker called him and said, "You can't buy a thrill in California". But a more logical explanation may be that they took it from the first line of 'It Takes A Lot To Laugh, It Takes A Train To Cry' from Bob Dylan's 1965 tour-de-force, 'Highway 61 Revisited' which was a particular favourite of Fagen's. The song opens with the line "Well, I ride on a mail train, baby/Can't buy a thrill."

Their original idea for the album cover was a photograph of a little girl looking into the window of a porn shop while the proprietor leers at her from inside. In fact, the shoot was completed and producer Gary Katz's young daughter was used in the photograph, but eventually good taste won through and the idea was dropped. Becker and Fagen then wanted to use a photograph from Billy Wilder's 1963 film *Irma La Douce* but due to copyright problems, that wasn't feasible. Instead, ABC's art department worked up a collage of other images which included a photograph of prostitutes awaiting clients.

When Steely Dan saw the cover art they took an instant dislike to it, but by then it was too late and they were unable to exercise their option to veto the cover. The liner notes were written in typical tongue-in-cheek fashion, and the nature of the language testified to the literary background of their author, Tristan Fabriani. Few people realised it at the time but Fabriani was, in fact, a pseudonym for Becker and Fagen themselves. They had occasionally used the name at Jay and The Americans' gigs: asking Black to introduce them as Gus Mahler and Tristan Fabriani was all part of their unceasing tomfoolery. They never worried which one was Mahler and which Fabriani. Significantly, Becker and Fagen failed to mention their stint with Jay and The Americans, attributing the group's varied apprenticeships to "infamous groups from past decades."

Another in-joke on the album was the assertion that 'Do It Again' was not a Becker/Fagen composition, but "traditional". When an interviewer later mentioned this, Fagen laughed. "You should never believe anything it says on a Steely Dan record," he said. "It's just a bunch of lies and bullshit that we write to confuse the listener."

Due to the rigid AM radio format which meant that records over three minutes would rarely be played on the air, ABC requested Steely Dan to edit the almost six-minute 'Do It Again' to a more radio-friendly length. That was the only compromise that Becker and Fagen permitted – and even then it was done grudgingly. "We were trying to widen the public's appreciation of some more interesting rock and roll than they'd been hearing," Fagen said later. " We couldn't get a bite until we did 'Do It Again', which I think is very good, but we'd like to start working from there."

Privately Becker and Fagen were surprised not only by the modest success that 'Can't Buy A Thrill' achieved initially, but also that ABC had released the album in the first place. "We had zero expectations," Becker said. "In fact, we were amazed that ABC bought the album at all. It was like a dream come true." The reason they were immediately successful on arriving in California, they said, was because they were now writing for themselves – their own band rather than for some unidentified person or group. Life, it seemed, was wonderful.

⁓

Becker and Fagen gave their first major interview in October 1972 to Chris Van Ness of the *Los Angeles Free Press*. 'Can't Buy A Thrill' was still to be released, but Van Ness had heard an advance tape of the LP and was sufficiently impressed to venture out to a small club in Glendale called Under The Ice House to witness Steely Dan's first-ever live performance. The ABC press agent's casual hype also intrigued Van Ness: "Listen to it. I don't know anything about the group, but I'm told they're pretty good," he said. Usually press agents described their clients with a great deal more hyperbole than that.

The six-piece Steely Dan was already on stage when Van Ness arrived at the club. He would later write that Steely Dan had... "More rock and roll energy than the J. Geils Band and The Faces put together". He requested an interview with "the group" and this, of course, turned out to be Becker and Fagen.

Van Ness very astutely opened by asking why David Palmer sang only two tunes on the album and yet sang all the songs live. Fagen must have spluttered before replying: "Well, he would have sung more, 'cause he sings better, but we got him late. But he'll be doing most of the singing." Fagen maintained that very shortly Steely Dan would be better represented in live performance. "I can see the way it's going and it's growing very satisfactorily into what we'd like it to be."

Van Ness asked some pertinent and searching questions; indeed, he asked Becker and Fagen if they thought they would be able to keep the band together, particularly since they wrote all the material themselves. "When we started out and when Donald was singing, it was our band," said Becker. "But as we play together more, it becomes more of a group effort. I think it's a sure thing that these six people will stay together," he added as an oblique afterthought.

But Fagen didn't make any bones about their monopoly on the songwriting. "As far as material goes, yeah, I suppose it is our band, and we'll always write the material. But as far as arranging goes, everyone makes a contribution."

Steely Dan made their first appearance in New York at Max's Kansas City in Union Square during November 1972. Their six-song, forty-three minute set previewed songs from the forthcoming album and *Variety*'s reviewer noticed their potential. Within a month of that gig, they were opening for The Kinks on a much wider touring circuit.

ABC were right behind Steely Dan and their music, but expected a tough time getting some of their more complex material played on radio – hence their insistence that they include a couple of straightforward cuts on the record. B/F didn't even want 'Dirty Work' on the album, which may explain why Fagen didn't sing it. Ironically enough, once radio programmers heard the album, they immediately latched on to 'Do It Again', one of the songs that ABC felt would be among the most difficult to secure airplay. One enthusiastic promotion man at ABC insisted on sitting with disc jockeys until they played 'Do It Again' all the way through and eventually the public warmed to its minor key mysteries and Fagen's nasal but interesting voice. Radio programmers clamoured for the song to be a single, saying that it was a certain smash.

On the flip side of Steely Dan's second single, which had been selected by the band themselves and then endorsed by ABC, was a very strange old song called 'Fire In The Hole'. The title was taken from a phrase used by American soldiers in Vietnam. When raiding a Vietcong village and uncovering a hidden bunker, the camouflage matting would be lifted and a grenade thrown down into the pit with the comment "Fire in the hole". Fagen's angry, strident piano dominates proceedings and the song also alludes to how so many students succeeded in dodging the draft back in the late Sixties and early Seventies. (Becker and Fagen included).

"Our first hit single wasn't a cheery thing," Becker ventured. "It's not something you'd normally pick for a first single. No promotion man at any record company would have picked 'Do It Again' as a single. They don't relate to songs composed in minor keys." But it was Becker's favourite song on the album at the time... "a good blend of commercial potential without being silly."

By reaching number six in the US charts in early 1973, it succeeded far beyond Steely Dan's wildest dreams. Even Katz admitted that they had seriously underestimated the song's appeal. "We had no idea that was a single," he said. "That was the farthest thing from our mind – that a long repeating phrase would be a hit song. It never entered our minds. The only reason it was the first cut was because it sounded great. We wanted to put something on that had a nice feel to it when they put the needle down."

Fagen: "But we did write it ['Do It Again'] sort of like a ballad, and it told a story."

'Do It Again' , the opening song on side one of 'Can't Buy A Thrill' and still one of Steely Dan's best known compositions, was recorded on the second take and it was the first "professional record" on which Donald Fagen sang solo lead vocals. But you would never know it. After the long intro, Fagen's voice thrusts into the song with all the confidence of an experienced singer. It featured Denny Dias's deft electric sitar solo and an equally deft organ solo from Fagen. Becker and Fagen's original idea was to have a drone in the background, but they couldn't locate an acoustic sitar and while they were listening to the track, they decided to settle for the electric sitar that *was* available. It represented a rare occasion when they settled for something which didn't possess *exactly* all the right qualities they were looking for in an instrument. Dias hadn't played an electric sitar before and hasn't since.

It was long and rambling and told a story of murder, lynch mobs and card sharps. The lyrics conjure up cinema-style images (as would many Becker/Fagen compositions) of a Sergio Leone spaghetti Western and could easily be a synopsis to one of his films.

'Dirty Work', which David Palmer sang, was another example of Becker and Fagen trying to be more commercial. And yet beneath the sweet and almost sentimental music, there were hidden barbs in the song. The narrator realises he is merely a sexual plaything at the beck and call of his lover, but is so infatuated he is powerless to bring their lusty trysts to an end. In the second verse Becker included a reference to the game of chess ("Like the castle in its corner/In a medieval game") which he has always enjoyed. Guest musician Jerome Richardson contributed a perfectly understated tenor sax solo.

'Kings', which Becker and Fagen described as a "vacuous historical romance", features a sizzling guitar solo by Elliott Randall. Becker, Fagen and Katz knew Randall from New York, having worked with him at a few Jay and The Americans gigs and on one or two of their demos. He was given free rein to interpret the solo as he wanted and due to some disruptions in his personal life, came up with what he called a "deliberate trip into schizophrenia land", a break which lurches from the very melodic to extremely obtuse whole tones and back again.

But Randall's real claim to fame – the terrific solo on 'Reelin' In The Years' – was pure coincidence. He'd been invited to stop by the Village Recorder by Jeff Baxter to say hi to "the guys". The others in the band didn't even know Randall was in town and as Baxter had been grappling with the solo for some time without getting Becker and Fagen's nod of approval, and knowing Randall's propensity for such interpretations, he graciously suggested that Randall should try. After a couple of takes the memorable solo was in the can without any punching in or editing. The rest, as they say, is history. Jimmy Page once nominated it as his favourite guitar solo of all time.

The day after his masterful performances on 'Kings' and 'Reelin' In The Years' Becker and Fagen actually asked Elliot Randall to join Steely Dan, but he declined their offer for two reasons: he didn't want to live in Los Angeles and he knew that Becker and Fagen were rigidly controlling the show. He foresaw a relatively short life span for the group as a six-piece.

In 1973 Becker and Fagen told Alison Steele on her *Nightbird And Company* radio show that they got the musical idea first on 'Reelin' In The Years' and added the lyrics later. If one song demonstrated Fagen's singing ability then 'Reelin' In The Years' was it. Fagen executes its rapid-fire lyrics and difficult verses with apparent ease, prompting Gary Katz to exclaim: "I would dare anyone to sing a verse of 'Reelin' In The Years'."

'Midnite Cruiser' again features a fine vocal by Jim Hodder and bears a first line reference to one of Fagen's adolescent jazz idols, Thelonious (thinly disguised as Felonius) Monk. Fagen's chorus drives the song along with warmth and vitality. The Latin influenced 'Only A Fool Would Say That' features Jeff Baxter speaking the Spanish line at the end of the song.

In what was to be the first of many such requests, Walter Becker was persuaded by a frustrated and puzzled journalist to elucidate on the impenetrability of the lyrics of 'Brooklyn', since he was having difficulty in unravelling them. Becker explained that the "charmer under me" was indeed the character mentioned in their cryptic sleeve notes: "President Street Pete is the beneficiary here." He and his family had lived in the apartment below Donald Fagen.

"The song is just a bunch of things that the guy and his wife had coming to them, you know, for the indignities that they had suffered living in Brooklyn, sitting on the stoop and just shooting the shit about the Mets and that kind of thing for twenty years. So as you see the song does yield to a valid interpretation."

"Change Of The Guard' is as bright and sunny a song as Becker and Fagen would ever write and it gave the Skunk a chance to shine on a guitar solo which climaxes with a slide that flits wonderfully from speaker to speaker. 'Turn That Heartbeat Over Again' closes the album with Becker, Fagen and Palmer all sharing the vocals in a unified chorus.

"I guess I am a perfectionist, but 'Can't Buy A Thrill' is the worst album we'll ever make," Denny Dias said soon after its release. And looking back on the album many years later, if anything, his opinion had hardened even further. "I don't know what we were trying to do. The music was intricate and we just weren't up to it."

Fagen eventually came to feel the same way, too. He said that the mistake they had made with 'Can't Buy A Thrill' was to try and correct things which sounded weak after they had cut the basic track. As Denny Dias said, the track had to sound good when it was put on tape. "Many times you think you can fix things in the mix, but you can't. You have to start with a solid drum track and a lot of those songs didn't have that; the time was strange or the performance wasn't good or it didn't cook, you know?"

Dias commended Gary Katz for his restraint in not forcing his own ideas on to the record in the way many producers would have done. If Becker and Fagen were convinced about what they wanted, Katz would willingly submit to their wishes.

Generally the reviews for 'Can't Buy A Thrill' were excellent. Naturally, on the emergence of a new group, critics tried to draw a parallel with existing bands and some of those rather stretched comparisons included Crosby, Stills, Nash and Young, Procol Harum, Spirit, Stephen Stills, Bread and even David Bowie.

In the UK, *Sounds'* Penny Valentine loved it: "A really superb album this, polished up like a diamond. More please." *Rolling Stone* ended their review with the quote: "'Can't Buy A Thrill' is distinguished by three top level cuts and scattered moments of inspiration, but there are those instances of Steely Dan coming on like a limp dildo. Too bad – great title."

'Reelin' In The Years' became Steely Dan's second hit single from the album. Coupled with 'Only A Fool Would Say That' and released in March 1973, it marginally failed to hit the Top Ten in the US. Despite some reverential reviews in the UK and extensive airplay, it failed to chart until some six years later when it was reissued. In the US, some confusion arose over the name Steely Dan and England's long established folk group Steeleye Span, and in February 1973 *Sounds* reported that Steely Dan was being forced to change its name for the American market! There was no basis of fact in the report.

Soon after the album was released Steely Dan snagged a job composing an advertising jingle for Schlitz beer. Becker and Fagen used the music from the Schlitz jingle as the basis for a commercial, but refused to let the beer company hear it until it was finished. They spent six to eight hours in a studio while a representative from Schlitz's ad agency waited out in the lobby. The props they requested included a giant sombrero and a tank of helium. (The photograph of Fagen and Denny Dias holding the helium eventually appeared on the back cover of 'Katy Lied' but was taken at the Schlitz session).

The ad involved a bilingual narration from Donald Fagen and Jeff Baxter. Fagen muttered things like... "When I get home from a hard day's work, I grab for all the gusto I can get, 'cause you only go around one time". While he was narrating in English, Baxter translated into Spanish, simultaneously breathing in the helium in order to give his voice a high-pitched cartoon-like quality. The ad was based around the slogan "When you're out of Schlitz, you're out of beer" and according to Denny Dias, Becker and Fagen wrote "the coolest beer commercial you're ever likely to hear".

Although Schlitz paid for the session and everything connected with it, it turned out that some of the English words had dubious meanings when translated into Spanish and the ad was never transmitted. Walter Becker was pleased about that. "The ad was done on a contingency basis and never hit the airwaves, much to my joy," he said.

After four years of trying Becker and Fagen were at last in business. Their début album was selling well and was about to go gold and they'd had two hit singles. 'Can't Buy A Thrill' eventually peaked at number 17 in the US in February 1973. With no hit single to promote the album, it made no show in the UK album chart.

Although Becker and Fagen were surprised by the *speed* of their success, they weren't surprised to have achieved it. "We were very arrogant teenagers – well, we were in our twenties, but we were still basically teenagers – and we always felt one of our things would hit," said Fagen. "It was very exciting. I think we probably downplayed it among ourselves in a way, because for one thing we figured it would be just a one hit deal. So we said, 'Well, it's a hit, but a lot of people have these one hit records and so what?' It was also frightening about becoming known."

But if the success of 'Do It Again' caught them by surprise, neither had anticipated the downside: the pressure to repeat that success. Their delight was short-lived. The real work was only just beginning.

❧

Thirty-Five Sweet Goodbyes

The accepted wisdom of the music industry in 1972 was that to translate success on the singles chart into album sales an act must tour extensively. To this end ABC appointed Joel Cohen, a partner in a company called Kudo III, to manage Steely Dan. Cohen's previous experience was as tour manager for Three Dog Night, a band to whom the road was their second home.

Although they were totally unprepared for the first tour, Walter Becker and Donald Fagen felt obliged to bow to corporate demands since ABC had given them their full support before and during the recording of 'Can't Buy A Thrill'. Cohen promptly put the tour theory into practice with a vengeance, managing to secure Steely Dan as opening act for some very big names and some very surprising names too. "The manager that we had used to road manage Three Dog Night... that was basically his concept of how things should be done. Constant touring... and singles," said Fagen. "We weren't well rehearsed at all. And the tours weren't well organized. We were always shuttling back and forth from the west to the east coast. He felt we owed it to our singles audience."

That singles audience had bought over a million copies of 'Do It Again'. "We had a million selling single, but an album – that's where the gold is," Denny Dias told one journalist. "All the members of this band want to keep on making good records, do bigger tours and get that million-selling album." Quite whether Becker and Fagen wanted to "do bigger tours" is a matter of conjecture.

In December 1972, Steely Dan were booked to open for The Kinks. They then went on to open for Elton John, The Beach Boys, Uriah Heep, The James Gang, The Guess Who, Black Oak Arkansas, Focus and, most surprisingly of all, British good time glam-rockers Slade who were attempting to translate their UK success Stateside.

Fagen, never the most robust of physical specimens, later admitted that opening for heavy metal acts was "very stressful" and that he was "very frightened of the personnel". He had light-heartedly mentioned in a press biography that he didn't talk to anyone over five feet eight inches tall – that throwaway comment now took on an altogether more ominous meaning.

The point was vividly illustrated on March 30, 1973, when Steely Dan shared a bill with Black Oak Arkansas and Dutch instrumentalists Focus at the Hollywood Palladium. Black Oak were a bunch of good natured, rowdy, beer-swilling Southerners whose biker-style audience consumed vast quantities of alcohol and other stimulants while bouncers carried unconscious bodies out of the gig by the truckload. The aesthete in Donald Fagen was offended; the scene left him feeling distinctly uneasy.

An incident in South Dakota seemed to encapsulate the reasons why Becker and Fagen loathed road life. Steely Dan were headlining a gig and in the process of changing over the equipment between soundchecks, someone stole Jeff Baxter's guitar amplifier. They knew who the thief was, but couldn't prove it. It caused much consternation in the

Steely Dan camp and Fagen could be seen behind the stage leaning against a power pole with a look of sad resignation on his face.

On another occasion Steely Dan were due to open for The Eagles at an open air concert in the midwest when a severe electrical storm hit the area in the afternoon. The winds whipped beneath the stage with such force that it buckled upwards with the equipment on top. One piano leg actually pierced the flimsily constructed plywood stage. The storm passed and Steely Dan's crew checked the weather forecast, only to be told more storms were on the way. Most of the Steely Dan entourage – including Becker and Fagen – thought it was far too risky to contemplate going ahead with the show, but by the time the soundchecks were scheduled the weather had turned clear and sunny. Tour manager Gary McPike was furious, but Steely Dan refused to budge and didn't play.

Fagen once talked about a gig where on taking the stage he somehow managed to plunge a speaker screw about three inches into his head and bled throughout the set. "It did give a Grand Guignol effect," he said.

The worst aspect of touring for Becker and Fagen was waking up in a different hotel room each day, and in Becker's case a particular dislike of being jostled awake much earlier than he preferred in order to travel on to their next destination. Fagen hated riding in rental cars, but by the same token he would have nothing to do with the rock'n'roll image of riding in long black Cadillac limousines. Becker and Fagen weren't seeking money, groupies or adulation; they thought of themselves as working musicians and songwriters, nothing more, nothing less. It was an attitude that most of their hedonistic peers in the rock world did not share.

Steely Dan enjoyed an excellent relationship with their road crew who took a great deal of pride in their work. But Becker and Fagen couldn't understand why roadies would willingly subject themselves to a gruelling tour and then come back for more. One day Fagen asked Englishman Jimmy Lewis why he did it. "Our job is to create an environment in which you can create," he said. The reply stopped Fagen in his tracks and instilled in him a respect for road crews that never wavered.

Steely Dan's live set at this point included certain songs – 'Megashine City', 'Take My Money' and 'Hellbound Train' – which had been written specifically as vehicles for David Palmer and which would never make it onto a Steely Dan studio album. Becker, Fagen and Katz especially did not want to be reminded of Palmer's brief and inapt contribution to the band.

Becker and Fagen had also written a tasty live guitar segue from 'Megashine City' into 'Dirty Work'. These segues and bridges eventually became the norm at Steely Dan concerts in order to give Fagen a break from singing. "Our shows," he recalled in his normal deadpan fashion, "were a constant din from beginning to end."

Steely Dan were great musicians but they were far from the most photogenic band in the land. Fagen had a slight stoop, Becker's long straight hair almost always looked in need of a trim and a vigorous shampoo, and their dress sense – or lack of it – in what was then a bizarre period fashionwise anyway was risible. Critics were quick to lambast Steely Dan for their lack of "visual style". After one of their early gigs at the Whisky A

Go Go in Los Angeles, one reviewer referred to them as "the ugliest band in the world". Of course, Becker and Fagen couldn't care less: they were in rock'n'roll for the music not the showbiz; they sought to emulate their jazz heroes, musicians who gave no thought whatsoever to what they wore on stage. Image was unimportant in jazz. "We were used to seeing a musician kicking over his bottle of beer," said Becker who would have been happy to turn his back to the audience for an entire set if he could get away with it.

The spectacle and theatricality which had crept into big time rock – smoke bombs, face masks, ostentatious light shows, outrageous glam-rock clothes and platform shoes – revolted Steely Dan, although Jeff Baxter was perpetually amused by the stage clothes worn by some bands. Denny Dias once said that he was amazed that Elton John could play the piano at all while wearing six inch heels. Of far more immediate concern to Fagen and Becker, and Gary Katz, was David Palmer's vocal interpretation of their songs. Despite his reluctance to sing live, Fagen soon realised that he was the best person to accurately convey the attitude of their songs and that he would somehow have to overcome his fear of fronting the band. He was going to have to learn to talk to an audience and even crack a few jokes. "It was very difficult to convince me to get up in front of people and sing," he told one interviewer. "But I finally got enough courage to do it, and I've been getting into it slowly. Now it's come together pretty well."

Another drawback with lead singer David Palmer was his propensity to wear very tight trousers and each time he bent over or stretched he ran the risk of splitting them. At one gig at a small club in Philadelphia, Palmer had met with friends before the show and drunk more liquor than was wise. With Palmer in a stupor, Steely Dan took the stage, but the singer was way beyond recall. Not only did he sing the entire set a half-tone flat, but he also split his tight pants right up the middle. The stage was just three feet above the floor and those seated directly in front were given a close-up view of Palmer's sweaty crotch. To make matters worse, he wasn't wearing underwear. On another occasion at the Whisky in LA, Palmer's split trousers were repaired with gaffer tape. The Philadelphia incident didn't help David Palmer's cause. Neither did another disastrous occasion when he missed his mouth and poured a can of beer over himself at an important press reception.

Fagen was steeling himself to face the fact that he was going to have to be the lead singer, but he was reluctant to over indulge in pre-show intoxicants. David Palmer was a nice guy and everyone in the band liked him, but artistic considerations outweighed social niceties. In April of 1973, Palmer's four-month reign as Steely Dan vocalist came to an end.

Fagen was backed into a corner; there was now no denying that his voice *was* the sound of Steely Dan. Occasionally, only half seriously, they would discuss getting someone else in to do the job. One voice that Becker and Fagen liked was Elliot Lurie, the singer from Looking Glass who had a US number one hit with 'Brandy (You're a Fine Girl)' in 1972. Another vocalist Becker and Fagen thought would work well in Steely Dan was Gerry Rafferty, singer on Stealer's Wheel's 1973 hit, 'Stuck In The Middle With You'.

But Gary Katz had no such doubts about Fagen's ability as a vocalist. At an open air gig in the Balboa Stadium in San Diego when Steely Dan opened for Elton John before a crowd of 30,000, Katz stood alongside Warren Wallace who commented how he loved to hear Fagen sing. "From the first time I heard Fagen sing, everything else in my life became secondary," Katz told Wallace.

"If we had known about Dave [Palmer] earlier, we could have incorporated him more fully into the Steely Dan sound," Fagen said, almost by way of apology. "He was a good singer for us early on, but he didn't really have the attitude to put the songs over. So I started doing it myself, much to my chagrin. It seems to have worked out."

ев

On January 30, 1973, Steely Dan interrupted their busy touring schedule to tape the NBC rock show *Midnight Special* which was aired on February 9. They played 'Do It Again' and 'Reelin' In The Years'. During the spring of 1973, they continued gigging extensively right across America. It was an exhausting schedule, arranged so they could record during the week and tour at weekends. The schedule took them from San Francisco to Denver, from Albuquerque to El Paso and from Baltimore to Seattle. Denny Dias remarked that at the weekends they needed time to recover from their recording sessions but they had to travel and perform, and during the week they needed time to recover from all the weekend's touring but had to press on with recording.

Becker and Fagen also found their non stop schedule was not conducive to their songwriting routine and often remarked on the effort that went into their tunes and how their songs couldn't be composed in one session at some Holiday Inn in the middle of nowhere. Becker and Fagen couldn't – or wouldn't – write songs while on the road.

Steely Dan now had a successful album behind them as well as two Top Twenty singles and they were adamant they were not going to be rushed with their second album. They began to establish a system of working which would continue to develop through the decade, right up to the sessions for 'Aja' and 'Gaucho'. "We've spent many years developing our writing style," Fagen told New York DJ Alison Steele in 1973, "but as far as the sound, we had never played live when we went in to record."

It was a double-edged sword because although their record company paid for them to fly from gig to gig (which in itself was unusual), they were sending them to places like Fayetteville and Hammond, Louisiana, deep south swamplands which, to confirmed city dwellers like Becker and Fagen, was like taking Eskimos to the Sahara. They didn't want to be there, period. A year later Becker and Fagen would immortalise their touring experience in the ironic opening line of 'Pretzel Logic': "I would love to tour the southland/In a travelling minstrel show."

"We may have been typecast from our first album but I don't think I know or anybody else knew what kind of group that was," said Fagen. "You know, it's funny, how you put something together like an album and people see some coherent strain running through it that was never intended or conceived or that we really don't see that way. I've noticed quite a few people don't know what to call it. It's certainly not too well defined in my mind."

In between the gigs Steely Dan worked on the album which became 'Countdown To Ecstasy' at the Village Recorder in West Los Angeles, maintaining the same studio team of Roger ("The Immortal") Nichols, Gary Katz and Dick LaPalm. Before he was fired, Palmer did record a couple brief sessions on 'Countdown' as a background singer, along with Royce Jones who would later be drafted in to augment the touring band. Also hired to sing on just one song on 'Countdown' was Michael Fenelly whose voice had a certain 'high' quality that Fagen liked.

One night, during the mixing of 'King Of The World' after Becker and Fagen had long since given up and gone home, Denny Dias, Roger Nichols and Gary Katz stayed behind to try and finish the song. They worked non-stop until eventually Katz fell asleep on the floor. Nichols said the mix they had sounded like sonic wallpaper; it was so perfect that after the song had been played you couldn't recall hearing it. "It was very complex and required a lot of level changes and manipulations on the board – there was no computerised mixdown then – so everything had to be done by hand," said Nichols. "Denny came up with a technique of just doing a verse and then doing just the chorus and splicing the two pieces of two-track tape together. This made it possible to do things that no human could do in real time."

But they were working in an unfamiliar room – Studio C instead of Studio A – and the combination of that, together with their exhaustion, meant that they ended up with a totally unsatisfactory mix. Dias and Nichols were still in the studio at 10am. the following morning when the group who were booked in that day came knocking on the door.

Dias never stayed up all night mixing again. "You should be well rested to mix," he said. He was a real audiophile and stereo buff and once inside a studio he couldn't resist the temptation to get his hands on the board. Dias knew his quest for perfection sometimes irritated the others, but he just couldn't help himself: "I really wanted everything to be in stereo perspective, perfectly balanced symmetry. I would occasionally annoy everybody, although some of the sounds that came out were pretty good."

Indeed, Dias must have been spectacularly successful because twenty years later Roger Nichols confirmed that Donald Fagen *still* carried around in his wallet a piece of paper on which Denny had written the eq points necessary to brighten, clarify or warm up sounds.

Becker and Fagen considered it essential that every song they recorded had a rock steady drum track. On 'Show Biz Kids' there were problems with the tempo which Roger Nichols solved with more inspired technological wizardry. "I remember we had a lot of problems trying to record a perfect, ultimately steady rhythm track. It was just one of those tunes that was so very difficult to play exactly in tempo, with every instrument in sync. What would happen was we'd get a great drum track and something else wouldn't quite cut it, or everything else would be spot on except for the snare. After a while, everyone got very frustrated, and they started trying different drummers, and then different combinations of players and still it never quite hung together properly.

"There were no drum machines in those days, so we made a twenty-four track, eight bar tape loop, which at 30 ips was a considerable length of tape, trailed it out through the door into the studio, around a little idler which was set up on a camera tripod, back into the studio and then copied that to a second 24-track machine. Everything was on the tape except the lead vocal and lead guitar. It worked like a dream."

Fagen admitted that some of the songs were completely his and some were completely Becker's, "but in most there isn't any cut and dried version. 'The Boston Rag', for instance, has my chorus and verses by Walter," said Fagen, attempting to explain how the song came to feature the lyric "You Were Lady Bayside". Bayside was a community in Queens where Becker once lived and where he formed one of his first rock and roll bands. He included it for no other reason than he liked the sound of it in the song. Just as Fagen's vocal comes in, the song features some very crisp 'Stairway To Heaven-esque' acoustic guitar from Ben Benay. The lines in the song "Lonnie was the kingpin back in 1965" and "Lonnie swallowed up all he found/It was forty-eight hours till Lonnie came around" refer to Lonnie Yongue, Fagen's room-mate at Bard. Strangely enough Yongue had never been to Boston, but Becker later commented: "The nice thing about 'The Boston Rag' is that it took place in New York. I haven't seen Lonnie in a long time. Hi, Lonnie!"

Jeff Baxter played the guitar solo in 'The Boston Rag'. He later described his perspective of the process to achieve what Fagen and Becker were looking for in a solo as "sort of a combination of exorcism, displays of technique and all kinds of things. My frame of mind during most of those solos was an extremely emotional emotionlessness. I was very into the music, but to get too involved would have been dangerous, because the idea was that nobody got that personally involved. Usually Donald would say 'Bend a lot of strings' and 'Go fast'."

Baxter added that sometimes Becker would push him to the point where he wound up wondering if one solo was any different from the next, but he still never had any complaints. He also said Gary Katz would never buy a solo unless he was turning purple doing it. Baxter wasn't a great lover of effects pedals, preferring to plug his guitar direct into the board and cranking his amp up to full volume. However, on 'King Of The World' he used an Echoplex.

'King Of The World' was written after Becker and Fagen watched the 1962 film *Panic In The Year Zero*, starring and directed by Ray Milland. "Typical devastation," said Becker. "Like, what you do at the end of the world. The sense of doom is overwhelming." The film focused on a family on a fishing trip in the mountains when Los Angeles is blasted by a nuclear attack. 'King Of The World' examines the behaviour and predicament of a survivor after a nuclear attack and asks whether he would be better off dead anyway.

Becker later laid beneath the drums in the far corner of the studio making random comments which were mixed into the song's instrumental section. His comments were heavily equalized and reverbed, and one of the barely audible things he said was "I think my face is on fire". This was Becker and Fagen's cryptic comment which accompanied the song on the lyric sheet of the Probe UK pressing of the album. Other comments ranged from "Ooh La La" on 'Pearl Of The Quarter' and "Enervated after an attack of unrelieved nostalgia, Jeff 'Skunk' Baxter sheds his outer skin and stands revealed as a Wild Boy" on 'The Boston Rag' to "Dias the Bebopper meets Baxter the Skunk beneath the Bo tree in this altered blues" on 'Bodhisattva'.

The impenetrability of 'Your Gold Teeth', another song recorded during these sessions, had every rock critic in America struggling to decode its significance. None managed it. The obscurity of the line "Even Cathy Berberian knows there's one roulade she can't sing" demonstrated Fagen and Becker's quest for anything and everything that was oblique. Many fans and critics thought that Cathy Berberian was a figment of Fagen and Becker's imagination, but she actually did exist. Born in New York of Armenian immigrant parents, she studied at the Milan Conservatory and adopted a singing style that required her to moan, snarl, snort, squeal and scream in imitating electronic sounds. She later said she was "terribly flattered by the tribute from Steely Dan", and bought several copies of 'Countdown To Ecstasy' for her immediate family. Becker and Fagen were never persuaded to reveal the song's meaning (if indeed it means anything) but their lifting of a lyric from Count Basie and Joe Williams' version of a song entitled 'Going To Chicago Blues': "There ain't nothing in Chicago for a monkey woman to do" *was* noticed and made public a few years later.

References to Bard College feature frequently in Becker and Fagen songs but 'My Old School' was the centrepiece. One wall of the Village Recorder building in Santa Monica had been painted in various shades of blue – depicting an earthquake with a hefty piece of freeway falling into the Pacific – and Becker and Fagen used the mural as inspiration for the line: "California tumbles into the sea."

There was a reference to the Wolverine, a train that ran up to Boston (and through Annandale-on-the-Hudson) from New York and Bard was compared favourably with William And Mary, one of the oldest colleges in America. But the song is best remembered for Jeff Baxter's blistering guitar solo, played on an instrument that he had only just finished making. "The guitar I played it on I built myself. I built it that afternoon; I finished that Stratocaster. I cut it out of a beautiful piece of board maple, cut the neck and fretted it, wound the pick-ups and stuck it all together and brought it into the studio. That guitar was only finished three hours before at the parking lot in Valley Sound."

'Bodhisattva' was written by Donald Fagen without Becker's input. Denny Dias recalled picking Fagen up on the way to the studio and Fagen telling him he'd only written the tune the previous night. "That's sort of a parody on how Western people look at eastern religion – sort of over-simplify it," said Fagen. "We thought it was rather amusing – most people don't get it." Like Duke Ellington, Fagen was (and is) eternally fascinated by the Orient, and he managed to incorporate both China and Japan into the lyric of the song.

Jeff Baxter later claimed that at the time 'Countdown' was recorded, he had just learned how to play Bach's 'Toccata And Fugue' on the guitar. "It is a beautiful piece of music... you hear it every time you see a monster movie. And there was one particular chord pattern, I was so hung up on it, I said to Donald we have to use this. The next thing I knew he came in with 'The Boston Rag' and he said 'You're gonna like this', and he put that actual chord change in it. It thrilled me to death, Donald listening to my ideas."

"This was a perfect example of the rest of the band developing arrangements," Becker said. "'Your Gold Teeth' was developed in a playing kind of context. Denny had the spotlight and I think it worked out rather well. By 'Countdown To Ecstasy' we would come in with the basic tune idea, play it down and develop the arrangement more with the band. Jeff, in particular, was able to contribute a lot more in terms of integral parts of the songs rather than add-ons. 'Countdown To Ecstasy' had kind of a unique flavour because of that."

Donald Fagen's girlfriend, Dorothy 'Dotty of Hollywood' White, who had been an aspiring artist for some time, designed the cover for 'Countdown'. Her watercolour depicted three almost featureless aliens looking blankly into the distance at some dazzling lights. When ABC boss Jay Lasker saw the painting, he immediately took exception to it, complaining that there were five members in the group and there were only three figures in the painting. "Dotty" argued that it wasn't a painting of the group, simply something which would look good on the cover. Lasker was adamant. So White went away, studied her watercolour and managed to incorporate two more vague shapes into the painting without altering its impact. The apparently disembodied hand which appeared in the back cover photograph of Steely Dan in ABC Studios' control room belonged to Roger Nichols.

As for the actual title of the album, Jeff Baxter explained that..."Steely Dan had been planning to write a whole mini-opera about a marine and the last thing was how he goes on leave and we were gonna write a song called 'Countdown To Ecstasy' because he finally got laid. We figured we'd be in big trouble with the State department so we didn't do it."

'Countdown To Ecstasy' was released in July 1973, together with the single 'Show Biz Kids' which had been selected by the group themselves. It was Becker and Fagen's stinging denunciation of the Los Angeles lifestyle and featured a superb slide guitar part from Rick Derringer, but it was an abject failure, only reaching number 61 on the *Billboard* singles chart. As with 'Do It Again' the five-minute plus song had to be edited, which conveniently enabled a four-letter word to be exorcised too. Strangely enough, critics and fans alike also had great difficulty figuring out the incessant vocal vamp beneath the song. One ridiculous music press suggestion was "We're gonna love sweeties". In fact, the girls were singing "You go to Lost Wages", a Fagen/Becker pun on Las Vegas.

At least two of the voices comprising the closing hubbub were those of road manager Warren Wallace and a member of the road crew, John Famular. With David Palmer already on the way out and Fagen unwilling, it's just possible to pick up Wallace asking a pertinent but facetious question: "Hey, is this the band that's looking for a lead singer?" Immediately after Wallace comes Famular who, by cupping his hands over his mouth, does his best imitation of a commercial airline pilot clicking on the microphone and saying: "This is your captain speaking!" When Fagen came to write the sleeve notes he made sure "Grunt" Wallace and "Pilot" Famular were credited for their respective contributions.

While recording 'Show Biz Kids' Becker and Fagen expressed mild concern at using an expletive, but when they briefly tried an alternative word it sounded silly and completely out of context, so their original lyric was allowed to stand. Katz was amused as well as relieved: "We did it with style and panache, I thought."

"We're sadder but wiser in relation to that," Becker said, "but it's always comforting to know that you've got something potentially obscene on AM radio."

ABC still allowed Steely Dan to pick their own singles and they naturally chose whatever happened to be their favourite song with little regard for commercial potential. The choice of 'Show Biz Kids' was their first big mistake. Even though Steely Dan were still touring extensively, they were unable to overcome the setback.

Katz was very disappointed. "We did think we had a hit single this time, though. It had a great repeating chorus, nice Motown beat and nothing happened. To this day, we can't figure out what's commercial."

Katz felt radio stations were partly to blame. "I don't think radio gave the second album or third single (he excluded 'Dallas' from his calculations) a chance. In one city where we were coming off the two Top Ten singles, they told us we couldn't get play until Dallas played the record. So the band went there, set for a 9,000 seat hall. They had to be moved to an 18,000 seat auditorium and they filled that. So we say, 'Obviously the public accepts the group, based on the last two records and the crowds. Why can't you play the record?' I don't care if the group is Steely Dan or Dawn, and I don't care if the guy at the radio station likes the record. If the public accepts an act, then the station should play it. Where else will the public hear a new group on the radio and what kid will pay six dollars for an album by a group he's never heard? This is my complaint."

Henceforth Becker, Fagen and Katz fought shy of choosing their own singles. "We'll leave that to someone who thinks they know the right thing to pick," said Katz.

In the UK, Probe Records adopted an aggressive point-of-sale campaign for the album, running a series of 45-second ads on Radio Luxembourg, taking full page ads in the consumer music press and distributing 1500 display cards to selected retailers. In a bizarre twist to the campaign, Probe also sponsored a Steely Dan balloon race at a Radio Luxembourg motor racing meeting at Brands Hatch in Kent.

English disc jockey John Peel reviewed the single in *Sounds* and liked it. He admired Rick Derringer's slide guitar playing and Becker and Fagen's "healthy cynicism with show biz and show biz groovers". Peel also lamented the omission of the rude word... "that might have prodded the more impressionable among you into raging, uncontrolled copulation in the high street."

As ever Fagen tried to play down his and Becker's roles in the creation of the music. In interviews he stressed the importance of the other musicians in the band: "My bass player and I write all the material, but the solos and arrangements come from the group. Walter and I think it out in advance and then we go into the studios and work on the tunes from there. I think of them as compositions rather than songs. They are structured, but there is room for improvisation."

In October 1973 'My Old School'/'Pearl Of The Quarter' became the second single from the album to flop, reaching no higher than number 63 in *Billboard*, although it sounded great on the radio and to this day remains a particular favourite among Steely Dan fans.

Steely Dan had blown their chance and they knew it. Having very nearly had two Top Ten singles from 'Can't Buy A Thrill', they had now released two miserable singles failures and 'Countdown To Ecstasy' suffered as a result. All the momentum they had gained from their début album had been lost at a stroke.

Nevertheless, reviews of the album were once again excellent. In the UK, *Melody Maker* lamented the lack of success of 'Can't Buy A Thrill' and implored fans to go out and buy this album. "If they don't happen here this time, there's something drastically wrong with this country's ears," bemoaned *MM*'s critic.

Rolling Stone cited Steely Dan as the American dance band alternative to Slade, a comparison that belies understanding. *Stereo Review* marvelled at their "potent and persuasive mix of rock, jazz and pop" and said it was "a really excellent album". *Records and Recording* rounded off their review by claiming that Steely Dan, along with The Band and The Grateful Dead, "*are* American white rock at the moment".

❧

Soon after the release of 'Countdown To Ecstasy' Jim Hodder was at a party in Pasadena when in the early hours seven or eight friends began singing old Motown songs. One of them was Royce Jones who was signed to Motown with a group called Odyssey (not the band which eventually had a hit with 'Native New Yorker') and Hodder asked him if he was interested in trying out for Steely Dan who were about to embark on another tour. Two weeks later Jones passed an audition at Modern Music Studios by singing 'Bodhisattva'. He was only a verse and a half into the song when Donald Fagen stopped him and told him that he'd got the gig. Royce Jones thus replaced David Palmer and made his début with Steely Dan at the Sopwith Camel club in Glendale.

As a direct result of the flak that Steely Dan had received in the press for their shabby looks, and also because of the departure of David Palmer, Fagen and Becker hired two female backing singers, Gloria Granola and Jenny Soule, affectionately nicknaming them Porky and Bucky, for the 'Countdown To Ecstasy' tour. Porky and Bucky liked to dress up in fetching go-go costumes which Becker and Fagen loved and they were equally as enthusiastic to have been invited to join Steely Dan.

Fagen was asked if they had thought about going the whole hog and putting the two girls in a cage and suspending it above the band in true Las Vegas style. "We thought about it," he said, "but you can only get people to do so many things."

"Sooner or later they will do the routine with the live python," added Becker.

Royce Jones soon realised that Fagen didn't especially want to sing live, and he was asked if he wanted to shoulder some of the responsibility. He did, and was given the opportunity to sing 'Brooklyn', 'Dirty Work', 'Any Major Dude' and 'The Boston Rag' as well as sharing vocals with Fagen on 'Bodhisattva'.

At the Santa Monica Civic Auditorium in September Steely Dan returned to the stage and surprised fans with an improvised encore of The Angels' 1963 US hit 'My

Boyfriend's Back', sung by Porky and Bucky. The song hadn't been worked up in rehearsals and Royce Jones was amazed when they suddenly began playing it. It never became a regular feature of their live shows, but when they were in the right frame of mind Becker and Fagen added it to their set list. When Becker and Fagen had performed at oldies shows with Jay and The Americans, The Angels were occasionally on the bill and it was Fagen's idea to include a tongue-in-cheek version of the song for the girls to sing.

Although they had only recently increased the size of the band, Becker and Fagen spoke publicly about adding further personnel to augment their live show. "We want to eventually have an orchestra on stage," said Fagen at one point. The buzz about Steely Dan's live show was really gaining pace now and after their stint as opening act, they were popular enough to attract an audience on their name alone. It was around this time (September 1973) that they played their first concert as headliners.

In between recording Steely Dan albums, Gary Katz and Roger Nichols produced and engineered an album for Katz's friend Thomas Jefferson Kaye. Kaye was descended from Indian blood and his self-titled 1973 album was virtually a who's who of Steely Dan musicians: Walter Becker played bass on two tracks, Donald Fagen sang background vocals with David Palmer on three tunes, Jeff Baxter guested on one track and other Dan session regulars included Rick Derringer, Victor Feldman, Clydie King, Venetta Fields and Sherlie Matthews.

Becker and Fagen were now heavily in demand for interviews, but they did themselves no favours by habitually describing their music as "smart rock". If anything was guaranteed to turn critics against a band, it was a couple of smart-ass college hipsters touting their own intelligence and musical integrity (albeit tongue in cheek). One Steely Dan bio from ABC describes a typical Becker/Fagen song as having "a penetrating verse, a rousing chorus, an inspired bridge and, of course, a no-holds barred instrumental of some sort".

"Pop songs with some kind of structure that's interesting and can be developed," was how Fagen described Steely Dan's music. "We're pretty traditional in that way, but the chords are usually more interesting than most rock and roll, I think."

Sure enough, some critics took exception to Becker and Fagen's conceit and sneered at their obscure lyrics and intellectualising. Becker called Steely Dan's music "planned diversity", and Jeff Baxter agreed: "I'd rather have people looking forward to a song they don't know anything about than looking forward to a song they know is gonna be the same as the last song."

But Becker and Fagen were confident that their particular brand of songwriting would be a hit with the critics if not with the public. They admitted that they wrote and recorded solely to please themselves and if other people liked it that was a welcome bonus. But Becker and Fagen's single-minded dedication and all-encompassing musical control was soon to have its inevitable consequences.

❧

CHAPTER V

Slow Hand Row

Once the novelty of space, warm weather and laid-back insouciance had worn thin, Los Angeles was a grave disappointment to Walter Becker and Donald Fagen. Neither was suited to the balmy Southern California lifestyle, they missed New York's artistic vitality and, in fact, Becker said that once they got to California they soon began writing about New York. 'Show Biz Kids' palpably demonstrated their feelings about Hollywood and its inhabitants, and the east coast/west coast, New York/Malibu dichotomy came up several times in interviews.

"I find it very difficult to relate to Angelinos," Becker told Jim Ladd, "even of my own age, who presumably have the same cultural backdrop that I do, but of course, they don't. All they know about is what kind of wax you put on your surfboard and what different kinds of neuf bars you can get for your Chevy."

Ladd played Devil's advocate and claimed that New York was so violent he couldn't imagine anyone voluntarily subjecting themselves to living there. Becker and Fagen sprang to its defence, comparing the Big Apple's intellectual and artistic vitality with the bland artificiality and intellectual emptiness of Los Angeles. Becker likened living in Los Angeles to "living in a morgue". "LA is marked by excesses of every kind and complete disregard for humanity, as if it were built for the automobile and hamburger stand operators."

In late 1973 and early '74, Becker and Fagen were faced with the same problem as with their previous album – trying to write songs between concert dates. With only six or seven months between the release of 'Can't Buy A Thrill' and 'Countdown To Ecstasy', and the latter's fairly moderate commercial showing, the pressure to come up with the goods was even more intense than before. Their decision to resurrect and update three old New York demos reflected the difficulty they had writing songs to meet their exacting standards. 'Barrytown', 'Parker's Band' and 'Charlie Freak' – as well as the Duke Ellington cover, 'East St Louis Toodle-Oo', and the throwaway 'Through With Buzz' – were all dusted off for future use.

It never seemed to occur to Becker and Fagen that the others in the band might be composers too. In a roundabout way, they did eventually hear that the others were writing, but Becker said that they were never shown the results. "For all we know they might take over," he said. One press release from ABC stated that "every facet of the collaboration is shared". No doubt if they had been asked, Baxter and Hodder would have disagreed.

Further unwelcome touring was on the horizon once Steely Dan's third album was out, and while Fagen and Becker were locked away for months writing new material, Jeff Baxter and Jim Hodder, and to a lesser extent Denny Dias, sat around twiddling their thumbs, adding to Becker and Fagen's unease by actually pushing for more gigs and longer tours. It was a kind of revenge: since Becker and Fagen had virtually frozen the others out of the record-making process, Baxter and Hodder decided to punish them by forcing them out on to the road.

During interviews after the release of their third album, 'Pretzel Logic', Becker and Fagen dispensed totally with any further pretence of enjoying life on the road. "I don't like the jock atmosphere of a travelling rock and roll band," Fagen said. "It's corny, boring and silly."

Becker was behind his partner wholeheartedly: "Donald has to sing and that's a tough thing to have to do. If you get a cold you still have to sing every night; I've seen that happen to almost everybody that I've been on the road with. It's like football players and their knees – it's just a matter of time." Ever the joker, Becker went on to say, "We were gonna get matchbooks and have a picture of Donald with the legend 'Can you sing like this man?' So we could get another singer. He'd just have to play piano."

While Becker and Fagen squirmed, Baxter and Hodder revelled in the applause and partying. Baxter even thought Fagen was a natural front man for the band: "I was actually enjoying myself, everybody in the rhythm section was enjoying themselves. Donald and Walter hated touring, hated it with a passion. [But] Donald turned out to be a great performer. There's a streak in Donald that runs to be a great stage presence, I mean he'd literally go nuts. He'd buy himself a plastic organ and go up there in a vest and drive people nuts. They couldn't believe this guy, you know. So I think somewhere down deep inside of Donald there's a – if not a love – a certain genetic understanding of live performing. No, they didn't like it, but they hadda like some of it, 'cause it was pretty funny. And one thing was really nuts, everybody really liked the band when we played. I guess we had something for everybody, 'cause we used to pound it out. I mean, everybody would sweat their brains out. Donald would work, that guy was out there working."

Fagen was also very cynical about the notion of a rock and roll band being interviewed. When interviews were scheduled to include all or just other members of the group, as opposed to just Becker and Fagen, he would advise the others: "Say anything you want, just don't say anything that's true." Needless to say, this was a tactic they used quite often, especially when an interviewer asked dumb questions, knew nothing whatsoever about Steely Dan or appeared to be merely going through the motions.

Steely Dan's road crew was very small in comparison to the huge tours that began to criss-cross the US during the Seventies. Their sound engineer was a Lancashire-born Englishman named Stuart 'Dinky' Dawson, who went on to found Dawson Sound. Dawson first toured the US in 1969/70 with Fleetwood Mac and eventually moved to the US permanently to work with The Byrds, The Mahavishnu Orchestra and Lou Reed. He devised the overhead vocal PA system which was separate from the stereo PAs on each side of the stage, and with Marshall Goldberg from Boston designed the "snake cable" which joined stage equipment to a mixing console amid the audience in the centre of the auditorium. He claimed to be the *first* person ever to mix live sound from the audience, a practice subsequently adopted by all touring acts.

As a support band, Steely Dan often experienced problems soundchecking. In late 1972, when they were opening for The Kinks, 'Dinky' Dawson always made sure that they got an uninterrupted soundcheck and when he mixed the band in stereo Walter Becker and Denny Dias were always very impressed.

Dawson was later struck down with pneumonia and had to come off the road, but Steely Dan had been so taken with his ultra hi-fidelity sound system that they eventually tracked him down and told their management and record company that they wanted to use his production company on every forthcoming tour. Employing Dawson's sound system actually inspired them to play better than ever. For his part, Dawson still maintains that Steely Dan played some of the finest live shows he's ever heard and was frequently amazed at the audience reaction. He cites Seattle in April 1973 as one of the most outstanding. Dawson said there was so much energy at a Steely Dan show that people jumped up during the first number and went absolutely crazy for the band's music for the rest of the set.

Gary Katz was in full agreement. "I would see shows that I thought were just incredible, some of the best rock and roll shows I ever saw. Then I'd go backstage and Donald and Walter would be sitting there with their heads in their hands complaining about how rotten they'd been."

"Everybody was high, but it didn't make any difference, they played incredibly," said Dawson in his broad accent. In fact, when Steely Dan quit touring Dawson pretty much also quit, because he knew that those live shows would be virtually impossible to better either soundwise or musically.

Jeff Baxter and Dawson became firm friends and both got great amusement from anything that was offbeat. "The guy who mixed our monitors was interesting, too," said Baxter. "He would set up the monitors so he could hear real well, and he'd get a nice sound that he liked and take out his violin and play with us throughout the set. Everything was really shaky." The violin-playing monitor mixer was named Jim Jacobs and he had a habit of incessantly playing a tape of Bob Dylan's 'Visions Of Johanna' through Steely Dan's sound system before gigs, a custom Becker and Fagen would refer to in 'Doctor Wu', one of the songs on 'Katy Lied'. 'All night long/We would sing that stupid song' referred to Dylan's 'Visions Of Johanna'.

All touring bands in the Seventies found drugs and intoxicants in plentiful supply, but Donald Fagen indulged only rarely. His one vice had a constructive use: he liked to down a brandy and a Valium before taking the stage to help him conquer his stage fright. Before the gig Fagen would gather up the band and lead them through an oldies singalong to loosen everyone up, often with Hodder and newcomer Jeff Porcaro drumming along on a wooden bench. Leiber and Stoller's 'Ruby Baby' (which Fagen eventually covered for his 'Nightfly' album) was a favourite warm-up song.

While the band wended their tortuous way across America – and prepared to head for England – ABC issued a press release which contained typical examples of the PR hyperbole which dogged Steely Dan. It described the group's members as "among the most literate in rock" and stated that Steely Dan's (or to be precise Becker and Fagen's) influences were existentialist philosopher Martin Heidegger, symphony conductor Pierre Boulez, saxophonist John Coltrane and novelist William Burroughs. ABC seemed to be encouraging Becker and Fagen to assert their apparent intellectual superiority over their audience.

Asked about their influences, Becker and Fagen would begin with a discussion about

Heidegger's *Being And Time* . "Existentialist metaphysics really offer a way of achieving authentic existence," Fagen was quoted as saying, a comment unlikely to be uttered by, say, Ozzie Osbourne or Ted Nugent. Of Burroughs' *Naked Lunch* Walter Becker said: "I'd like to send a copy to every executive in the country." Discussing New Journalism, they opined that Hunter S. Thompson, the drug-abusing proponent of gonzo journalism whose hilarious *Fear And Loathing* reports often appeared in *Rolling Stone*, was a much better writer than Tom Wolfe.

Often during interviews, discussions about literature and philosophy actually preceded talk of musical influences, and at a press conference in early 1974 Fagen was approached by a music journalist who compared the lyrics of 'Rikki Don't Lose That Number' to the poetry of T. S. Eliot. "Don't take them too seriously," retorted Fagen, accepting the unwelcome compliment with an enigmatic smile.

ABC nevertheless took Steely Dan very seriously indeed and concluded one of their many press releases with the rash claim: "To many people they are the established spokespersons for the contemporary rock audience."

Spokesman or not, Fagen still hated doing interviews.

℘

The recording of Steely Dan's third album took them into another phase of their career. The album was again recorded mainly at the Village Recorder, with overdubs and mixing at Cherokee Sound in Chatsworth but this time Gary Katz – with the active encouragement of Becker and Fagen – decided to adopt the "workshop situation" whereby outside session musicians, usually the best in the business, were brought in to perform specific and varied parts. It was a method of working which Steely Dan would eventually take to its absolute limit – by sometimes not even playing on their own records.

Names like Chuck Rainey, Michael Omartian, Dean Parks, Jim Gordon, Jeff Porcaro and the already established Dan sideman Victor Feldman, all became regular contributors to Steely Dan albums. In fact, very soon Steely Dan sessions became *the* talking point among LA studio musicians. They were definitely among the better dates to be asked to play on, not just because the chord changes and rhythms were invariably more challenging but because the sessions were great fun, too. In amongst all the hard work and intense pressure, Becker, Fagen and Katz sought to extract – and demanded nothing less than – the absolute pinnacle of a musician's performance. If he still didn't come up to scratch Katz would soon be on the 'phone to the next player in line. For an LA session musician, to have some Steely Dan credits on his CV was the ultimate accolade.

During the early stages of recording, Becker and Fagen actively encouraged the musicians to express themselves within the structure of each tune. For solos, they usually began with a brief description of the kind of thing they were looking for and would then resort to "virtually anything, including jumping up and down and verbally abusing the guy", according to Becker. Almost certainly this statement contained a good deal of exaggeration, because Fagen and Becker – who were both terribly shy – later admitted that they could barely talk to the musicians about non-musical matters and to have treated professional players in this way would have been tantamount to artistic suicide.

In fact, Becker and Fagen usually trod very carefully, seldom emerging from the control room with "an attitude" toward a musician. If, as frequently happened, a player was unable to execute the part to their satisfaction, they would more than likely lay the blame squarely on themselves by saying that they had stylistically mismatched the player to the part in the first place.

Steely Dan's regular drummer and occasional vocalist Jim Hodder was an early victim of this musicians' pool policy. Like David Palmer, he was a popular guy much liked by everyone in the band, but he wasn't steady enough to satisfy Becker and Fagen's desire for the perfect drum track. He also had his fair share of problems, the most notable being an inability to curb his alcohol intake. The final nail in Hodder's coffin was hammered home during the recording of a song called 'Night By Night' at Cherokee Sound in Chatsworth. Becker and Fagen wanted pinpoint accuracy for the drum track and Hodder was unable to provide it. When the request went out for an alternative, Denny Dias suggested a prodigiously talented teenage drummer of his acquaintance called Jeff Porcaro.

Porcaro was only nineteen, the son of percussionist Joe Porcaro, and had been making substantial money on the road with Sonny and Cher. Dias called Porcaro and within forty-five minutes he was there. The personable, bespectacled drummer and Steely Dan megafan walked into the studio, looked up at an ornamental rope and noose hanging from the rafters and, knowing Steely Dan's reputation, said, "I know you guys have a rough reputation on musicians, but this is ridiculous!"

One of Jeff Porcaro's many drumming idols was session drummer Jim Gordon, who ironically enough ended up playing on the majority of the tracks on 'Pretzel Logic'. A session veteran, Gordon had already worked with artists like John Lennon, Eric Clapton, George Harrison, Traffic and Carly Simon. He was most famous, however, for writing the coda to Eric Clapton's classic Derek And The Dominos' track 'Layla'. 'Parker's Band', Becker and Fagen's tribute to Bird, featured the double drums of Jim Gordon and Jeff Porcaro and the latter was delighted to be playing with the elder statesman. "Gordon was my idol," said Jeff. "Playing with him was like going to school. Keltner was the bandido in town. Gordon was the heir to Hal Blaine."

Another studio player invited to contribute to a Steely Dan session for the first time was bassist Chuck Rainey who'd already worked with The Supremes, Aretha Franklin, The Crusaders and Roberta Flack and Donny Hathaway and was now *the* session bass player in the US. Rainey and Katz happened across each other on a freeway in Los Angeles and, within a week, Katz had called to invite him to play on Steely Dan's record. It proved to be the launching pad for a long term association between Steely Dan and Walter Becker's all-time favourite bass player.

Having adopted the "workshop situation", Becker and Fagen themselves were somewhat reticent about playing in front of the cream of LA's studio musicians. In fact, Michael Omartian can never remember Walter Becker playing guitar or bass while he was in the studio. Both songwriters were modest about their respective techniques and consequently insecure about sitting down and playing with hot session musicians. "I play good enough for what we do, but I wouldn't like to get in a blowing contest with Rick Wakeman," said Fagen.

Becker, Fagen and Katz kept a tight rein on the comings and goings of musicians at sessions with the outside players kept apart from Jeff Baxter, Jim Hodder and even Denny Dias. Baxter was only called in to do solos and overdubs and obviously resented the fact that he now had no say in the arrangements of any tunes. Denny Dias was usually present and encouraged to air his musiacal views but henceforth he averaged only one or two solos per album; although he was a very distinctive musician, he could not play screaming rock guitar convincingly enough for Becker and Fagen. Dias spent his time contentedly observing Becker, Fagen and Katz at work in the studio, only to bring himself to the fore as soon as mixing began. In fact, 'Pretzel Logic' was the last album on which Dias had any serious mixing involvement. Despite Roger Nichols' technical and scientific gifts, Steely Dan soon began employing Elliot Scheiner to assist Nichols with the mixing duties.

By employing session musicians – in particular drummers – Becker and Fagen were sometimes able to arrive at whatever they were looking for much quicker than would have been possible with less accomplished players. The drummers they used also widened Becker and Fagen's imagination and brought to their songs parts that they would never have conceived themselves. Yet it was still Fagen and Becker's names on the composition at the end of the day. Only Bernard Purdie, the great New York session drummer, ever dared to suggest that he should been given a co-writing credit on a Becker and Fagen's song.

Becker, Fagen and Katz's perfectionism became legendary. And yet the interesting thing was that when Becker and Fagen decided to shelve a song, very seldom did the studio musicians feel that it was not "happening". The problem invariably existed somewhere in the composers' heads. Many of the musicians thought they had nailed it and couldn't understand why a track was being cut again and again. When Becker and Fagen finally decided on a take, the players often thought an earlier one was every bit as good.

What went on in those heads, no one dared to try and guess. Walter Becker was extremely cynical and difficult to get a reading on; Donald Fagen was introverted and even more difficult to understand and, until they knew better, some players interpreted his aloofness as a sign of disapproval. Becker and Fagen's interests never coincided with those of the musicians they employed. Most of the musicians simply came to accept and understand the tremendous peculiarities about their personalities.

The sessions for 'Pretzel Logic' weren't as experimental as the first two albums. This time around Becker and Fagen realised each song more fully before entering the studio and Katz helped them to hire the right musicians to execute their ideas. "I felt that they had everything together enough that they didn't need to experiment," said Michael Omartian.

The guitar solo on the title track is a prime example. It was played by Becker, and as usual took a long time to piece together, often "an hour per bar", according to Roger Nichols. But there seemed to be an element of divine guidance in the way they worked. One night Becker and Fagen were working on one part of the solo and after he'd played it Fagen said, "Yeah, I think that was all right." When they played the tape back and Becker heard it, he was astounded. "Did I play that?" he asked incredulously.

Walter Becker's obsession with hi-fi meant that he was often suggesting new equipment and gadgets that Steely Dan might employ in the studio. During the 'Pretzel Logic' sessions he suggested using some giant, imposing speakers called Magnaplaners. Although they measured over five feet tall, Steely Dan obtained a pair and recorded the whole album using them in the Village Recorder. Unfortunately, what sounded good on the Magnaplaners didn't always sound good on ordinary speakers; indeed, Michael Omartian thought the Magnaplaners themselves were "paper thin" and sounded "just goofy".They did try using them again for 'Katy Lied' but the Magnaplaners didn't sound as good in ABC Recording Studios and were discarded.

A particular favourite of Becker and Fagen's was Duke Ellington and The Washingtonians' theme song 'East St Louis Toodle-Oo' which on 'Pretzel Logic' became Steely Dan's first – and last – cover version. Wah-wah guitar sounded exactly like a muted trumpet and was also great fun to play, so Becker and Fagen went out and obtained the three available versions of Ellington's song, each one slightly different in detail and arrangement, which they combined into one for their own version. Many critics jumped to the conclusion that Steely Dan had covered it simply because of its mention in Burroughs' *The Naked Lunch*, but Fagen and Becker steadfastly denied this was the case.

"Without having a missionary attitude about it, we still thought it would be interesting for the audience to realise that that kind of expression is not a new thing," said Fagen. "In 1926 a trumpet player was doing with his lip what it takes a complicated set of electronics to do on an electric guitar. Walter had been putzing around with that song for years. We wanted to hear it with all the expertise of modern hi-fi."

According to Becker, the piano solo in Steely Dan's 'East St Louis Toodle-oo' was a composite of "four bad clarinet solos with notes changed only where absolutely necessary. Duke didn't have a good clarinet player in that period; a few years later he hired Barney Bigard."

In addition to the substitution of Fagen's piano solo for Rudy Jackson's clarinet and Becker's wah-wah guitar for Bubber Miley's trumpet, Steely Dan's version also utilised Jeff Baxter's note-for-note pedal-steel-guitar-through-a-Fuzztone rendition of Tricky Sam Nanton's trombone and a sax/guitar duet for the horn ensemble. Donald Fagen also played the alto sax – the one and only time he played his beloved saxophone during Steely Dan's seven album recording career.

'East St Louis Toodle-Oo' also provided Walter Becker with his first appearance on a Steely Dan record, playing six-string guitar. Making up the rest of the band were Jim Gordon on drums, Becker on bass *and* guitar, Dean Parks on banjo and Roger Nichols banging the gong at the end.

Fagen, obviously very proud of Steely Dan's version, sent Duke Ellington a copy of the record for his 75th birthday that April, saying "I would have been very flattered if he heard it, but I don't know if he did." Unfortunately, the great American jazz composer died within a month of his birthday, so the chances are that he didn't get to hear Steely Dan's tribute.

The one-and-a-half minute 'Through The Buzz' was Becker and Fagen's shortest song and also their worst. Laden with strings and a repetitive lyric, it was, according to Fagen, about... "a more or less platonic relationship between two people. There's nothing really sexual about it until one of the young people realises he's being used and starts having paranoid fantasies and breaks off the relationship. There's no symbolism or anything, we never use puns. It's a very saccharine sounding track with a very cynical lyric. We often do that for an ironic purpose. That is, to juxtapose a rather bitter lyric against rather sweet music."

Denny Dias and Jeff Baxter shared the guitar part on 'Any Major Dude Will Tell You', a delicate song about madness and insecurity. The tune contained a guitar line which repeated itself three times with variations, so Dias – who strictly avoided the use of vibrato in his own playing – played the first part, then handed the guitar to Baxter who then played the last five notes which absolutely did require vibrato. Roger Nichols then punched it in on the tape machine. The guitar solo was actually written by Becker and Jeff Baxter together.

While recording 'Any Major Dude' some of the musicians were wandering around the studio furtively asking each other about the line "Have you ever seen a squonk's tears?" "What the hell is a squonk?" they inquired. Being unfamiliar with literature, they were all reluctant to ask Becker and Fagen directly for fear of ridicule, but a squonk, they later learned, is a mythical woods animal that has the ability to cry himself into a bag of tears.

As a result, or perhaps because – in their perverse way – they simply wanted to annoy people, Becker and Fagen were seldom persuaded to divulge what, if anything, any particular song was about. On one occasion, however, Fagen was induced into explaining that the title song on 'Pretzel Logic' was about time travel. "When it says, 'I stepped up on the platform/The man gave me the news', we conceived the platform as a teleportation device. And there are other key lines like, 'I have never met Napoleon/But I plan to find the time'. What we're actually saying is that I plan to find the time that he lived in," said Fagen. It was a logical explanation, but then again Fagen could easily have been making it up as he went along.

Explaining 'Rikki Don't Lose That Number' Fagen said: "That's a very simple love song to a young lady. I always thought it was a rather erotic, decadent sort of thing. Here you find a guy, a rather rich gentlemen living in a resort and he somehow manages to capture this young lady."

One interviewer in America was convinced that the 'number' referred to in the single was a marijuana cigarette. Becker denied this was so, or even that he and Fagen knew of this usage for the word number. "I think that's San Francisco slang," he said, "but we didn't know that." Fagen picked it up from there: "The fact is we were simply referring to a phone number, so I think people should take the lyrics more literally and [it'll] be on the safe side."

The reality was really quite simple: there had been a student at Bard College called Rikki who had made quite an impression on Becker and Fagen and they decided to utilise her name for the opening song of the album. Jeff Baxter again played the excellent guitar solo without use of an amplifier – his instrument was plugged straight into the board. And what a solo it was – funky, fluid and perfect in length and execution. However, while recording the solo Steely Dan had encountered some very unusual technical problems. When they played the solo back there would be a little blip underneath the guitar, so they changed to another track and the same thing happened. They only had three tracks empty and on the last track the dropout still occurred. When Roger Nichols examined it closely he found some little lumps on the tape which he cut out and sent back to the manufacturers, 3M, for analysis. Their response suprised everyone: it turned out to be mustard from a workman's sandwich.

Michael Omartian played piano on the track and on the night they finished the song there was good reason for an impromptu dual celebration. Another track was successfully in the can, but even more significantly Omartian was about to get married, so Steely Dan ordered in some champagne and held a party in the studio. Omartian's fiancée picked him up at around eleven o'clock that night, they drove to Las Vegas to plight their troth and he was back in the studio again the next day. Despite the scepticism surrounding Vegas marriages, Omartian was pleased to report that it's still going strong today.

'Rikki', Steely Dan's first single from the album, was actually one of the last tunes to be mixed. Fagen said, "If it comes out good enough, we'll make it the first tune." With its flopanda (a marimba type instrument) introduction, it borrowed heavily from Horace Silver's jazz composition 'Song For My Father'. But Fagen defended the similarity to the intro of the Silver composition. "It was supposed to be a Brazilian bassline and when Jim Gordon saw the chart he naturally started playing that type of beat," he said.

The album was completed by 'Monkey In Your Soul' with its growling backdrop and funky saxes, 'Barrytown' (the name of a hamlet very close to Bard College) which Becker and Fagen used as a target for denigrating small town America, and 'With A Gun', a galloping depiction of a man whose way of settling a business debt is to ambush his partner.

Many critics saw 'Pretzel Logic' as being more accessible than 'Countdown To Ecstasy', but Fagen denied it was ever a consideration. "We really don't think about it. The record company was starting to get annoyed with us because they couldn't get a single off 'Countdown To Ecstasy'. The only thing we did was tighten up the arrangements. The songs weren't quite so long. And 'Night By Night' was basically written for commercial purposes." Obviously Becker and Fagen's idea of what was commercial clashed with the record company's since the cut was not even released as a single.

It was Becker and Fagen's intention to use a title which would form a sort of bawdy trilogy with 'Can't Buy A Thrill', and 'Countdown To Ecstasy'. However, they were unable to come up with anything remotely appropriate and so resorted to naming the album after one of its songs: 'Pretzel Logic'.

The idea for the cover came from Fagen and Gary Katz, who thought it would be interesting to take a photograph of a pretzel vendor in New York's Central Park. Los Angeles based photographer Ed Caraeff was assigned to take the cover photograph, but on the appointed weekend (when snow was on the ground) he was unable to spare the time to fly across the country, and Raenne Rubenstein, a New York photographer, was commissioned to do the job instead. The weather at that time was particularly bad, but ABC couldn't wait for it to improve and when the photo had been taken (complete with misspelt sign) they asked the vendor in question to sign a release form for the rights to use the photograph. When he refused to do so ABC did some snooping on Steely Dan's behalf and discovered that he was operating without a licence anyway. It was therefore unlikely that he would sue, so they decided to use the photograph regardless. In the event there were no legal comebacks.

The inside cover photo of Steely Dan posing beneath a large carved eagle known as the Eagle Throne was taken at photographer Ed Caraeff's house-cum-studio in the hills of Coldwater Canyon. Instead of projecting the photo on to a flat piece of paper, Caraeff, who did all his own developing, manipulated the photo in his darkroom by tilting one end of the photo paper to get the elongated effect. Although all five members appeared in the picture, the reality was that Jim Hodder did not play drums at all on the album, being confined to some background vocals on 'Parker's Band'. Jeff Porcaro had augmented the group live and even if Hodder did foresee the inevitable, he was unable to prevent it.

On March 20, 1974, just before they embarked on another extensive US tour, Steely Dan recorded a live radio broadcast from the Record Plant for KMET, one of the most progressive stations in Los Angeles at that time. The show was eventually bootlegged and it became, for those that never saw them in concert, a rare chance to hear how the band sounded live. The bootleg was called 'Rotoscope Down Pleasantly Retired (A Peak Behind The Curtain) – The 1973 American Tour' on the Amazing Kornyfone label. It contained ten songs and was a typical example of a Steely Dan live show from that era. Opening with 'The Boston Rag' they ran through extended versions of 'Do It Again', 'Pretzel Logic' and 'King Of The World'. There were two as-yet unreleased songs, 'Mobile Home' and an 'Untitled instrumental' which Becker and Fagen eventually modified into 'Your Gold Teeth II'. There was confusion over the actual title of 'Mobile Home', since the sleeve notes referred to it as 'Mobile Heart'. Becker resolved the confusion by describing it as "a song about a trailer". (In the early 1990s slight variations of this album appeared on bootleg CDs from the EEC under different titles – 'Steely Dan Live', 'Reelin' Through The Years' and 'This All Too Mobile Home' – but each one features the same show.)

❧

'Pretzel Logic' was released in March to huge critical acclaim. In the UK the *Melody Maker* cited Steely Dan as "probably the best new band to emerge in the last two years" while in the rival *New Musical Express* Ian MacDonald had even higher hopes for them.

"Steely Dan must surely break through to the wider audience soon, and sometime in the future cut one of rock's definitive albums," he wrote.

"In the US, *Downbeat* wrote that "there are probably no better rock recording groups in America, and damn few worldwide." Richard Cromelin in *Creem* ended his review with the statement: "Steely Dan are the best band in America. 'Pretzel Logic' is great. Connect." What few reservations were expressed were very trivial ones: Bud Scoppa in *Rolling Stone* had been knocked out by Steely Dan's live show and maintained that their records did not equal their live performance, at least not on a good night, despite their lack of a visual identity. "As pop personalities they're practically anonymous," he wrote, probably unaware that nothing pleased Becker and Fagen more than anonymity. *Stereo Review*'s writer had admired 'Countdown To Ecstasy' but thought that with 'Pretzel Logic' Steely Dan were treading water. He did add, however, that he would... "rather hear Steely Dan treading water than most bands at full stroke."

Gary Katz dreaded reading praiseworthy comments about his production because any such remarks inevitably presaged two or three days of good-natured abuse from Becker and Fagen. But however much their reputation gathered pace and however much their live performances contributed to that reputation, nothing could halt the internal power struggle within Steely Dan. Now, as success loomed on a large scale, Becker and Fagen lined up against Hodder and Baxter with the touring schedule as the principal bone of contention.

"It was unfair for us to spend eight months writing when Jeff Baxter and the others wanted to tour," admitted Becker. "We weren't making very much money and everybody wanted to be touring a lot. We didn't. That was that."

By now Baxter and Hodder had even discussed going out on the road together, leaving Becker and Fagen behind. Dias was left with the casting vote and he would always lend his weight to Becker and Fagen's cause. "I could never do anything to hurt those guys," Dias told Baxter and Hodder. "We don't want the band to become a circus," they said.

Fagen never missed an opportunity to carp on about his dislike of travelling and one-nighters and constantly described hopping around the country on tour as "a nightmare". By now he and Becker had reached a point where they could dictate exactly what they were going to do and putting an end to the "nightmare" was at the top of their list.

Inevitably manager Joel Cohen backed Hodder and Baxter. His whole philosophy of management was to maximise profits in every way possible so the idea of stopping touring was complete anathema to him. Indeed, he knew of no other way to manage and failed completely to comprehend Becker and Fagen's attitude or their musical integrity. But Cohen's status as a manager was compromised by the manner in which he came by the job in the first place. Had he grown up with Becker and Fagen in New York, supporting or championing them when times were hard, then things might have been different. As it was, Cohen had simply been appointed to the job by his friends at ABC Records (which raised suspicions about a conflict of interest anyway), and he never enjoyed the respect that many rock performers had for trusted managers who combined business acuity with a long standing paternal sympathy for their charges' artistic endeavours.

In some respects the tension caused by the rift inspired some great performances in the studio. Jeff Baxter played some truly great guitar solos on 'Pretzel Logic', particularly on 'Rikki Don't Lose That Number', 'Any Major Dude' and 'Night By Night'. It was almost as if his supercharged playing was inspired by a desperation to maintain his position in this most respected of contemporary rock groups.

Immediately after the release of ' Pretzel Logic' rumours about the imminent dissolution of the band were rife and Fagen did his best to scotch them. "That's all ridiculous bull," he said. "We're more or less fairly stable now as the five humanoids that started this thing."

Of course, by now there were far more than five musicians involved and as well as the nagging dispute between the studio heads and the tourists, there was an instability within the band caused by a certain top-heaviness. Becker and Fagen had auditioned various musicians in Los Angeles with the intention of augmenting the band. They'd hired young prodigy Jeff Porcaro as a second drummer as well as keyboardist/vocalist Michael McDonald, the latter for his ability to blend vocally with Fagen and handle the high parts. Becker, Fagen and Dias began referring to their extended line up as the Steely Dan Reserve Flotilla.

Despite his non-appearance on the album and the hiring of Jeff "The Beat Goes On" Porcaro, Jim Hodder didn't seem the least bit concerned about the threat to his position as Steely Dan's number one drummer. But beneath his front, Hodder *was* worried. He told *Melody Maker* that Fagen had wanted two drummers since the band was formed. "I was against it at first, but what the hell, we had two guitarists and (now we've got) two keyboard players, so why not two drummers? And one of my favourite bands had two drummers – Frank Zappa and The Mothers. It can work like a locomotive, especially on tunes like 'Do It Again'. It gives us time to relax in different parts and we can concentrate on the next fill."

"I like having the two of us drumming. It doesn't always work in groups and you have to forget about your ego. With us it sounds like one guy playing at times, but it makes for a better combination of sounds. What we have to watch out for is when Donald conducts those long endings. It's great material to play in this band and we only clash occasionally – not so anyone in the audience would notice."

The only way to effectively dispel the split rumours was for the band to tour. In the spring of 1974 Becker and Fagen wearily packed their bags for more US dates and Steely Dan's first and only visit to Europe. It was to be their final tour together and it was marked by contrasting performances that, as always, reflected the perverse nature of this most peculiar of groups.

Things started disastrously in New York where sound problems at the prestigious Avery Fisher Hall in Lincoln Center almost shattered their collective confidence once and for all. Steely Dan were opening for The Electric Light Orchestra at what was basically a home town gig for them, so Becker and Fagen were especially anxious to put on a good show. Gary Katz flew in from Los Angeles expecting to see something special, but Dawson Sound wasn't scheduled to start mixing the shows until Steely Dan's next gig and as they were soundchecking, Dawson and his crew showed up anyway to witness the confusion. The band were allowed no time at all in which to carry out their soundcheck and when the sound crew brusquely whisked them off stage, Steely Dan refused to perform.

By the time the dispute had been resolved, the show was an hour late in starting and when they saw the crowd eagerly awaiting them, Steely Dan took the stage and ran through a rollicking 45-minute set. But their performance was marred throughout by the failure of a monitor and constant feedback, which at one point became so bad that they were forced to stop in mid-song. The audience were sympathetic and brought the Dan back for an obligatory encore, but it was a disastrous evening for everyone concerned. The incident provided more grist to the mill as far as Fagen's arguments against touring were concerned, but first there were the UK dates to play – and, in contrast to the New York show – many fans still feel that these were among the finest Steely Dan ever performed.

Steely Dan arrived in England in May on the back of an extensive run of US concerts. During the tour they were scheduled to film an *In Concert* special for producer Stanley Dorfman and make an appearance on the BBC's *Old Grey Whistle Test*, introduced by "Whispering" Bob Harris. However, fate intervened to prevent either appearance taking place.

There was confusion over the actual tour dates which changed each time they were published in the music press, but the mix-up over their schedule did not harm attendances. The reason for the changes was that each time promoter Howard Rose and manager Joel Cohen came up with an itinerary, Dinky Dawson would dismiss it as impractical. Dawson had by now taken on almost guru-like stature in Becker and Fagen's eyes and they listened very carefully to everything he said. Dawson and his associates Keith Robertson and Jimmy Lewis had extensive knowledge of the touring circuit in the UK and they told Becker and Fagen in no uncertain terms that... "These Yanks don't know what they're talking about". Dawson advised Becker and Fagen to start their tour in Manchester, avoid certain venues and play Leeds early on in the tour. The increased participation of the audio engineers now became another source of tension, particularly between road manager Gary McPike and Joel Cohen, who generally saw eye to eye, and the rest of the crew, who respected Dawson. When Dawson's judgement proved absolutely correct, McPike and Cohen didn't stand a chance.

When the twelve dates *were* eventually finalised, the tour was set to open at Manchester's Palace Theatre on May 17, and would then take them to Bristol, Leeds, Glasgow and Southampton, with two mid-tour dates at the Rainbow Theatre in London. From there they had an option to play key cities in Continental Europe.

Steely Dan's long awaited arrival in the UK had been eagerly anticipated by the all important UK music press since their 1972 album début. *New Musical Express* ran a full page advertisement announcing the tour dates with supporting group The Kiki Dee Band. The tour was called 'Steely Dan Slips Into The UK' and Becker and Fagen were tickled by the logo, which depicted an astronaut sitting astride a penis-shaped spaceship. And although their name may have given them a useful thrust at the start, it failed to give 'Rikki, Don't Lose That Number' so much as a nudge and the single flopped in the UK, unlike in the States where it cruised into the Top Ten, peaking at number four in May, and it was later nominated for a Grammy for Best Pop Vocal. 'Rikki' was Steely Dan's last UK single on the Probe label before they moved on to the recently established Anchor label, another subsidiary of ABC Records in Los Angeles.

Anchor arranged a rather sumptuous press reception at the Global Village in London, but Steely Dan's schedule was so tight that when their equipment was held up at the airport the entire affair was cancelled. The problem of how to dispose of the food awaiting a horde of hungry journalists was solved by donating it to the Salvation Army. Unfortunately, a reporter from *Record Mirror* took exception to the cancellation and erroneously reported that Steely Dan refused to perform."We can tell ourselves how good you are, you don't have to keep ramming it down our throats," he added, echoing a similar stance taken by certain US critics.

Expectation was so high that when Steely Dan opened the tour at Manchester, you could hear a pin drop while the audience waited for the band to take the stage. When they did, the sound of their footfalls on the boards were clearly audible. Jeff Baxter announced that... "We've never been here before but we're gonna do the best concert of our lives," which was greeted with roars, screeches and whistles of approval. Then, when the noise had subsided, the silence was broken by the dual pounding of Hodder and Porcaro's drums as they launched into 'Bodhisattva'.

In the twelve song, one and a half hour set, Donald Fagen sang less than half the solo lead vocals and joined Royce Jones for the choruses on 'Bodhisattva' and 'Show Biz Kids'. The show was a heady mixture of inspired improvisational guitar work from Dias and Baxter, the rich vocal blend between Fagen, Jones and McDonald and some unusually long intervals between some songs.

Jeff Baxter alone injected some animation into Steely Dan's static stage show with his exaggerated facial expressions and energetic bounding around the stage. The versatile Baxter switched to a Gibson Les Paul for the blues based 'Pretzel Logic', played a steel guitar on 'Brooklyn' and even played an extended conga break on 'Do It Again'. Fagen introduced 'King Of The World' as "a very frightening little piece of music" and by the time Hodder and Porcaro's drums kicked in, the band had really warmed up and was flying. The only low point of the evening was a rather lame version of 'Dirty Work' which was sandwiched between spirited versions of 'My Old School' and 'Reelin' In The Years'. The band encored with 'Show Biz Kids' sung by the white-suited McDonald and the trailer song, 'Mobile Home' which Fagen introduced by saying, "This is a new one you've never heard before, but you're gonna dig it".

Chris Welch in the *Melody Maker* described it as a "sensational set" and declared that "Steely Dan have made many English bands sound five years out of date". The *NME* critic was equally impressed: "There's so much to hear at a Steely Dan concert it's necessary to go back for more."

'Mobile Home' concluded with Jeff Baxter's guitar solo which was based on 'Theme From A Summer Place', Percy Faith's 1960 number one instrumental smash from the film of the same name. It was a gag Steely Dan pulled many times on stage. As for the song itself, it provided a high energy end to Steely Dan's live show and Becker and Fagen admitted that if the song had been at the stage it was now, they might not have failed to record acceptable versions of it for both 'Countdown to Ecstasy' and 'Pretzel Logic'. SD's Manchester set was almost exactly the same as the one they had been playing back in America.

The long musical interludes which had been designed to give Fagen a break from singing weren't received too well but he still took every opportunity to avoid singing. "I didn't think most people wanted to hear a Jew sing," he explained at one point. So Royce Jones took the lead vocal for 'The Boston Rag', 'Brooklyn', and 'Dirty Work'. Jones now sang all the songs that had previously featured David Palmer on lead vocal, but 'Megashine City' and 'Take My Money' had been dropped along with the singer.

Despite the disagreements. Jeff Baxter's enthusiasm was unbounded and he maintained his sense of humour. "Sometimes in the States the kids just shout for 'boogie.' We just wait for them to shut up and then we can start to play. Boy, is that funny! I love that," said Baxter.

"It's true that we play more to ourselves than the audience sometimes but we have a lot of fun. After the show we scream at each other if we have made any mistakes. But I've never been in a band that has played so many different kinds of music before. I used to have to be in five different bands at once to get this kind of experience."

Dias and Baxter were from opposite ends of the spectrum, both musically and in terms of personality. "I play as if I were a jazz musician," said Dias, "except I'm working in a rock context with its feel and excitement. There are no problems, except I'd like to play more. Jeff can play all the wide vibrato sounds and bend the strings, and he's really good. We only met up through the band and we're on opposite ends of the stick, we're so different. I play the jazz and Jeff is so much more experienced as a rock player."

To end their '74 concerts in style, Steely Dan adopted the old idea of having the band leave the stage in pairs. Towards the end of their second encore, after 'Mobile' had become a jam, Royce Jones and Michael McDonald would leave first, followed by Denny Dias and Jeff Baxter, leaving Becker and Fagen and Porcaro and Hodder in the spotlight. Becker would then walk off, Fagen would thank the crowd most sincerely for coming to the gig and exit himself. Finally, to end on a high and send the audience home buzzing, Porcaro and Hodder would play a lick for lick five minute drum duet which was beefed up even further when Dinky Dawson introduced an outboard tape effect.

After the undisciplined scenes at Steely Dan concerts in America, the attentiveness of British audiences impressed Steely Dan almost as much as the band impressed the critics and fans. "UK audiences were exemplary," said Denny Dias. "I've never played for a better audience than a British one. If I was gonna pack up an audience and take them home with me it would be a UK audience. Nobody spoke while the music was playing and when the music stopped, they made more noise than you ever heard in your life and then quietened down again for the next one."

He marvelled at how at one gig the first few rows stood up in their excitement and Fagen had to ask them to sit down so the people behind could see. When everyone complied, Fagen was astonished. Audiences in the US were just not willing to acknowledge – let alone obey – requests from the stage.

Dias: "I remember playing one town in America where a guy was standing at the side of the stage with a beer in one hand and he was banging the stage in what he thought was in time to the music and the whole stage was shaking. He was swinging the beer over his head and dripping it on everyone around him and he was just typical of the whole audience. They scream while you play, they scream while you don't play and they try to tell you what to play. They're not polite about it at all." No such problems occurred in the UK.

In London for two Rainbow dates Steely Dan were booked into The Curzon Hotel. Dinky Dawson and his associates were familiar with the hotel and didn't like the idea of staying there. They told Becker and Fagen they knew a much better place – Blakes in Kensington, where most touring American musicians stayed and where the action was considerably faster. Blakes was fully booked at the time, but Dawson's smooth tongue wangled Becker and Fagen into the hotel. Dawson and company soon followed. Porcaro, Hodder, Jones, McPike and Cohen remained stranded in The Curzon.

Denny Dias wasn't impressed with The Curzon either, and he too managed to relocate to Blakes. "It was like staying in a brothel," he said. "All the upholstery was pink and they had button couches in the rooms." Jeff Baxter and Jim Hodder never got out of The Curzon but when Jeff Porcaro got wind of Fagen and Becker's secretive transfer, he packed his own bags and arrived at Blakes Hotel at about 2.30 am, asking "Where's the party?" The chopping and changing between hotels seemed to accurately reflect the rifts between the various cliques within the Steely Dan touring party.

In interviews conducted in the UK Walter Becker gave unstinting praise to Dawson's sound system, a factor much commented on by reviewers. "Our sound system is designed for small halls like the Palace Theatre at Manchester and we'd rather work in those situations than sacrifice the sound quality in a bigger venue," he said. "Dinky Dawson is our sound designer and he's brilliant. He's worked with us from our first gigs when we used to support The Kinks and The James Gang. That was terrible, bands used to play tricks on us in those days like not letting us on stage for a soundcheck or turning the lights off. When Dinky joined us, I couldn't understand a word he said but I knew he was an intelligent, professional guy."

A bizarre incident occurred in Leeds where Steely Dan stayed at the Dragonara Hotel, close to the main railway station. Walter Becker's mother, who at the time taught dance in London, somehow managed to persuade Steely Dan's UK record company to ferry her to Leeds in a limousine to see her son play. Accompanied by another young girl, Becker's mother ran up an enormous bill at the Dragonara and an Anchor employee was fired from his job as a result. Mrs Becker was an unwelcome guest, by all accounts.

Michael McDonald later said that Steely Dan unanimously thought that their Manchester concert was the best gig they had ever performed. And in a rare show of enthusiasm, Becker and Fagen also declared that the personnel on their UK tour, and the degree of musicianship they showed, was the best of their various touring line-ups.

The praise they received from critics wasn't entirely unqualified. Steely Dan's

Rainbow gig was slagged on several counts by the *NME* critic. Under the headline 'Thumbs Down For The Dan', Ian MacDonald expressed his disappointment with the unprofessionalism of a long and tedious last minute soundcheck. He criticised the sound, arguing that there was far too much drums (Jeff Porcaro blasted Jim Hodder off the stage for sheer volume), no bass at all and a complete lack of separation between the guitars of Baxter and Dias. He said Baxter had a bad night for solos with the exception of his second break on 'Reelin' In The Years' but enjoyed the second encore, 'Mobile Home', during which all the musicians left the stage until only Hodder and Porcaro were left for their closing five minute drum duet.

In contrast, Peter Harvey of *Record Mirror* loved the Palace Theatre show so much that he wanted to listen to them for hours. Harvey called Steely Dan… "the most exciting and inventive American rock band since The Mothers and Steve Miller and the best performers bar none."

Donald Fagen was an avid historian with a particular interest in Napoleon, and he and Jeff Baxter visited Radio Luxembourg's studios which had been used as Gestapo headquarters during the last war. But Fagen wasn't keen on going to Germany itself. The group and crew were assembled in a hotel room one afternoon when Fagen said in mock horror that he would not go to Germany; or that if he did go to Germany, Gary Katz would have to go with him. And even then Fagen said he would be afraid to go to sleep 'cause he'd likely wake up with his teeth as the rheostat in somebody's Porsche!

In the event, the tour never got beyond England. Steely Dan had played only five dates of their British tour when Donald Fagen was taken ill. He contracted a serious throat ailment and although he went to see a Harley Street doctor and waited a week for the illness to improve, he was so sick that specialists advised him that he might do permanent damage to his voice if he sang again on the tour. Initially concerts at Glasgow, Sheffield, Scarborough and Southampton were postponed, then the following week the rest of the gigs were called off. Other members of the band suggested Fagen might like to take a trip to the French Riviera to get some sunshine and recuperate, but Fagen was so poorly he only wanted to go home. The whole band headed back to Los Angeles and on landing at LA International Fagen looked so pale, thin and gaunt that he was strip-searched on suspicion of being a junkie.

The cancellation of Steely Dan's outstanding dates was a bitter blow to their hopes of continuing the momentum of their visit and building on the reputation they had established. Probe Records hinted that Steely Dan might return to the UK in October after a series of US dates.

They weren't to know how close Steely Dan were to their last gig for a *very* long time.

❧

The Kiki Dee Band followed Steely Dan back to America and continued to support them when they resumed their touring schedule on Fagen's recovery. They had lost a small fortune by having to cancel the rest of their UK dates and as soon as Fagen was well enough, they embarked on a series of Californian dates in Fresno, Santa Barbara,

San Jose, San Bernadino, San Diego and Long Beach. On the back of the success of 'Pretzel Logic' and 'Rikki Don't Lose That Number' demand for tickets was high and this enabled them to recoup some of the funds lost during the English tour.

On stage during Steely Dan's last weeks as a concert band, the line-up usually consisted of Fagen's piano squarely in centre stage, from where he could conduct the long endings to songs, with Walter Becker wearing headphones and largely hidden behind Jeff Porcaro's drum podium. Never before had any two rock musicians so disliked the attention and adulation that goes with being in a famous group, nor had any two musicians made this so evident by their lack of on-stage profile. When questioned about his anonymity, Becker was surprised. "You've noticed that? The reasons are it takes the heat off me and I don't have to make my presence felt. As long as I can hear Jeff Porcaro's snare drum and hi-hat, I'm happy. I moved up there about ten gigs ago. I just want to hear the drums and it's all cosy up there. I have a seat and it keeps me comfortable and happy."

Steely Dan used to record every live show they played and the tapes of all these shows were entrusted to Walter Becker for safe keeping. However, for reasons known only to him, he either misplaced them or perhaps intentionally destroyed them so that he and Fagen would never be faced with the prospect of having to listen to their live performances again. Since they later hated hearing some of their earlier studio recordings, one can only begin to imagine their reaction to hearing live renditions of those songs. The only official version was the token (and very belated) Santa Monica Civic version of 'Bodhisattva' which would emerge as the B-side of 'Time Out Of Mind' and 'Hey Nineteen' seven years later.

On their 1974 US tour Steely Dan had hired a truck driver cum emcee called Jerome Aniton. He was a character quite unlike his employers with an unquenchable thirst for alcohol and a devil-may-care attitude that, perversely, Becker and Fagen admired no end. His fondness for alcohol did wonders for his introductions, and on more than one occasion he crashed the equipment truck. At the prestigious Kennedy Center for the Performing Arts in Washington DC, where at that time Steely Dan were the only 'rock'n'roll' group permitted to play, Aniton did thousands of dollars' worth of damage driving their equipment truck out of the building, smashing a massive hole in one trailer which housed most of Dinky Dawson's personal possessions. It was raining torrents as Steely Dan's crew drove on to their next gig in Boston so someone had to crawl up on to the top of the trailer and try to patch the hole over before the gear inside was ruined.

On another occasion Aniton drove from Baltimore to Washington at night without headlights accompanied by two fifteen-year-old girls in the front seat. He was accident prone and incessantly intoxicated, and ought not to have been allowed to continue with such responsibility, but Becker and Fagen had taken a shine to him and insisted he be retained in some capacity.

So Aniton became the comedian of the party, sending the band into paroxysms of laughter with unconventional behaviour he considered normal. Aniton was given the responsibility of introducing the band on stage and his introductions were exaggerated interpretations of what an emcee might say at black soul reviews. Aniton was a truck driver doing his take on a black emcee while under the influence of alcohol and presenting a white band... but it worked a treat. He gave some memorable and hilarious introductions, and even became something of a favourite among fans who relished yet another unexpected quirk of Steely Dan. The first time he introduced them, the band enjoyed it so much they played the opening song better than ever before.

Part of the fun was that Aniton didn't even understand Steely Dan... he actually thought Donald Fagen's name was *Stevie Dan*. On one occasion, ever unsteady on his feet, Aniton stumbled into Fagen's grand piano on stage and said to one of the other players, "I bumped into Stevie's piano."

His introductions varied nightly from 'Stevie Dan' to 'Mr Stevie Dan and Whatever'. The more Aniton drank, the more hilarious his introductions became so everyone encouraged him to partake as much as possible. Aniton might go on and do a rambling two-minute-plus introduction replete with expletives while the band members laughed aloud behind him, encouraging him with audible asides. At a gig in Cleveland, Aniton's geography deserted him and he referred to the city as being on the east coast.

If Aniton's wayward behaviour provided light relief on the road, then sitting through interviews was a chore that Becker and Fagen could happily have done without. The release of 'Pretzel Logic', in particular, seemed to open the floodgates for critics to start unravelling Becker and Fagen's lyrical "code". One Los Angeles critic, Richard Cromelin, "exclusively revealed" that 'Pretzel Logic' was about suicide. His reasoning was based on a UCLA lecture on that subject by a Dr Paul Pretzel!

In an interview with *NME*, Fagen and Becker were accused of deliberately confusing their listeners with their obscure lyrics. "We don't necessarily try to communicate any specific thing to the listener. It's more or less us trying to communicate an impression, and the listener has the freedom to interpret as he wants," Fagen explained patiently. "When you're trying to cram a lot of information into what is basically a popular song form, you have to leave some holes. It's impossible to add that many details. We always have a story in mind and try to present it in the most entertaining way we know how. Sometimes we leave a few holes, that's all."

Most interviews wound up with them discussing their love of jazz and listing their numerous jazz influences. In one 1974 interview these included John Coltrane, Miles Davis, Sonny Rollins, Charlie Parker and Tubby Hayes. They rubbished most contemporary rock groups, took a hefty swipe at Yes and said the popularity of groups like Black Oak Arkansas, Uriah Heep and Slade amazed them. (SD had opened shows for all three so their dislike was formed at close quarters. "How they (Slade) ever managed to get enough money together to come here and tour is a miracle," said Becker.

Most acts play their favourite music during soundchecks, and Steely Dan's preference seemed to be a mixture of soul and non-Fagen lead vocals. At a soundcheck in the Sopwith Camel club in Glendale, they ran through 'The Boston Rag' and several other Dan tunes along with some surprising choices of covers: a fast boogie version of Marvin Gaye's 'Ain't That Peculiar', The Champs' instrumental hit 'Tequila', and Royce Jones wound it up with an a capella version of the sentimental Chi-Lites' hit soul ballad 'Have You Seen Her?'

After this gig Fagen told *Zoo World* magazine that... "as a rule we don't like to play nightclubs, but we always play here. It's a good place to break in new material, get comfortable with it before we take it on the road." (Indeed, SD had played four successive nights at the Sopwith Camel in early March to warm up for the current tour.)

Becker continued: "It's not like a jazz band where you just give the guys a set of charts. Last time out we had two women singing with us. This time we've got a new vocalist, a keyboard player and a second drummer. They had a lot of things to assimilate, phrasing to learn, things like that."

And Fagen was still bemoaning the fact that he had been elected the lead singer of the group. "I'm just not a natural singer," he said. "There's born singers and I had no training and the combination of things leads me to think that I'm not that good."

Becker could see the funny side: "He still firmly believes that if the good Lord had meant him to sing, he wouldn't have taught him how to play the piano."

ఴ

Becker and Fagen wanted to close the US tour – and their live career – with shows at the Santa Monica Civic Auditorium on July 3 and 4, but Independence Day was already booked so they had to settle for the 3rd and 5th.

Since Becker and Fagen were drawing salaries from ABC, they envisaged enormous difficulty in breaking the record company financial stranglehold which required Steely Dan to exist in a perpetually repetitive cycle of recording albums and touring to promote them. The only way out, they decided, was to dismantle the band completely. With no group, logic dictated that touring would not be possible.

Very soon after Steely Dan's last gig of the 'Pretzel Logic' tour at Santa Monica, it was announced that Jeff Baxter and Jim Hodder had left Steely Dan. Baxter had already guested as a session player on a couple of Doobie Brothers' albums and had been playing gigs with Linda Ronstadt and The Doobies between his Steely Dan commitments. On occasions when Steely Dan supported The Doobies, the ever enthusiastic Baxter would play all Steely Dan's set and then half The Doobies' set, too.

Fagen and Becker encouraged Baxter to play with other artists, claiming that it made him a more interesting musician when he returned to Steely Dan. More significantly, perhaps, it also got him off their backs for a while and Baxter was playing at the Knebworth Festival in England with The Doobie Brothers when Fagen called him with the news that he and Becker wanted to continue without him and Jim Hodder.

According to Denny Dias, Becker and Fagen had put off the decision for as long as possible so that both had the time to develop a career away from Steely Dan. Though they often appeared cynical and aloof, Becker and Fagen had no desire to hurt anyone.

When the announcements were made, Steely Dan manager Joel Cohen described the split as "completely amicable". He went on: "Eventually the members want to have an orchestra on stage - they want to get larger and larger." Baxter was expected to join The Doobie Brothers, while Hodder was officially listed as "looking".

"We took the band apart in a decisive fashion," said Becker, "so that it could not be put back together and we could not be sent out on the road. What were they gonna send, me and Donald with banjos?"

ℰℐ

Within a couple of months, it was reported that Steely Dan had six tunes finished for their next album and that Becker and Fagen would be continuing with Denny Dias and hiring outside musicians. Fagen and Becker were now free in many senses of the word. Using the workshop situation, the studio became just another instrument for them to experiment with.

Fagen: "The situation just sort of evolved into having a band and making records with them. Our producer, Gary Katz, was instrumental in putting it together. But after a couple of records, we decided that the situation was too limited for the kind of music that we were writing so we arranged to have other musicians brought in. And that finally evolved into a situation where we could hire whomever we wanted to play individual songs. It's probably more like the movies than popular music."

September 1974 saw the release of Steely Dan's second single from 'Pretzel Logic', the title track itself backed with 'Through With Buzz', which charted at number 59 in America, but continued the dismal showing of Dan singles in England. Steely Dan won numerous music press awards in 1974, figuring in almost everyone's Top Twenty list. But Becker was as unimpressed by the honours as he was by the majority of the competition. "Awards don't impress me," he said. "It depends on who is choosing. All I have to do is look at the name above and below us and the credibility is gone."

Only two months after the announcement that the band had split, *Rolling Stone* reported that Steely Dan were now suing manager Joel Cohen for $2 million for defamation, breach of fiduciary duty and libel, and spreading false rumours that the group was breaking up, inferring appearance dropouts and damaging their relationship with ABC. Cohen in turn blamed Steely Dan's business managers and attorney Michael Shapiro for poisoning their minds and filed a $3 million slander suit against them.

Denny Dias remembered it thus: "Joel Cohen wanted us to do whatever would make the most money. Donald and Walter wanted to do whatever would make the best music. Whenever Cohen could force the issue, he would. Walter said he was only interested in lining his own pocket."

Becker and Fagen lost the case and it was eventually settled out of court, with Steely Dan being forced to pay Cohen a substantial sum by way of compensation for their being allowed to break their contract with him. Having finally rid themselves of Cohen, Becker and Fagen elected to manage themselves.

Without the pressure of touring and with Cohen out of the picture, Becker and Fagen could now settle in their houses and write songs to their hearts' content. They were in their element and were determined not just to expand their musical and lyrical vocabulary but to set themselves even more ambitious goals.

ℰℐ

CHAPTER VI

Laughing At The Frozen Rain

There was a nine month gap between Steely Dan's last gig at the Santa Monica Civic and the release of 'Katy Lied' in April 1975, but it was never suggested that their decision not to tour was as final as it turned out to be. (They wouldn't play live again for nineteen years.) Their aversion to the concert stage did encourage interviewers to delve deeply into the reason for their absence. "We're not the least concerned about touring," said Fagen, barely disguising the relief in his voice. "We've never been that highly motivated about going out on the road. We enjoy performing, but I'm not sure it's worth the inconvenience for a frail person such as me. The tour problems can be overcome by routing and planning. We don't write when we're on the road. We have a lot of things to do and say and touring detracts from that."

"We try to avoid gymnasiums. You'll never see us at the LA Forum. We don't make any money on tours. We play in places that accommodate a limited number of people. Beyond that you can't be assured that the sound is occurring. Our expenses are usually equal to the profits."

Becker felt that the high standards they had set for themselves would almost certainly deteriorate if they continued on the gigging merry-go-round. "I don't want to meet the audience. You have a more direct and intimate relationship with someone who's sitting alone, listening to your records. Playing live isn't that personal. When we played, it was as direct as possible. No one was sitting more than three miles away. The trend for rock and roll bands now is to play the biggest halls around. Also, I've noticed that bands who stay on the road for an extended time, or for most of their career, the quality of their show often suffers from the lack of new material. Then the quality of the records is even worse."

As ever Becker had no qualms about expressing his contempt for his peers. "The quality of rock music presented is appalling. Neither Donald nor I go to rock and roll shows. There's not much to see," he added.

Steely Dan had recorded their first three albums almost exclusively at the Village Recorder, but when they were ready to begin recording their fourth, Walter Becker and Donald Fagen accepted Roger Nichols' suggestion to try a different studio and booked into ABC Recording Studios in North Hollywood. They had no particular reason to be disgruntled·with the Village and moving to ABC was a decision they would eventually regret. Becker and Fagen ensconced themselves there during the latter part of 1974 and early 1975, delighted and relieved to be free of the pressure of going out on the road again in the immediate future.

Prior to the sessions, Becker and Fagen instructed keyboard player Michael Omartian to buy them a new piano. Being avid listeners to all kinds of music, they had noticed the superb sound quality of Bosendorfer pianos on classical records and wanted to use it for their own music. They specifically asked Omartian to get them a Bosendorfer and he wasn't about to argue since he, too, was a tremendous fan of that sound.

The upmarket piano shop David Abell Music was located opposite the studio and Omartian played several pianos before settling for a very expensive seven-foot-six Bosendorfer with an exquisite tone. The piano was delivered to the studio that same afternoon. Becker and Fagen duly informed the record company that they had bought a new $13,000 piano for the studio and, *erm*, would they mind footing the bill? With Steely Dan's albums selling like the proverbial hot cakes ABC could hardly refuse and they paid up without any fuss.

The Bosendorfer became the central instrument for the whole album. Omartian played some beautiful Becker and Fagen melodies on that piano during the 'Katy Lied' sessions, and its rich tone provided the perfect underpinning for Becker's guitar solo on 'Bad Sneakers' and Phil Woods' alto sax solo on 'Doctor Wu'. Omartian was livid when he returned to ABC Studios a year later to find the piano covered in cigarette burns. "How anyone could treat such a beautiful instrument in such a way was beyond me," he said.

As with its predecessor 'Katy Lied' was Steely Dan's second album of short pop songs. Every track except 'Your Gold Teeth II' was less than four minutes long, which was most unusual for Becker and Fagen; their albums almost always had a couple of tracks coming in at over five or six minutes. The album's cover, again the work of Fagen's girlfriend Dorothy White, was an extreme close-up of an abundant US grasshopper called a katydid. When Fagen saw the blurred photograph, (which came about because the film froze) he liked it and realised a loose connection with their chosen album title and the play on words it evoked. The photographs on the rear of the sleeve were taken by photo enthusiasts Walter Becker and Roger Nichols and the album design was consciously based on the format adopted by the Fifties West Coast jazz label Contemporary Records.

One of the most frequent observations of Becker and Fagen's music was that they put jazz changes into pop song structures and wrote hooks. But when he was asked about it, Becker played it down. "I think we used to tell people something that ended up coming out like that. I think we were just trying to suggest on a much smaller scale that we would occasionally use a slightly different way of getting from key to key, and slightly different chord qualities than were heard in ninety percent of the music on rock and roll radio stations."

Becker and Fagen maintained that they never consciously set out to write hits, but at the same time they were well aware that the classic structure of their songs was ideal for radio and chart success. Walter Becker couldn't resist a little gloating over their recent achievements by harking back to their years of struggle: "We were given many reasons to believe that our music would be vastly unpopular by people we approached over the years."

"It was mainly the lyrical content that put people off," Fagen explained, "and possibly at the time the kind of harmony. What we ended up doing was writing the kind of lyric we like superimposed over a traditional song structure, which made sense to people. Which made sense to me. Traditional song structure is extremely serviceable."

Becker attributed their penchant for listening to jazz records and jazz radio as being responsible for putting them both "on intimate terms with how songs work. That's probably one of the reasons why we wrote so many bridges in our songs."

Becker and Fagen were always at pains to stress that their songwriting process was a fifty-fifty operation, but Fagen did admit there were occasional exceptions. "Musically, we think very much the same, but otherwise he has his life and I have mine. Usually I'll develop the germinal idea for a song and take it over to Walter... We more or less put both our names on all the songs, but I've written a few myself; I can't recall any except 'Barrytown' on the 'Pretzel Logic' LP. I don't think it came off so great anyway, so I don't know if it's a good idea to do stuff by myself. 95% of our songs are collaborative."

Fagen praised Becker's creative strengths and expanded on their relationship outside the working environment. "He's a good editor also. He'll suggest improvements on my original idea, and then we'll work on lyrics together."

"We actually never discuss each other's life in any particular detail," said Fagen. "We have a sort of psychic... I hate to use that word... I don't know, we both know the direction that we're going, and it doesn't matter that we know the actual circumstances behind it. We just discuss it as what we want to do with the narrative. We're friends but we're not the closest friends in the world. We've known each other for a long time and we understand each other's working habits and needs and limitations. But we aren't hanging out together that much."

Their songwriting method usually began with Fagen coming up with a musical idea – a fragment of lyric, a chord sequence, a possible chorus – then getting together with Becker and kicking the ideas around, joking about it, smoking Turkish cigarettes, laughing a lot and developing a story. Fagen could start songs but often needed Becker to finish them; with Becker it was vice versa.

Becker said that he liked "swatches of colour, images that don't necessarily make much sense" and was less concerned with tying everything together; Fagen, on the other hand, would argue endlessly to exclude or replace something from a first draft if he thought it shouldn't be there. Their rabid imagination and love of the obscure was all that informed their lyrics. "Because of the lack of input, experience that's available in the United States of America, or the world in general these days, we more or less rely on pure imagination for song ideas," said Fagen. "And we like to make them original, and we'll set up a framework, no matter how bizarre it may be, and proceed to write a song on that basis.

"I'll come up with an idea and he'll come up with a scenario, and we'll decide what we think the song is about and which part of the exposition is happening in each verse and get a title together and no matter how strange the idea may be we just go along and hope that we can finish the song and that it actually emerges as something.

"When we go in the studio it's further refined by the studio musicians who are playing on it. Both of us in concert write the music and the words. You know, it's a lot of pacing around the living room. Whenever Walter has some free time he'll drop over, show me what he's got, I'll show him what I've got and kick it around a little bit. It's very informal.

"There's a lot of stuff packed into the records musically. We try to make it 'unboring', that's one of the main things we go for. If it's boring that's the main indication that there's some failure."

A popular misconception within the music business was that Becker and Fagen's exceptionally high songwriting standard was due to the fact that they wrote at least one song every day. In fact, Becker said that their songwriting sessions were confined to "a couple of hours, a couple of times a week", usually in the evenings or nights. And when they were in the studio their songwriting diminished even further to the point where they wrote only what was needed to finish an album.

In *Downbeat* Fagen told Jim Bickhart: "One of us generally comes up with the germinal idea, usually from the same type of inspirations other writers draw upon. We usually work things out on the piano. It's easier to develop harmonic interest that way, though you can sometimes find a nice tune without it.

"I think of each piece as a composition, so the arrangements are integral to the actual composition. It's a classical approach, not so much formal as traditional. It's more traditional to western music than modal, formless rock and roll. I'm fond of the pop structure and blues structure. It's fun to adhere to certain rules about length and structure and still put them through twists and grotesqueries. One of the most interesting things in pop music certainly is to set limitations and then take occasional liberties. Because of those liberties, people sometimes don't realize how much blues we do; usually at least one per album."

ℰℐ

'Katy Lied' contained at least one song – 'Your Gold Teeth II' – which the musicians thought was particularly intricate and difficult, with bars of 3/8 and 6/8 thrown in, so Becker and Fagen started out with the idea of having just Jeff Porcaro, Chuck Rainey and Michael Omartian run it through in the studio. They practised the tune over and over again without achieving the take that Becker and Fagen had visualised. Eventually, late at night after playing the song countless times, they decided it had been played to death, abandoned it and agreed to return refreshed another day for a second shot.

All too aware of the difficulty the musicians had been having with the song, Fagen gave Jeff Porcaro a Charles Mingus record with Dannie Richmond on drums which featured similar odd time signatures. Porcaro listened to it several times and when the three players returned to the studio they nailed it quite quickly. Porcaro later described 'Your Gold Teeth' as pure bebop.

Talking about his drumming on 'Katy Lied' in *Modern Drummer*, Porcaro rather modestly said: "All that went through my mind was Keltner and Gordon. It was do or die for me. All my stuff was copying them. For instance, on 'Chain Lightning' all I thought about was the song 'Pretzel Logic' which was Gordon playing a slow shuffle.

"On 'Doctor Wu' I was thinking of John Guerin, especially those fills going out between the bass drum and the toms. He'd do it in bebop style. Guerin was on Joni Mitchell's 'Court And Spark', which was in that same Steely style. On 'Black Friday' I was again thinking of Jim Gordon, my shuffle champion. I got real frustrated trying to play this, and I just threw a big tantrum. 'I'm the wrong guy! You should get Jim Gordon!' I told Gary Katz. After walking around the block three times, cursing myself, I came back in and cut it.

"The ride cymbal on 'Katy Lied' is an old K Zildjian my dad gave me," Porcaro added. "Unfortunately, all the cymbals are clipped and phased because the DBX didn't work. That was real heartbreaking for the guys."

In 'Bad Sneakers' the piano part and the vocals follow each other, another cool Becker and Fagen touch. The song, which has an agonisingly beautiful melody, seems to be about their longing for New York. They had by now grown very tired of the Californian sunshine and had serious difficulty relating to people from the Golden State. Walter Becker in particular was emulating Charlie Parker, William Burroughs and numerous other artists by experimenting with a variety of drugs and living an increasingly nocturnal lifestyle. It took him a while to realise that if he didn't curb his propensity for abusing his body, he would in all likelihood wind up laid to rest in... "that ditch out in the valley/That they're digging just for me".

Gary Katz told WLIR-FM that 'Bad Sneakers' proved a fairly straightforward song to get on tape. McCracken locked it into a great groove on rhythm guitar and Michael McDonald was drafted in for his first appearance on a Dan album. His keyboard skills weren't utilized however; Becker and Fagen wanted him solely for his distinctive vocals and he added his voice to 'Bad Sneakers' and particularly 'Any World That I'm Welcome To', yet another old song which had originally been written with a female vocalist in mind (Walter Becker later mentioned Dusty Springfield by name). It also provided drummer Hal Blaine with his only credit on a Steely Dan album.

Denny Dias didn't spend nearly as much time in the studio with Steely Dan as he used to but he recalled an occasion when they needed an instrumental melody for a song and Fagen confidently predicted he'd have something ready by the next day. Becker joked that Fagen had been writing fugues and, indeed, when they came into the studio he had written a fugue, 'Rose Darling', with counterpoint in the vocal parts.

Outtakes from the period include 'Mr Sam', another old song from their pre-Steely Dan days and a song intriguingly entitled "Gullywater".

Speaking about 'Katy Lied' in particular, Fagen said: "Each song is seen from a different viewpoint. Some, I imagine, have an idealistic tone to them, while others are someone who's obviously suicidal. Obviously the narrator, if you will, is really in the deep stages of severe depression. And, of course, I probably was when I was performing them. Everybody's personality is just a symptom of the times. I always seem to see both sides of things simultaneously, for which reason I never have an opinion about anything."

In 1975, Fagen was 27 and Becker 25 and throughout their twenties – certainly for the last few years – they had spent almost all their waking hours in quiet rooms writing songs or in darkened studios recording those compositions. Fagen was clearly a workaholic and though he didn't admit to it at the time, all the indications were there. Asked what kind of life he lived, Fagen replied: "I rarely step over the portals of my door to the outside world... I watch TV, I listen to old records and play the piano a lot."

"I'm a jazz fan," said Fagen. "I listen to my local jazz station (KBCA) but I haven't heard anything really new at all since about 1965. I still like to listen to my old Blue Note and Prestige albums; the best records are the Fantasy re-releases of old stuff. You might say that both Walter and I have a rather narrow spectrum of taste when it comes to that sort of thing. I like Sonny Rollins, John Coltrane up to the point where he self-destructed jazz. He got a little too smart and ventured into realms where man should never tread. I also dig Mingus, Duke Ellington, Charlie Parker, Eric Dolphy, sax players in general and great rhythm sections. Also Miles' quintets.

"None of it matters. We're in it for ourselves anyway. To become excessively popular you have to cater to the whims of mass taste, which I don't feel we've done. Popularity is relevant to business but irrelevant to music, and we're only in business to the extent that we have to stay in business so we can afford to make music for fun. I'm pleasantly surprised at the level of acceptance we've attained. It's far beyond my mother's wildest dreams."

Neither Becker, Fagen nor Katz ever showed up at showbiz or record company parties. It just wasn't their scene; they felt uncomfortable with the forced bonhomie and refused to go along with it. "I think we insult people unintentionally," said Fagen. "We keep getting invited to this and that, like the Grammy awards. I got a thing that said 'Wear beautiful clothes'. I don't have any beautiful clothes! Now I know what they wanted me to come like, they wanted me to come dressed like Cher!"

At least one of the Steely Dan studio musicians felt that Gary Katz, too, was uncommunicative in the studio, and he took that to mean that Katz wasn't impressed with his contributions. Other musicians felt the same way, but kept their mouths firmly shut for fear of losing a lucrative engagement and future session fees.

Despite their hostile reputation, which Becker and Fagen thought amusing to encourage, they very seldom adopted an attitude when a musician made a mistake. But when Michael Omartian blundered musically, he would go into the control room and light-heartedly say, "Man, I'm really sorry, I shirked my responsibility as a musician to really practise and be prepared." This became a standing joke between Omartian and Becker who, each time he played a wrong note or chord, would smile and say, "You're shirking again." Christopher Cross eventually hired Michael Omartian to produce his multi-Grammy winning début album purely on the strength of his work with Steely Dan – 'Katy Lied' in particular.

The usual routine at the 'Katy Lied' sessions was for Fagen to sit at the piano and play a tune while Omartian, who has perfect pitch, stood alongside transcribing it. Omartian would then write out the voicings that were necessary to pull off the chord immediately before the session. The band then learned the song from a combination of Fagen playing it a few times on the piano and from the charts which Omartian had just prepared. Becker and Fagen invariably came in psyched up to work exclusively on one song per session and stuck rigidly to that routine.

If they were stuck for ideas, Omartian offered suggestions for certain parts of songs. Fagen and Becker were always receptive to a musician's suggestions and Omartian was given freedom to play around with bass lines and elaborate on Fagen's basic piano parts.

Becker admitted that the superimposed triads which end 'Throw Back The Little Ones' were Omartian's idea. Sometimes Becker and Fagen made crude demos with Fagen's piano and singing and occasionally Becker's bass line. Since neither could read nor write music, this still entailed someone writing out the charts. At other times, if the studio players were having difficulty, they would request Fagen to go into an isolation booth. To assist everyone he would sing a reference vocal as they rehearsed the tune so all the musicians knew the feel of the tune and the direction in which Becker and Fagen wanted to go.

Most studio musicians who played on Steely Dan sessions remember Fagen as the originator and more musically organised. Becker would concentrate on the lyrics, and tended to improvise on Fagen's suggestions with an excellent sense of overdub possibilities. Typically, Becker would be in the booth observing through the glass, while Fagen would be in the studio, guiding musicians and suggesting things.

Becker and Fagen had written a sequel to the 'Countdown To Ecstasy' version of 'Your Gold Teeth' by appropriating a strange series of chords from an extended instrumental version of 'Do It Again' which Steely Dan used to perform live on stage. They later described this extended instrumental as "an overture" and admitted that it was vastly unpopular with audiences and "received such an unenthusiastic, soggy welcome" that they were eventually "bullied out of it". "'Your Gold Teeth I and II', the second version, much more closely resembles the original version which we never recorded. It was just a simple sort of waltz," Becker said.

Rose Darling' is yet another example of a Becker and Fagen tune with all their characteristic elements of deceit, an illicit affair, drugs and even murderous intentions. As usual, not enough of the story details are filled in to allow an accurate assessment of the plot and, indeed, Becker and Fagen's structure allows several vastly different interpretations to co-exist alongside one another. Usually Becker and Fagen only gave the musician certain guidelines when playing a solo, allowing them room to improvise, but in 'Rose Darling' Dean Parks played a specific solo transcribed note for note.

'Doctor Wu' contains an absolutely divine alto saxophone solo played by Phil Woods. Woods was booked in for what Steely Dan anticipated would be a long and demanding session, but he floored Becker, Fagen and Katz by nailing it in the first take. It was rumoured that Fagen was so dumbstruck by the performance that he asked Woods to play it a couple more times just so that he could hear it again.

A couple of years later Fagen was happy to give his version of the story. "'Doctor Wu' is about a triangle, kind of a love-dope triangle. I think usually when we do write songs of a romantic nature, one or more of the participants in the alliance will come under the influence of someone else or some other way of life and that will usually end up in either some sort of compromise or a split. Okay, in this song a girl meets somebody who leads another kind of life and she's attracted to it. Then she comes under the domination of someone else and that results in the ending of the relationship or some amending of the relationship. When we start writing songs like that, that's the way it usually goes. In 'Doctor Wu' the "someone else" is a dope habit personified as Doctor Wu. In 'Haitian

Divorce' it's a hotel gigolo. The details of 'Rikki Don't Lose That Number' and 'Through With Buzz' are vaguer but the pattern is the same."

Queries about their lyrics continued to dog them in almost every interview they gave. Sometimes Becker and Fagen delighted in playing the game and one such occasion concerned 'Chain Lightning', the haunting, modulatory blues from 'Katy Lied'. Challenging Richard Cromelin and their audience to unravel the song, Becker said: "No one will ever come close to 'Chain Lightning'. No one will ever touch 'Chain Lightning'."

"Even the clue wouldn't have helped," Fagen continued. "I'll tell you what the clue was. In the guitar break just before the second verse, I was gonna say, 'Forty years later', but we decided it wasn't a good musical idea."

The mystery remained intact for many years and Becker and Fagen never did divulge the song's subject matter. Then, during an interview to promote "The Nightfly' some seven years later, Fagen finally admitted that 'Chain Lightning' in their minds described a "visit by two guys to a fascist rally". Given Fagen's supposed fascination with Hitler, it came as no surprise – and they *had* talked flippantly several times about composing a song about his beer-hall putsch in Munich in November of 1923.

Less of a mystery was the Latin style arrangement of 'Everyone's Gone To The Movies', originally copyrighted in 1971, which takes a comic look at teenagers corrupted by watching blue movies "in Mr LaPage's den". But Becker and Fagen took the story a stage further with the allusion to a far more serious undercurrent: Mr LaPage's covert goal was to deflower some of the nubile young virgins.

Although 'Katy Lied' contained only ten songs, Becker and Fagen found it necessary to use seven guitarists and they flew in New York based Rick Derringer and Hugh McCracken especially. Only Walter Becker takes two solos, on 'Black Friday' and 'Bad Sneakers'; Denny Dias played the solo in 'Your Gold Teeth II'; Dean Parks played 'Rose Darling'; Rick Derringer played 'Chain Lightning'; and Elliot Randall resurfaced to play 'Throw Back The Little Ones'.

Becker and Fagen heard about Larry Carlton, who was working with The Crusaders (probably through Wilton Felder who also appeared on 'Katy Lied'), only when the album was almost finished and he was invited to add rhythm guitar parts to 'Daddy Don't Live In That New York City No More'. It was to be the beginning of a long and rewarding relationship.

❧

The reviews of the album were surprisingly poor. The *Melody Maker* critic thought 'Katy Lied' was a good album but not as "masterful" as 'Pretzel Logic', then he added that Becker and Fagen's songwriting partnership had grown in stature and that in the long run 'Katy Lied' might be seen as their best album. *Rolling Stone*'s John Mendelsohn hated it; he felt Fagen's singing lacked passion, said he didn't care if he never again heard another Steely Dan song and described their music as "essentially well crafted and uncommonly intelligent schlock". Nick Kent in *New Musical Express* described it as "easily their worst album to date" and predicted that unless Becker and Fagen built a new group identity, "things may deteriorate further".

This was all water off a duck's back to Becker and Fagen. Criticism never bothered them. They wrote and recorded for themselves anyway and if other people liked it all well and good. If they didn't, too bad.

"We write for effect," Fagen said of their songwriting technique. "Lately, we've been getting into the social protest thing, like 'Black Friday' on the new album. We may even do a song about Gerald Ford, the Kennedy assassination or Da Nang." Fagen's tongue was surely firmly in his cheek. "We write topical music. I don't think audiences have a problem relating."

Of course, most of the audience *did* have a problem understanding Becker and Fagen's lyrical sketches. But it was as much the sound of the words in the context of a song as their actual meaning, and ninety percent of those who enjoyed their music probably couldn't care less what individual songs were actually about. Most Steely Dan fans were happy just to listen to the music without worrying too much about what story, if any, the lyrics told.

If, as Walter Becker said: "Steely Dan is a scribe who writes upon the wind, in search of fertile ground," then a great deal of the seed was spilled in the desert.

Fagen: "Our heart is still on Second Avenue and that's what we like to write about. Our lyrics are basically experience combined with a little fantasy."

"I think there's a lot of New York, urban type imagery and settings and so on," added Becker. "Even the language in our songs is imitation thereof."

The first single to be lifted from 'Katy Lied' was the opening tune, the ominously titled 'Black Friday'. In US history the first real Black Friday occurred on September 24, 1869, a day of panic in the securities market which was repeated nine years later. The term is often used on both sides of the Atlantic for any day of crisis, financial or otherwise, but there is no evidence to suggest that Becker and Fagen were referring to any particular occasion. They had simply used their collective imaginations to create a fictitious incident.

Becker and Fagen's tale is of a crooked speculator who makes his fortune and absconds to Australia with the proceeds to live in the lap of luxury and seek forgiveness for his sins. As well as Omartian's piano it features David Paich playing a Hohner electric piano. It wasn't typical Top Forty fodder, but it hit number 37 in the US... not bad for an act that wasn't touring, wasn't about to tour and wasn't making any secret of it either.

They chose Muswellbrook, a town in New South Wales, Australia, for the lyrics of the tune. "It was the place most far away from LA we could think of," explained Fagen... and, of course, it fitted the metre of the song and rhymed with "book".

Becker and Fagen were now in their absolute element: touring was off the menu, they had no internal personnel problems to deal with and they were able to hire and work with the *crème de la crème* of session players. "It's a luxury to use Larry Carlton and Wilton Felder," said Fagen. "It was a logical outgrowth to have different sundry musicians on different tracks. Specialisation pays off. We always used outside singers of some sort. Given the basic personnel, there weren't enough voices to sing all the notes in the chords, especially the harmonies."

The question most critics and fans wanted answered was what made Steely Dan so different from other groups? "Harmonically we're a little more complicated," Fagen explained diplomatically. "Perhaps we're a little more careful in the studio. We strive for all the songs on an LP to be of equal quality. The music, the writing, the recording. We have some sort of framework which helps us write songs. When the songs come out people have some pretty bizarre interpretations. A chord with four notes isn't really better than one with three notes. We like to throw in a ringer once in a while. It makes things interesting."

Becker and Fagen recited the musical doctrine according to Steely Dan: "We write all the music and arrange it and show it to the musicians. We provide the framework for them to work with. We try to bring out the best in them. I think we've been very successful, especially this last album."

Despite Jeff Baxter's departure some six months earlier, Becker and Fagen were still being questioned about their future prospects without him. "I saw him the other day," said Becker. "He wanted to play live more 'cause he likes the action. With The Doobie Brothers he's got a 38 city tour lined up. That's work. The Doobie Brothers are doing very nicely. He'll be in Oxford, Mississippi before us."

Yet when Fagen told *New Musical Express* that... "the only reason Jeffrey didn't play on the last album was because he was on the road with The Doobie Brothers," he was not being honest. "And we missed him on the dates where we could have used him, so somebody else did it."

Although they reckoned that the return of the "Skunk" was a possibility, he and Hodder never played another note on a Steely Dan record. Baxter's contributions had been an integral part of the early Steely Dan sound – he played outstanding solos on some of their greatest songs – and their flippant comments testify to the deterioration of their relationship with him. Baxter was everything Becker and Fagen weren't: extrovert, a practical joker and truly in love with life on the road.

There was even some speculation in the press that Baxter and Hodder's departure might lead to the end of Steely Dan as a group. Becker and Fagen smiled incredulously at the suggestion and Fagen responded: "If you think of it more as a concept than a group of specific musicians, there's no way it'll break up." It was too early to discuss the next configuration of Steely Dan and Baxter's name was even included in the list of possibles. "We're always meeting new musicians," said Fagen. "There are certainly some that are well qualified. Including Jeff."

If there were to be any future Steely Dan tours, Becker said, "You'll see two Steely Dan shows on different tours, it'll be different bands and a different kind of musical presentation. The nucleus of the band has always been the same."

Fagen: "We have a bunch of satellite performers who are more or less interchangeable from time to time. Usually we pick musicians that we think will fit the particular song. Sometimes we'll just hear somebody on a record and hire them for the date, and if it works out it's all the better...

"You know, we grew up listening to jazz musicians and they're always playing with different musicians, so I don't see why the same thing can't happen here. It makes it much more interesting."

"I remember Rick Derringer," Becker said. "'Chain Lightning' has all the aspects of a straight blues, except the chords constantly modulate, and he was sort of freaked out by that for about three or four seconds, and then realised he had to do something a little different from what he usually does."

Derringer, by now a regular on Steely Dan sessions, rose to fame in The McCoys, whose 'Hang On Sloopy' was a number one 'garage' smash in 1965, but more lately he'd appeared with Edgar Winter's band White Trash. McCracken's more illustrious session credits included Paul Simon and a stint with Paul McCartney's Wings.

They admitted that before they even considered another tour they were going to record another album. "The idea," Becker said "is to get an ongoing recording process going and not have to be interrupted by a tour. 'Cause what usually happens is just as you're finishing an album, you have some ideas on how you'd do it differently, things that you'd like to do while it's still fresh in your mind, and it's always been for us that immediately on completion of the album, we were always pressured by various forces, internal and external, to go back on the road. As if we're going to make some money or something."

Asked to explain the concept of Steely Dan, they couldn't, or wouldn't, define it. The word games continued. Fagen: "We've been working on it and as soon as we can articulate it properly, it'll appear on the record probably. See, all we can do is give clues, 'cause we're too close to it. It's all on the record, you know. It's all there. There isn't much to say about it."

"Even if we could answer the question," Becker said, "you know that we would lie. We would deliberately lead you off the scent."

Fagen: "We do have rather venomous personalities at best, although we try to keep it to ourselves."

Henceforth the sum total of promotion for a Steely Dan album was however many interviews Becker and Fagen were prepared to tolerate. One journalist in particular who regularly championed their cause and gave their albums laudatory reviews was Richard Cromelin. Whenever Steely Dan released an album, Cromelin was always among the first in line to interview Fagen and Becker about it, and their relationship seemed to be one of mutual admiration.

But Becker and Fagen's friendship with Cromelin was soured once and for all years later when he interviewed Fagen about the 'New York Rock and Soul Revue' album. When the article appeared in the *Los Angeles Times*, he referred to Becker as a "baby-faced sadist". Cromelin also – quite justifiably – questioned Fagen about his partner's drug addiction and induced him to discuss Becker's unreliability during the 'Gaucho' sessions. Becker was incensed by the article and in the wake of it both he and Fagen wrote letters to the *LA Times* castigating Cromelin and attributing his "outburst" to a desire for revenge for all the teasing to which they had subjected him over the years.

'Katy Lied' reached number 13 in England and on the strength of this Steely Dan's UK record company Anchor reissued 'Do It Again' in late summer which finally gave Steely Dan a long overdue, albeit minor, English hit. Despite heavy airplay on local radio stations, it only scraped into the Top Forty at number 39.

In interviews to promote the album and single, Becker, Fagen and Katz were very secretive about what actually went on during Steely Dan recording sessions and when asked for anecdotes about those sessions, Katz laughed and said, "Well, every night someone falls down and I spill a cup of coffee, usually on a piece of equipment, which drives Walter berserk."

Fagen: "It's obvious to anyone really interested that Steely Dan is a conceptual group, like jazz bands have always been. Not that I'm saying we're a jazz band by any stretch of the imagination. But whoever's in the band is in the band. We use different people for different purposes, and people we like to work with tend to reoccur in rotation. It's a good way to avoid stagnation. That's a chronic problem with pop music, the stagnation caused by using the same people over and over. We choose the band to suit the piece.

"It takes a process of getting to know who's around and where to find them when you need them. Once you find people who will subordinate to your trip, you can get somewhere. The best musicians will be able to subordinate either to themselves or to someone else. It comes down to discipline.

"I find it hard to look for trends in what we're doing. We write whatever we write and arrange however we arrange. But I think it's fair to say we're getting more spontaneous, going with the flow in the studio more than we used to. But it's never been a matter of contriving anything to be commercial; the most obvious examples like 'Reelin' In The Years' were not contrived. They were composed and then improvised upon."

Fagen's ambitions were non-existent outside music. "I don't have any goals. I just enjoy making records. It's fun, it's something to do, you make a little bread you know? I just bought a new synthesizer to fool around with, an ARP Odyssey. It's not too overwhelming, but the one I had before was even more elementary."

Ironically enough, during one exceptionally frustrating session at ABC Studios Becker took exception to the sound of an ARP String Ensemble and smashed it into a hundred pieces. He and Fagen then had the shards mounted on the wall as a kind of monument to his work.

ABC put 'Bad Sneakers'/'Chain Lightning' out as the second single in August 1975 but once again Steely Dan had completely misjudged the singles market. Gary Katz belatedly realised the extent of their miscalculation. "It was a terrible mistake not putting that out as the first single," he said. 'Bad Sneakers' made not the slightest dent on the US singles chart. By then Becker, Fagen and Katz were already back in the studio working on songs for the follow up and Gary Katz had put his disappointment behind him and was more than confident: "We have songs in the can you wouldn't believe."

When the album was finished Becker and Fagen, as ever, were eager to use the latest technology and, not keen on the Dolby sound reduction system, put into effect another of Roger Nichols' ideas to put the 'Katy Lied' mixes through a DBX sound reduction system. It proved to be a disastrous decision.

Once mixing was finished and they played the songs back, the sound reduction system was pumping and sounded odd. They tried everything to correct the fault but, despite Roger Nichols' expertise were unable to do so. There was only one answer: one night Nichols, Katz, Becker and Fagen flew to the DBX factory in Boston to see if the makers could succeed in getting the damaged mixes to play back properly. They made countless adjustments to the equipment, but even they were unable to recover the sound.

The maker's final resort was to make a special set of DBXes that had external controls for some of the adjustments that were usually internal. Under normal circumstances this meant that the equipment would have to be periodically sent back to the DBX factory to be realigned, but DBX responded to Steely Dan's request by giving them external control of those adjustments so that they could listen to the mixes and adjust the controls at the same time.

They returned to ABC and remixed the album using the new DBX-adjusted equipment, a very tortuous and painful experience, and everyone connected with Steely Dan maintained that the album never sounded as good again. "If you had heard that album the way it originally went down on tape," Becker said, "you would have heard something else."

Katz, it seemed, was even more crushed by the sonic damage than Becker and Fagen. "We had to decide whether we were gonna scrap the album or put it out. It was close." Katz said the album suffered 85% and placed the blame squarely on the studio. "I can't listen to it. I hate to hear an album that we're involved in that's not up to our standards. It was the best sounding thing I'd ever heard before it was mixed. ABC Studio is a mess. But we feel we can go on and do a better one next time." Eventually he became philosophical about their problems in the studio, saying that any group who spent as much time recording as Steely Dan, was likely to suffer with similar difficulties. Nonetheless, Katz moved to Warner Bros at the first opportunity afterwards.

Then, typically for Steely Dan, Becker and Fagen wrote some tongue-in-cheek sleeve notes for the album demonstrating the extreme care and attention which they took with each album, only to have this havoc wreaked upon them.

Initially Fagen was so angry at their misfortune that he refused to even discuss the problem: "There was a technical problem which I don't want to get into. These are things the public doesn't want to know." However, the questions persisted and he eventually relented and spoke about the disaster, telling Harvey Kubernik: "It took us a long time to figure out what it was and then undo it. Machines ten, humans nil."

Becker also conceded defeat. He admitted that he couldn't even listen to the record, adding "I'll get back to it later."

Becker and Fagen's quest for technical perfection had rebounded in their faces and ruined the album. They had been taught another very costly lesson; don't be so hasty to use the latest and greatest piece of equipment.

℘

Luckless Pedestrians

Steely Dan's fifth album, 'The Royal Scam', was released on both sides of the Atlantic in May 1976. It was a nine song collection which, despite Gary Katz's criticism of ABC Studios, had again been recorded there with additional sessions at A & R Studios in New York.

By now, Fagen and Becker's pool of musicians had expanded into a veritable orchestra of session players. They thought nothing of flying a guitar player or a drummer – or indeed both – across the country to play little more than a few bars of one song which might not even make it onto disc. Expense didn't enter into it; their foremost consideration was to find the right stylistic match and to create as perfect a rendition of each composition as was humanly possible. Within a few years they would take their obsessiveness even further, using the latest technology to create absolute millisecond-perfect drum tracks, using either a drum machine, a computer, a live drummer or a combination of all three.

At the sessions for 'The Royal Scam', Fagen and Becker began to record each tune with six or seven different rhythm sections, switching the players around to try almost every configuration possible. They would record all the songs with Rick Marotta and then record them all over again with Bernard Purdie to see what each drummer could bring to the tunes.

Bass players, guitar players and keyboard players would flit in and out of a variety of studios so often they never knew what was going on. Different combinations of musicians were playing all the songs on successive nights and no one knew in advance – including sometimes Becker and Fagen – who (if anyone) would end up on the final track. On some frustrating occasions, after countless unsuccessful takes, a song would be dropped because Becker and Fagen decided that none of the multitude of efforts had come close to their vision of the song. Often Becker and Fagen's microscopic fastidiousness bewildered the session players, who thought every facet of the track sounded fine but which for some reason Becker and Fagen refused to accept. And no amount of talking could persuade them otherwise.

Fagen and Becker took their controlled experimentation further with each album; it would reach its limit on 'Gaucho' when it became increasingly unlikely that they would *ever* be satisfied with virtually any basic track. During 'Gaucho' they employed an astonishing forty musicians and singers and worked on one song for so long and listened back to it so many times that they actually wore the oxide off the tape.

Recording for 'Scam' began in 1975 in Los Angeles with Elliot Scheiner at the controls. His first experience of working with Becker and Fagen had been on Jay and The Americans' 1970 album 'Capture The Moment'. In 1975 Scheiner had engineered 'Destiny', the second solo record by ex-Rascals vocalist and keyboardist Felix Cavaliere. The sound of 'Destiny' impressed Becker and Fagen enough for them to ask Scheiner if he was available for their forthcoming project. They were also looking for a different sound for this album and with Scheiner acting as tracking engineer, they spent two weeks working at a new studio (for Steely Dan) on Lankersham Boulevard in LA called Davlin. But after two frustrating weeks Fagen and Becker hadn't got a single satisfactory basic track so they abruptly flew to New York to try some of the tunes at Scheiner's home studio, A&R.

Up to that point Steely Dan had been using one-inch 24-track tape, but Scheiner had heard about a new recording technique called the Eicosystem, whereby two 16-track machines could be linked up together to provide 32-tracks. The mixing problems they encountered with 'Katy Lied' had not deterred them from experimenting with new technology, and when they got to New York Scheiner persuaded Becker and Fagen to try cutting the tracks for the album using the Eicosystem.

Becker and Fagen not only changed the studio, they changed the musicians, too, except for Larry Carlton who accompanied them on the trip to New York. The change of scenery and studios seemed to do the trick; the A&R sessions were successful beyond their wildest dreams compared with their Los Angeles dates, and in another two week period they managed to get more than half the album's basic tracks on tape.

But then Steely Dan's technical gremlins intervened again. When Scheiner began to edit the tape, it became clear that the Eicosystem wasn't working and Steely Dan abandoned the sessions. The system was absolutely brand new so they had expected some teething troubles, but what the makers had failed to tell Steely Dan was that they couldn't edit the tape if two machines had been linked up together. Almost immediately after one technological disaster, Becker and Fagen had been plunged into another. Their scant consolation this time was that at least this problem could be rectified and didn't affect the sonics of the final record.

Nevertheless, Becker, Fagen and Katz held Scheiner personally responsible for the chaos. They went back to Los Angeles and transferred all the 16-track material back to old-fashioned 24-track. Scheiner was put on the "shit list" for the rest of the 'Scam' sessions and later, when it came to mixing the album, Roger Nichols and Barney Perkins carried out that task. However, Scheiner was soon forgiven and reinstated to mix Steely Dan's next album.

Scheiner was disappointed by his enforced exile. In their two week spell at A&R Studios he had successfully recorded six or seven basic tracks for the album before Becker and Fagen returned to California. In sharp contrast to their fruitless LA sessions, they got a first night take on 'Kid Charlemagne' with a band consisting of Bernard Purdie, Chuck Rainey, Don Grolnick on clavinet, Larry Carlton and Victor Feldman.

For 'The Royal Scam' Becker and Fagen hired Garry Sherman to write the charts. Sherman was a veteran of New York commercial dates, but during the sessions his abrasive manner and condescending attitude toward the other musicians led most of them to develop a strong dislike of him. He also irritated Becker and Fagen one evening by arriving at the studio with a photographer and requesting his picture be taken flanked by the duo. Becker and Fagen, who weren't renowned for their tact, refused to cooperate and Sherman didn't get his picture.

They were also pretty annoyed that Sherman should expect this of them, especially at a critical time during recording, so notions of revenge began to form in their minds. One Friday night, when Steely Dan were finishing up at studio A1 (which could be locked from the outside), they put into operation Elliot Scheiner's idea of getting all the musicians out of the studio, sending Sherman back to pick something up and then locking up and leaving him imprisoned for the weekend. At the last minute they decided that perhaps the stress might cause the middle-aged conductor/arranger to have a heart attack, so the idea was abandoned.

While Steely Dan were working on 'The Royal Scam' in October 1975 and before the Eicosystem debacle, Elliot Scheiner had separated from his wife with little hope of a reconciliation. Scheiner's lawyer told him that if he was going to seek a divorce, then for tax purposes he should do it before the end of the year. Scheiner asked how the hell he could possibly achieve that in only a couple months. The lawyer went on to advise him that there *was* a way to accomplish this before the deadline – go to Haiti where real "quickie" divorces were available.

Scheiner mentioned to Fagen and Becker that he wanted to take some time off from recording in order to fly down to Haiti and get his failing marriage annulled. They were amazed and intrigued by the idea, and encouraged him to spill more of the relevant facts of the story. What Scheiner didn't realize was the reason for their undue interest in his predicament.

He duly flew to Haiti, where his US lawyer had arranged for a Haitian lawyer to meet him at the airport and drive him to his hotel. The lawyer explained the procedure and the next morning both men were in a courtroom listening to a magistrate reciting the official procedure in French. This was translated by the lawyer and Scheiner answered briefly in English. After only about five bewildering minutes Scheiner's divorce was complete. He had beaten the deadline with time to spare and celebrated by staying in Haiti for another couple days exploring and soaking up the atmosphere of the island.

On his return to the studio Becker and Fagen continued to pump him for information about his visit, pressing for some of the finer details of what had happened. It all became abundantly clear some time later when Scheiner was surprised and delighted to hear they had written and recorded a song, 'Haitian Divorce', based very loosely around his experiences. Becker and Fagen had used extensive creative licence on the song: they injected some fictitious elements to spice up the story and made the protagonist of the song a woman in order to add the "semi-mojo" twist in the final verse.

℧

Becker and Fagen were looking for a different drum sound for 'The Royal Scam' and Jeff Porcaro, who had played on all but one song on 'Katy Lied', was passed over in favour of two Steely Dan débutants: Bernard "Pretty" Purdie and Rick Marotta. But Porcaro was a very personable guy as well as a great musician and certainly didn't hold his exclusion against Becker and Fagen.

Steely Dan used three drummers – Purdie, Marotta and Herb Lovelle – on the tracking dates. The latter played on sessions for 'Sign In Stranger' but his contribution didn't make the final record and Becker, Fagen and Katz liked his snare drum sound so much that they wanted to retain it on a two-bar drum loop for possible use on a later album. Lovelle's snare was eventually put through Roger Nichols' self-built drum machine, Wendel (who got the credit), and used on a song for 'Gaucho'.

After the melodic Bosendorfer piano approach on 'Katy Lied', 'The Royal Scam' took an altogether ballsier point of view. "It's got a stomping mood to it compared with 'Katy Lied'," said Becker. Fagen also acknowledged this: "We were looking for a bigger bass and drums than we've had. I think there were probably less overdubs in general as far as the basic rhythm tracks. Almost everything was there and everyone played it."

Of the two percussionists appearing for the first time on a Dan album, the most famous was Bernard Purdie, a very strong-willed and boisterous character best known for his work as Atlantic Record's in-house session drummer but who later claimed to have played on several early Beatles tracks. Purdie liked to carry three signs around with him reading "Bernard 'Pretty' Purdie", "The World's Greatest Drummer" and "The Hitmaker" and, depending on his mood, displayed them in the studio where he was working. He also had a neon sign proclaiming "Another hit being made" which he plugged into the mains at the studio, and he often displayed hit albums, on which his playing was featured, on the floor around his drum kit. At one point he even claimed he should have received a co-writing credit for 'Home At Last' because his drums were such an integral part of the song.

Purdie tuned his own drums to perfection to suit his own taste and wouldn't normally alter the tuning but, perhaps inevitably, Becker and Fagen wanted him to try a different sound for one song on 'The Royal Scam'. He absolutely refused to do so. Determined to have things their way, Becker and Fagen arranged for Dinky Dawson to crawl into the studio on his belly in pitch darkness and fix some pads under Purdie's drum heads to dampen the sound a little. Hence Dawson's credit for "Techno" on the album sleeve.

Gradually Purdie was persuaded to come around to their way of thinking – to tighten or loosen his drum heads as requested – but the drummer always ensured they knew he was doing them a special favour. He could afford to be arrogant; he was an excellent sight reader and an incredible time-keeper, and he often seemed to have an innate sense of a Becker and Fagen composition which he would nail in the first three or four takes. But even after what he deemed an acceptable take, Becker and Fagen invariably wanted more and Purdie found this hard to accept.

"With me they always wanted something specific," he said later. "They had already recorded 'The Royal Scam' with other drummers so I had to overdub. I stuck to the original patterns, but they wanted what I could do. They knew my earlier work, so they wanted to hear my own take on their music. They were very strict to the point of super precision. Really picky. They wouldn't take no for an answer and they wouldn't accept mistakes – period. It was truly frustrating in the beginning. I come from the school that when you feel good about what you've done, it's hard to do better. It only goes downhill from there. I learned to curtail my own feelings and just wait. They wanted it their way, so you had to do many takes."

Sometimes Purdie would nail it during an early take, but Becker, Fagen and Katz wouldn't be happy with one or some of the other instruments. Then Purdie would start goofing around, not concentrating and even, one studio insider suggested, deliberately make mistakes to demonstrate his musical superiority and vent his frustration. Despite his occasional bouts of sulking, Purdie was most impressed by Fagen and Becker, admitting that he thought they were "the closest thing to genius I've seen". He was impressed by how incredibly precise they wanted their drum tracks; they would allow him some leeway to express himself in the early takes, then make their own suggestions. In some of their songs, Becker and Fagen would tell Purdie they didn't want a shuffle, but Purdie considered his shuffle to be unique and he often played variations on it and managed to get away with it. Becker and Fagen had long since learned how to get the best out of any particular session musician and with Purdie it was no use mentioning another drummer's name as a stylistic guide as doing so would more than likely cramp his own creative input.

The second drummer making his début on a Steely Dan record was Rick Marotta and in an interview with *Modern Drummer* he maintained that he didn't even know who Steely Dan were when he sat down to record 'Don't Take Me Alive'. "I remember I wanted to get in and out as soon as possible. Larry Carlton and Chuck Rainey were there – pretty much business as usual. Then they counted off this tune... the first thing I heard was the lyrics 'Agents of the law/Luckless pedestrians' and I almost stopped playing. I thought I'm listening in my 'phones to this guy who can really sing, and the tune sounds amazing, and the band is amazing. It was just different. You have to kiss a lot of frogs when you're a studio player. After that I had to stop and collect myself. This is real. Every time I went in with them, I knew it was going to be something really historic. They were the most demanding of anybody I've ever worked with. Donald was like the Prince of Doom. For instance, I'd walk into the control room and it would sound unbelievably great and he'd be looking at the floor, saying 'Yeah, I guess it's OK'."

Marotta illustrated Fagen's incredible ear for the minutest of flaws. "On 'Don't Take Me Alive' there's one backbeat in the 16th or 17th bar that was a little softer than the others. I'd say, 'Donald, show me where'. He'd wait for the tape to come around and he'd point it out. 'Right here'. He'd pick the same spot each time. He wasn't crazy, he was just microscopic. Walter was as well. It was beyond my imagination how anybody could be so focused for so long."

Becker and Fagen were so attuned to the same wavelength in the studio that it became a talking point among the studio players. Rumours of an uncanny telepathic link even began circulating. On the rare occasions when they disagreed about a musical component and were both adamant about their respective views, Gary Katz usually told the musicians to take a break and when they came back the difference had invariably been resolved.

The consensus of opinion among various studio musicians trying to sum up the difference between Fagen and Becker's studio personae was that Becker was vocal about what he wanted, while Fagen would quietly direct musicians, maintaining his professional composure, but stalk around with a look of dejected resignation when he was unhappy.

Another musician who helped to shape the sound on 'The Royal Scam' was Larry Carlton. Becker and Fagen flew him to New York and placed him firmly at the forefront of the material, not only to play some blistering solos (seven in all) but to add to the rhythm dates as well. Carlton helped fill in Becker's bass lines where necessary, too, although he was quick to point out that he could take no credit for the arrangements.

Becker spoke effusively about Carlton's musical ability as well as his temperament. "With Larry, every pass he made was something good. His disposition was so even that it always seemed fairly easy, even if it took a while to get what you finally wanted. It was mostly just a question of stating clearly what the idea was that you had in mind. If we had something in mind that was even remotely appropriate for Larry, he could do it well. It was never like pulling teeth with Larry, as it had been with many other people.

"If that is the definitive Steely Dan guitar album, then Larry Carlton is the reason why. He contributed quite a bit to the tunes. There would be a lot of volatile people with volatile musical styles in the room and in a lot of cases, it seemed to me that Larry, more than anybody else, was holding things together rhythmically and in other ways."

Certainly one of Carlton's best solos on 'The Royal Scam', and arguably one of the best he's ever recorded, was on the opening tune and first single from the album, 'Kid Charlemagne'. He admitted that it was his claim to fame: "I did two hours' worth of solos that we didn't keep. Then I played the first half of the intro, which they loved, so they kept that. I punched in for the second half, so it was done in two parts and the solo that fades out in the end was done in one pass."

In some of their earlier interviews Becker had hinted at the lengths to which they would go to achieve the effect – or solo – they were seeking. They had attracted an ominous reputation for some of their more hostile methods of encouragement for a musician. But the truth of the matter was somewhat different, although both men encouraged the myth: "Donald and I have resorted to almost every possible mode of communication or demonstration to get soloists to do solos. Usually we'd start with a brief musical characterisation. A little discussion of some of the pivotal points of the piece and some sort of extra musical description as well. Something like 'fiery' or 'fluid', 'spirited' or 'subdued' or 'bluesy'."

The rhythm track, with its original back east groove, was a revelation. Becker and Fagen knew that if Chuck Rainey didn't play the bass part, then Becker would, so as usual they didn't need to have a part written for the song. Chuck Rainey was just given the chord changes and 'Kid Charlemagne' brought out the best of Rainey's musical instincts; using all his experience and imagination to improvise, he incorporated as much of his rhythmic and melodic knowledge as he could into the song. Rainey later wrote in *Bassics* magazine how he based the part on the James Jamerson school of thought, on rhythm rather than melodic notes. He also generously gave full credit to the drummer for allowing his bass part to work so well.

'Kid Charlemagne' is set in San Francisco and is about a drug dealer who, in Fagen's words, "had been overtaken by society and was left standing in the road with nothing."

Becker, Fagen and Katz variously described the main protagonist in 'Kid Charlemagne' as a maker, an artist, a chemist and a chef: "Someone who makes consciousness-expanding substances of the most dramatic, sensational kind no longer in vogue." Becker said that they didn't use any particular model for the song; Fagen said he thought it was more about the age – the late Sixties – and the reflections of someone who found himself in a decade where he's no longer of any use. They denied that 'Kid Charlemagne' was based on a Timothy Leary or Charles Manson type character, saying that he would probably be much less of a celebrity than those two examples. Becker claimed that there *was* an individual on whom the song was based, "who hung over the song like the Sword of Damocles" but he refused to name names.

"I think our songs are about people who exist all the time," said Fagen. "Occasionally there is a reference to someone who actually exists, but by and large the characters are largely fictitious. There's more topical material on this record. We wrote about 1976 more than we usually write about the time that we're living in."

'Kid Charlemagne' also contains a unique vocal interpretation from Fagen – the line "Yes, there's gas in the car" – with very distinct vibrato and an almost falsetto emphasis on the last word. Denny Dias was not present for many of 'The Royal Scam' sessions and so hadn't been around when Fagen cut the vocals. He can clearly recall listening to the album for the first time and when he heard Fagen's unbelievable vocal leap he was so astounded that he sprang right out of his favourite armchair.

Backed with 'Green Earrings', 'Kid Charlemagne' reached only a dismal number 82 in the US singles chart in July 1976, and yet again a Steely Dan single failed to make any impression in the UK chart. Donald Fagen didn't sound too disappointed, though, and wasn't any more optimistic about its successor. "I really thought that single was gonna go. It didn't. They've put 'The Fez' out, hoping they could get a disco hit. Well, you can dance to parts of it, you just have to stop in the middle once in a while."

'The Fez' was released in October 1976 but even when Becker and Fagen put out what was unashamedly a dance track – albeit a parody of disco music – at the height of the disco era, they couldn't crack the Top Forty. But they weren't considering chart success; it was another of their inside jokes – normally disco songs tended to hang on one chord, so they took up the challenge to compose a disco type song with plenty of chord changes. They certainly succeeded on that score, but it didn't succeed as a chart single, only reaching number 59 in the US.

'The Fez' is unique in another way. A veteran of sessions with Bob Dylan, Van Morrison and much of the New York soul of the Sixties, keyboard player Paul Griffin is the only other individual ever credited as co-writer on a Steely Dan song. Becker and Fagen were always fair in recognising and praising a musician's contribution where appropriate but in Griffin's case there was some disagreement as to his exact role in 'The Fez'. "He wrote the main theme," Fagen replied tersely when asked about it. Becker disagreed. "I wouldn't call it the main theme," he said. "He wrote a melody that is featured. At least, he *says* he wrote it."

Fagen said they had set up a riff at the session which Griffin picked up on and started noodling around with and which eventually became the main keyboard hook of the tune. Becker denied that the song was written in the studio. "But there is an instrumental melody which Paul started playing in the session, and when we decided to build up that melody to a greater position, since we had some suspicion that perhaps this melody wasn't entirely Paul's invention, we decided to give him composer credit in case later some sort of scandal developed and he would take the brunt of the impact."

Paul Griffin remembers it differently. He claims that Fagen already had the keyboard line and that he recognised the classical piece which had perhaps subconsciously inspired it, and so Griffin deliberately chose to move away from the original pattern in order to defeat any potential plagiarism suit. That similarity was to a classical piece by a European composer – the first four notes are exactly the same, but Griffin took it elsewhere completely.

Indeed, Becker and Fagen had made a demo of the song but the groove on the demo of 'The Fez' was less catchy than the final recording. Even today, Chuck Rainey still maintains that Jeff Porcaro played drums on the song, but Bernard Purdie received credit on the album. Since Purdie did overdub drum tracks for Steely Dan on some of the later albums, it's possible that Porcaro played the part, then Purdie added his unique feel to the track later.

The album contained the usual intoxicating mix of intellectually obscure lyrics and tight playing.'The Caves Of Altamira' was an old song which Becker and Fagen had written and demoed with Kenny Vance around seven or eight years before in New York. It was very unusual subject matter for a pop song and once again Fagen's taste for historical knowledge informed the lyrics: the Altamira Cave is in northern Spain (just west of Santander) and is famous for its prehistoric paintings and engravings; the roof of the cave is covered with paintings of bison and elsewhere there are black-painted or engraved figures of deer, horses, wild cattle and goats. In the 1976 version of the song Becker and Fagen omitted the third verse in which the narrator reflects on his childhood adventures and returns to the caves only to find that many others have discovered what was once his own secret little world.

'Don't Take Me Alive' was set in mid-Seventies America; it dealt with Fagen and Becker's unease about the regular outbreaks of violence in Los Angeles. Gangland shootings, wanton murders and armed sieges were so commonplace that Becker and Fagen felt compelled to reflect it in a song. They saw it as violence for its own sake, and in interviews they became involved in discussions about the relative merits and drawbacks of life in Los Angeles and New York.

"In Los Angeles and throughout the world in general, terrorism is a way of life, actually, for a lot of people," said Fagen. "The song was inspired by a run of news items where people would barricade themselves inside an apartment house or a saloon with an arsenal of weapons. It's about individual madness rather than political situations."

Becker and Fagen admitted that their literary backgrounds led them to write short story type plots into many of their songs. Obscurity came from their editing out superfluous information to avoid the danger of creating "a lousy or pretentious song". They also stressed the importance of taking the music and the lyrics together, because by putting a sweet melody to a subversive lyric, or vice versa, they were creating irony, one of their favourite tools.

Becker and Fagen always enjoyed writing about people who were "at the end of their proverbial tethers" ('Do It Again', 'Charlie Freak', 'With A Gun' etc.) or who were "in a life or death situation". "It goes back to Greek drama," said Fagen. "They didn't write about people who were having a lot of fun."

Neither Becker nor Fagen played an instrument on 'Don't Take Me Alive', but they weren't in the least bit concerned – in fact, they actually relished it. Becker even refused to exclude the future possibility of their not playing at all on an entire Steely Dan album and Fagen was in total agreement: "If we ever received an award, we'd like to receive it for songwriting. At least we'd rather be recognised for that than our musicianship, although we both feel we have interesting styles as musicians."

In a 1979 interview with Dennis McNamara on WLIR-FM in New York, Gary Katz explained how they told Larry Carlton to make the guitar intro as "nasty and loud as possible". McNamara told Katz that the song made him think of Al Pacino in *Dog Day Afternoon*; Katz responded by saying: "I think of *much* nastier things than that when I hear it."

Fagen had been a science fiction fan since he was a kid and had once belonged to a sci-fi book club. This was reflected in 'Sign In Stranger', a song based on an imaginary planet where criminals, gangsters and murderers were banished for their crimes. "That's true," Fagen said. "Of course, it does take place on another planet. We sort of borrowed the Sin City/Pleasure Planet idea that's in a lot of science fiction novels, and made a song out of it." Paul Griffin improvised a suitably interplanetary piano solo after Fagen had given him some idea of what they were looking for.

"'Green Earrings', for example," Fagen continued, "has a very contemporary vamp which leads into a cycle of fast progression and another section which is actually from another era." Despite the sparseness of the lyric with its one word lines, a story can be gleaned about a relationship blemished by a compulsive thief who shows no remorse for stealing his partner's prized jewellery. Denny Dias's short chiming guitar solo is punctuated by some machine gun bursts from Bernard Purdie's snare and hi-hat before Elliott Randall launches into the second solo which starts off just quirkily but then becomes increasingly deranged as the fade approaches.

'Haitian Divorce' was recorded with Walter Becker altering Dean Parks' guitar notes with a voice box. In contemporary interviews, Becker made absolutely no mention of Elliot Scheiner's experience in Haiti. "It's a divorce you get in Haiti and they're not hard to come by, let me tell you," he said. But over the years Becker and Fagen would make more cryptic comments about 'Haitian Divorce' than any other Steely Dan song. "It's a fierce and terrible ritual," said Fagen, sounding for all the world as if violent and painful self-mutilation was part of the process. "You wouldn't want your sister to have a Haitian divorce, believe me. It was a quick divorce, without too much red tape. If you can say 'incompatibility of character' in French, you're as good as gold. But we added a few moments to the ceremony itself."

Becker and Fagen liked nothing better than leading interviewers up the lyrical garden path and into a maze of allusion and perplexity. So Becker added another level of intrigue to the conversation: "The thing is now, I know a lot of people don't believe in voodoo and all that, but people like that shouldn't go to Haiti. Because they'll just nail you with that stuff. That's powerful medicine. We did a lot of research."

They refused to elaborate further and the word games began again, this time on operatic lines. They told Richard Cromelin, who duly reported in *New Musical Express* that... "Donald and Walter are well aware of the fact that Aida is not joking with you", whatever that meant. Being slightly more realistic, they said they simply wanted to hear how a reggae song would sound with lots of jazz chords. Needless to say, they were amused at the result.

'Haitian Divorce' wasn't released as a single in the USA, since its slight reggae feel convinced the record company that its likelihood of success was small; reggae had hardly any commercial appeal in the US at this time and its most famous exponent, Bob Marley, never had a hit in the US under his own name (although Eric Clapton had topped the charts with Marley's 'I Shot The Sheriff' in 1974).

This was not the case at all in the UK where the tide had finally turned for Steely Dan. Contrary to what ABC had decided across the water, Anchor really went out on a limb by issuing 'Haitian Divorce' as a single. With eleven singles and three Top Ten hits behind them in America – but only one Top Forty hit in the UK – it inexplicably struck a chord with English singles buyers and sailed into the Top Twenty, reaching number 17. Ironically enough, 'Haitian Divorce' was to be Steely Dan's biggest UK hit and their solitary Top Twenty entry. Fagen was pleasantly surprised, "because it's quite an exotic number," he said.

Although at the time the tune was recorded the US Government recognised a Haitian divorce, the rules changed from one period to another. On other occasions a divorce obtained in the Dominican Republic would be recognised, while a Haitian one would not. But Becker was at pains to point out the legitimacy and factuality of their song. "Of course, you can't get a Haitian divorce any more," he said. "You used to be able to go to Haiti and get a divorce real fast. They give you this document in French with ribbons and plumes and everything, and it's recognised by the American government. In a way that's enlightening. It's a situation people thought we probably made up. There are people out there who probably think we made up the name Haiti. We've been accused of everything else." As this comment indicates, the incessant accusations of lyrical obscurity occasionally irritated Becker and Fagen and Becker went on to accuse some of the Steely Dan audience of being intentionally dumb.

Ostensibly, 'The Royal Scam' is about Puerto Rican immigrants coming to New York with the expectation of a better life and eventually discovering that it was nothing like they'd been led to believe, especially for Latin Americans with little or no money and poor English.

In an interview with Steve Clarke of *NME* Becker and Fagen were in their element again when it came to discussing – or refusing to discuss – their lyrics, particularly of the title cut. A measure of the fun and revelry they enjoyed can be gauged by comparing Becker's responses to Clarke's questions. When he was asked what 'The Royal Scam' was about, Becker set the tone for the conversation when he replied: "About four and a half minutes". Interviewing Becker and Fagen when one – or both – of them was in this mood must have been a nightmare.

Turning serious for a moment, Becker admitted that Puerto Rico and New York City both featured in the lyric, then seemed to regret his honesty and began to argue that divulging what the song actually meant would be doing the song a disservice and would be "lending credence to the notion that in order to enjoy a song, you have to know exactly what it means. Or that it does mean exactly one thing. And it doesn't really. None of these things are true." Almost in the same breath Becker denied... "that Puerto Rican nonsense that someone over here (the UK) invented" and complained that the speculation was getting out of hand.

When Michael Watts interviewed them for *Melody Maker* and asked them to confirm this Puerto Rican theory, Fagen's response was almost as if he was disappointed that their lyrical puzzle had been solved: "Because the interpretation is so accurate, I wouldn't even want to comment further."

Fagen maintained that Dan fans could enjoy the song on many different levels and that that was the biggest part of the fun anyway. As with the word pretzel, scam wasn't an everyday word in England and Fagen was occasionally required to explain its meaning.

"Particularly because that song does have a topical aspect and because of that it's dangerous to give specifics and it is an allegory and it is written in rather a Biblical argot, I can tell you that," Fagen said. "The song does have rather a poetic way of expressing what we wanted to express. I'm very fond of that lyric. I wasn't totally satisfied with the way the actual track came out."

There was nothing unusual about that, but Fagen *was* pleased with their lyrics, which he felt were getting better – and tighter – with each album. "Just generally more charming and wonderful in every way."

One critic suggested that their lyrics on 'Katy Lied' were not their best. Fagen disagreed. "I thought they were good. I just think that from 'Pretzel Logic' on, all our lyrics have been superior to what we were doing before. More adult, if you will – not that that's such a good thing for rock and roll music, but make of that what you want."

"'The Royal Scam' isn't the key song," said Becker. "It's regrettable that if you call an album after one of the songs, which is something we don't do all the time, people take it for more than it is. We like each song to be listened to individually without relating to the whole album, although if you record a certain selection of songs the album will have a certain character. Generally the cheese stands alone."

Real people as well as places were also mentioned. In the song 'Everything You Did', Becker and Fagen included the lyric "Turn up The Eagles/The neighbours are listening" and far from being seen as a put-down, many people (The Eagles included) regarded it as a compliment. Asked by interviewers which contemporary groups they admired, Fagen and Becker, tongues firmly in cheek, occasionally listed The Eagles among their favourite rock acts.

But Fagen denied that they were harbouring some sort of vendetta against The

Eagles, a band whose album sales far exceeded those of Steely Dan. "Oh, no. We enjoy their music very much, we think they're swell. There is something funny about them, though. They're imitative of a lot of late Sixties bands. At one time a lot of critics spent a lot of time lumping us together with them. We both started at the same time and we were all white guys who sang in 3-4 part harmony. So we have a running joke about how The Eagles are our only competition." Becker and Fagen later referred to The Eagles as The White Drifters.

Within a few months of hearing 'Everything You Did', Don Henley and Glenn Frey returned the "compliment" and included a line in 'Hotel California' to acknowledge their own namecheck and send a message back to Steely Dan. "We liked the way they would say anything (in a song)," Glenn Frey explained. "That's why we used the words 'They stab it with their steely knives/But they just can't kill the beast'."

Comparing Steely Dan to other acts was becoming a harder and harder task for rock critics. Steely Dan knew full well they sounded nothing like the country rock influenced Eagles, and such comparisons might have sparked off the ill natured banter in the first place. During their visit to the UK comparisons were drawn between Steely Dan and 10cc, perhaps because both acts tended to use the studio as an instrument in itself. Fagen refuted the suggestion by saying that 10cc were "more in a Beatle-type bag than we are" which must have seemed like a compliment to the Manchester quartet. Becker simply dismissed the comparisons and reminded journalists of the fact that on their last visit they were being compared to The Doobie Brothers.

❧

Once the recording of 'The Royal Scam' was finished, Becker and Fagen urgently needed some artwork for the cover. Fagen called their photographer buddy Ed Caraeff and asked him if he had anything to hand. Fortunately, Caraeff had been working with Van Morrison who had told him that his new album was to be called 'Naked In The City'. Accordingly, Caraeff had asked a friend called Zox to paint some Los Angeles-type skyscrapers as the basis for the cover. Caraeff and Zox had already tried out numerous ideas, all of which included Zox's 8' x 6' painting: one idea entailed photographing a young Rae Dawn Chong and her little brother in front of the painting; in another Caraeff and Zox devised a way of making it look like dollar bills were falling from the sky. As things turned out, Morrison returned to Europe, eventually abandoning his own recording plans so Caraeff now had no use for the painting.

After speaking with Fagen, Caraeff came up with the idea of using Zox's painting with, superimposed upon it, a photograph of a sleeping vagrant on a Boston bus bench taken by Charlie Ganse, a Caraeff house guest. They took it to Hollywood where a specialist was able to match the tone of the photograph to the painting. Three of the buildings in Zox's painting were based on photographs he had taken of real skyscrapers on Wilshire Blvd in Los Angeles, the fourth was based on an old snapshot of the Prudential building in Chicago. Towering above the man were ominous skies and the skyscrapers which metamorphosed into a variety of snarling animal heads. The centrepiece was a king cobra just about to strike at a mongoose on its neighbouring edifice. It proved to be one of *the* great album covers of the Seventies.

"We had the title, but we didn't have a cover, so we went to see this photographer who we'd worked with before," Walter Becker explained. "We said 'We're in a hurry, 'cause we have deadlines, what do you have lying around the house?' And he had a photograph of the painting that's on the cover of the album." The painting has hung in a number of different places in and around Los Angeles: it spent some time in the Museum of Rock Art in the San Fernando Valley and most recently was on display in a gallery on Main Street in Santa Monica. It is for sale but only for the right price.

Fagen added that coincidentally it had... "a rather delightful relation to one of the tunes on the album. Also it had a nice colour. It looked vaguely purple; royal, regal." That coincidental relation is almost certainly to the cave paintings referred to in 'The Caves of Altamira'.

ℰℐ

Becker and Fagen came to London to promote 'The Royal Scam' immediately after its release. They were particularly looking forward to the visit, but certainly not to the interviews they would have to endure. Fagen planned to visit the Napoleonic Museum in Monaco and Becker was headed to the Monaco Grand Prix. While in London they were supposed to be looking at recording studios (they purported to want a change of scenery) and were seeking inspiration for songs, but it's pretty unlikely that either of the latter two conditions were ever realistic proposals. Fagen justified his visit to the Napoleonic Museum by saying that he wanted to get some of the atmosphere of the place for a song they were planning to write about the Congress of Vienna!

Needless to say, the visit proved fruitless as far as finding a suitable studio outside their list of favourites in Los Angeles and New York. Almost everything about the idea was impractical: for one thing, recording in London would have meant extortionate bills for transporting session players across the Atlantic and accommodating them in fine hotels, and for another Becker, Fagen, Katz and Nichols were unfamiliar with the studios which would have set them at an immediate disadvantage.

With the release of 'The Royal Scam', discussions about a Steely Dan comeback tour were rife. It was rumoured that they would be back in Britain in 1977 and touring America before that. This depended on how fast they could record their next two albums, which would fulfil their contractual obligations with ABC. At the time of their promotional visit to the UK in early summer 1976, they were already one album behind with two more to finish before January 1977. With Steely Dan's predilection for working on an album for however long they deemed necessary, there was never any way they would be able to fulfil their contractual requirements ahead of the deadline.

In order to improve on their original contract, Fagen and Becker had negotiated a new one and although this improved their royalty rates, it also brought a new form of pressure. "At one time we had no deadlines. We just had a number of albums to deliver. Our royalty rate was non-existent. This is true," Becker assured Steve Clarke of *New*

Musical Express. "At the time we were in England, we had never gotten a royalty statement which showed a plus. In other words, every penny we earned in record royalties was taken up by recording budgets – which were not inordinately large by any means – and by loans to buy amplifiers to keep us on the road, which was something else that we weren't making any money out of.

"We renegotiated that contract, so that instead of getting no record royalties we'd get *virtually* no record royalties. And in return for that we'd get deadlines for albums. When we were working on this one we started getting all this legal mail, harassment type mail from the record company, threatening to do things to us if we didn't finish the album by a certain date."

Becker concluded his overt statement with a wisecrack. "Some of your big heavy groups, when they hand over an album, the record company has to hand over x hundred thousand dollars. When we hand in an album, they just say "Thank you.'" But at least this provided them with the excuse, if they needed one, not to tour. "Caesar wants a record every three months, it turns out," Becker said, "so we have to render unto him before we render unto the concertgoer."

Aside from Keith Moon regularly bragging that he was a millionaire when he probably wasn't, very few rock musicians ever discussed money in their interviews in case it came to the attention of the taxman, but Steely Dan had no qualms about mentioning the perilous state of their bank accounts and bemoaning their lack of financial security. "I don't make any money whatever," said Fagen. "I live in a sort of financial limbo. When we were young and innocent, we signed a contract that was less than sensible in the sense that we could have a lot of success and not make much money. And our studio costs have to be paid back through royalties. All the same the single will help us to sell more albums so more people will hear the music, which is good."

Questioned about the expense of using top session players, Fagen and Becker bounced their answers back and forth like a scripted ping-pong session: "Some of them are very expensive," Fagen said. "Some of them are *outrageously* expensive," Becker elaborated. "Although we usually spare no expense." Fagen wound it up by joking that as the album had cost so much at least people would be getting their money's worth.

Despite all their complaints about the life of a touring musician, Becker and Fagen had submitted to the incessant requests and were realistically considering touring again. "We've never gone out with the same band twice," Becker said. "It's always been different. So there's no reason to start duplicating ourselves now." But although they wanted fresh faces as well as the top notch players, Fagen and Becker weren't about to desert their old friend Denny Dias: "Denny's got staying power vastly above that of most of his comrades," said Fagen. "He's actually shown an amazing dedication to our vision, if you'll allow me to use that, for many years. Although he plays with outside groups quite a lot while we're writing or working on something else, he's always ready to play with us."

Indeed he was. Dias would always make himself available for whatever musical venture Becker and Fagen were about to embark upon.

For once, Becker and Fagen didn't completely rule out a tour, but they did decline to name names, merely stating the obvious – that the line-up would probably include some of the musicians who had appeared on the recent albums. Their most satisfying touring aggregation had been their 1974 outfit with guest players of the calibre of Mike McDonald and Jeff Porcaro, but now they were looking at hiring players like Bernard Purdie, Chuck Rainey and Victor Feldman and that would be a very expensive business.

In August 1976 Becker and Fagen were featured in *Newsweek* under the headline "Recluse Rock", and were called "perhaps the best and certainly the most imaginative American rock group of the Seventies". But the *Newsweek* writers obviously hadn't even spoken to Becker and Fagen first hand and the article had very little substance, relying on secondary sources and ridiculous hearsay for their research. It centred on the "prolific pair's forbidding menace" and their alleged surliness and anti-social behaviour towards anyone but their immediate circle of musical colleagues. They took Walter Becker's tongue-in-cheek quote about their "direct one-to-one hostile attitude toward fellow members of the race" seriously and held their non-attendance at showbiz parties and lack of TV appearances against them. Gary Katz responded to the latter charges by admitting that it was simply because they weren't asked that often.

Becker and Fagen defended themselves against allegations of hostility and also denied they were difficult to work with. "If a musician likes a lot of freedom and he's not doing what we want, sometimes we can be constraining," said Fagen. " But I don't think we're difficult. We're not mean."

Becker tried to illustrate the point further by suggesting that the average producer was more difficult to work with than they were. He was quick to add that he didn't include Gary Katz in that category.

Another constant enquiry which dogged them was why it took them so long to record an album. Fagen denied that that was even the case and fell back on the (true) excuse that they had experienced technical problems. "It doesn't take us that long to actually work in the studio, but we do write all the songs which takes a while, and the last two albums we've run into technical trouble. When we were recording 'The Royal Scam' there was a lot of dead time waiting for studios to become free. We'd book a studio and it was no good or we'd do some sessions that didn't pan out. We weren't quite happy with the results."

Becker and Fagen would book studio time only when they were absolutely convinced that they had enough strong songs to make up an album. They had to be absolutely convinced of a song's structure and lyrical content before they began recording it. A common method in the Seventies was for a band to book a studio and then try to construct a song around some guitar riffs or a jam. With the high cost of studio time, even Steely Dan could not afford to waste money on it for musicians to merely experiment with what might well turn out to be a less than inspired song. "I remember one occasion when we were lacking a verse, but that's about it," Walter Becker said.

Fagen told *NME* that they threw a lot of material away. He skirted around their difficulties with the Eicosystem by saying that the equipment in a New York studio was not compatible with that in LA, "so we had to order some new equipment". However, this statement was not corroborated by studio staff which indicates that Fagen was disguising the true reason for their tardiness. While they were allegedly waiting for this to arrive, Becker and Fagen composed yet more songs. "It is the songwriting that actually takes most of the time," said Fagen. " It is three or four months to write enough material and two or three months to record it." But despite the advances in technology, each Steely Dan album actually took longer to complete than its predecessor.

'The Royal Scam' charted higher in the UK – number 11 – than it did in America, at 15. Even though they just missed the Top Ten in England, it was a remarkable achievement, especially as there had been no hit single at that stage. No doubt their European promotional visit, some impressive spreads in *New Musical Express* and particularly a lengthy and detailed interview with Michael Watts in *Melody Maker*, contributed to the album's good showing.

It soon followed all the other Steely Dan albums and was certified gold. And with another "comeback tour" failing to materialize, all Becker and Fagen had to do was summon enough energy to write sufficient material for their next studio venture.

And not even scholars as wise as Becker and Fagen could predict how long it would take – or how successful it would be.

ూ

The Crimson Tide

Becker and Fagen's January 1977 deadline for another two albums passed without so much of a hint that even one album was in the offing. In fact, there was to be fully a sixteen month gap between the release of 'The Royal Scam' and its follow up, 'Aja'.

It was even reported in the music press that Steely Dan were recording enough material for two albums to fulfil their contract with ABC after which they would be free to join Warner Bros. Becker and Fagen offered to do one live album (with half the material new) as well as a studio album, but ABC refused, fearing damage to the inevitable greatest hits package. Several midsummer dates came and went as ABC jockeyed for exactly the right time to release the album. Ironically 'Aja' was released in September, 1977, on the same day as the long-awaited but ultimately disappointing Rolling Stones' live album 'Love You Live'.

'Aja' was the record that finally realised Becker and Fagen's artistic vision and catapulted Steely Dan into the platinum bracket. It surpassed all their previous sales figures by a long way, eventually going on to sell around five million copies and spending more than a year on the US album charts.

On 'Aja', Becker and Fagen's extensive studio experience meant that they were able to exploit the full potential of the musicians that they hired. By now, they had certain musicians in mind for specific parts or solos even during the preliminary stages of composing a song. Another reason for 'Aja's' excellence was the simultaneous realisation by those favoured musicians of what Fagen and Becker had spent five years aiming toward. In effect, Steely Dan was almost a band again, albeit a studio band with a multitude of members, all of whom were actually the cream of the session world. Now, the composers and their hired hands were all moving forward as a single unit.

Steely Dan tried not to recognise any time or budget constraints, and simply kept on recording until they had either achieved exactly what they were looking for (or as close to it as was humanly possible) or decided that the idea was a bad one in the first place.

Most Steely Dan songs boasted either a guitar, sax or piano solo, but when Becker and Fagen included a solo in a song it wasn't just a throwaway or an opportunity for an instrumentalist to indulge himself, it had to make sense, have a purpose and relate to the rest of the song. By the same token, Becker and Fagen understood that they could get away with lyrical and musical murder on a verse, but when the chorus came in they had to have a melodic and memorable hook. Two prime examples of songs where complex but interesting verses open up into hookline choruses are 'Doctor Wu' and 'Bad Sneakers' from 'Katy Lied'.

In attempting to deny the widely held perception that they were inaccessible as both people and musicians, Fagen tried to lay the blame on their record company's publicity department. When Steely Dan were in the studio recording they didn't want outsiders watching the often long and laborious process of getting takes. "A lot of the requests we get are to 'observe us in the studio or to watch us write'," Fagen explained, shaking his head in disbelief. "We reject that sort of thing. It's boring, what we do. Also there have been periods when for personal reasons we weren't up to interviews. If we're involved with a project that isn't going well, we don't want to present it to the public."

Nevertheless, the requests wouldn't go away and ABC's publicity department persisted in passing them on until Fagen and Becker finally relented. In December 1976 Susan Shapiro from *Music Gig* magazine was invited into the Village Recorder to hear some of Steely Dan's new material. She listened to two songs tentatively titled 'When Josie Comes Home' and 'Asia' (sic) [which were scheduled for Steely Dan's forthcoming LP]. Becker was supposed to be there for the interview but had gone missing for a couple of weeks, during which time neither Fagen nor Katz knew his whereabouts.

In his partner's absence, Fagen was talkative and sincere. Shapiro asked him how he and Becker had reacted to some of the criticism that had been levelled at 'The Royal Scam'. "The reason that the critics were disappointed is that they get tired. The first LP is always the easiest to like, the second they still like, the third they think is pretty good. The longer you last as a group, the harder the critics are. That accounts for some of the disappointment with 'Scam'. Myself, I think it's one of the best ones we've done. I think, in fact, each record is a little better than the last." Fagen told Shapiro that his favourite part of record making was still to come – sequencing the tunes once they had all been cut.

As for sequencing their albums, Fagen and Becker would decide where each tune went on the record based on the key of each song, while Gary Katz argued in favour of songs with similar tempos being kept together. Fagen said the songs were sequenced for sound rather than narrative potential, but Katz admitted that to a large extent sequencing was down to pot luck. "There's no science to that at all, except first cut first side, " Katz said. "It's probably as important as making the record in that it sets the feel in the same sense that you would edit a movie… so that it flows from beginning to end. And it's a very difficult thing to do, 'cause everyone feels another thing. Lots of lists, lots of lists."

In the summer of 1977, Becker and Fagen were lured into listener-sponsored radio station KPFK in Los Angeles for an in-depth interview with disc jockey Captain Midnight (Steve Tyler), the writer Harvey Kubernik (who amongst other things was *Melody Maker*'s West Coast US correspondent) and the omnipresent Richard Cromelin. The incentive for their visit was the opportunity to play some favourite jazz sides from their own record collections. Becker and Fagen christened it Radio Free Steely Dan and said they were still open to other deejaying offers.

It also proved to be quite a coup for the station, since one of the 'Aja' songs ('Black Cow') was exclusively premièred on air that night – several months before the album came out. KPFK also threw the phone lines open for listeners to call in with questions for the jovial duo. The jokes flew thick and fast and Becker and Fagen enjoyed themselves a great deal, especially towards the end when they stopped taking calls and double handedly took over the airwaves with some of their favourite jazz selections. They played music from the Bill Evans Trio, Miles Davis, Charlie Parker, Bobby 'Blue' Bland, Charlie Mingus and Duke Ellington.

Fagen very rarely spoke ill of the session players whom they used, but on this occasion he showed his frustration: "I can't mention any names, but we've been greatly disappointed by a lot of people who we thought were more versatile. They're all good musicians, but we have them in mind for ten tracks and it'll turn out they were only good for two."

At the time of the phone-in Becker and Fagen had been living in Los Angeles for almost six years and they made no secret of the fact that they were now looking for a way out. They had resumed recording in New York with 'Scam', and it seemed that whenever things weren't running too smoothly they headed back to New York for a much-needed shot of energy. Becker was more frustrated with life in California than Fagen, and when he was asked why he had stuck it out for so long if he disliked it so intensely, Becker replied: "Convenience". "And inertia," Fagen said with great honesty. But they were about to shed their convenience and inertia within months they had sold their Malibu homes and were homeward bound.

Another example of Fagen and Becker's inertia concerned their promptness for interviews – if indeed they showed up at all. "We are sort of a pain in the ass to get to places on time," Fagen admitted. "If it's not directly related to working, we have a tendency to have very selective memories."

The amount of time Steely Dan spent in the studio perfecting their songs was a common topic among interviewers and Becker and Fagen seemed always to be explaining reasons why each LP took longer to make than its predecessor. "Before, we used to knock off two in an evening and that was that, but now it's really hard. Now when we come into a session the sheets are like this," Fagen said, stretching out his arms to maximum width. "We're not trying to be more complicated or anything. They're still almost pop song forms, but there's little things you can do to make it interesting by way of development of the themes that are stated in the popular part of the song."

Another worry for ABC was Steely Dan's recording budgets, which had been increasing steeply and which had prompted the record company to start hassling them during the 'Scam' sessions. But Fagen didn't regret anything: "It just takes time to get something to be good, to get eight or ten songs that are all good. Most rock and roll albums will be padded with less than wonderful material. We want every bar of the thing to be good. It's all time and we just eat it up. We're not total perfectionists in the studio, we just have aspirations in that direction."

Reportedly 'The Royal Scam' had cost over $100,000 to produce, which in the light of what was to be spent on 'Aja' and particularly 'Gaucho', was chicken feed. Steely Dan's deadline was eventually extended to March 1977 and Fagen suggested that a new Steely Dan style would emerge after their contact with ABC expired. He also hinted at a "slick, stylistic change", and warned that the new album's lyrics "would have no social significance".

☙

All the basic tracks for 'Aja' were cut in Los Angeles, except 'Peg' which was the last tune to be recorded in New York while the rest of the album was being mixed. Elliot Scheiner cut the basic track for 'Peg', then Becker and Fagen took it back to Los Angeles for overdubbing and Al Schmitt mixed the song.

'Peg' featured a fantastic groove from Chuck Rainey and Rick Marotta, which the latter described by saying, "We had done stuff with them before so we knew what to expect, so we just started playing. Chuck and I had played together so much that we got into a groove. I don't remember everything about it exactly, but I remember I was very sick, and Don Grolnick had to take me to hospital in the middle of the night during a rainstorm to get a shot. Anyway, once Chuck and I started playing, you could have hung your coat up on the groove." Marotta went on to say how flattered he was to learn that Jeff Porcaro loved it so much he made a tape loop of it and rode around in his car for hours on end listening to their stupendous playing.

While a few of the less tolerant studio players complained about the length and repetitiveness of Steely Dan sessions, the vast majority enjoyed the experience and said that the songs were such fun to play anyway that they didn't care how many times they were required to play them. Chuck Rainey, for one, didn't mind and perhaps that's why he turned out to be Aja's most used muscian. He recorded every song on 'Aja' – plus most of the outtakes – at the Village, at Producer's Workshop, and at various studios in New York. He was virtually the sole constant in each experimental rhythm section. Becker and Fagen continued with the method they had adopted during 'Scam', spending perhaps a week recording all the tunes with six, seven, or even eight different drummers.

They were somewhat reluctant to use Bernard Purdie extensively again because his distinctive stamp was all over 'Scam', and they didn't want to repeat themselves. But eventually, after some unsatisfactory rhythm tracks, they couldn't resist calling him into the studio to see what he could bring to the tunes. In the end, six different drummers were used on only seven songs and Purdie was the only one to appear on more than one cut.

Each studio player had his own little foibles: Chuck Rainey liked to hear the demo (if there was one) in his earphones; Jeff Porcaro liked to hear it in the studio and look at the chart at the same time. The musicians would listen to the demos and either play along with the song or learn it directly from the chart. In the days before decent home studios, Becker, Fagen and Katz would often record a basic demo of a song as a guide for the players. Chuck Rainey claimed that their demos of 'Peg' and 'Josie' were so good that they could have been released without any further embellishment. It's doubtful whether Becker and Fagen felt the same way, though.

Becker and Fagen had at various times made it quite clear to Chuck Rainey that they didn't want him to slap his late '50s Fender Precision bass on any of their songs. A session player of considerable experience and renown, Rainey felt somewhat annoyed about this precondition and what he saw as Becker and Fagen's inflexibility. He felt more than qualified to determine when it was appropriate to use his thumb on a bassline. Thus, while they were recording 'Peg' in New York, Becker and Fagen told Rainey that despite its slap-type groove, they didn't want it to sound like a lot of other current records that featured such a technique. Rainey felt that a slap line would be perfect for 'Peg' and when the recording of actual takes started, he turned his back to the glass of the control room and *did* slap the part. Becker, Fagen and Katz didn't realise. They thought his bassline was really neat and everyone left the session happy.

Later on, during the recording of 'Aja', Rainey had serious problems with his lower back and couldn't make some sessions. Gary Katz told him that he couldn't get a bass player at such short notice and rather than cancel the session suggested that Rainey send somebody over just to hold the part down in his absence. They could then overdub the bass part later when Rainey had recovered. He was delighted that Katz wasn't about to hire another bass player and not just because he would lose two or three weeks' worth of double scale session fees.

Rainey taught bass guitar in Los Angeles, and he prepared one of his more talented and adaptable students for the Steely Dan session and sent him along to the Village Recorder. Unfortunately the student, in trying to appear as a hardened studio professional ignored all Rainey's advice and very quickly became a target for ridicule. He took three basses instead of only one; he arrived two hours before the scheduled one o'clock session instead of immediately before the start time; and he scattered hand-written notes all over the floor around him. He also broke the golden rule of professionalism which is not to bother any of the players with questions about past projects. Chuck Rainey went on to suffer a couple of years' worth of good natured kidding about the incident.

However, there were times when things did not go according to plan. Many of the hottest guitar players in Los Angeles tried to play the legendary guitar solo in 'Peg' to Becker and Fagen's satisfaction. In all about eight different guitarists (exaggerated estimates varied from thirteen to over twenty) attempted it in what Becker and Fagen described as a "pantonal thirteen bar blues with chorus". Larry Carlton tried it, Robben Ford tried it, Walter Becker tried it himself twice but in the end it was Jay Graydon who nailed what they were looking for.

Gary Katz explained why they found it so hard to get a solo that everyone was happy with. "Everyone had their own idea of what that solo should be and it just wasn't matching up to what Donald and Walter expected of it. Jay Graydon was their last ditch effort – it became Jay Graydon's solo by default. It came out pretty much the way they had in mind, though."

Becker admitted that though they demanded the utmost from guitar players, the ends justified the means. "In the past it has been Larry who played most of the guitar solos. We're probably hardest on guitar players. But we get the best work. We've real charts and everything. It's more productive. The musicians enjoy getting asked to do something that's challenging. We like working with an overview, too. It's difficult, but it's fun. It's not stupid music."

Despite the fact that Larry Carlton's solo was one of those rejected, he later borrowed the opening chords to 'Peg' for his own composition, 'Room 335' and when playing this song live would introduce it by saying, "This is the tune that I stole from Steely Dan." In fact Carlton hadn't stolen it, but had obtained Becker and Fagen's permission to use their chords beforehand.

Marotta also described how, on the same song, he was amazed when Walter Becker called him and said "'Man, the difference between the verse and the chorus is that you opened your hi-hat about a billionth of an inch every couple of beats.' He called to ask if I did it on purpose. It was just for a little lift."

Michael McDonald's distinctive background vocals also helped make the song what it became. In fact, another well known singer tried McDonald's parts but it didn't turn out to Steely Dan's satisfaction. Quizzed about the identity of the singer, Katz refused to name names for fear of embarrassing him. Paul Griffin *did* feature on background vocals on 'Peg' and that came about purely by chance. Griffin played electric piano on the session and had a habit of singing along with playbacks in the control room and when Katz heard Griffin blend with Michael McDonald, he pointed it out to Becker and Fagen who suggested that he should go out and try it in the studio. It came out perfectly.

In 'Black Cow', the opening song of the album, Becker and Fagen used a veteran studio drummer named Paul Humphrey from Motown sessions with The Four Tops and Marvin Gaye. Humphrey's snare drum sounds beautifully dry amid Chuck Rainey's thick, lubricious bass. Fagen told Jim Ladd that 'Black Cow' depicted the floundering of a relationship when a certain incident will stand out in a person's mind and in this particular case it was "this luncheonette in Anywhere, USA – it was probably in Brooklyn, I would imagine – where the shit hit the fan."

The wilting sax break on 'Black Cow' was by Tom Scott and Fagen commended him for his work as horn arranger on the album. "We consulted with him about the sort of thing we wanted; sometimes we'd sing him some lines that we wanted in a certain spot – it was really a collaborative thing and then he would fill in a lot of the voices. He's a real expert arranger for small bands – well, for any kind of band really – and he took it very seriously, tried to do a great job and he really knew how to match the kind of harmony in the rhythm section with the horn charts. It really sounds like it was of a piece, although a lot of it wasn't planned until the tracks were done."

"We went over the tunes very carefully with him," Fagen continued, "and told him what we wanted. And generally his voicings follow the piano voicings. He does have a very fine working knowledge of how to do the proper voice at the right time."

Walter Becker admitted that Scott had contributed substantially more to the horn charts than any of their earlier horn players. Usually Becker and Fagen specified almost every detail, but in Scott's case, they gave him an idea of what he definitely should and shouldn't do, while still allowing him a certain amount of freedom. They used a mixed horn section of five saxes, two trombones and a trumpet, as required by Becker and Fagen's complex jazz chords.

Tom Scott was himself delighted to have been asked to work with Becker and Fagen. "I tried to bring a real advanced harmonic conception in the horn writing to their thing, and that has never been quite done before – at least with that size of band. You know, when you've got five saxes and there are only three notes in the chord, sometimes I would throw in a few funny notes. And they seemed to dig it. I was just trying to add some kind of different harmonic intention that would enhance what we already know about Steely Dan and their sound."

Walter Becker played some great guitar solos on 'Aja', including 'Home At Last' and 'I Got The News', but a candidate for the best must surely be 'Josie', which was a real stormer. Usually both Fagen and Becker were unduly modest when discussing their own musical contributions to Steely Dan records, but some time after their split when Fagen was asked about Becker's guitar playing, he said: "Self-loathing is really our specialty. He is a great guitar player; he doesn't have the kind of technique that a Barney Kessel or someone has, but he's very inventive and his touch is fantastic and I always thought that his solos were really my favourites, even though we were using the best players in the country. I think even so his playing – at least stylistically – is so perfectly matched to what we were trying to do. I guess that it's back to the word attitude."

On 'Josie', Chuck Rainey was given a rare written bass part but asked to improvise and improve upon it using his own creativity. As with 'Peg' he employed a right hand technique of palm slapping in the verse to add colour and variety.

Even before they started recording the title song, Fagen and Becker's vision of it featured a drum solo, and they admitted that initially they had Tony Williams in mind for the part, but they eventually called New York-based Steve Gadd out for the session. They had heard several good reports about him recently and Becker admitted that they may have mentioned Williams' name to Gadd as a stylistic indicator. "Fortunately he didn't take that too seriously," Becker said later.

There was never any explaining the vagaries of a Steely Dan session. Some supposedly straightforward tunes would need endless takes to achieve the track that Becker and Fagen were looking for, while others that were long and complicated pieces would be nailed in the first or second take.

On this occasion the latter applied. The whole studio was astonished by Steve Gadd who, Fagen said, had "really invented a new kind of drumming in those days." When the band came into the studio the chart for the song was pretty awe-inspiring itself. The song moved from section to section like a suite and Becker and Fagen wanted each part to be extremely precise. "We figured we'd rehearse it for a day 'cause it was quite difficult, but when we got to the studio, it must have been six or seven pages and we just decided to run it down once and, Steve Gadd aside from being a fantastic drummer, is a fantastic sight reader and didn't really need to rehearse and neither did the rest of the band. They were really good readers: Larry Carlton, Michael Omartian, Chuck Rainey and they just went through the first take and there was a little mark on the chart for Steve Gadd to ad-lib through a certain part and a couple different parts which we figured we'd talk about and so on, but they just ripped through it on the first take and we kept it." In fact, Gadd "ripped off" the drum solo so much that some of the other musicians were mesmerised into looking at him and not concentrating on their own playing. Consequently some of the other parts had to be re-recorded and punched in later.

As well as Steve Gadd's drum solo, 'Aja' included a masterful tenor saxophone solo by Wayne Shorter which was an excellent example of economy and restraint. Fagen described how Shorter's solo was compiled in the studio. "On the song 'Aja' Wayne did two or three takes. The first was kind of a rehearsal, then he wrote down the changes, because they were tough and hard to remember, so he wrote out the scales and did two more takes, which we later combined. If Larry Carlton found a guitar part complicated he'd play a bit and then we'd come up with a couple of suggestions. It seemed like we were doing a lot of takes, but we were recording on tape."

In order to complete the title song, Becker and Fagen inserted parts of another discarded composition entitled 'Stand By The Seawall' into it. Michael Omartian couldn't understand why Becker and Fagen had given up on it – he thought the song was "totally cool". The long guitar solo on 'Aja' was played by Denny Dias and Becker played some nice little blues phrases the second time it went through the main theme.

It was one of their most outstandingly successful pairings of musician and song. But more often than not it didn't turn out that way: "There were many instances," Becker said, "when we conceived what we thought were dynamite solo sections, but then nobody was comfortable with it. We were wrong in thinking that so-and-so would rip this one right off."

'I Got The News' was originally written for 'The Royal Scam' sessions, and in many ways is almost as sparse lyrically as 'Green Earrings', but is decidedly more erotic. Originally, the tune didn't work out to their satisfaction so Becker and Fagen rewrote it and changed the lyrics but still retained the keyboard part with Victor Feldman in mind. "We let him play rather freely on the date," Fagen said. Fagen failed to mention another occasion when Steely Dan had Feldman doing nothing but shaking a salt-cellar for an entire six-hour session.

When Becker and Fagen were writing the songs for the album, Becker called their ex-tour manager, Warren Wallace, a big sports fan and close friend, and asked him for the names of some successful college football teams. He reeled off a few names and was surprised months later to find the most lyrically appropriate – Alabama, the Crimson Tide – used in 'Deacon Blues'.

Later ABC asked Becker, Fagen and Katz to edit 'Deacon Blues' for a single, but they refused on the grounds that the song would have been totally destroyed it. Pete Christlieb's sax solo was such an integral part of the song that to edit it out would have made a mockery of the whole tune. 'Deacon Blues' did come out as a single in April 1978, backed by 'Home at Last'. It peaked at number 19.

Pete Christlieb was located by a process of trial and error. "He came about because we liked the sax player on *The Tonight Show* and we found out who it was," said Gary Katz. "We kept hearing this one guy who was great, but never could figure out who in the band it was. We had one player come down thinking it was him and when it wasn't, we called the other one and it was Pete and he was great. Pete's a free spirit, there's not much controlling Pete, which is exactly what we want. So you just run the music by him and he blows his brains out. He's just a great player. That was just a very uninhibited session with Pete because he just wants to play. And we like that sort of spontaneity."

Katz also admitted that recording 'Deacon Blues', as with 'Doctor Wu', was "emotionally crushing" to him. Once again Becker and Fagen's adolescent hipsterism and jazz ideology formed the basis of a Steely Dan song. Some years later Donald Fagen explained the intent behind the song: "Well, the idea of the song was about this kind of alienated kid out in the suburbs who was looking for some sort of alternative values and turns to jazz and hip culture as something to grab on to. And the basic idea is that there's a kind of culture of losers that he'd rather be part of than the general way of life in America.

"You know, they've got a name for the winners in the world, and the losers should have some sort of franchise as well. And the name which he has chosen which conveys a certain power is 'Deacon Blues'."

'Aja' was mixed at A&R Studios in New York, which was still a favourite of Becker and Fagen's. "It's a real old studio, great echo. The whole album with the exception of 'Peg' was mixed there because we like the engineer that works there, Elliot Scheiner, who did the mixdown on all the tracks but one. And there's some players in New York that we particularly like. Sometimes it's easier to go there rather than get players to come out from New York."

Fagen explained that both Becker and Nichols were "deeply into the golden age of hi-fi. Our model was not the rock sound but Rudy van Gelder's Fifties sound, the sound he got on his Fifties Prestige recordings. We'd mix our records to sound as much as possible like a Fifties Miles Davis recording. We got so into that sound that at one stage we tried to persuade Roger to forget stereo and mix everything down into mono. He refused. For good or ill, it all came out of our own personalities, that East Coast Beat sensibility. The be-boppers had a way of dealing with the white world that amounted to a kind of intense irony and that influenced us.

"There's something very funny about smooth sounds, they go along with the whole American idea of slickness and smoothness, the idea of *faux-luxe*, Mantovani, Mancini, the soundtrack of the '50s. And we rejected that whole '50s sensibility... more of an insensibility really... and looked for some authenticity in beat and blackness."

Becker and Fagen's legendary perfectionism in the studio meant that they consigned many wonderful songs to the scrapheap. "It's happened to more songs than I care to think about," Gary Katz confessed. Songs which didn't make it on to 'Aja' included the aforementioned 'Standing By The Seawall', 'Shanghai Breakdown' and 'Were You Blind That Day?' Indeed, they already had one version of 'Gaucho' written, but it wasn't perfected until three years later, during the sessions for the album of the same name.

☙

'Aja' received a million dollars' worth of advance orders in the US alone and while the LP was selling by the truckload on both sides of the Atlantic, the rising tide of punk rock began to rock the boat for many older established groups. 'Aja', with its smooth, pristine production, was the absolute antithesis of the unproduced, raw-edged records being made by The Sex Pistols, The Clash and The Damned but Steely Dan went largely ignored by the punks who spewed invective on the likes of Led Zeppelin, Yes and Pink Floyd, the old dinosaurs – or old farts – of rock, as they called them. Becker and Fagen did say that punk music was of no interest to them, though they did concede that as a sociological event the upsurge may have had its benefits.

In truth, the punks' scorn made little impact on the old guard's record sales, especially in America, and by the end of the year 'Aja' had become the third best selling album in the country, surpassed only by Fleetwood Mac's multiplatinum 'Rumours' and Linda Ronstadt's 'Simple Dreams'. It won a Best Engineered Recording Grammy for Roger Nichols and was nominated for Best Rock Album of the Year by the National Academy for Recording Arts and Sciences.

'Aja' received unprecedented initial airplay and sales. It entered the *Billboard* album chart after only three weeks and virtually every song on the album was being programmed while ABC were readying 'Peg' as the first single. Eager Top Forty programmers even cast aside their usual reticence to play album cuts.

Eventually 'Peg'/'I Got The News' became the lead off single from the album in November 1977 and justified its selection in the new year by providing Steely Dan with their first Top Forty hit for eighteen months. It was also to be their biggest hit from the album. ABC wanted Steely Dan to edit 'Peg' – which was less than four minutes long anyway – but after a lot of consideration and one abortive attempt to do so, they refused.

Reflecting on the album's phenomenally successful musical marriage some years later, Fagen said, "I think the album reflected a wish on the part of a lot of players to do something a little more sophisticated, more mature, just expand the vocabulary of pop music." But they were only expanding that vocabulary within Becker and Fagen's parameters and Becker placed more emphasis on their own input, "The way we did it we were kind of the auteurs of the record in the sense that a director is the author of his film."

Becker put the success of 'Aja' down to the fact that they now had the luxury of being able to throw away everything that didn't work in the studio. In the past, despite their perfectionism and because of budget constraints, they often were forced to allow certain things through which they knew they – and indeed the studio musicians – could improve upon, given the time. On 'Aja' Fagen and Becker simply kept throwing material away until they had an entire album's worth of wholly satisfying performances.

Becker also attributed the success to the general conditions of the record buying market at that time. He modestly maintained that during certain periods of the year some records sold far more than at others. He put it down to good timing and didn't claim any personal credit for Steely Dan's skyrocketing sales figures.

Fagen admitted he was surprised by the number of units shifted and thought the reason the LP may have achieved such huge success was because... "the audiences are being conditioned to getting more used to jazz harmonies because of all this fusion business – that may have something to do with it. I had assumed our audience would not go much beyond 500,000 for an album, which it was up until 'Aja'."

With the passage of time, Fagen was justifiably proud of the album and called it "a wide range of listening experience". A few years later, Walter Becker admitted to thinking that 'Aja' was "dangerously ambitious".

Throughout its recording – before 'Aja' clocked up record sales figures – Steely Dan experienced business problems with ABC. They were trying to renegotiate their contract with the record company anyway, but their relationship had deteriorated to the point where what really worried them was the thought – which Becker confessed in public – that the company might actually have confiscated the master tapes as a penalty for going over budget in studio costs. They had been in the studio for a very long time and after some modest rumblings during 'The Royal Scam', ABC were now making loud noises over 'Aja's' spiralling costs. Becker even talked about finding a secret hiding place for their masters. They officially put the difficulties down to a failure of communications between them and the label, without specifying who was actually at fault. But their confiscation fears proved to be totally unfounded.

"Generally, I would say that ABC didn't mind the fact that we didn't tour that much, because each album sold more records than the last. It seemed like the more invisible we were the more albums we'd sell, so that wasn't much of a problem," said Fagen. "They complained about the budgets, but not that hard. They realised that a lot of people go into the studio and spend $100,000, some $200,000 and then some half a million dollars and come out with something you can't sell. But if we went in and spent a lot of money at least they knew we'd come out with something good. There was some trouble over it, but not that much. Eventually we got an offer from Warner Bros – we actually signed with them while we were making 'Aja' or just before – the idea being we'd have one more album to do, then go over to Warner Bros. It turned out we had two more to do and by the time we got to Warner Bros there *was* no more Steely Dan."

"Our record budgets are large and our record sales are moderate," said Fagen. "These days we probably spend maybe half what the profit is."

Becker and Fagen's inexorable drift away from ABC had picked up a considerable head of steam. Then current ABC president Steve Diener commented: "I hope they stay with the label. I have a lot of respect for those guys. I really mean that. The reason I tolerate and even encourage them is it's necessary for their own creative perfection. But when they deliver... they deliver. They are a very special breed of cat, and that includes their producer Gary Katz." Diener demonstrated his enthusiasm and admiration for Steely Dan's music by writing half of the liner notes for 'Aja'. Comparing Becker and Fagen to medieval troubadours and placing them on a "very special level", Diener exposed ABC's desire to keep Steely Dan with the label, but his attempt was in vain. Ironically, Diener himself was soon to be ousted from ABC (and his failure to keep Steely Dan on the label may well have been a contributing factor) and Jerry Rubinstein put in charge.

'Aja' was also far and away Steely Dan's most successful album in the UK; it charted in the top five, even without the benefit of a hit single. The only significant interview Becker and Fagen granted was to Sylvie Simmons from *Sounds* and they were in top form: joking about merchandising the Steely Dan name with breakfast meats and Kewpie dolls and citing their fondness for Bugs Bunny and Daffy Duck – both Warner Brothers characters – as their reason for singing with Warner Brothers Records.

ABC International's Elaine Corlett faced obvious problems breaking Steely Dan worldwide: there were only two relatively anonymous uncharismatic members, they didn't tour, they didn't like having their photographs taken and hated doing interviews – and even when they did an interview they often insulted the interviewer. Steely Dan albums were selling very well, but ABC knew they would sell in even greater quantities if Becker and Fagen would deign to do some dates, but nothing ABC could do would force them on to the road. "The situation is not yet where I'd like to see it," Corlett said. "If they would tour or do a film, it would improve." As things turned out, the increasing pressure contributed to Steely Dan moving over to Warner Bros.

The relative success of both 'Peg' and then 'Deacon Blues' on the singles charts inspired ABC's creative services chief, Herb Wood (a former executive at Motown where his experience of TV advertising included Diana Ross and Stevie Wonder) to arrange for a second advertising blitz on 'Aja'. Wood was a very strong advocate of the success of television marketing and the two-week campaign ran during the first two weeks of July and cost $275,000 in all – ABC's most extensive television advertising campaign to date. The original TV ad had plugged the album with an audio excerpt from the title song and a visual play on the LP cover; the second ad concentrated on linking the album to the hit singles and followed a plotline supposedly taken from both songs concerning a glamorous movie star and her forgotten lover. In fact, as ABC didn't want viewers to tire of the new commercial, they ended up mixing it with the old one.

The third single within a year from 'Aja' was 'Josie'/'Black Cow' which was released in August 1978. It peaked at number 26 the following month. 'Josie' details the return – probably from a prison stretch – of a highly regarded ringleader and all the celebrations which will herald her reappearance. She's a hellcat, a thief, a motorcycle freak and easy with her virtues, but she's also violently loyal to her friends and disciples. It contains another allusion to a Charlie Parker and Dizzy Gillespie composition 'Scrapple From The Apple'. Jim Keltner played on the song (he also tried 'Peg' without success) and told *Modern Drummer* how Becker and Fagen wanted something weird to overdub on the breakdown. Keltner had been given a garbage can lid with rivets in it for Christmas and played that, hence his credit for percussion. Becker and Fagen liked it and left it on the song.

Gary Katz still couldn't understand why Steely Dan's singles weren't bigger hits. "I have a sense that we put people off. There's something cold that puts people off, whether it be the lack of touring, the lack of interviewing or the lyrical content. I don't know why."

Steely Dan's harmonic complexity and strange lyrical puzzles didn't sit easily alongside the majority of simple pop tunes which usually populated the Top Forty in both the US and the UK and most of their fans were somewhat older than the average singles buyer anyway. Also, since all Steely Dan singles (with the exception of 'Dallas') were taken from their albums so, it's no surprise that the vast majority of Steely Dan fans didn't buy the same song on two different formats. As Fagen later admitted, he came to view singles simply as an advertisement for the album.

❧

Generally the critics heaped praise upon praise on 'Aja'. *Billboard* said 'Aja' may well rank as the year's most polished album, *High Fidelity* called it "easily the best album released thus far this year" and Richard Walls in *Creem* described it as "one of the most satisfying albums of the year. In the UK Steve Clarke of *New Musical Express* wrote that 'Aja'... "stands as simply the finest and certainly the most sophisticated and intelligent rock album to be released this year."

In an interview with *Melody Maker* Fagen cryptically described Steely Dan's new album as "quite a departure, considering our past tawdry records. This is the first album to include the elusive combination of the soak, the salta, the awn and the alder."

He was less cryptic about 'Aja's' lyrics, "I think we're steering a little bit away from melodrama. The tunes we ended up with are in a somewhat lighter vein than the last album." As he had earlier promised, the album contained... "some basically erotic material [but] not heavy breathing or anything."

"A lot of people don't give a tinker's damn what in particular you're singing about, and we're aware of that," said Becker. "So it should work that if, theoretically, some portion of the audience didn't understand the English language to any significant extent – which may be true, for all I know – these things would actually sound good."

Some critics had scrutinised Steely Dan's albums so closely that they felt they had discovered a theme linking all the songs. But Fagen denied there was ever any grand concept to a Steely Dan album. "We do it song by song," he said. "We don't really plan the shape of an album, except perhaps subliminally. First in this album we had too many medium or slow tempo songs, so we went in and cut a couple of up-tempo ones. 'Peg' was the last cut. We had a song slated for it [called] 'Here At The Western World' that had originally been cut for 'The Royal Scam' album. It was laying around and we liked it a lot, but it didn't fit on 'Scam' and we thought we had too many songs in that tempo on this album, so it's still sitting around. We'll get it out sooner or later."

Despite all their experience Steely Dan still did not know where to start looking in the search for a hit single and were glad they were no longer saddled with that responsibility. When he was asked if they were bothering to release a single from the album, Becker took the opportunity to take a swipe at programming restrictions, saying: "I'm sure we will, but I don't know which one it will be. When we write the songs and prepare the album, we really don't concern ourselves with that, because we're not a good judge collectively of what's going to strike the public's ear in that way. And a lot of our things are too long – there's all kinds of restrictions in radio here, it can't be more than two minutes or something."

Steely Dan were now being bracketed in the fusion category, but Becker denied that they had found a new direction. "It's not more jazz or less pop. It's just rock. We write rock songs, because when we were starting, rock was the most exciting field. It was actually more interesting melodically than jazz in the post-Coltrane period, before a lot of the new jazz started."

೮

Becker and Fagen had deliberately made a point of keeping their faces off Steely Dan album covers and Fagen admitted that they did this specifically to try and avoid any image making. "We wanted it to stand on itself ..." Both men enjoyed their privacy and were very keen to remain faceless, and this anonymity also served to deepen the mystery surrounding the band. Likewise their habit of wearing sunglasses in photo shoots (it was another in-joke between them), their long unkempt hair and shambolic clothes maintained their anti-image stance. But looking back on it years later, Fagen's stance had shifted."We could have been much looser about the whole [image-making] thing," he said.

The anonymity was exacerbated by their continuing aversion to touring, although there were serious talks about going on the road again around the time 'Aja' was released. After a three-year hiatus and all the will-they-won't-they rumours, Becker and Fagen finally conceded and agreed to some dates. Just as for the 'Katy Lied' sessions, Becker and Fagen hand-picked a seven-foot Yamaha piano for their planned post-'Aja' tour and installed it in Denny Dias's house, where rehearsals were due to take place. But after precious few they called the whole deal off. The piano still resides with Denny Dias and his family in Los Angeles.

Donald Fagen was adamant about wanting certain crack musicians on the tour and allegedly said that if they didn't go, he wouldn't either. These studio players knew of their indispensability and all wanted enormous amounts of money to sign up. Being the *crème de la crème*, they were entitled to ask for those sums, but what none of them knew, though, was that as a mark of respect to Denny Dias, Becker and Fagen intended paying him more than any of the hired guns as a kind of grand gesture. Certain estimates asserted that the tour would be bound to lose money. Others voiced the opinion that Donald Fagen didn't think he could perform well enough vocally. Whatever the true story, Steely Dan was being offered an awful lot of money and Katz was trying his damnedest to persuade Fagen to do it. "I push them so much," he said. "I hate to see Donald turn that money down, I really do. It's selfish. They may not owe it to anybody, but they do owe it to themselves to go out and play."

But as Fagen had told Katz on several occasions, "You don't have to go out there and make a fool of yourself." Fagen still had strong reservations: "All we can do is please ourselves and then assume the average fan is something like us. We can't try to please the fans because we really have no idea who buys our records.

"We'll go out on tour eventually. As soon as we get all this business stuff straight. Do maybe twenty dates. I don't like to travel, but I'd like to do maybe twenty dates. We'll see how it goes. If it's a good band, we'll probably take it out again. It depends how sick I am after the twenty dates."

After the aborted rehearsals, Fagen disguised the real reason for their abandonment. "We had rehearsed a few musicians, but it became apparent that we just didn't have enough time between the album and the tour. The whole thing was going to be more complicated than we had expected."

Amongst all the confusion, even Walter Becker didn't seem to know what exactly was going on. "We had planned to do it, to tour, but at this point I'm just not sure what we're going to do. The album was originally going to be released considerably sooner and when we did finish it, the record company wanted to hold it for a while. So the tour that had been planned was completely inappropriate, because it was going to happen before the record came out. And we decided we'd put it on the back burner for the time being." Becker even went on to suggest that they would begin rehearsals again soon, having underestimated the amount of time necessary to start from scratch and work the songs up to an acceptable standard.

Incredibly, Fagen then declared that when they realised that the audience would expect them to play 'Rikki Don't Lose That Number', 'Reelin' In The Years' and other Steely Dan chestnuts, they just weren't interested in recreating their old hits live on stage. "We're interested in new material. Once it's done... get rid of it."

Very little had changed since Steely Dan's earlier tours. Before it had been, in Fagen's words, "bridges between almost every song" and "a constant din from beginning to end". For the post 'Aja' tour, Fagen mentioned having written a 45-minute medley of songs from the first three Steely Dan albums. He never actually specified which songs were included in that medley, but it would have made interesting listening nonetheless.

Despite all their imaginative excuses as to why the rehearsals were abandoned, Becker and Fagen eventually came clean on the real reason – the salary arrangements. "There was a sliding pay scale with that based on the amount of money to be lost by various musicians leaving town. When this became evident to some of the members who had, uh, slid considerably from the top of the pay scale, they had things to say like 'How come him ...?' and 'And me?' And we said, 'Oh, shit', we felt like capitalists exploiting and repressing these musicians, so we cancelled the band after the first rehearsal."

At one stage Becker and Fagen claimed to have been looking for some young musicians to feature on their album, but had been disappointed and had had to resort to the same studio clique again. Although they failed to find any new and exciting players there were no less than eleven new names on 'Aja' that hadn't appeared on previous Dan albums. They included Steve Gadd, Wayne Shorter, Lee Ritenour, Steve Khan, Pete Christlieb and Jim Keltner, any one of whom could have commanded a touring salary of at least $1,000 a week.

∞

After they had finished working on 'Katy Lied', Becker and Fagen had agreed to produce an eponymous album by their old Bard friend Terence Boylan. Label boss David Geffen had just signed him to Asylum Records and when Becker and Fagen heard Boylan's songs they were impressed. If they were going to produce the album, Becker said, they would stipulate which studio to work in as well as which musicians to use: Jim Gordon, Victor Feldman, Dean Parks and Chuck Rainey.

Becker worked on a Boylan song called 'Rain King' but after booking some sessions a month or so ahead something cropped up which prevented the Steely Dan duo from attending. Boylan went ahead without them, and when Becker and Fagen eventually showed up they said he'd done just fine and suggested he might as well continue without

Donald Fagen, aged 7.
(Courtesy of Elinor Fagen)

Donald Fagen, aged 16.
(Courtesy of Elinor Fagen)

Donald Fagen at Bard College.
(Boona Collection)

Walter Becker playing guitar at Sottery Hall at Bard College.

(Boona Collection)

Steely Dan in 1972, just after the recording of 'Can't Buy A Thrill', left to right: Jim Hodder, David Palmer, Denny Dias, Donald Fagen, Jeff Baxter and Walter Becker. (London Features International)

Jay and The Americans, for whom Becker and Fagen played as back-up musicians between 1969 and 1971. Leader Jay Black is on the far left and Kenny Vance, who was Becker and Fagen's first manager, is seated left. (London Features International)

Jerome Aniton, Steely Dan's unofficial MC (top left, Randall Kennedy)*;*
Guitarist Jeff 'Skunk' Baxter (above, Retna)*;*
Guitarist Denny Dias (left, Randall Kennedy)
and Michael McDonald with
Royce Jones (below, Randall Kennedy)*.*

Donald and Walter, camera shy as ever, in 1975 (opposite) and 1976 (this page).

Donald and Walter in 1978 above (Courtesy MCA), and in 1979 below (Katz Pictures).

Donald Fagen with his mother in New York's Central Park in 1985 and giving piano lessons to his niece Emily Pfaff, his sister Susan's daughter. (Courtesy Elinor Fagen).

Fagen, left (Retna).

Fagen (right) and Becker on stage with the Jimmy Vivin(
Band at the Lone Star Cafe in 1989 (Pete Fogel).

Rosie Vela, who re-united Walter Becker and Donalo
Fagen on her 1986 début album, Zazu (A&M Records).

Becker in the recording studio (Retna).

Becker and Fagen playing the vibraphone together in 1993
(London Features International).

Becker and Fagen during Steely Dan's re-union tour, 1993.
(top: LFI above; bottom: Retna).

them. Fagen contented himself with playing piano on two songs, 'Don't Hang Up Those Dancing Shoes' and 'Fame'.

Once the Boylan album was finished, Asylum wanted to hold it until the fall of 1976; then Boylan decided to add another song which meant the deadline was missed and spring of 1977 was mooted instead. Then Asylum changed their minds again and the album didn't appear in the shops until the fall of 1977.

In December 1977 ABC in the UK released a Steely Dan 12" in the Plus Fours series which included 'Do It Again', 'Haitian Divorce', Steely Dan's first and rarest single, 'Dallas', and another previously unreleased Becker/Fagen song called 'Sail The Waterway'.

Only two days after 'Aja' had been certified gold, Fagen called Paul Griffin and asked him to attend a studio in Los Angeles to work on some new tunes. Griffin was astonished by Fagen's dedication; if he had just released a gold album he admitted that he would almost certainly have been on a beach in the South of France or some other exotic destination rewarding himself for his hard work and achievement.

In the wake of 'Aja's' success, Walter Becker confirmed that, as had been rumoured, Steely Dan were intent on following Gary Katz to Warner Bros. but admitted that ABC did own the rights to a greatest hits album. But they couldn't be serious about it: among their suggestions for possible titles were 'Steely Dan: The Golden Years', 'I Remember Steely Dan', 'That Was The Steely Dan That Was' and 'The Good Songs'.

It was also time to sort out two pressing matters: Denny Dias and their lack of management. Dias officially left Steely Dan after 'Aja' was released. He was glad that it was finally over, because he felt he had been holding on under false pretences. His contributions had grown progressively more sparse with each successive album and in the meantime he had been playing with other groups, notably The Hampton Hawes Quintet. When Fagen and Becker asked Dias what financial requirements he had, he asked for a guaranteed minimum for a of couple years just so that he could get himself on his feet and without hesitation they agreed generous terms.

Having been managerless since their acrimonious split with Joel Cohen, Gary Katz wanted to see Steely Dan's business affairs put in the hands of an experienced manager with plenty of clout in the industry, and he mounted a small campaign for them to adopt a higher profile in this regard. Katz arranged a meeting for them with Irving Azoff, whose company Front Line Management handled The Eagles, Dan Fogelberg, Boz Scaggs and Jimmy Buffett. "We were ready to go blissfully through life without a manager," Becker admitted.

The meeting convinced Becker and Fagen that Azoff was indeed the man who could give Steely Dan the lift they needed to get to the top of the league. "We were doing fine, you know," Becker said. "Going out and looking for managers is like going out and looking for rattlesnakes. Irving impressed us with his taste for the jugular... and his bizarre spirit. He thought we could do much better about making America Steely Dan conscious. He wanted a new hobby. We figured, sure, take a shot."

Azoff, rich, short but powerfully built and a big noise in the US rock industry, was a very big Steely Dan fan already, and he immediately put into motion a plan to push sales of 'Aja' high above the million mark. "Here's how we did it," he explained later. "Simple strategy. Think of the biggest American supergroups: Fleetwood Mac, The Eagles, Chicago... and Steely Dan. Everybody knows Steely Dan. They belong in that list. All we had to do was make it official.

"I used my power base and called all my rack-jobber friends – the guys in the field and the record chains – and I offered them 'Aja' for a suggested $6.98 instead of the $7.98 list price. Most of them knew they could stock up early and retail it as if it were $7.98. They all bought two, three, four times as many as normally. I told them the offer would last two weeks. We never raised the price. And they kept selling. So here's this album that's number three in the country. What radio station isn't going to play a hit Steely Dan album? It's been the most played album for weeks. We killed the Stones, didn't we? It was fun. Those guys would have gotten there sooner or later anyway. They deserved it sooner."

The album cover also proved to be a strong selling point, featuring a stunning and enigmatic photograph of a Japanese model called Saeko Yamaguchi by Hideki Fujii. Becker and Fagen finally got the go-ahead to use an expensive finishing process called "liquid lamb" which gave the cover more depth and gloss. They had wanted to use it on earlier albums, but it had proved to be too expensive.

In the short term, Becker and Fagen stayed in Los Angeles to write the theme song for the film *FM*. Steely Dan's new manager Irving Azoff was originally the movie's executive producer, but once shooting was complete he asked for his name to be dropped from the credits. It was an early indication of the quality of the film which soon reached Fagen and Becker, but they were already committed. They penned the title song, 'FM', which was built up layer by layer from a click track and featured their old "buddies" from The Eagles, Glenn Frey, Don Henley and Tim Schmit, on backing vocals.

'FM' was their first film song since 'You Gotta Walk It Like You Talk It'. "We wrote a song that would sound good with a big production, and an overdub of strings (arranged by Johnny Mandel), that would sound good coming out of movie theatre speakers," said Fagen. "If it had been a mystery film it would have worked out better. I feel like we didn't compromise on the song at all to make it programme music. But then, we still haven't seen the movie."

Bearing in mind the title of the single, AM radio stations naturally wouldn't play the song, but then in an amazing display of initiative, they took the 'A' from 'Aja' which was harmonically compatible and edited it into the song so that where 'FM' should have been, 'AM' came out instead.

Boasting another fine sax solo from Pete Christlieb, 'FM' was a sizeable hit for Steely Dan in America – number 22 – and a minor one in England, but Fagen was not necessarily impressed by chart placings. "The song was a hit, but I think we should have seen the movie before we committed ourselves. But I enjoyed doing it, and I thought it was a very successful piece of movie music. As you know, it wasn't a successful movie."

Roger Nichols won another Grammy for Best Engineered Recording for 'FM/FM Reprise' – his third Grammy and the only time any engineer has won a Grammy for a single song.

Becker and Fagen decided to take a year off in 1978 and used the time to work on a couple of projects which were really labours of love. Woody Herman had heard Steely Dan songs on the radio, but when one of his musicians gave him a cassette of 'Aja', he loved it and became a true fan. Then Dick LaPalm, who had worked with both parties, and knew that the big band leader was looking for material to stand alongside a suite written by Chick Corea, played him some of Steely Dan's earlier material. Herman was impressed enough to decide to devote an entire side of an album to their compositions.

The Village Recorder donated studio time free of charge and the engineers and technicians also worked for nothing. Becker and Fagen, who had long been Woody Herman fans, got together with him and selected five songs, 'Green Earrings', (arranged by Joe Roccisano, for which he was nominated for a Grammy), 'Kid Charlemagne', 'I Got The News', 'Aja', and 'FM'. The fifteen-piece Thundering Herd orchestra recorded all five songs at Wally Heider's Hollywood studio in just two days during January 1978 and they were mixed the following month. Becker and Fagen were delighted to be able to attend the sessions. "They were the happiest two days of my life," said Becker. The album was called 'Chick, Donald, Walter and Woodrow' and was released on the Century label. When BBC Records in the UK issued a CD of the album in the early '90s an extra track, 'Deacon Blues', was included on the list.

"The tunes that came out the best, like 'Green Earrings', were the ones that were most reworked for the big band," said Fagen. He joked that it could end up with Steely Dan music being rearranged for marching bands. Becker and Fagen wrote some humorous sleeve notes based on Dick LaPalm's habit of dangling a quarter attached to a length of nylon fishing line from his third floor office on to the sidewalk below and pulling it away from anyone's grasp if they bent to pick it up.

The same year Becker and Fagen snagged the job of producing their first out and out jazz album by tenor saxophonists Warne Marsh and Pete Christlieb. Marsh and Christlieb hit upon the idea of playing together and their recordings of some tenor duets found its way into the hands of Becker and Fagen. The band was a quintet with piano, bass and drums completing the line up. The record was called 'Apogee' – Dick LaPalm came up with the title. Becker and Fagen wrote a song especially for the album called 'Rapunzel,' which was based on a particular Fagen favourite by Dionne Warwick and written by Burt Bacharach and Hal David called 'In The Land Of Make Believe'. They asked Robert Palmer to write the sleeve notes for the album. "We heard the song on a Dionne Warwick record and thought it would be nice to blow on," Fagen said, adding that the album "is basically for tenor freaks."

Other compositions on the album included Charlie Parker's 'Donna Lee', Jerome Kern and John Mercer's 'I'm Old Fashioned', a song written by Joe Roccisano and Christlieb's own 'Magna-tism'.

Since they had found Pete Christlieb in *The Tonight Show* band, Becker and Fagen decided to send Johnny Carson a copy of the album, but it appears that even if he got to hear the record at all, he was singularly unimpressed. "His secretary wrote back saying he'd listen to it," Fagen said. Of course, B/F never heard from the chat show host.

Originally due for a late October shipping, ABC released a double album of Steely

Dan's 'Greatest Hits (1972-1978)' in November 1978. There was one previously unreleased song on the album, a divine song about a brothel featuring Michael Omartian's exquisite piano playing called 'Here At The Western World'. Becker and Fagen overdubbed the background singers during the same period when they were mixing the 'Apogee' album with Elliot Scheiner in New York.

The album featured another enigmatic cover photograph, this time by Image Bank's Pete Turner. The inside photo of Becker and Fagen was taken by Anton Corbijn in the lobby of the Hotel de L'Europe in Amsterdam in the summer of 1976 when Becker and Fagen were in Europe promoting 'The Royal Scam'. The photograph also featured a mystery piano player in the background and accompanied an interview Becker and Fagen gave to *Oor* (translated the word means ear) magazine in Holland. As usual, Becker and Fagen were reluctant subjects, but they liked Corbijn's photograph so much that after *Oor*'s editor had taken the shot to the USA and *Rolling Stone* bought it for use in a December 1977 piece on Steely Dan, Becker and Fagen then asked for it to be used on the forthcoming 'Greatest Hits' package. The album was a sure fire winner, ultimately racking up platinum status, reaching number 30 in the US and 41 in the UK.

Becker and Fagen had taken great care in selecting the songs for the record, but Fagen was still sure... "that somebody will find something to object to our leaving off the album". Then he adopted his less serious mode: "We were going to put 'FM' on our 'Greatest Hits' album, but we decided not to. But they sent us over all the tracks from the soundtrack, so we were thinking of putting 'More Than A Feeling' by Boston on our 'Greatest Hits', too."

After the fun that Becker and Fagen had working on 'FM' they were already supposedly considering some other offers in that same sphere. "We have also recently been talking to a German animator named Klaus Gorman about doing music for an animated film he's making tentatively titled *The History of the CIA*," they told one interviewer, but whether they were serious is anyone's guess.

Buoyed by 'Aja's success, the fun projects they had undertaken and their time off, Becker and Fagen were in fine fettle. The only dark cloud on the horizon was the difficulty of living a fulfilling life in Los Angeles. They simultaneously decided to return to the east coast to live. Although they were not planning on recording, they continued to write songs together and in an unusual display of loquaciousness, Donald Fagen called *Rolling Stone* to inform them that he and Becker were thinking of moving back to New York.

Their plans then called for the next Steely Dan album to be recorded by two different studio bands, each playing one side of material. All the songs were to be written in New York, followed by one of the bands then touring under the Steely Dan banner. It would be easier to teach one of the groups all the songs, but this turned out to be another grand idea which never came to fruition.

☙

CHAPTER IX

Bodacious Cowboys

When Becker and Fagen finally did return to New York, Fagen especially was delighted to be back in his adopted home town. "I moved into the Stanhope Hotel and from my window I could watch steel drum bands, Latin, salsa and even bagpipe groups playing in front of the Met," he said with something approaching cheerfulness, although this was never a state of mind much associated with Steely Dan. "Then I'd go outside for a walk and all the way down to 43rd Street, one tenor sax would fade into another. It's nice to have music in the streets."

Eventually they moved into the same luxury apartment building on Central Park West, Fagen on the third floor and Becker on the eleventh. Like John Lennon and Paul Simon, both of whom lived nearby, they could look down on Central Park's sylvan delights, and choose between the solitude of their remote castles or the street life at ground level.

Soon after their return, Fagen discovered a bad taste blues singer called Root Boy Slim and The Sex Change Band with The Rootettes through a friend at a radio station. With time on their hands, they took their enthusiasm for the band to unusual lengths – even attending recording sessions at Criteria Studios in Miami while on vacation and going down to Washington DC to see him perform live. Gary Katz produced his eponymous album which contained such delightful titles as 'Heartbreak Of Psoriasis', 'Too Sick To Reggae' and 'Boogie 'Til You Puke'.

Steely Dan's patronage had no impact whatsoever upon sales of his album and Warner Bros dropped the band. They signed to Illegal Records and followed their 1978 début with an album entitled 'Zoom' a year later which was also a flop. (Root Boy Slim's own life was an unhappy one, too. He became an alcoholic and drug addict and was admitted to various institutions several times. He turned to writing poetry, but eventually died in 1993, aged 48.)

A previously unreleased Becker and Fagen composition appeared in 1979 on the eponymous début album of a jazz funk band called Dr Strut. The album was released on the Motown label who were at the time trying to broaden their musical horizons and featured 'Countdown to Ecstasy' assistant engineer Tim Weston on guitar. Dr Strut was comprised of four other hot session players and songwriters and 'Canadian Star' was the only song on the album not written by the band themselves. It was a superbly melodic instrumental boasting some lovely guitar and sax interplay between Weston and David Woodford. The band never achieved the recognition they deserved and followed it with an LP called 'Struttin'' in 1980, but faded rapidly from sight after that.

Becker and Fagen began recording again themselves sometime in 1979. The sessions flitted between Soundworks, A & R Studios, Sigma Sound and Automated Sound in Manhattan, but they occasionally flew cross country to Los Angeles for sessions at their favoured Village Recorder and Producers Workshop.

A variety of circumstances, most of them unfortunate, caused the next – and final –

Steely Dan album to be the longest, most expensive and certainly most difficult to complete. First and foremost, Becker and Fagen were under enormous pressure to top 'Aja's' runaway critical and commercial success, but several other factors would weigh them down. Becker and Fagen both underwent private, personal crises; there were lingering legal hassles to be resolved with their former record company; and, most disturbing of all, there was the complete loss of one of the best tracks for the new record. In the end, after working steadily for five days a week for just under two years, 'Gaucho' was complete – but the price they paid was the end of their partnership.

"There was a long getting-to-know-you phase with the New York musicians, a courtship," Fagen offered as a none-too convincing excuse for the delays. "We would put in a lot of work just to find out that ultimately something wasn't going to make it, whereas in the past we could tell on the first layer of work. On 'Glamour Profession' we must have spent three times as much time and effort making versions that turned out to be just demos."

Years later Fagen's terrible memories of the record still lingered. "The writing was hard, the recording was hard, everything about it was like pulling teeth," he said in 1993. That album is almost a document of despair. We were running out of steam as far as our youthful energy was concerned and we hadn't matured enough to deal with it. We were still adolescents."

Fagen went on to say that they had "made more use of layering than we have in the past. Some of our experiments with tunes became more than experiments – we thought they became more than experiments – we thought we had a record for a long time. We didn't realise that we didn't really. Then we had to start from scratch."

Gary Katz was behind them all the way when it came to justifying their long stint in the studio. He stressed the testing nature of Steely Dan sessions. "The songs are all really hard to play well. There are a lot of changes, and we demand more than some people do in the final product. Session musicians come from fourteen jingle dates or whatever, and they sit down and see these chord changes, and they have to, like, sit for a while and play. Negotiating all the rhythmic nuances of the chord changes correctly and as a unit, it's time-consuming. Most of these guys are used to going in, seeing a track, and ripping it off in two or three hours. That never happens. The only time that ever happened was 'Aja'; Steve Gadd ripped that off, solos and all. That tune was done in an hour and a half, the only tune that has happened with in all the years. It freaked us out."

During the same 1979 interview with Jon Pareles in *Musician*, Katz said that he was already throwing away two tracks for the current album that were sixty percent complete. "Either it's great till the minute it's done," he said, "or it's as worthless as never having been done. We punch in everything, anything, anywhere."

They were always on the look out for new and exciting players to incorporate into the Steely Dan sound. Consequently they were frequently being encouraged to check out this guitarist or that drummer. But they needed more than just the plaudits of friends before they could contemplate using a musician on one of their songs. "People will say that so-and-so is a great player," Becker said, "but usually they're not descriptive enough about what it is he does, not enough to give us an idea of what's appropriate or how to use him."

Most of the regular studio players were more than familiar with Steely Dan's methods and knew how to handle the pressure. But during the 'Gaucho' sessions Steely Dan utilised the skills of at least one novice as far as session work went – Dire Straits' guitarist (and singer and principal composer) Mark Knopfler. Becker and Fagen had first heard and been impressed with his guitar playing on Dire Straits' début album in 1978.

Knopfler was asked to take a crack at the solo on 'Time Out Of Mind', but he was not a sight reader and had to ask Becker and Fagen for a tape of the song so that he could take it back to his hotel and work on it. It was his first studio session outside of recording with his own band and here he was in New York with one of the most demanding outfits around. It was no surprise to learn that Knopfler was intimidated by Becker and Fagen's reputation. Once the session was under way, he didn't appreciate that their demands to try things over and over again, and persistent requests to try something different, were standard Steely Dan behaviour, and no reflection on either their dissatisfaction with his efforts or his ability as a guitarist.

Becker gave Knopfler a copy of the tape, but didn't make it clear which sections of the song they wanted him to play over – and he didn't know all the chords either. "When he came in we could tell he was worried," said Becker. "He got set up and said there were some sections he didn't know. We said 'Don't worry, because that isn't where we're going to have you playing'. But what came out was good. Anyway, it takes a long time for us to do things and maybe he felt like he was some kind of remedial guitar player, because it took hours for us to do the stuff. But that happened with everybody."

Initially, when Knopfler was questioned about the session, he wasn't able to disguise his disappointment. It was, he said, "a strange experience – like getting into a swimming pool with lead weights tied to your boots." Knopfler wasn't used to the brash New York manner and how they would discuss his efforts – in complimentary fashion or not – right in front of him. But the tape operator came up to him at the end of the session at about four in the morning and said, "Man, you did great. I've seen musicians crawling out of here after their sessions."

Becker and Fagen weren't able to allay Knopfler's nervousness and frustration. "I think he definitely felt that, because he would play something and it was okay, then we'd say 'Let's try one more'. Occasionally it happened where a jazz player played something and we'd say that sounds good, let's try one more and he'd say 'What was wrong with that?' The answer to that question is that there was nothing wrong with it, but we wanted to achieve some other effect. So I think there was a bit of that and probably a little culture gap there as well. Anyway, I'm glad that it worked out."

In his review of the album, Richard Evans in *Melody Maker* wrote that Knopfler's solo was barely audible and likened it to "employing Michelangelo to paint your ceiling with Dulux". The solo was overshadowed by Rob Mounsey's stabbing brass parts and didn't do justice to either Knopfler or Becker and Fagen..

Producer Katz was Becker and Fagen's main line of communication with the session musicians and singers. Fagen later said that he and Becker were often too shy to talk to players and that Katz's task was to put the musicians at ease by making small talk, more often than not discussing baseball and hockey, and thus get them in the mood to play.

Since Katz himself was a sports fan who set up several video recorders to tape various baseball, football and hockey games and who insisted on never knowing the result before watching them, this was no problem.

"We try to run Steely Dan sessions like jingle dates," Katz said of their methods. "Everyone loves jingle dates. They go so quickly, they sound so great, everything is laid out so clearly. They don't go quite so quickly for us, but that's what we try for. With Donald and Walter right from the first it was serious business. At the beginning we knew exactly what they wanted in their music, but they had to learn the technique of making it work. It took work in the studio to bounce it back, to refine it. After the basic rhythm track is done, the rest is trial and error, apart from a little bit of an idea. We try everything we think might work and reject them if we don't like it later."

Becker and Fagen fully intended the 'Gaucho' album to herald a return to shorter songs in the mould of 'Pretzel Logic' and 'Katy Lied'. But things didn't turn out that way and Katz later sounded almost apologetic. "Before we even went near the studio and before most of the tunes were written, one night we said, 'Listen, this album we're gonna make short pop songs, we'll put ten songs on the album'. But the tunes wound up being longer than that. To this day I couldn't tell you what happened. Donald said, 'Look, all right, I mean, it's a verse, a chorus, a verse, a chorus, an instrumental and out – I mean, what's so big?' And it comes out to be five and a half, six minutes. It's not like excess, it just works out that way. There isn't a lot of dead space in their songs now, everything that we use from bar to bar has a good reason for being there. They're much tighter pop songs now, even though they run six minutes."

When Becker and Fagen were composing material for their albums, their prime consideration was Fagen's vocal ability and his honest but modest self-appraisal of it. "I don't have a large range," he said, "so it has to be within a certain interval." However, occasionally Becker and Fagen must have overlooked this because on one song slated for 'Gaucho' called 'Heartbreak Souvenir', which featured some classic Bernard Purdie and Anthony Jackson, Fagen discarded the track because he said it was "too hard to sing". As a result of this habit, Fagen gave Roger Nichols a piece of paper personally signed on which he promised not to write songs he couldn't sing. Nichols admitted that he's had to show Fagen the note several times since.

During the recording of 'Gaucho', the atmosphere in the studio was distinctly uneasy all round. Walter Becker was wrestling with his drug problem and Fagen, too, was depressed and tetchy about the slow and painful progress of the sessions. They were beginning to have their first serious disagreements; Becker's problems led to unpunctuality and sometimes even failing to arrive for recording sessions at all, and even Fagen, himself not the most reliable of time-keepers, wasn't prepared to tolerate his partner's sloppy agenda.

Fagen later put it as delicately as he could without offending him. "Music wasn't his first love at that point, I think," he said. "He was kinda leaping toward destruction." Fagen explained that the problem had spun out of control in California and said that since Becker didn't like himself, he was headed for trouble no matter where he chose to live. Not only did he find Becker difficult to work with, he didn't know how to begin to address the situation… and decided that it was best for him not to interfere at all. Hopefully, once 'Gaucho' was finished, Becker would eventually figure out a way to resolve his problems.

Christmas 1979 was a very bleak time for Becker and Fagen but for different reasons. They had been working on a song called 'The Second Arrangement,' which was the first tune to be finished for the album. It had been a dream to record – the track almost fell together and it was Roger Nichols and Gary Katz's favourite song on the album at the time.

One evening Fagen asked Gary Katz to get an engineer to prepare the song for listening when they next returned to the studio. Unfortunately, in the process of carrying out this task, the engineer thought he was at the tail leader of the tape and put all twenty-four tracks on record. In actual fact, he was at the head leader and he inadvertently completely erased all 24 tracks three-quarters into the song.

That night Katz was having dinner at the Stage Deli with his young son. Midway through the meal Roger Nichols burst into the restaurant and informed him that 'The Second Arrangement' had been erased. Katz knew Nichols wasn't the type to joke about such a serious matter and when he returned to Soundworks he found the engineer in tears in the middle of the studio. Many weeks and thousands of dollars' worth of effort had been erased at the careless flick of a switch, and although Becker and Fagen tried to re-record the song, they could never recapture the spontaneity of the original and it had to be shelved. (Steely Dan had long since decided never to make safety copies of tunes due to the inferior sound quality.)

The responsibility for telling Becker and Fagen the bad news fell to Roger Nichols and when Fagen heard it, he didn't utter a word – he just turned around and walked out of the studio.

Tracking engineer Elliot Scheiner could never understand why Becker and Fagen used a different band when they attempted to recut the song. The original featured Ed Greene on drums, Don Grolnick on keyboards, Will Lee on bass and Hiram Bullock on guitar, but when they tried it for the second time they brought in Steve Gadd instead of Ed Greene – and two more different drummers would be hard to imagine.

Fagen eventually got over his disappointment and was pretty matter-of-fact about the incident. "He was aligning the machine making record tests, and he was making the record tests on the same reel the tune was on. He went past the tape leader – he must have fallen asleep or something – and into the tune. And when he woke up it was somewhere in the last quarter of the song. And he had all 24 tracks on record. We tried to do the song over, but it was too depressing. We decided we'd either do it sometime in the future or forget about the whole thing."

The loss of such a gem was a tragedy. 'The Second Arrangement' was another Becker and Fagen cracker and would have set well with the other songs on the album. Hiram Bullock's majestic guitar hook masked a tale of loneliness, adultery and sexual jealousy. The song contained their usual references to unusual objects: in this case a yellow Jag and a Gladstone bag.

"I would like to think that the next album won't take this long," Katz said midway through the sessions. An engineer accidentally erased a completed track. That was one of the most serious emotional setbacks we've had in the studio. We started it again from scratch, building up the rhythm arrangement, the guitars, the voices, and when that didn't pan out, we had to start another tune from scratch." That "new" song turned out to be 'Third World Man'.

Becker and Fagen had the erased song in a variety of forms and were using 'The Second Arrangement' as its working title. Eventually the dummy lyrics they had been using in the studio took on greater significance and became the basis for the actual lyric. This was by no means an unusual occurrence; sometimes when Fagen was singing to assist the musicians with a tune, if he sang impromptu lyrics occasionally they became so used to them that they sometimes wound up retaining them anyway.

Rob Mounsey had also been involved in the recording of the tune and during an encounter with Donald Fagen some years later, began quoting the lyrics to Fagen who was astonished that they were still lodged in his brain. Fagen could barely remember them himself; but what really amused Fagen was that the words that Mounsey remembered were the dummy lyrics that they had used for the scratch vocal.

❧

In January 1980 Walter Becker was devastated when Karen Stanley, his girlfriend of many years, died from acute mixed drug intoxication in their shared Upper West Side apartment. She was 31. One year later her mother, Lilian Wyshak, a lawyer from Beverly Hills, hit Becker with a massive $17 million lawsuit claiming that he had caused her death by introducing her to heroin, cocaine, and encouraged her to live with him in an intimate relationship.

Becker's close friends countered with information that had not been made public previously – that he had paid numerous very costly hospital bills for her in trying to assist her to get off her dependency and gone into seclusion after her death. Becker's grief turned to anger that he should be blamed for his girlfriend's death and he aggressively countersued. The case was eventually settled out of court in Becker's favour, but his troubles continued to dog him for some time afterwards too.

"The reason why the album cost so much," Fagen said "and why it took so much time was first and foremost bad luck. We had numerous technical problems in recording the LP. We lost what was to be one of the album's most up songs when the tape was mistakenly erased. We also moved back to New York from LA and were unfamiliar with the musicians and the studios."

Being unfamiliar with the players hardly bears examination, since the only mainline musicians on 'Gaucho' who had not previously appeared on a Steely Dan album were bass player Anthony Jackson (who wound up on only two songs anyway) and keyboard player Rob Mounsey. As for the studios, Steely Dan did much of the work for 'Gaucho' where they had logged countless hours on earlier albums so that also proved to be a rather poor excuse.

Fagen eventually offered what was perhaps a much more accurate and true assessment of the reason for their tardiness. "It can also be attributed to the fact that we were going through a pretty dry period creatively. We were writing songs, but it took us a while to get enough songs that met our standards. We would have worked on it longer, but we didn't want to go over a million dollars, because we felt it would be too excessive and self indulgent. We went into the studio before we had a selection of songs that met with our standards and some misconceived ideas."

Fagen had often lamented the shifting nature of their band and the fact that he and Becker had never been fortunate enough to know other like-minded musicians from their early days in their own neighbourhoods. "A perfect situation for me is the Duke Ellington Orchestra which stayed together for 60 years. Unfortunately, we write such a variety of material, it's best to finish it and then decide stylistically who would be the best for it. I do miss not having a band now. Having musicians there who are always ready to try things out, that sort of thing. But the original band was thrown together rather haphazardly. It was never as satisfying a relationship as some groups have. It never gelled like The Band or even something like The Grateful Dead, where it's guys who have played together for years and have developed a relationship as people as well as musicians."

It was during the making of 'Gaucho' that Nichols' growing interest in computers and Fagen's desire to have a machine that could fulfil extremely precise drum patterns led to him designing a beast they christened Wendel. Working in his living room at weekends and around Steely Dan sessions, Nichols designed and built Wendel almost entirely by himself.

"We found there were certain feels that we couldn't get out of real drummers – they weren't steady enough," he said. " So we had to design something that would do it perfectly, but with some human feeling, the right amount of layback. Instead of just one hi-hat sound that repeats machine-like, over and over, we had 16 different ones, so it had the inflections. Wendel can play *exactly* what the drummer plays – if he plays it a little early or hard, Wendel plays it a little early or hard. Play it once and Wendel memorises the song, then you play it again and it repeats what it hears."

The first version was an 8-bit machine, similar to a Linn drum machine. "Roger Linn was working on his at the same time I was working on Wendel. I decided to use mine for studio application because of the extra high fidelity we needed and the amount of memory it took to do that – it was a pretty expensive machine. The first Wendel would've been twenty grand. It takes a lot of memory to have a higher sample rate, which gives you an 80kHz frequency response – today's consumer units have only 20kHz. Just one snare drum beat takes 48k of memory. One crash cymbal takes $12,000 worth. We just used the brute force method so we could get it done. The new improved Wendel has a megabyte of memory, 32 megabyte hard disc, higher sample rates and it's 16-bit. I use it quite a bit these days."

Drummer Chris Parker was called in to play his first Steely Dan session during 'Gaucho', but he, like Mark Knopfler, found it a particularly difficult experience; Becker and Fagen spent an eternity getting exactly the right snare and bass drum sounds and then when they commenced recording the track, Parker said that there were so many varying suggestions being offered from all sides – from Gary Katz and Elliot Scheiner as well as from the composers – that he lost all sense of the tune. Parker said he couldn't get a clear indication as to which direction he should follow and combined with his lack of experience he wasn't surprised when his efforts didn't make it to wax.

When Becker and Fagen were unhappy with a musician's contribution they would usually leave the dirty work to Gary Katz and head out to a nearby diner giving terse instructions to the effect that they wanted the guy gone by the time they came back. Very rarely was the situation reversed, when a session player could not tolerate Becker and Fagen's fastidious, perfection-seeking methods. One such musician was New York-based bass player Will Lee. Although Lee eventually appeared on Fagen's 'Walk Between Raindrops' on his first solo effort, he wasn't as tractable as many of the other session players and neither was he afraid of letting Steely Dan know it. His work on 'Gaucho' never made the final cut.

All the musicians hired by Steely Dan knew the score. Steve Khan: "When you record with them, no matter how much you like what you did, you never get your hopes up, because it will easily get erased tomorrow."

The title song of the album, recorded at A & R Studios, developed into a twelve hour endurance test. "'Gaucho' was a five-minute plus song with seven pages of score, that took up three music stands," said Khan. "We had tried a couple of versions with different bands and failed. Then a band of Anthony Jackson (bass), Jeff Porcaro (drums), Victor Feldman (percussion), Rob Mounsey and myself tried it one night for four hours. Just before dinner I thought we had a good take, but they didn't like it. We returned from dinner and tried again unsuccessfully, and Donald and Walter gave up on it.

"The musicians can get attached to this stuff, and we had a feel for it and didn't want to give up. So after Donald, Walter and Victor left, I asked Gary if the rest of us could try it a few more times. We stayed till five in the morning, completing eight full takes and some extra pieces Gary wanted. The next night during a break they listened to it. We thought they were going to laugh at us, and they did, but it was because they liked it. Then, like most of the songs, they kept the drum track and rebuilt it to their idea of perfection, in some cases using different players. To the musicians, it means more than the money to see that this music comes out."

Becker and Fagen were looking unhappy when they left around midnight. Victor Feldman went back to his hotel and after several more takes with a click track the next musician to leave was Jeff Porcaro who had to go to the airport to catch a flight to Oklahoma for a Toto concert. The players thought it sounded great; no one had made any mistakes and were praying that Becker and Fagen could find something they could live with. When they returned and listened to all the takes, they thanked the band for staying on and said, "There might be something here we can work with."

Becker, Fagen and Katz then cut the multi-track over forty times and edited together a drum track only. Becker played a new bass part, Steve Khan overdubbed some new guitar and over the course of a couple of nights Rob Mounsey recorded new acoustic and electric piano parts.

The saxophone solo on 'Gaucho' also posed problems. "Where that sax is," said

Becker, "on that site had been erected many things. Various piano things, things more thematically integrated with the rest of the song. Although it seems like an obvious conclusion, that sax took months to arrive at. As for the verses, it's really a very simple thing. If you ever listen to the most primitive blues, there *is* no twelve bar blues. There's thirteen bar blues and thirteen and a half bar blues, they'll throw in an extra beat of 'ahh-ha, hammmm', and that's what 'Gaucho' does. Just use a little space where you have something to say, and if you don't have something to say, just skip right ahead to the next thing."

"Although that song is extremely angular rhythmically," said Fagen, "it's very comfortable sounding. I don't think it's awkward. Generally, if there's something that just doesn't make sense musically, we'll change it. It's a matter of taste. We stay away from anything where the musical effect is basically to shock; I don't like harsh nasty-sounding things just for some kind of cultural shock or political statement. The intention when we were writing it was that it would have a horn-like melody and be kind of jagged. We felt there could be great humorous potential for putting lyrics to a melody like that, providing it didn't become too humorous. I think it worked out quite well."

'Gaucho' was typical Becker and Fagen imagery: the two homosexual partners live together quite contentedly in a luxurious apartment high above Manhattan until their relationship is threatened by the arrival of a handsome young South American cowboy wearing a "spangled leather poncho" and "elevator shoes". Becker and Fagen later said that if, when they were listening back to one of their songs, it didn't make them howl with laughter, they regarded it as a failure.

They weren't at all keen on discussing the lyrics on 'Gaucho.' The only explanation Walter Becker was prepared to give (and even then only semi serious) was the definition of the Custerdome. "It's, ah, one of the largest buildings in the world. You know, an extravagant structure with a rotating restaurant on top."

But Fagen was more forthcoming. "It exists only in our collective imagination. In the Steely Dan lexicon it serves as an archetype of a building that houses great corporations..."

For 'Glamour Profession' Rob Mounsey overdubbed the piano at Automated Sound and he was pleasantly surprised that in the space of only an hour and a half he'd constructed a solo that Fagen instantly liked. Mounsey began by improvising it and then he and Fagen together decided on parts to develop around his improvisation and the more formalised rehearsals.

Although Mounsey was credited with arranging the horns on 'Babylon Sisters' and 'Time Out Of Mind', he admitted that the basic ideas for horn arrangements usually came from Fagen. According to Mounsey, Fagen's ideal horn section was three saxes and a trumpet; the method they used was for Fagen to sing his ideas to Mounsey, who would chart them, then consult with Fagen as he filled in the spaces.

The horn arrangement on 'Babylon Sisters' features two bass clarinets and some alto flutes, because Fagen was keen to get some woodwind instruments on the record. During the session, Fagen came out into the studio and squinted at Rob Mounsey's score, looked at Mounsey, turned to Gary Katz and said, "It's perfect. The arrangement's perfect." Mounsey thought he sounded almost disappointed.

George Marge and Walter Kane were the reed players on 'Babylon Sisters'. The latter had been one of the best and most in-demand studio reed players in New York over the past twenty or thirty years. Of all his impressive studio credits, nothing Kane had played on up to that point impressed his now grown-up kids, but when they heard he was playing on a Steely Dan record, they were prouder than they'd ever been.

As with 'Don't Take Me Alive', neither Becker nor Fagen actually played on 'Babylon Sisters'. "We've got it all except the fingers," Fagen said. "Both of us have terrific feel. I think we get a lot of points for style, but technique and execution are weak. There tend to be a lot of mistakes and inconsistencies. If we can't find a musician who's comfortable with a particular feel, *then* we'll haul out our instruments."

Katz was wholeheartedly behind Becker and Fagen in wanting absolutely the best players available. "I guarantee that if John Coltrane was alive, Donald would be down on his knees," he said.

"The B band is me and Donald. The A band is anyone else – professionals," said Becker. "I prefer to have someone else play bass – someone I know who's better than me – unless all else fails. The way I feel about my guitar playing, to be perfectly honest with you, is that it's to be used only as necessary or 'taken as directed'. If there's anybody else we think can do it, we get him first." He did concede that his innate understanding of the songs had found him choosing that last resort more often.

Asked about a stylistic shift on 'Gaucho' to electric piano and synths from the acoustic piano sound of 'Aja', Fagen claimed that that was simply happenstance. "Some of that was just a matter of practicality. The studios we were working in didn't have particularly good sounding acoustic pianos. At one point we rented a Steinway and got a lemon."

❧

Late one Tuesday night in April 1980, Walter Becker was walking near his home with a friend when he stepped off the kerb and was hit by a speeding yellow cab. He fractured his right leg in several places. The breaks were severe and henceforth collaborations with Fagen and Katz had to be conducted over the phone, with Becker listening to tapes in the hospital. The actual recording had just about been completed; all that remained were some overdubs and the final mixdown. But mixing was a crucial element of the Steely Dan sound and Becker had always had a considerable influence on it in the past.

Becker was in real pain for a long time and suffered fever and secondary infections. He was in a cast for seven months, but nonetheless retained his sense of humour, telling *Rolling Stone*: "That car and me, we were attempting to occupy the same space at the same time. We were definitely in violation of certain fundamental laws of physics – we were quantum criminals."

In fact, he did make one wheelchair-bound attempt to attend a mixing session, but the sheer impracticalities of getting to the studio over Manhattan's potholed streets meant he was in so much pain before he even got to the studio that he could not tolerate any more than about thirty minutes at one time. Although the album was mixed with his consultation, his hands-on input at source was badly missed.

As they had done with 'The Royal Scam', Steely Dan allowed a journalist into the studio to observe them at work. Robert Palmer described in the same *Rolling Stone* article, about how, in the summer of 1980, Fagen, Katz and Nichols worked on fifty seconds of music for four hours. They were mixing the fade of 'Babylon Sisters' and after some sixty-plus attempts, Fagen was not satisfied. During further attempts Fagen asked Nichols and two assistant engineers to add minuscule amounts of echo and delay to the background singers' voices, but he was still not happy. He then wanted to try it with and without the girls. Finally Fagen was happy with the results. "This is the happiest night of my life," he said.

Later that same year, Rick Derringer was working on 'My Rival' at Soundworks. Becker was still absent, so Fagen, Katz and Derringer worked on the song's eight bar introduction for an hour before everyone was happy with Derringer's phrases. The same night, Derringer spent another hour playing a guitar solo for the same song, but was not surprised to find that eventually the solo was played by Steve Khan. "The parts Rick did were voted yes, but the solo was voted no," Fagen said tersely. Khan recalled that while recording the solo for 'My Rival', Fagen told him he wanted the guitar to sound "like Howlin' Wolf's guitar player – *if* he could play these chord changes." Khan wound up using a Telecaster and tried numerous different amps before they settled on the appropriate Hubert Sumlin-like sound.

The amount of time they spent working on 'Gaucho' caused problems with oxide shredding off the tape because it had passed across the heads so many times. It got to the point where one tape which featured the song 'Time Out Of Mind' had deteriorated so badly that as they approached mixing Steely Dan had to cut down on the number of times that they ran the tape, but they succeeded in mixing the tune before it finally fell apart.

Roger Nichols and Elliot Scheiner also finally succeeded in persuading Becker and Fagen to use a computer to mix the album, and they spent about three weeks just mixing 'Babylon Sisters' in Los Angeles. It was the highest amount of mixes that the computer had ever undertaken and Neve, its manufacturers, threatened to award Steely Dan the platinum floppy disc award for the most mixes.

In a *Musician* interview with David Breskin published in March 1981, Fagen explained to him their songwriting technique and his obsessive habit of hoarding ideas and anything that might prove useful for a future song. "I usually come up with the harmonic framework and then Walter comes over and we take it from there. Also, a lot of the songs are a sort of testimonial for saving things. I still have cassettes left over from college that contain ideas, little snatches of things. They sometimes come in useful in other contexts if you keep them around long enough. For example, the chorus in 'Glamour Profession' – I can't even remember when I wrote that."

Becker remembered all right. "We wrote the hook [to 'Glamour Profession'] when we were in college and now just changed the words." It was yet another song about

Hollywood highlife; a famous basketball star is hooked on cocaine, smuggling in large quantities from Colombia and throwing very expensive parties with the profits. The final line of the chorus, "Living hard will take its toll", was to prove uncommonly prophetic.

Breskin challenged Becker and Fagen over the similarity of the title song to a Keith Jarrett composition called 'Long As You Know You're Living Yours' which appeared on a Jan Garbarek/Keith Jarrett 1974 ECM album called 'Belonging'. Becker admitted that he loved Jarrett's song and they eventually approved their off the record comments for publication with Fagen admitting, "We were heavily influenced by that particular piece of music." Jarrett later sued them for plagiarism, and, given the circumstances and their admission, won the case. He was granted a co-writing credit and royalties on all future pressings of the song.

Except for the obvious influence of Horace Silver's 'Song To My Father' on 'Rikki Don't Lose That Number' Becker and Fagen had never been confronted with any similarities between their own compositions and those of other writers. But now there were some surprising admissions in the pipeline. "We haven't invented everything we've ever done," said Fagen. "We've borrowed ideas, but they're good ideas. They may sound fancy, but not contrived. We have different values from most rock and roll composers."

Fagen jokingly suggested that "we are the robber barons of rock'n'roll" but went on to admit quite seriously that... "The bridge on 'Glamour Profession' is a take on the bridge of Kurt Weill's 'Speak Low', and that it was influenced by disco music in general." Breskin also pointed out its similarity to, of all bands, Dr. Buzzard's Original Savannah Band and Fagen confessed to having bought their first album.

'Hey Nineteen' deals with a thirtysomething hepcat trying to get inside a musically naïve teenage girl's pants, but he finds they have nothing in common except their taste for 'Cuervo Gold' and the 'fine Colombian'. Fagen said: "Sentimental love is the stock in trade of every songwriter. Actually, we use it quite often, but we just try to change the angle a little and change the quality of the relationships a bit. It's innuendo and innuendo is a tradition in rhythm and blues."

Listening to 'Hey Nineteen', some critics suggested an even greater sense of alienation than usual beneath the surface. Becker and Fagen had both passed thirty and the majority of their audience were much younger. "At one time I felt I would be morally obliged to blow my brains out at this age," said Becker. "But I no longer feel that."

"'Hey Nineteen'... we had a lot of trouble with. We couldn't get a track we were happy with and we ended up doing it from the bottom up, starting with the drum track and overdubbing the rest of the stuff. That's a real pain in the ass. Part of the reason we did it that way was that we didn't want a real live sound. We were looking for a kind of mechanical version of early rhythm and blues. It was our intention to let it sound a little machine-like, with Hugh McCracken's warm obbligato guitar juxtaposed against that."

Evidently, Becker was not in one of his more informative or affable moods during an interview with Mitchell Fink. "I don't know how many songs we've written about whores – it must be every other one. It's all very deliberate. You can only say so much about love. I don't see anything unreasonable about 'Hey Nineteen'. I think that song's self-explanatory, if not strictly autobiographical. I figured a lot of people could identify with it."

"We felt we could get more freshness and divergence if we had some new players," said Katz. "The chemistry of cutting a track as far as we are concerned depends on having the right guys in the room at the same time, and having everybody tuned into the music at the same time. It is not too dissimilar from everybody else, but we are more demanding, more exacting."

Fagen went on to say that despite this approach... "We allow the musicians the freedom to play within the structures of the tunes in the style for which we hired them. We have pretty complete charts when we come in. It's basically where takes one through 10 will be rehearsals and takes 11 through 50 will be takes."

Recording 'Gaucho', Steely Dan kept regular hours in the studio, working in the evenings (usually from 3 p.m. till 11 p.m.) and leaving it free during the day. Nevertheless one unnamed source said, "It can get pretty boring hearing them play the same things over and over again for a year."

Walter Becker played only one guitar solo on the title track of the album but admitted that he would have played a lot more if he had been able to attend the later overdubbing sessions. Due to his immobility, most of that responsibility fell to songwriter Sammy Cahn's son, Steve Khan.

One song on which Steve Khan didn't get to play the solo was 'Third World Man'. The reason was that the solo had been recorded at the 'Aja' sessions by Larry Carlton for a song entitled 'Were You Blind That Day?' which Fagen had described as a third world fantasy. The song didn't quite come up to Becker and Fagen's expectations and so was left off 'Aja' at the last minute. When 'The Second Arrangement' was erased, Steely Dan then pulled the song out of the vaults, reworked the lyrics and re-recorded it under the title 'Third World Man'. Larry Carlton's original and moving guitar solo remained intact and indeed an integral part of the new song.

A song which surprised Becker and Fagen by being nailed early on was 'Babylon Sisters'. Bernard Purdie's genius came into play once again. Becker used the song as an example to refute criticism that Steely Dan albums were bland, overproduced and didn't sound like a bona fide group. "What really takes so long are the things on an album that don't work. And it's never the musicians' fault. It's always our fault," Becker said. "When a musician comes in and looks at a piece of material that he's never seen before, sometimes it can gel. When it does it's the best thing in the world. We got 'Aja' on the second or third take. On 'Gaucho', 'Babylon Sisters' was a second take. It doesn't sound as if it's been read or played by studio hacks. It doesn't sound as if it's been made by old men. It doesn't sound commercially motivated. It sounds like good music to me. Take some old Charlie Parker records. On certain days his band sucked. It can happen to anyone."

During the making of 'Gaucho', Roger Nichols had been working on a video of Steely Dan in the studio, which was done from an offbeat angle, to say the least. There were no regular shots of musicians or singers – it featured a hand moving a fader on the board and shots of Donald Fagen's leg as he left the studio. Although Nichols mentioned its commercial possibilities, the video was put on hold because of all the legal hassles and never got beyond Nichols' home collection.

Nichols explained how they approached getting the right sounds for a Steely Dan album. "Instead of using EQ on the board to change a drum sound, for instance, we'll bring in 52 different kick or snare drums to try to get the sound we want. We found it's better to make the adjustments at the instrument end rather than try to fix it with EQ and things. So we'll try many different instrument and microphone combinations with minimum EQ or no EQ at all to get something that sounds right."

He continued to describe their mixing techniques and the equal attention to detail Steely Dan employed even when recording was finished. "When we're mixing we'll use a lot of limiters, because they're nice and fast and you can't hear them doing anything. We'll use those on most of the vocals just to level things out. We try not to bounce tracks together. A lot of the other people I've worked with will take backgrounds, which might be on five or six tracks, and bounce them together onto two tracks or one track, just as a matter of course. Or they'll ping-pong all the guitars together or the horns together, just because it's easy that way; one knob for the guitars, one knob for the horns and so on. But bouncing is a generation down and if you listen you can hear the difference, no matter how good the machine is. And the ambience disappears when you ping-pong things together. So if at all possible, we try to keep all the instruments apart on the separate tracks they were recorded on, so that you get true hi-fi, with the least amount of generations before it gets to the record."

For Steely Dan's next album, Nichols was eager to experiment with the 3M digital machine and had persuaded Walter Becker of its advantages and benefits. "We had the Soundstream people come in, since they were in town for another project. They did a little demonstration for us with our tapes, but it was unsatisfactory for us," Katz explained. Steely Dan were thinking of mixing to the Soundstream, but it never materialised and they eventually decided to stick with analogue – this time.

"We decided that it didn't sound any better than the Studer conventional analogue two-track. Digital sounded a little different, but not necessarily better," Becker said. Greater editing problems with digital also swayed them back to analogue. Katz also found digital had a harsher high end.

With all the technical difficulties which continued to dog them throughout the making of 'Gaucho', Gary Katz was already keen to establish a studio expressly for use by Steely Dan. "Had you asked me about this last year, I would have given you the same answer. But we're talking about it now, along with Elliot and Roger. We'd like to put up a room, or buy an existing facility, to serve as a workshop, primarily for overdubs and mixing. There are more than enough rooms for basic tracking, and we're not interested in being in the studio business. We wouldn't lock everybody else out, but it would basically be there for us, so we wouldn't have to worry about other people coming in the middle of a project."

Eight years after the formation of Steely Dan, Becker and Fagen hated hearing some of their early records on the radio or in restaurants. Fagen said "We started out imitating as most people do," and that if he happened to hear one, his general feeling was one of humiliation. "I don't really understand some of our earlier stuff."

To a lot of people on the outside 'Can't Buy A Thrill' was a sensational début album, with at least five really great, inspirational songs and five good songs which virtually any other act would have been proud to have had on their album. Walter Becker didn't think so. "There were a lot of things that were very shoddily done, and a lot of things that were just bad, but probably different things for me than for Donald. We were doing the best we could, but fuck it, it wasn't very good. It's like looking at yourself in a mirror, it's not really how you look. I don't know whether it's ultimately good or not, I really don't."

℘

As 'Gaucho' neared completion and before ABC was absorbed into MCA, Irving Azoff tried to find out exactly how many albums Steely Dan had sold over the years. This was a ploy often used by managers attempting to re-negotiate or break record contracts, and record companies often had difficulty giving exact sales. Most artists' contracts contain a clause which enables the act to send in auditors once a year to check sales figures against royalties paid, but this is complicated by contracts which only pay royalties on 90% of sales. The remaining 10% of 'sales' are actually records that are given away, promotional copies to radio stations, review copies to critics and miscellaneous 'complimentary' copies that somehow float out of record company offices into the hands of 'friends'. Many of these wind up being sold anyway, a big bone of contention with most artist managers, and the difficulty lies in coming up with an exact figure of how many records have been sold – and how many given away.

According to Azoff's accounting Becker and Fagen were owed several million dollars in unpaid royalties, but MCA in turn claimed that payment of these royalties was not its responsibility. The matter of the royalties became linked to a separate dispute over whether 'Gaucho' was rightfully MCA's album, and Steely Dan found themselves in court arguing the toss.

Becker and Fagen had signed an agreement with ABC in January, 1979, for one more album with the company, so when MCA bought out ABC in March 1979 they automatically acquired the rights to Steely Dan's next album. But having completed the album, Steely Dan wanted to put the record out on Warner Bros. MCA naturally tried to block Becker and Fagen's defection and went to the Superior Court in Los Angeles where the judge ruled in MCA's favour. Steely Dan, however, claimed that their MCA contract was void, because the audit of MCA's books revealed that they were indeed owed several million dollars.

"There were some inaccuracies and it was discovered that some bookkeeping records were lost in the MCA-ABC transition," said Azoff. MCA, in turn, claimed that they had spent a million dollars on Steely Dan's new LP and were therefore entitled to release it.

MCA's auditors did experience difficulties in going through their books and could not disprove Azoff's claim that Becker and Fagen were owed royalties. The auditors entered into negotiations over the audit, but wanted to postpone them for a year, a delaying tactic which could have put back the release of 'Gaucho'.

Just before completion of the album, Front Line Management approached MCA for a settlement of the issue. When MCA did not respond, Azoff wrote a letter claiming "material breach of contract due to non-payment of royalties". MCA countered by taking the case to LA District Court seeking a temporary restraining order. They scored the first success when they were granted such an order preventing Steely Dan from releasing the album on any other label. After that the negotiations between Front Line Management and MCA were pursued with much greater urgency since both parties realised the necessity of getting the album out before Christmas.

MCA settled partial claims to the audit which they said related to MCA and not ABC. Becker and Fagen were a little concerned that MCA would not give the album their full promotional and advertising muscle, but MCA's Gene Froelich said the record company was right behind Steely Dan: "We're going to give this album our maximum effort. We consider it one of the most important releases of 1980," he stated.

With that settled, 'Gaucho' was in the stores in a matter of days. The album had been tentatively scheduled for release in September 1980. Gary Katz said: "We are meticulous in our work and we have had some mishaps. There were some personal things, Walter broke his leg a while ago, though it is hard to say how much that slowed us up, since we did continue to work."

Steely Dan actually delivered the master tapes for 'Gaucho' on October 28, 1980 and MCA had pretty much everything set for a rush release. They wanted the album in the shops before Christmas, but they outstripped themselves by a clear month, having the album out on November 21.

One of the conditions of MCA being awarded the album was that Steely Dan still had total quality control over the material. Gary Katz went to a special plating facility called Europadisc in New York to oversee the initial pressings and these were used for disc jockey and promotional copies. Similar monitoring continued for the regular production run. The need for haste also added to the cost of the album.

MCA had planned a basic advertising campaign well in advance and production of the album jackets was started immediately. They shipped out 5,000 retail streamers which simply stated that the album was finished and called 'Gaucho'; they simply couldn't wait any longer for the graphics.

Gary Katz told Sam Sutherland in *High Fidelity* that they had cut twelve songs for the album which was general operating procedure and gave them the option of more choice on the final work. In addition to the seven songs on the record, there was the infamous erased song 'The Second Arrangement', 'Kulee Baba' (on which Rick Marotta had played and said was "really unbelievable"), 'I Can't Write Home About You' and 'Heartbreak Souvenir'.

As for the embarrassing need to scrap performances by highly-regarded performers, Katz saw that happening "less and less – it used to be more guys on the floor than were left on the tape in the machine. But I think our experience is reducing that somewhat."

The album was finally issued in November 1980 and went platinum in the US, peaking at number nine in January 1981. Reviews ranged from the accusation of its being 'Aja' part two in *Melody Maker,* to Sam Sutherland in *High Fidelity* who voted it "a stunner" and his "candidate for best of the year". *Musician's* reviewer urged readers to spend the extra buck and buy the album, but *NME*, now staffed by hawkish young punk rock fans whose lack of taste often ranked with their inability to spot a winner, called it "an almost perfect blandness".

When it was released 'Gaucho' retailed at $9.98, the first non-soundtrack album in history to sell above the $8.98 suggested list price. A very angry Irving Azoff said, "They (MCA) went to $9.98 over my screaming objections". He blamed the high price for the album's failure to match the incredible success of 'Aja'.

Becker and Fagen were also outraged by MCA's pricing of the record and suspected it to be pure spite. "We pleaded with MCA not to put the album out at $9.98, but their position was 'We price the record, you have nothing to say about it or else we shelve it'," Fagen said. "I really regret it, because we've been getting a lot of flak about this. I know that our audience will blame us for being avaricious when, in fact, we did the best we could to prevent it. We had no legal recourse; MCA won the court battle."

When he was asked about the controversy, Walter Becker didn't mince his words: "I think they're the Mafia. I really do. I don't like them. We said please don't make it $9.98, that's too much. But we didn't matter. I feel like I'm robbing somebody, even though I benefit from it – I don't want it. It has nothing to do with recording artists. I don't think any recording artist says 'Make the records a dollar more so I can make more money'."

In their defence, MCA claimed they were trying to recover some of Steely Dan's exorbitant recording costs.

Gary Katz argued that the production costs for the album were considerably less than a million dollars, but he did admit... "It is an inexcusable amount to pay for a record album." The trend in music at that time was moving away from exorbitant studio costs towards the punk ethic of making records simply and cheaply, but Katz said: "We are not part of the trends, so it is not applicable to us."

↻

Although Becker and Fagen suffered more than their fair share of "jerk-off interviewers" they had always resisted the temptation to really tear into any particular one. But during a round of promotional interviews for 'Gaucho' at the Park Lane Hotel in New York, Becker (whose disposition wasn't helped by the fact that he was still on crutches) was in a vituperative mood, while Fagen was trying to moderate the conversation by cracking jokes.

When *New York Times* journalist Kristine McKenna's turn came, she likened the encounter to being a new kid in school thrown into a room with a cruelly cool in-crowd. After a long day of repetitive questioning, Becker and Fagen were in no mood to continue and it was McKenna's bad luck that she arrived at the end of the day. She wrote that the duo found most questions too insipid to merit serious thought, and when she asked if they thought competition in popular music had gotten stiffer over the last few years, Fagen quipped, "Yeah, it's gotten stiffer; rigor mortis has set in."

But the question that flipped Becker over the edge was prompted by a lyric ("But I'm just growing old") from 'Hey Nineteen'. McKenna asked if they were going through a mid-life crisis and caught the full brunt of Becker's contempt. He snapped: "Are you a journalist or a whore? Sheeesch!" The interview was curtailed rather swiftly and when McKenna's piece appeared in the *New York Times* it was entitled "Steely Dan: A (Very) Brief Encounter".

A month later, when Becker and Fagen taped a live radio interview with hip Jewish comic Robert Klein in front of an invited audience of some 200 people at RCA's recording studio on West 44th St, they were in a much better frame of mind. On his nationally syndicated show Klein interviewed pop stars of the day, featured some live music and reeled off a five-minute monologue, cracking plenty of jokes. It was the only public appearance Becker and Fagen made in support of the album, but it was strictly limited to an interview only. Klein joked that this was the Steely Dan 1980/'81 tour. "Yeah, that was it. And believe me, it was better than the band was," Fagen said.

Matching Klein joke for joke, Becker and Fagen facetiously explained how they fired all their roadies in order to once and for all terminate Steely Dan's touring period and how Steely Dan's last live gig in July 1974 was the last time they saw a smoke bomb go off. Referring to their staff writing job at ABC, Fagen described Hamilton, Joe Frank and Reynolds as "another audacious group of the time and also registered nurses".

Becker and Fagen also responded to a claim by Mitch Miller – one of the world's best selling recording artists in the 1950s who lived above Becker – that he had apparently been forced to endure a lot of guitar practice at very unsociable hours. Miller, who once worked as an A&R chief at Columbia Records and whose antipathy for the music was largely responsible for their late (and economically disastrous) entry into rock'n'roll, was alleged to have said: "This guy from Steely Dan – (Walter) Becker? He lives in my apartment building in New York City. He plays the same licks all night long. I feel like calling the cops on him. To get into rock you don't have to be a very good musician." Never ones to bypass an opportunity to respond to such claims, Becker and Fagen had the last laugh at the Klein taping. "We get all our ideas from Mitch," Fagen said. "We have a little microphone that we've snaked through the pipes and when he's practising his oboe we just flip on the recorder."

Becker and Fagen's infamous reputation concerning interviews was testified to by an attempt by *Melody Maker* writer David Fricke to set up a telephone interview with the pair. It involved a personal introduction at the Robert Klein taping, two weeks of phone calls and several missed deadlines. Finally having arranged the interview, Walter Becker called once, Fricke's line was busy and that was the last Fricke heard of him. However, when Fagen called he spoke amiably and frankly for an hour on a host of topics.

"I like my privacy. I love writing songs and making records. Records for me have integrity. I didn't even know there was any live music until I was old enough to get into bars where they played jazz."

Talking frankly about the time they spent making 'Gaucho', Fagen admitted that at one point the record company's patience ran out, they cut off the money and refused to pay for any more studio time. Becker and Fagen sent the bills to their manager, who footed them for a while until MCA relented and finally agreed to fund more sessions.

Fagen was in a particularly communicative mood and was willing to discuss the influences on their songwriting techniques and admitted quite frankly that much of their output was derived from music of the Thirties, Forties and Fifties as well as jazz and big band. This was music with which, he said, the vast majority of the pop audience was not familiar. Indeed, he admitted that they managed to obtain just enough information about it so that they were able to adapt the various techniques to their own purposes.

During other interviews for 'Gaucho' Becker and Fagen for the first time referred to their so-called "travelogue concept" of songwriting. In Fagen's words this was ... "aimed at transporting the listener to foreign lands and foreign worlds. Many of the songs show that attraction for exotica that Duke Ellington had. They're concerned with unexplored territories, the crowded streets of foreign lands – the romantic frontier."

A close examination of Becker and Fagen's lyrics does reveal an extraordinary number of places scattered liberally throughout each album. In particular, they seemed to have a morbid fascination with Hollywood, which crops up several times in 'Reelin' In The Years', 'The Caves of Altamira' and 'Glamour Profession'. Other more diverse places include Paraguay, Guadalajara, Peking, Biscayne Bay, Lhasa and Bogota. But Becker and Fagen's "travelogue" wasn't nearly as international as they would have us believe: a very large proportion of the places referred to in their songs are in the US, with the streets, districts and neighbourhoods of New York and Los Angeles featuring by far the most frequently, proving that although their stories might have been imagined the locations they chose to set them in were taken from first hand experience.

Fagen was under no illusions about Steely Dan's success. "Our success is an accident in a way. We have so many more traditional influences and are more uncompromising than most rock'n'rollers. We've taken our style from jazz, early 19th and 20th century serious music, R & B, blues and to some extent white rock'n'roll and simply played for ourselves. I guess we appeal to a certain audience that dances, a certain audience that likes the backbeat and yet another one that can pick up on the nuances. We never expected to sell as many records as we have recently, we just lucked out really."

℀

Becker and Fagen songs had never been a popular choice among other groups and artists as far as cover versions were concerned. Much of their output was simply too hard for many rock musicians to play anyway. Those who did record versions of Steely Dan tunes could hardly be termed big name bands: Birtha and Jose Feliciano both covered 'Dirty Work', Herbie Mann did 'Do It Again' and Deodato recorded a version of the same song. In the UK in 1984 Tom Robinson had a very minor hit with a version of 'Rikki Don't Lose That Number'. (In early 1979 ABC had reissued Steely Dan's version of 'Rikki' which peaked at a miserly 58 and within three weeks had disappeared from the top 75; amazingly, Tom Robinson's cover peaked at exactly the same position and for the same number of weeks.)

Fagen was mystified by the Herbie Mann and Deodato cover versions. "We seem to be big with the lightweight jazz crowd, for some reason. We didn't write it with those kinds of bands in mind, it's just that that song lent itself to that kind of treatment."

Becker lamented the fact that other groups were somewhat reluctant to cover their songs and reckoned it was because of some of the attitudes expressed within those lyrics. Those that had gone out on a limb and covered one, Becker said, "make it sound like a worse idea than it was in the first place. Even 'Dirty Work' which I think we didn't execute well, everyone else executes at least as badly as we did – which is inexcusable – and usually worse. I haven't heard a good version of 'Dirty Work'. There should be one."

With all the literary allusions in their lyrics (Becker and Fagen were often asked to list their favourite writers), it was only a matter of time before they would be asked about developing their mutual or individual storytelling techniques into a full-length novel. Becker admitted to writing poetry "a long time ago", but said that they intended to stick to lyrics and had no plans to write a book. Fagen admitted he'd thought about writing a book, but said, "I have no talent for that sort of thing... too lazy".

One thing which did please Becker and Fagen was the knowledge that Steely Dan's music encouraged their fans to investigate their jazz influences further. If Steely Dan opened people up to the music of John Coltrane, Thelonious Monk and Sonny Rollins, Becker and Fagen viewed that as a reward for their efforts in many ways more pleasing than the royalty cheques which dropped through the mailboxes. They must have been acutely aware, if not slightly embarrassed, that Steely Dan records outsold records by their jazz heroes by about twenty to one.

The first single to be taken from 'Gaucho' was 'Hey Nineteen' . This was pretty much an all Wendel track, but wherever possible, a live drummer was credited and Nichols' invention got credit for sequencing and special effects. It was scheduled for release the same week as the album, but at least three radio stations in Los Angeles and San Francisco somehow managed to obtain copies of the single almost two weeks before the actual release date and two of them began airing it as an exclusive. Many other programmers claimed to have had a copy of the single and in some cases the entire album. This caused an investigation to be launched at MCA to try and determine how the tapes were leaked. Both MCA and Front Line Management denied having been responsible for the "exclusives". But Donald Fagen didn't give a damn who was responsible. "Who cares? The music business works the way it works. It's a mentality that means nothing to us."

In a similar vein, when MCA staff received advance copies of 'Gaucho' on cassette, some immediately rushed to their favourite disc jockey to ensure that he was the first to air the new Steely Dan album. Fagen might not have cared, but Irving Azoff, who liked to control the marketing of his acts with an iron hand, was once again livid.

'Hey Nineteen' was backed with a previously unreleased live version of 'Bodhisattva' which had been recorded at Steely Dan's July 5, 1974, concert at the Santa Monica Civic Auditorium. 'Bodhisattva' was released complete with a rambling two-minute plus Jerome Aniton introduction, recorded when he was almost blind drunk and slurring his speech, and numerous expletives had to be bleeped out. Fagen could be heard laughing aloud in the background at Aniton's ad libbed intro. The single reached number 10 in the *Billboard* chart.

An unexpected bonus came about through their use of the lyric "The Cuervo Gold/The fine Colombian" which gave some very handy publicity to the Heublein Spirits Group, the importers of Jose Cuervo tequilas, who by way of gratitude sent Irving Azoff a case of the stuff. Azoff, ever mindful of the chance to earn an extra buck or two, brazenly asked Heublein what royalties Steely Dan could collect from the deal.

Yet another dispute erupted between MCA and Steely Dan in March 1981 when the second single taken from 'Gaucho', 'Time Out Of Mind', was released with the same live version of 'Bodhisattva' that had appeared on 'Hey 19' on the B-side. Becker, Fagen and Gary Katz had already agreed that 'Third World Man' would be the B-side. However, MCA had also already decided to use 'Bodhisattva' again as the supporting song; the duplication didn't harm the single's sales which still reached number 22 in the US.

At this point Irving Azoff seemed to be conducting an ongoing feud with MCA. He said: "To add insult to injury, they've now maliciously removed 'Third World Man' from the B-side of 'Time Out Of Mind' under the pretext that since there are only seven cuts on the album, it would hurt the LP's sales to include another album track as the next B-side." Azoff viewed the move as one with dire implications. "I contend that they're foolish enough to be considering seven singles from the album."

Bob Siner of MCA Records dismissed that forecast, saying the decision to use 'Bodhisattva' had stemmed from radio stations' demands for a new single, not from any formal sales strategy. According to Siner, a delay in finalising production plans led to a minor crisis when several radio stations, including WABC-FM in New York, began airing 'Time Out Of Mind' prior to its release as a single.

Siner also cited 'Gaucho's' multiple platinum predecessor 'Aja' as having only seven tracks, but that album spawned three hit singles: 'Peg', 'Deacon Blues' and 'Josie'. Gene Froelich of MCA said that 'Third World Man' was... "never the B-side – it was simply up for consideration. At one time they (Steely Dan) wanted it for the B-side, but at another time they didn't care what it was." He added that several radio stations were already playing 'Time Out Of Mind' and... "since we already had a B-side mastered, we decided to use that. There was no malice involved in removing anything. There was nothing to remove."

At that time Tower Records were also in dispute with MCA and were not carrying their product, so no Steely Dan records were available in their stores.

'Time Out Of Mind' was one of the tunes which had been written a couple of years earlier at Fagen's home in Malibu and during recording of the song, Fagen played piano and electric piano/synth for most of it, but Rob Mounsey played the same instruments in the instrumental section. It was far too complicated to credit it that way on the album sleeve so they compromised by simply listing Mounsey as the piano player and Fagen as the electric piano and synth player.

❧

'Gaucho' was voted the Rock/Blues album of the Year in *Downbeat* Magazine's 46th Annual Readers' Poll. Steely Dan were also voted the leading Rock/Blues group, narrowly beating out Earth, Wind and Fire. They also came a surprising second to Manhattan Transfer in the Vocal Group category. As for sales, 'Gaucho' went platinum in the US, reaching number nine, while in the UK, again without the benefit of a hit single, it just scraped into The top Thirty at number 27. It won Roger Nichols his third Grammy in five years for Best Engineered Album.

But despite the many plaudits, all was not well between Becker and Fagen. Once 'Gaucho' had been completed, Fagen spotted an ad in the back pages of a Los Angeles newspaper which stated that Bob Dylan was looking for musicians to accompany him on the road. Using his real name, Fagen answered the ad and a few days later Dylan's bass player, Rob Stoner, called Fagen excitedly and said what a great idea that the co-creator of Steely Dan was interested in a musician's job with Dylan. "I will definitely talk to Bob about it and I'll get back to you in a few days," Stoner said. But Stoner never called back and Fagen never did become Dylan's keyboard player. "As far as I'm concerned Dylan passed up a good thing," Fagen said later. "Sorry, Bob, I'm not available any more."

Fagen's interest in joining Dylan on the road probably had a twofold purpose – an attempt to jolt Becker into realising that life could go on without him, and to gain some time and space away from their deteriorating relationship. Nevertheless, for a musician with such an aversion to life on the road and who allegedly suffered from acute stage fright, it seems the unlikeliest of ambitions. Dylan, after all, played more concerts in six months than Fagen must have played in his entire career. Obviously the deciding factor was not being required to sing.

Fagen later dismissed the application as "basically a whim" and stressed that he was "secure in my own endeavours". But all the signs were there; Steely Dan had spent two years making a record, Walter Becker badly needed to sort himself out and Fagen had obviously had enough of watching his partner self-destruct while he was left to take all the critical decisions and responsibility for the album on his own shoulders. Fagen clearly needed to escape from the chaos that now enveloped Steely Dan.

Since Steely Dan no longer toured, time spent recording in the studio was Becker and Fagen's only means of communication. Their deep commitment came at the expense of other areas of their lives; they expended so much time and energy striving to make every last bar of every last song as close to perfection as possible that they were in danger of becoming robots.

Nevertheless, Becker and Fagen would not allow themselves the luxury of putting out a disappointing album. "We make mistakes and some of the mistakes get on the record," Fagen explained. "And no matter how long we work on it, not every song comes out the way we want it to. I'm not pleased with every last bar on 'Gaucho', but it's up to a standard that pleases us. This is music, music we care about. We don't make records to find girls. We already have girls."

Becker and Fagen's concentration in the studio was unsurpassed; they would stay focused for hours on end. But occasionally even they had to admit defeat and change track to gain some light relief. One such night at Soundworks Fagen and Katz pitched a baseball to and fro across the studio; another night Fagen had complained that he couldn't listen any longer after hours of concentrating on the finer points of a mix and strolled into the studio, sat down at the piano and ran through some jazz standards, including a favourite Thelonious Monk tune.

Nevertheless, the writing was on the wall for Becker and Fagen in the early part of 1981, although Fagen wasn't admitting it just yet. He said there *had* been times when they were about to call it quits "but the way it looks now, it looks like we'll probably stick it out a while. You have to have a certain amount of tolerance to keep something like this going for so long – to get through when times are sticky," Fagen said.

However, on June 17, 1981 it was announced in the *New York Times* that Becker and Fagen had indeed split up after fourteen years of writing and recording together. Fagen exclusively broke the news to Robert Palmer and described the parting this way: "Basically, we decided that after writing and playing together for fourteen years, we could use a *change mondaire* as the French say. We wanted to do something fresh." Fagen refused to be drawn on whether or not they would ever do another Steely Dan album. "We just kind of left that up in the air. It would be fun but it depends on our mutual inclinations further down the line. Nothing is planned; we'll see."

A Front Line spokesman said that both would be embarking upon solo projects, with Walter Becker likely to produce outside acts, and indeed Fagen had already composed an instrumental piece for the animated Columbia film *Heavy Metal*. The film was based on the comic Heavy Metal book characters and Fagen told Palmer how he came to snag the deal: "They sent me the script and the comic book, and frankly it didn't make much sense to me, but I took it as a jumping off point to do a five-minute piece that's mostly instrumental, with a little harmony vocal, if it got me back in the studio."

The album's executive producer was Steely Dan manager Irving Azoff and with Howard Kaufman (founder of HK Management – future Fagen representatives) and Bob Destocki he compiled the album. Accompanying Fagen on the soundtrack album were Black Sabbath, Grand Funk Railroad, Eagles guitarist Don Felder and Stevie Nicks. Named after a spaceship, 'True Companion' was recorded at Automated Sound Studios in New York and featured Fagen himself on synthesizers (with Ed Walsh), and on kalimba and lead and background vocals (with Zack Sanders) with Steely Dan regulars Don Grolnick on Rhodes piano, Crusher Bennett on percussion and Will Lee on bass, but the central piece of the song was another great guitar solo by Steve Khan. (The musicians' credits on the subsequent Steely Dan release 'Gold' were incomplete and also incorrectly identified Steve Jordan as the drummer.) Gary Katz was busy with another project, so Fagen asked Elliot Scheiner to co-produce the song with him.

"I should be ready to start recording my own album before the end of the summer. Working on it has been interesting. The fact that it's not a Steely Dan album has freed me from a certain image, a preconceived idea of how it'll sound. I hate to use the word 'personal', but I do think it's going to be more subjective. The album has a theme that all the songs relate to in one way or another, although I would hate to call it a 'concept album.' The theme has a lot to do with the blues."

The final irony of Steely Dan's career occurred when just a week or two before the official announcement of their separation was made, 'Babylon Sisters/Gaucho' became the third single from 'Gaucho' and the final Steely Dan single. It failed to chart in both America and England and fittingly marked Steely Dan's demise.

∾

CHAPTER X

New Frontier

Only a year after Steely Dan had officially announced their split and while Donald Fagen was busy recording his first solo album, a tribute to their music was being planned in Gresham, Oregon, at the first annual Mount Hood Jazz Festival. On August 7, 1982, a band at Mount Hood Community College devoted an entire set to Donald Fagen and Walter Becker compositions.

The idea was conceived by rabid Steely Dan fan, Dick LaPalm. Since so many jazz musicians had appeared on Steely Dan albums throughout the years, he thought it would be fun to show the musicians' appreciation of their writing skills. LaPalm was unstinting in his admiration: "To me, Donald and Walter are the Rodgers and Hart of this generation. I think we're putting together what will prove to be a magic afternoon." The band consisted of Chuck Rainey playing bass, Victor Feldman on keyboards (he also wrote all the arrangements), Paul Humphrey on drums and Mitch Holder on guitar. The reed section included Ernie Watts and Jerome Richardson, on brass was Slyde Hyde and Chuck Findley, and conducting the band was Joe Roccisano.

Among the songs rehearsed for the performance were 'Babylon Sisters', 'Green Earrings', 'Sign In Stranger' and 'Black Cow'. As the concert was being finalised, LaPalm said that the tribute didn't necessarily end there. "I just got off the phone with Gary Katz and he will be co-producing the album of Mount Hood with Al Schmitt. And I spoke to Donald last night. Gary and Donald have been working in New York on Donald's solo album. They both seem very excited about the project. We don't have a record deal for this yet, but I'm talking to Arista, Warner Bros and others."

But the question everyone wanted answering was whether Fagen would demonstrate his approval for the concert by actually making an appearance in Oregon himself? Knowing Fagen's reluctance to even be seen in a public place, let alone on a stage, LaPalm said: "I have a hunch Donald might want to show up. He's excited, yes, but he's also a last-minute kind of guy. I talk to him every other day, but I don't know for sure whether he'll show. I said to him 'Donald, you won't have to sing. Maybe you can just play keyboards on a couple of tunes'. He said, 'What do you need me for when you have Victor Feldman?'"

Due to time constraints, the band could not rehearse as much as they would have liked and, in fact, only managed to have a very brief soundcheck before their spot arrived. They preceded Bobby Hutchinson on stage and although the performance lasted about an hour and the audience appeared captivated, it was difficult for the musicians to tell exactly how well it was received. Chuck Rainey was under the impression that as the concept was never pursued, perhaps it wasn't as successful as they would have liked. Gary Katz and Al Schmitt did go to Oregon and record the show live; Fagen didn't show up which was no surprise to anyone.

Even with all their contacts and music business experience, LaPalm and Katz had great difficulty in selling the idea of the album to a record company. Eventually it was bought for MCA by Irving Azoff, Steely Dan's one-time manager, who by this time had jumped the fence to become the President of MCA Records, but it wasn't released for fully six years. It came out under the title 'The Hoops McCann Band Plays the Music of Steely Dan', the name taken from the character in 'Glamour Profession', but instead of a live recording of the actual tribute all the tunes were re-recorded at the Village Recorder with basically the same band, one notable exception being the absence of Chuck Rainey, who was replaced by Chuck Berghofer on bass. On a sad note Victor Feldman (who is the only musician to have appeared on all Steely Dan albums besides Becker and Fagen) had died in May 1987, and by way of tribute to him the band used Feldman's 1982 arrangement of 'Babylon Sisters' for the album.

A few months before Fagen's album was due, MCA put together a second Steely Dan greatest hits package. Called 'Gold' and released in July 1982, it was a disappointing collection of tunes which hadn't appeared on 1978's 'Greatest Hits'. There was nothing from 'Can't Buy A Thrill' or 'Pretzel Logic', there were no sleeve notes and although when a compact disc version was released it had been improved to contain full musician credits, which had previously been unavailable for some songs, the credits for 'True Companion' were inaccurate and incomplete. After Steely Dan's superbly imaginative album covers, the artwork on the countless compilation albums that would follow showed no such imagination.

Coming less than four years after the 'Greatest Hits' double, 'Gold' was not well received by critics who not only detected the odour of MCA cashing in on Becker and Fagen's split, but also recognised a slick marketing ploy when they saw one. In the UK the first twenty thousand albums sold included a limited edition four track 12" single containing Steely Dan's four most popular singles, the turntable hits 'Rikki Don't Lose That Number', 'Haitian Divorce', 'Do It Again' and 'Reelin' In The Years'. The ploy was only marginally successful because the album could only manage to reach number 44.

Donald Fagen's début solo album, which would be released in October 1982, was originally to be called 'Talk Radio' but eventually came out under the title of its key song, 'The Nightfly'. The name represented a fictitious all night "jazz jock" character – a composite of many of the disc jockeys that Fagen had spent so much time listening to, and imagined himself as, when he was an adolescent twenty and more years ago.

These DJs filled the young Fagen's night with the music he was so passionate about, speaking in what would later become "FM-type voices, very slow, cool, reassuring" and Fagen included a brief statement on the inner sleeve as to the effect they had on him. "The songs on this album represent certain fantasies that might have been entertained by a young man growing up in the remote suburbs of a north-eastern city during the late Fifties and early Sixties, i.e. one of my general height, weight and build."

Despite several requests from various TV shows, there was no way Fagen could be persuaded to appear on any of them. He was brutally honest about his shyness, saying, "I'm too scared. There's millions of people looking at you. Also, as you can tell, I tend to let a lot of dead air go by." As with Steely Dan, Fagen's promotional round included only press and radio interviews. In *Off the Record* broadcast in January 1983 with Mary

Turner, when she read out his brief sleeve note on the air, Fagen feigned a little embarrassment, saying: "It was cute when I wrote it."

In the same interview but on a far more serious note, since Fagen had indicated many times that writing and recording was his "strongest suit" and what he enjoyed the most, when she asked him if he liked recording as well as writing, Fagen's answer indicated the difficulties which had begun to haunt him during the latter stages of writing 'The Nightfly' and which would continue to haunt him for many more years. "Actually, I've slowly been losing interest in the writing and recording aspects. As soon as I get the idea I feel like I should be finished somehow and the rest is basically a job, filling in the blanks. Periods of recording are punctuated by great performances by musicians which gives you the impetus to keep going."

Even with 'The Nightfly's' autobiographical concept and his own experiences liberally sprinkled throughout, Fagen found writing songs without Walter Becker to offer ideas and alternatives a much harder task, and the seeds of what would eventually turn out to be a bad case of writer's block were already being sown. "Actually, I wrote six songs that came rather easily, at least the ideas did, but I had a little trouble with the last two – filling them out. But I think the concept was strong enough to support a whole LP."

Fagen explained that the genesis of the album came from the reasons why he became a musician in the first place. He looked back nostalgically to the late Fifties and early Sixties when his attitudes were formed by the whole jazz/hipster ethic in general and decided that his "jazz jock" character represented the ethos of the era and built all the songs around that idea.

The album contained seven new Fagen compositions, plus his version of Leiber and Stoller's 'Ruby Baby', originally recorded by The Drifters in 1955 and then again in 1963 by Dion. When Lieber and Stoller appeared on Charlie Gillett's UK radio show in 1982 playing their favourite records, they selected Fagen's version of 'Ruby Baby' which pleased him no end and vindicated his decision to cover the song.

Becker's absence made no significant difference to the methods Fagen employed in making the album. Once again recorded in New York and Los Angeles with a similar array of crack session players, 'The Nightfly' was an immediate hit in America and, bolstered by the success of the first single, 'IGY', climbed to number 11. The subsequent singles 'New Frontier' and 'Ruby Baby', however, did not emulate 'IGY's' success. In England, Fagen solo fared no better than Steely Dan in the charts; all three singles flopped and the album itself barely made the Top Forty.

Because of the personal nature of the album's subject, Fagen broke with Steely Dan tradition and actually appeared on the cover of the record – the first time he had ever done so. "It was an autobiographical album so it seemed like I might as well go public with it," he said. The front cover depicted Fagen's fantasy concept, while the back was a straight depiction of a typical US neighbourhood in the Fifties.

Fagen had moved across town by now and the radio studio mock-up was erected in Fagen's Upper East Side apartment (close to the Whitney Museum) by photographer James Hamilton. After the first shoot, an assistant engineer at Soundworks, Mike

Morongell, noticed that there was a basic error in the photograph: the RCA microphone was facing the wrong way, with the wire coming out of the rear of the mike and towards Fagen. A second shoot had to be arranged to correct the mistake. One of Fagen's favourite albums, Sonny Rollins' 'The Contemporary Leaders' featured in the shot, along with the character's favourite brand of cigarettes, the Chesterfield Kings mentioned in the title song.

Steely Dan had been the critics' darlings for most of the Seventies, and there was every likelihood that a critical backlash would hit Fagen this time. However, most reviewers loved the album, despite being unable to discern the difference between the Fagen record and its Steely Dan predecessors. Citing the note perfect playing by the army of session players, the jazz influences and the sheen of Gary Katz's production, critics raised the inevitable but blatantly unfair question: "So what was Walter Becker's contribution to Steely Dan?"

In Fagen's mind the difference between Steely Dan albums and his record was clear. "In all the albums I did with Walter, we never said 'We're going to write about a certain period or a certain motif'. And I think that accounts for a lot of the difference right there."

Fagen continued to rebut the suggestion that Becker's input into Steely Dan must have been minimal by saying that they developed the Steely Dan sound together over the years and that there was really no way to separate how much of the style came from either one of them. Because Fagen used many of the same musicians and because his voice was the focal point of the record, Fagen admitted that it was basically the same sound and that there was not much difference until "you start looking at some of the details".

In documenting his adolescent fantasies, Fagen imagined himself to be that distant night-time jazz disc jockey playing the hippest records by Sonny Rollins, Miles Davis, Thelonious Monk and Charlie Parker. The message was clear: the Fifties and Sixties were an enormously important period in Fagen's life. "I was a member of that minority that thought, because of the cultural climate, life in the suburbs was arid. Jazz and black music in general, late night radio, hipster culture and the whole jazz ethic seemed like a vital alternative to the life I was leading," he said.

"There was a great emphasis on technology at the time. The Cold War was going strong, as it is again. Kids, through the media and what the government and their parents wanted them to know, grew up with a certain vision of the world. I think my discovery of black music and the hipster culture really broke all that apart. It made me see it a different way. And that's basically what the record is about."

'The Nightfly' was Fagen presenting a "kid's eye view of the way things were then and their expectations of the future." The record covered roughly the period from the International Geophysical Year, when he was ten years old, through the early Sixties when he discovered jazz in his early teens, to the assassination of President Kennedy in 1963.

"I used to like Chuck Berry and Fats Domino when I was a little kid. But then something happened when I was about twelve or thirteen. Something happened to rock and roll, actually; it became more mainstream - more *white*. I don't know if I was conscious of what was at work there; in fact, I probably didn't connect it to a racial thing. And it didn't appeal to me any longer. About that same time, I discovered these late night radio shows, and it seemed to have a vitality that rock and roll, by the early Sixties, didn't have. So I started listening to that. I was a lonely kid, and I guess jazz was probably a symptom."

At the time he was promoting the album, Spielberg's *E.T.* was cleaning up at the box office, and Fagen drew a parallel between the film and his own situation twenty years earlier. "The *E.T.* in my bedroom was Thelonious Monk. Everything he represented was totally unworldly in a way, although at the same time jazz to me seemed more real than the environment in which I was living. It was one of those developments with a thousand homes that all looked exactly the same. It was pretty barren actually. But jazz was an escape, not only from the architecture and the landscape, but also from the climate of thought at the time, the Cold War mentality and all that."

When Fagen and Roger Nichols were ready to start work on the album, they decided that the first Wendel model wasn't hi-fi enough, so Nichols set about building Wendel II, which had sixteen bits as opposed to the original Wendel's eight. Wendel II also plugged straight into the 3M digital machines, so there was no degradation of recorded sound. On 'The Nightfly' Wendel ended up "playing" on 'Ruby Baby', 'IGY' and 'Walk Between Raindrops', as well as embellishing the rest of the tracks and repairing various bits and pieces.

While he was perfecting Wendel II, Daniel Lazerus engineered 'Nightfly'. He was recommended by Nichols and had worked on an Eye to Eye album which had been produced by Gary Katz. 'The Nightfly' was his first full album as engineer.

At first Fagen was nervous at the thought of embarking upon a solo career. He'd always had Walter Becker there to fall back on and to bounce ideas off, both in the studio and during the writing process. Now although he still had most of the team behind him, he was strictly on his own. Certainly the lyrics on 'Nightfly' lacked the bite of Steely Dan, but this may have been as much due to Fagen's choice of subject matter as Walter Becker's non-participation in the lyric writing process. "I was sort of striving for a lack of irony. A lot of the songs are from a teenager's viewpoint, so I wanted them to have a certain innocence. I thought that the period and some of the concepts that I was trying to get over deserved that kind of treatment. Of course, there's a limit to how *little* irony I can pull off at this point."

Fagen's decision to record an autobiographical album caused him some misgivings. In retrospect he occasionally appeared to regret the temporary abandonment of his traditional defences and expressed concern that he might have revealed too much about himself. In one later interview, he contradicted his earlier comment by insisting that the album was *not* strictly autobiographical. "I play myself as I was twenty years ago. But it is not me *exactly*. It is a composite character of myself, what I remember and people I knew. Plus it includes my feelings in retrospect."

Fagen became very touchy about his lyrics being recognised as a reflection of something that actually existed and therefore open to closer – and probably more accurate – scrutiny than those on Steely Dan records. In 'The Goodbye Look' he changed a line to "Behind the big casinos by the beach" because the previous line reminded him of a line from a well known poem. He also expressed anxiety over the line "late line, night line" because of the Ted Koppel TV show of the same name in the US.

Fagen produced simple demos for 'The Nightfly', mostly with just a drum machine and keyboards, but he deliberately held back on the lyrics which he would be altering and amending when he was in the studio. Lyric writing was the chore where he missed Walter Becker's input the most, but musically he had everything worked out in his head and knew exactly what he was looking for with each tune when it came time to record.

The first of 'The Nightfly' sessions were held at the Village Recorder in Los Angeles and one of the first decisions taken by Fagen, Katz and Nichols was to bring in a 3M 32-track digital machine as backup to the analogue Studer. Nichols was so surprised by the difference in sound between the two that he embarked on a series of rigorous experiments. "One was exact and the other was... you could tell that it was the analogue tape. And that's when we decided to do the album digitally."

Despite the sophistication of the digital technology, Nichols had found that they could be fixed with surprising components. "The 3Ms are like Fords – you can repair 'em with baling wire and paper clips and parts from Radio Shack. The Mitsubishi and Sony are like the next generation: they've got the better error correction, but if they go wrong they're harder to troubleshoot, because each circuit does nine different things."

Nichols was an immediate convert to digital recording and became a crusader for the benefits and advantages of digital as opposed to analogue. Punch-in and punch-out was infinitely easier. "You can punch out in the middle of a note without any glitches or holes left in the tape. With digital you can combine different tracks with no degeneration," he said.

Nichols first became aware of a problem after Fagen's album was finished. Stevie Wonder, of all people, called him and told him that the CD of 'The Nightfly' sounded "funny". When Nichols played a copy of the CD he discovered that it sounded inferior to the analogue LP. Comparing 'Nightfly' with a CD of Billy Joel's 'The Nylon Curtain' confirmed Nichols' worst suspicions: third and even fourth generation masters were routinely being used to manufacture CDs. Nichols was outraged and wrote a detailed article in the December issue of *Recording Engineer and Producer*, demanding that record companies tighten up their downright careless attitude to their artists' product and only use original two-track masters to make CDs, especially if they intended to imply to the suspect masses that digital was superior to analogue.

As long ago as 1984 Nichols, ever at the sharp end of sonic technology, had invented a digital microphone which digitised air pressure changes, but his attempts to go further proved frustrating due to existing patent laws. He was informed that he couldn't patent his invention until other associated areas had been filled in. (As of 1993 Nichols was about to again submit his microphone for consideration, since other inventions have now filled in the blanks around the digital microphone.)

Although Fagen had heeded his engineering staff's recommendation to commit himself to digital recording, they had more than their usual share of technical problems, not least because of the newness of the machines. "The machine was up on the rack a lot, although toward the end we were using it with total freedom from problems. It's a matter of getting to know the machine and not abusing it. They need a lot of maintenance. If you really take care of them, there are no problems; the problem is finding out how to take care of them."

One persistent headache for Fagen and Nichols was an alignment problem between the digital machines in Los Angeles and those in New York. The west coast 3M representative would come in with his alignment tape, align the machine and swear it was perfect. Then back on the east coast the New York guy would do the same and swear his was perfect, but the machines wouldn't line up exactly right. Eventually their patience ran out and they decided to learn how to align the machines themselves. Roger Nichols, Jerry Garsszva and Wayne Yurgelun went to 3M's Minnesota headquarters, stayed in a sleazy motel, attended classes in the daytime and when they came back they knew enough about the machine to know if it had been aligned correctly. The problem turned out to be a very slight difference between east and west coast alignment tapes.

Fagen admitted that while working on 'The Nightfly' he was bitten by the machinery bug and moved away from the tried and tested Steely Dan method of putting a rhythm section together in a room and instead built up the tracks layer by layer. They completed the recording of 'Nightfly' in eight months, and compared to the three months they spent mixing 'Gaucho', 'The Nightfly' was mixed in ten days.

Nichols explained that when Fagen came to recording a vocal all the performances tended to be very good and that it was difficult to choose between three or four excellent ones. "Then we'd spend a lot of time doing a 'beat the computer', where he'll (Fagen) perform it again and again. Here's a phrase or a couple of words and he likes the way he sang them better than what's on the computer. So we'll put those in and periodically we'll go back to the song when he feels like it and try it again and he'll sing the whole song two, four, six or eight times. Then we'll listen to lines and 'Oh, this is a new way he did this line' and he likes this better so we'll pop this stuff in. It's a long process, but it keeps improving it a little at a time, but as far as the general public is concerned the first or second take would have been just fine and everybody would have been happy with it except Donald."

'IGY' – an acronym for International Geophysical Year – wasn't simply a figment of Fagen's imagination. It actually covered an eighteen-month period from July 1957 – December 1958 when an intensified programme of geophysical research was carried out throughout the world. It was a massive effort involving co-operation among more than 70 nations, the participation of several thousand scientists and observers and the operation of an equal number of scientific stations from all over the globe. The measurements and observations fell into three main categories: the physics of the upper atmosphere, and the heat and water regimen and the earth's structure and interior. 'IGY' was a strange choice of subject for a song, but Fagen used it as an example of how optimism can soon turn sour and of how his own hopes were dashed.

"'IGY' is a child's view of the future, with technology solving the world's problems, a gleaming future," Fagen explained. "Very little of that came about and we found that technology creates more problems than it solves. I guess I just wanted to look back." Fagen's optimistic ten-year-old view of International Geophysical Year included an undersea rail tunnel which linked Paris and New York by a ninety-minute journey and in a 1983 interview he still held out a little hope for such a dream. "Who knows? Maybe they'll start that project any day now.

"With 'IGY' we started out with a rhythm machine to get the feel, then used a sequenced synth for the backbeats, then I put down a bassline for reference using the piano, then Greg Phillinganes came in to put the basic thing down with the Rhodes. At that point we had the basic track."

After the idealism of 'IGY' came the Chinatown romance of 'Green Flower Street' (Fagen's nod to the jazz standard 'On Green Dolphin Street') in which Jeff Porcaro and Chuck Rainey were reunited on drums and bass. With Kennedy and The White House at a permanent stand-off with Khrushchev and the Kremlin and the threat of nuclear war hanging over the nation, Fagen wrote an upbeat song, 'New Frontier', about having a good time underground before the "reds decide to push the button down". "I was trying to show how ridiculous fall out shelters were," he said. "The concept that there was any real life possible after an all-out nuclear war. I thought having a party was a good way to display that in a sort of funny way."

Fagen always seemed particularly pleased with the title track. "'Nightfly' uses a lot of images from the blues: that hair formula gets its name from Charley Patton, the old delta blues guitarist, and Mount Belzoni gets its name from another old blues lyric: 'When the trial's in Belzoni/No need to scream and cry'. It's music I associate with a time of innocence, and in a way I can say goodbye to that now."

Fagen took the idea for 'Walk Between Raindrops' from an old Jewish folk tale about a famous rabbi/magician who could perform this remarkable feat. The song was recorded almost as an afterthought when the rest of the album was finished, and was interesting in that Fagen allowed a flawed – but ultimately enchanting – instrument track to get through his rigorous screening process. "The organ at the studio where we were working was very funky sounding which is unusual. I think it was broken, which is probably why it sounds so good," he explained.

The song, which swings along as befits a man obsessed with Duke Ellington's swing theorem, also features a keyboard bassline played by Greg Phillinganes which was doubled by Will Lee on bass guitar so that it sounded like an authentic upright bass. This was an early example of the doubling of basslines that would eventually become common practice on many records. Whether it was the intention to have the bass replace the keyboard bass is irrelevant now; it sounded so good that they chose to keep both parts in the final mix.

Daniel Lazerus was surprised when Fagen started a completely new song at Soundworks when the album was virtually complete. It gave him the opportunity to engineer the track alone and in fact the "Oh Miami!" exclamation was Lazerus's last minute idea as they were mixing the song. He'd always enjoyed the "Oh, rock!" breaks on some old records and Fagen suggested that they try "Oh, Miami!" Gary Katz, Lazerus and Fagen sang the parts with Katz most audible among the three voices.

Fagen had always loved bossa nova – particularly Luis Bonfa and Astrud Gilberto – and 'The Goodbye Look' was inspired by this music. A tale of military upheaval on a Caribbean island, the title bore no relation to the 1969 Ross McDonald detective novel of the same name and Fagen also denied it was inspired by the Bay of Pigs incident in 1962.

Fagen was still putting musicians to the test in the studio. One of the hardest songs to record as far as Michael Omartian was concerned was the title track. Fagen had Omartian sitting at a piano in the middle of the room at the Village Recorder playing with nothing except a "nauseating quarter note click" in his earphone, expecting him to play as if he were part of a group. Omartian found that very difficult because he had no other instruments to play off and Fagen wanted him to set the groove that way. Omartian said that Fagen would be standing in the control room with the advantage of knowing what he wanted the complete track to sound like, while he could only read the dots and try to imagine what Fagen was going to mould around his keyboard. After several hours of frustration, Omartian uncharacteristically threw down the music, exclaimed "I can't do this", and started to walk out. Fagen followed and convinced Omartian that he was sounding great. He coaxed him back and eventually his persuasion paid off, because although it took about six hours they eventually got the track they were looking for.

But if Omartian thought that was difficult, then he had another surprise in store. For the piano part of his version of 'Ruby Baby', Fagen wanted isolation between the right and left hand parts. It seemed he wasn't satisfied with the placement of the chords in the right hand coming down at the same time as the left. He wanted the left hand to be more laid back than the right so he asked Omartian to play the left hand as if he was playing with his right as well, which was virtually physically impossible, since any pianist has to play off his other hand.

"I tell you there's no piano player on the face of the earth that could accommodate that," Omartian told Fagen. Eventually they achieved the effect Fagen was seeking by seating Omartian and Greg Phillinganes at the piano together, with Omartian playing the low part and Phillinganes playing the high part. Fagen had decided that as Phillinganes was going to play the solo, he may as well play the right hand parts so he could place them where he thought fit.

Sure enough Phillinganes' solo didn't disappoint Fagen; it was a stupendous instrumental break. But once again their problems were just beginning. The piano by itself sounded fine, but when the synthesizers had been recorded and put over the top they found small tuning discrepancies underneath Phillinganes' solo. He later said that he based his solo on the riff from The Kinks 'You Really Got Me'. Fagen loved Phillinganes's solo almost as much as he had done Phil Woods' alto sax break on 'Doctor Wu'.

After the synth tracks were stacked up it sounded like they were rubbing with the piano, so they had to go back and take the whole track apart to figure out what was causing the problem. Fagen was adamant that he would not replace the piano solo. What they found was that the tuning increments of synths were too big; one notch would be too flat and the next notch would be too sharp. So Fagen and company rented a high-tech piece of Hewlett-Packard equipment to change the clock frequencies on the machine so they could move the tuning around in tiny increments. Then they took some of the piano, put it into Wendel, looped it so they could get a tuning reference on a rota tuner and started again from there tuning the synths. The song caused plenty of headaches and for a long while things were touch and go, but much to Fagen's relief the synths worked out at the third attempt.

"'Ruby Baby' is a rearrangement of The Drifters' version," said Fagen. "I liked the innocence of the lyrics. We needed party noises for it, and since our studio was right next door to Studio 54, we surreptitiously suspended a mike from the ceiling of one of Jerry Rubin's 'business parties'. But it sounded more like a stadium crowd, so we threw a party in the studio. A lot of people got very drunk, and we got our party noises." The first digitally recorded party in history was at Automated Sound and saw Fagen himself getting into the spirit of things by standing on a chair waving his arms like some insane conductor. The studio party was fun and provided them with the hubbub they were looking for.

'Ruby Baby's' 'love is blind' theme fits in well with Fagen's memories of his adolescence and his concept of innocence, and he listened to several other '50s records to get a general atmosphere of the period and jolt his memory. "I threw in a lot of other jazz chords and basically made it sound like a big R'n'B party situation. But it has a lot of dissonance – it's pretty strange, in a way," he added.

During the recording of one song, Ed Greene played drums on a track which Fagen didn't think was working, but he loved Greene's drum track so much that he took the tape away and eventually came back with a new song and lyrics ('Maxine') totally rewritten around the old song's drum track. Even with his limited experience at that stage, Daniel Lazerus was amazed by the dedication which Fagen put into rewriting that song.

'Maxine' dealt with an "extremely idealised version of high school romance", the ordeals of growing up in the remote suburbs and seeking any form of escape, be it through fantasy or love. Fagen said that he was a crooner – "I think that's basically the way my voice sounds over lots of changes" – and confirmed that the rich choral backdrop of both 'Maxine' and 'Ruby Baby' were "takes on typical four and five-part harmony of the period."

Knowing Fagen's propensity for the perfect drum track, it was not surprising to find two drummers credited on 'IGY'. James Gadson was the live drummer – he played the kick, snare drum and hi-hat, which was looped to become the track; then Jeff Porcaro came in and overdubbed tom-tom fills. The situation was reversed on 'Ruby Baby'. Fagen succeeded in getting strong performances from both players but was still unsatisfied, hence the reason Wendel was also involved in each song.

After his non-appearance on 'Gaucho' (his solo on 'Third World Man' had been cut during the 'Aja' sessions) Larry Carlton flew to New York for five days, spent four days working on the album and in a few hours was homeward bound. On 'The Nightfly' he used a late Fifties Fender Tweed amp with only one speaker. At one point Carlton was getting an extremely bad case of hum while recording his guitar and the engineers couldn't find any AC problems in the studio. They went on a neighbourhood hunt and eventually found the cause of the problem – a huge magnet on the other side of the studio wall that formed part of the New York subway system.

One day when Fagen was recording vocals at Soundworks, he noticed a bad smell which became worse as the day went on and gradually permeated the control room as well as the studio itself. Over the course of the next two days it became so bad that Fagen and his crew were unable to work until its source had been located and eradicated. Initial searches failed to find the cause of the stink, so the studio staff masked it by burning candles and sticks of incense. They went right through the air conditioning, removed the console, took up carpets and finally gutted the studio until, when they took up the floorboards, they found the cause: in the corner of the room, in a small drainpipe, was a big, moist, dead rat which had died from eating rat poison. The rat caused Fagen to lose a week's work and Soundworks to lose considerable revenue.

Chuck Rainey was living in Colorado when he received a call from Gary Katz to fly into LA for the sessions. When he arrived they weren't ready for him, so he sat in his two-bedroom hotel suite in Westwood for three days waiting a call. This had never happened before – being paid double scale fees without having to play a note. Not that he was complaining. Eventually he was put to work on 'Green Flower Street', his only appearance on 'The Nightfly.'

℃℈

'The Nightfly' was nominated for a Grammy in seven categories: album of the year, song of the year (for 'IGY'), best pop vocal, best instrumental arrangement with a vocal, best vocal arranged for two or more voices, engineer of the year for Roger Nichols (yet again) and Katz was nominated as best producer. As ever, Fagen was very reluctant to attend – he had refused to do so in the past for Steely Dan nominations – but since the album was nominated so many times he seriously considered breaking with his tradition.

'New Frontier' was released as the second single and Rocky Morton and Annabel Jankel of Cucumber Studios in England made a video for the song based on Fagen's party in a fall-out shelter scenario. Morton and Jankel had directed award winning commercials and went on to direct a remake of the classic 1940s thriller *D.O.A.* with Dennis Quaid and Meg Ryan. The video combined animation with live action and featured a bespectacled, nerdy Fagen lookalike partying in a New Jersey fall-out shelter with his girl. In their Rock Videos Hot 100 *Rolling Stone* described it as "warm and witty and stunningly crafted" and nominated it as possibly the greatest rock video ever.

Fagen didn't appear in the dip and when he aired his views on the medium it's easy to see why. "The animator seemed very excited about doing it. As for myself I'm not interested in video. When you listen to a record you have to bring your imagination to it. It's more interesting to me to hear pure music. I don't need any visual imagery to go with it, especially if it's like the kind you see on MTV."

167

Once 'The Nightfly' was out, Fagen again faced questions about a possible tour. He proclaimed the unlikelihood of "any grand tour", but did mention that he was considering doing some local club gigs in the New York area. He was obviously speaking out of turn because they didn't materialise for fully seven years.

'The Nightfly' didn't sell as well as 'Gaucho' and Fagen was critical of Warner Bros' marketing of the album, saying that they didn't get behind it as perhaps they could have done.

When Gary Katz read the reviews of the album, he wasn't sure about the so-called "left turn into jazz" which many critics sensed and said that although songs like 'Maxine' and 'Walk Between Raindrops' did have the sense of another era about them, he reckoned that some songs on 'Nightfly' could have worked on earlier Steely Dan albums, particularly 'Katy Lied'.

The eighteen month gap between 'Gaucho' and 'The Nightfly' wasn't such a long hiatus by usual Steely Dan standards. But Fagen was still asked why it had taken so long to come up with the album. "I'm a slow writer. It took eight months to write and a year to record – there were lots of technical breakdowns with the digital equipment." Fagen pushed himself hard and expected the musicians and engineers to do the same, and when long and demanding sessions extended beyond their scheduled hours, he came to regularly refer to it as "being on the night train". In several post-'Nightfly' interviews Fagen half-jokingly said the reason he loved recording studios so much and why he spent so much time in them during the Seventies was because "they remind me of my parents' house; wall-to-wall carpets, bland colours, Swedish furniture. I find them very comforting."

Fagen explained that the inspiration behind the record was that as he approached his mid-thirties, he began thinking about why he became a musician. "I was headed toward a different kind of life really, maybe an English teacher or something like that. I studied literature at college and basically had my course set out for me. When the Sixties came along I perceived that there were other options and, since music was my hobby, I decided to try to make a living at it."

Despite his reputation as an aloof and cold individual, Daniel Lazerus found Fagen to be a very good friend, almost like an elder brother to him. Lazerus was young and in awe of New York, but they went to the movies, walked home from the studio together and, most surprising of all, ran together in Central Park. Fagen's jogging route took him around the Central Park reservoir. The Fagen of Steely Dan days didn't look like a man who would eventually come to participate in keeping fit.

Once he was settled back into his daily life in New York, Fagen discovered that the problems he'd had completing the last two songs for 'The Nightfly' had extended beyond that and into his total songwriting routine. Although he wrote songs every day and found time to play some jazz standards and perhaps go through some scales, when he listened back to the material he had managed to write, he either didn't like it, found it repetitive, or it just didn't move him. It was the beginning of a seven year creative drought.

℘

CHAPTER XI

Big Noise, New York

With 'Gaucho' finished and nothing on the horizon for Steely Dan in the near future, Gary Katz had spent his time listening to as much new music as possible. Among the records he particularly liked was one he'd been sent by an American group called Eye To Eye on a small English label called Renegade. The group was built around the songs of keyboard player Julian Marshall and vocalist Deborah Berg, and when they discovered that Steely Dan's producer was interested in them a deal was struck.

Katz must have secured the band a considerable budget since the credits read like a Steely Dan album: Chuck Rainey, Jeff Porcaro, Jim Keltner, Rick Derringer, Elliott Randall and Dean Parks to name but a few. The songs were catchy and had quirky lyrics and no doubt due to Katz's involvement, Donald Fagen made a very brief appearance playing a synthesizer solo on the closing tune called 'On The Mend'. Their eponymous début album was recorded between February and July 1981 and released the following year on the Warner Bros label, but even with Katz's name in the credits it failed to chalk up any significant sales.

During the lull after 'The Nightfly', an unexpected skeleton appeared from Becker and Fagen's cupboard: an album entitled 'Walter Becker/Donald Fagen – The Early Years', introducing Steely Dan fans to such long lost gems as 'Brain Tap Shuffle', 'Let George Do It', 'I Can't Function' and 'Old Régime'. Put together by their old mentor Kenny Vance and licensed to Aero Records in New York, these old demos were welcomed by Steely Dan fans, but as far as Becker and Fagen were concerned, they were a most unwelcome reminder of their early days. They had never imagined for one moment that these primitive demos would ever become available to the public and Fagen's vexation was apparent in his comment about "some greedy little record people" making them available.

The cover photograph, taken by ex-American "guitar owner" Marty Kupersmith showed Fagen looking appropriately wasted and uninterested and Becker looking much younger than his 18 years, in their bare-walled office inside JATA's production office in the Brill Building. Their upright piano was just visible in the background.

Fagen had mentioned during promotional interviews for 'The Nightfly' that Robbie Robertson had asked him to write a "jazzy ballad" for the upcoming Martin Scorsese/ Robert de Niro film, *King Of Comedy*. Fagen obliged with a beautifully melodic outtake from 'The Nightfly' called 'The Finer Things'. As with 'True Companion' it was an instrumental enhanced with harmony vocals from a female chorus. Alto saxophonist David Sanborn took the lead and Fagen sang backgrounds, arranged the strings with Rob Mounsey and co-produced with Gary Katz. It was eventually revealed that Fagen had a deep seated anxiety about large string dates and always liked to get someone in to share the responsibility.

In the years that followed, with Becker and Fagen spectacularly inactive musically, Steely Dan's back catalogue continued to sell so well that neither of them needed to produce material or work in any way simply to survive. Whatever they thought about it personally, the music they produced with Steely Dan would provide a substantial and lasting pension for the two composers. Indeed, with the advent of compact discs, hundreds of thousands of Steely Dan fans went out and replaced their black vinyl records with the new silver digital formats and this alone secured their financial futures once and for all.

Fagen speculated that each new year thousands of college kids, newly introduced to Steely Dan's music, went out and bought copies of their albums, so steadily did they sell throughout the Eighties. At one point Fagen said that if the compact disc hadn't been invented, he would probably be playing in a lounge somewhere. Once Becker was back in harness producing pop and jazz acts, he said that the sales of the eight Steely Dan albums made everything else he did look like a hobby.

Even when Becker and Fagen were recording they didn't work every day, so if Gary Katz wasn't on the lookout for other interesting projects, he would have been semi-retired and he wasn't ready for that just yet. In an unlikely combination, the ex-Steely Dan producer snagged the job producing one side of an album by former Supreme diva Diana Ross for RCA and he asked Fagen to write a song specifically for her. Fagen was already writing material for his second solo album, but he came up with a *ménage à trois* song called 'Love Will Make It Right', and played synthesizer on what for him was a rather weak tune, especially lyrically. It was a song that looked at the revelation of an adulterous relationship between two married couples, all of whom had been close friends up to that point. It boasted the customary thick, squeaky synth sounds and washes of keyboards of early Eighties period Fagen.

Gary Katz later admitted that he didn't enjoy the experience of working on the 'Ross' album, wasn't fond of the result and accepted most of the blame for it. Katz felt his true forte was working with artists who knew in what direction they wanted to go and then assisting them to achieve their goals. Diana Ross expected her producer to find the songs, put the musicians together and then virtually create the record in the studio, so that all she had to do was simply turn up and sing the material. Katz was unused to working with an artist who required so much input in so many different areas.

Fagen, Katz and Daniel Lazerus spent plenty of time on the song, working on some experimental drum sounds with Jeff Porcaro at Media Sound Studios, which used to be an old church. Later Fagen and Lazerus spent two days mixing his composition at Soundworks using some new SSL equipment, but the studio was experiencing problems with "burn in". After all their diligent work they had a superb mix, but it was lost to the computer. They worked on a second mix and that was also lost to the computer. Finally, the third mix survived to make it on to the album. But Lazerus maintained that the third mix in no way matched up to their original.

Eye To Eye's follow up LP was called 'Shakespeare Stole My Baby' and came out in 1983. Once again Gary Katz produced and once again the same impressive list of session players was featured. Donald Fagen made his obligatory appearance on a Katz-produced album, adding an additional keyboard to the track 'Jabberwokky', but as with their début, the album didn't sell and lost Warner Bros a small fortune.

Marshall and Berg put together a band of mostly British players for some gigs rehearsed in New York and were offered the support band slot for a forthcoming Fleetwood Mac US tour. But by then Warners calculated that they had spent enough on the band and refused to put up any more money. Berg and Marshall quietly dissolved Eye To Eye soon afterwards.

In 1984 producer Hal Willner, knowing Fagen's penchant for Thelonious Monk, asked him if he was interested in performing a Monk composition on a tribute album to be titled 'That's The Way I Feel Now' and to be released on the A&M label. The concept involved an array of artists performing their favourite Monk compositions and the cast list also contained Todd Rundgren, Joe Jackson, Was (Not Was), Dr John and Carla Bley.

Fagen was a fan of guitarist Steve Khan (he'd written sleeve notes for Khan's 1979 album 'Arrows', they'd called him in for much of the work on the 'Gaucho' sessions and he particularly liked Khan's 1981 album, 'Evidence') and he asked Willner if he could record something for the project with him. Khan was delighted to be offered the opportunity to work with one half of Steely Dan. As most of the other artists had chosen medium or uptempo numbers, Khan thought it would be nice to treat one of Monk's ballads to show how beautiful his writing could be. They recorded 'Reflections' at Media Sound Studios in Manhattan. Steve Khan's acoustic guitar took centre stage in the first half of the song with Fagen lending a supporting role before coming into his own during the second half.

In the summer of 1983 Fagen went to see a show at the Next Wave Festival in New York called *The Gospel At Colonus*, which was based on an adaptation of *'Sophocles' Oedipus At Colonus'*. The show was set in a black Pentecostal church and Fagen loved it so much that he paid for engineer Daniel Lazerus to go and see it too. While he was there, Lazerus wondered if anyone had approached the show's writer and arranger Bob Telson about recording it. Afterwards Lazerus went up to the orchestra pit and asked Telson if anyone had proposed a recording deal. Telson said no, but told Lazerus there had been a considerable buzz about the show and that David Byrne for one was also interested.

Lazerus reported back to Fagen who then approached Warner Bros about the project. Anything that Fagen suggested received very careful consideration and eventually Fagen, Lazerus and Telson were in Clinton studios producing an album. Fagen and Lazerus's inexperience in dealing with budgets and paying for everything meant that Gary Katz was soon involved, too. Bob Telson had his powerful vision of the show, Lazerus took care of the engineering side and one of Fagen's main contributions – because it wasn't featured in the original show – was to get Hugh McCracken in to do all the slide guitar and harmonica work on the song 'Lift Me Up (Like A Dove)'. The album was recorded quite quickly, but there wasn't a large market for gospel music and even with the Steely Dan connection, Warners were unable to get a handle on the record, which didn't get the exposure it deserved.

Fagen was scheduled to begin recording in early 1984. Gary Katz had called Roger Nichols in California to inform him of the start date and he packed up his family and headed to New York. Eager for a date, when he didn't hear anything further Nichols called Katz back, but was told that the start date had been delayed because Fagen was having problems finishing the songs.

This problem wasn't evident when Fagen was interviewed by Bruce Pollock in *Guitar* magazine in February 1984. Fagen outlined his current working routine: he said he worked mostly in the daytime in a sunny room, spending five or six hours almost every day composing at the piano. Fagen admitted that he had managed to diminish his workaholism and said, "I have six tunes finished and when I get two or three more I'll record. It'll still basically be a personal record like the last one, but I'll be working more with blues material."

Although Fagen was booked into Soundworks in the early summer, the sessions still didn't materialize and this delay eventually went on for nine months before Nichols' patience ran out and he went back to California to work on another project. Fagen finally began recording in 1985 and after Elliot Scheiner had cut four or five basic tracks in New York, Fagen and company went to Jeff Porcaro's home studio in Los Angeles ('The studio that "Africa" built', as the drummer called it) to work on overdubs.

Fagen had given Daniel Lazerus some Howlin' Wolf records and told him that that was how he wanted the snare drum to sound on his album. Fagen had laid down the basslines on synthesizer and among the musicians booked were Rick Marotta and Greg Phillinganes, and bassist Jimmy Haslip was waiting in the wings. Wendel II was being utilized to shift beats around and fly things in and out of choruses and verses, and Fagen was considering doing another standard oldie.

One tune which was cut was called 'Big Noise, New York' which was co-credited to Fagen's then girlfriend Marcelle Clements, who wrote part of the lyric. The tune eventually surfaced seven years later on Jennifer Warnes' Elliot Scheiner-produced album 'The Hunter' and then Fagen's own demo version of the song was released on the CD single of 'Trans-Island Skyway'. Although about five tracks were recorded, after they went back to New York again Fagen decided not to use any of the tunes they had cut.

Greg Phillinganes recorded an album entitled 'Pulse' for Planet records in 1984 and Fagen contributed a tune called 'Lazy Nina'. It was a good song, but the album was produced by Richard Perry and was too keyboard heavy and relied too much on programming. Fagen's song had no bass or guitars; it was basically only drums and synthesizers with background vocals and would have been vastly improved by some "real" instruments. Also on the album was a song called 'Countdown To Love' written by Fagen's old buddies from Jay and The Americans, Kenny Vance and Marty Kupersmith.

✧

Toward the end of 1982 Walter Becker sold up in New York and moved right away from the city to what was for him the most unlikely of locations – the island of Maui in sun-drenched Hawaii. He wanted to escape from the painful memory of his girlfriend's death, get right away from New York and to make a fresh start in a totally new and different environment.

The change of scenery and the easy pace of living turned out to be just what he needed. He cut off his waist length hair, straightened out his drug problem, took up yoga, formed a steady relationship with his yoga teacher and waited for musical inspiration to return.

Becker re-emerged publicly as the producer of Liverpool group China Crisis, gladly pronouncing that "I feel like all my troubles are behind me". He had by then been living in Hawaii for three and a half years and had cleaned himself up physically and mentally, got married and became a father for the first time.

He made no secret of his troubles and admitted that had he not succeeded in making changes, he was sure he would be dead by now. Prior to that making records had been all-consuming: "I'd wake up, have a cup of coffee and head down to the studio. I spent my twenties in smoke-filled rooms with no windows. To suddenly wake up one day living in Hawaii seemed like an invitation to some other kind of life, which I accepted. It was like a new start for me. I learned to enjoy other things. My whole attitude changed and I got into a much better frame of mind.

"Then once I was in that better frame of mind, well, there I was driving in Hawaii in my truck and I started to think 'Gee, I kind of miss those big speakers and leather couches and the lights that dim'. Eventually I got antsy about it, and finally I found something I wanted to do."

During his rethink, one of the things which Becker reconsidered at some length was the unnatural amount of time he and Fagen had spent slaving away in recording studios. "I think that part of what was going on was we just liked to be in recording studios. We were in charge. We felt everything good was there. And our circumstances afforded us the rather rare luxury of just going on ad infinitum until we had something that was such a fucking incredible jewel that we would deign to present it to the public. I thought that was a good thing. But I also think we developed a perfectionist attitude that became more of a problem than a solution."

Now Becker returned to basics and had no such luxury. "Being forced to do the China Crisis record in eight weeks was a tremendous experience for me. You don't have the time or money to be indulgent, so you do things differently. Listening to English records, I can see that they're not so concerned as in America about that tightness of production – they tend to sketch out their musical ideas with bold strokes. After a while that appealed to me. I can see the value of making records with that kind of immediacy. And so I've come to the conclusion that too much repetition in the studio often translates into a loss of musical ideas and that's what's really important. Sometimes you hear people's demos and then you hear the records and most of what you liked about the demo is gone. Also I'd done all that studio stuff before, and once you know how to achieve an effect that way, it's no longer so fascinating."

After Steely Dan's demise, Becker stopped writing songs completely, but as time passed he began to feel his way gradually back into a writing and recording routine. After a few years' enforced break his creative juices began to flow again and stimulate his appetite for the whole routine of recording. "Well, I was very seriously distracted so it helped me make the break. Nothing relieves creative anxiety like unconsciousness. But since this project ('Flaunt The Imperfection') I got myself a little synthesizer and started doodling around on it. I think I might go down and buy myself a drum machine and maybe one of those four-track recorders like all the other kids."

Becker denied that he and Fagen were considering a reunion so soon after they had split up, but did concede that they spoke regularly on the telephone despite bad connections, echo and the time delay. Becker admitted to being surprised by the concept of 'The Nightfly' and at Fagen's choice of 'Ruby Baby' as the cover song of the album.

Bearing in mind the subject of Fagen's 'Nightfly' and his choice of a first production job with a mellow group such as China Crisis, Becker was asked if they tended to give each other an edge. "I think we're probably just getting older. It's hard to maintain that frantic adolescent humour well into your thirties, though we did. But maybe you're right, we did feed off each other in that way, spurred each other on. Now we're getting mellow."

Becker's association with China Crisis came about when they were touring the US to promote their 'Working With Fire And Steel' album. They were having lunch in Warner Bros Burbank offices when they were asked if they had any idea who they wanted to produce their next album. Eddie Lundon jokingly said, "Someone from Steely Dan", but he was actually thinking of someone like Gary Katz or Michael Omartian. Time passed and having forgotten about this off-the-cuff remark, China Crisis eventually got a call from Warner Bros asking them if they would like to work with Walter Becker. The Dan bass player and guitarist had been looking for an act to produce and having been appraised of China Crisis's interest had listened to 'Working With Fire And Steel'. Becker picked out 'Papua' as his personal favourite. It was a song about a nuclear holocaust, subject matter that may have reminded him of Steely Dan's own end of the world sketch, 'King Of The World'.

Becker jokingly explained that another reason he chose China Crisis as his first solo outside production job was that they weren't built around their clothes or their haircuts and that they were primarily interested in enhancing the song. "Plus their lyrics didn't make much immediate sense so, of course, I was drawn to that in a big way. I saw that as pure genius."

Becker also wanted to come back in as a producer with a group who could benefit from his kind of acumen. He felt that some of Garry Daly and Eddie Lundon's songs could indeed benefit from being enriched a little. Becker came to England to work on the album at Parkgate Studio in Sussex and was as nervous as the band themselves. His creative input was soon firing; he was able to contribute to the songs and suggested the synthesizer parts at the end of 'Gift Of Freedom', which were inspired by Miles Davis's 'Kind Of Blue' period. But Becker also admitted that they ran out of time; having reached week seven of the eight-week recording schedule, and time to begin mixing, China Crisis had still to put percussion on the album (the player they had brought in turned out to be terrible, Becker said) so they were left with no option but to almost totally dispense with percussion. Becker himself played some cowbells and they used a drum machine for a tambourine effect. The stripped down sound of the album was through necessity not choice.

In fact, when the Kick Horns arrived at the studio for 'Flaunt', Becker didn't like any of Eddie Lundon's horn arrangements – he said they were all too predictable – and asked each player to play their second instrument, so that instead of the usual two saxes, with a trumpet and a trombone there were some different voicings altogether.

China Crisis were on Warner Bros in America and since it was their idea for Becker to produce the group, bass player 'Gazza' Johnson was justified in expressing his disappointment with the marketing of the album. "Warners just couldn't find a peg to hang the record on," he said. Strangely enough, much more was made of the Steely Dan connection in the UK than in the US. In fact, Warner Bros knew so little about China Crisis that when they first met the group they were expecting a two-piece outfit. They also described China Crisis as a Scottish band in their original publicity promo.

Becker returned home to continue his... "groovy little lifestyle in Hawaii, which I'm now rather attached to. I'm a new daddy, you know, so most of my time is spent burping and changing. Basically you find very healthy, happy people who want to preserve their good mood. At this stage of my life I value that."

It would be hard to imagine more of a contrast between the new Walter Becker and the one of old.

❧

In 1986 while Katz was recording with ex-model Rosie Vela at the Village Recorder, Becker stopped by to say hi and also to play back the China Crisis album to Katz. Fagen was also there – he was playing on Vela's album – and Becker liked what he heard. He ended up hanging out for a few days and one day, while Vela was nervously trying to play keyboards in front of one of her all time heroes, Becker started noodling around with a little Casio keyboard. Vela gestured to Katz to get him plugged in and Becker added a snaky little synth line to a song called 'Tonto'.

Once word got out that Fagen and Becker were playing together again the inevitable Steely Dan reunion rumours began. In December 1985 with typical tabloid exaggeration and wild inaccuracy *The Daily Mirror* – of all newspapers – printed a brief piece saying that Steely Dan had indeed re-formed ("after a bitter power struggle between Becker and Fagen") and were planning a world tour in the following year!

Unbeknownst to either of them, both Becker and Fagen had individually selected 'Interlude' as their favourite tune on Vela's album. Their symbiotic relationship was still intact. After that, Vela and Katz schemed to get Fagen and Becker back together in the studio again. Eventually Fagen ended up playing on seven out of the nine songs and Becker on three.

After one session, Becker and Fagen walked about sixty blocks home together and that night everyone present knew that the musical and personal bond between the two songwriting partners had in no way been severed.

Vela's 'Zazu' came out in 1986 and A&M's marketing department didn't flinch from using Becker and Fagen's names in the publicity blurb. "What brings Steely Dan's Walter Becker and Donald Fagen back into the studio under the production of Gary Katz, after almost five years' absence?" they asked in bold letters on accompanying Vela biographies. The album was very well received despite some natural critical misgivings about a model-turned-singer. But the doubts were unfounded because she was a talented songwriter with a musical and lyrical quirkiness and a damn good singer, too. The first single, 'Magic Smile', received plenty of airplay and did very well in England, cracking the Top Forty to reach number 27 in January 1987.

"Some of her songs are weirder than Donald's in structure," Katz admitted. "Rosie had never made a record before and didn't really have much of an idea about what went into making one. So we spent a lot of time in preproduction. She had numerous variations on a lot of her songs. In one version, a given section would be a certain length, and in another version it would be a different length. We made decisions on exactly how long each section was going to be and began picking musicians for the project."

As with most of Gary Katz's productions, the session musician list was very long, even more so than the Eye To Eye project. Katz was angry that most reviews stressed the Becker and Fagen connection – this despite the fact that 90% of it was done before they set foot in the studio – or the fact that "this is a Steely Dan warm up".

In the aftermath of the Vela LP, Katz was tired of refuting rumours of a Steely Dan reunion and refused to elaborate any further on the reasons why. "When we go in to record, then I'll tell you about the Steely Dan record."

On the other hand, Vela's interviews were riddled with references to Steely Dan. "To people of my generation", she said. "Steely Dan were The Beatles of America". She explained she had been slowly purchasing recording equipment with her modelling fees and storing it in her New York apartment. Her brother, Chat, was a recording engineer so she'd had plenty of good advice. Vela had received classical training on the piano as a child, so this wasn't simply just another example of a model exploiting her beauty for success in the music business. She had now given up all modelling assignments in order to concentrate on her music. A tape containing some of her demos was passed on to Jerry Moss of A&M and he thought 'Fool's Paradise' could be a potential hit single, so he signed her up to do an album.

Soon after that Fagen and Becker resumed writing songs together. Becker would fly to New York for a month and then Fagen would fly to Maui for a similar amount of time. Rosie Vela was now being talked about as the girl who re-formed Steely Dan. However, although they did "write a few good songs", they just as promptly abandoned the idea and left the new compositions in limbo. Becker admitted that they had been working on some tunes together, but also quickly added that they wanted to do it with as little fanfare as possible.

MCA released Steely Dan's first greatest hits CD compilation, 'A Decade Of Steely Dan', in 1985. It was a reasonable cross section of material and included song by song musician listings of some of the early songs which hadn't been available up to that point. But as with previous compilations, the packaging of the CD was terrible; for some inexplicable reason the front cover featured a picture of a crumpled paper bag.

Despite Steely Dan's dissolution and their inactivity, Becker and Fagen's influence in the UK in the Eighties was as great – if not greater – than it had ever been. Up and coming bands like Danny Wilson, Deacon Blue (who took their name from the 'Aja' song), The Kane Gang whose 'Motortown' single was a direct nod to Steely Dan, Roachford, Go West, Curiosity Killed The Cat and Nick Heyward of Haircut 100 all admitted being inspired by the Dan.

As well as the music, there was something else about Steely Dan which impressed the more serious up and coming young pop and jazz musicians of the Eighties. There was an almost complete absence of hype surrounding their career which, in the image-conscious Eighties, appealed very much to those artists and fans to whom the glitziness of the immediate post-punk era was particularly unattractive. Although they were never an 'indie' band – MCA are about as major as you can get – Steely Dan had carried themselves in a manner that befitted most of the acts signed to Rough Trade or any of the up and coming independent labels of the Eighties.

The Dan were much admired for having maintained such a low-profile in contrast to the overblown, often macho, image mongering that infected so many of their Seventies contemporaries. Becker and Fagen had always maintained a dignified distance from the crasser aspects of the record industry, and this attitude – which at one time may have cost them a few record sales – was now rewarded with a genuine respect from fans old and new.

℘

Seemingly having given up on both ideas of another solo album and a Steely Dan record, Fagen now found something else to occupy his time. Unlikely as it may seem for someone so antipathetic towards the press in general, he landed a job as movie and music writer on Rupert Murdoch's *Première* magazine. His first article appeared in August 1987 and in it he wrote about his oft-to-be-discussed writer's block and how a request to write some film music seemed a good idea to get him away from the frustration of his home studio.

His articles appeared at irregular intervals right up until 1991 and during that time he conducted an interview with Ennio Morricone (for which, embarrassingly, his tape recorder failed to work – and Morricone couldn't speak English anyway) and wrote about his admiration for Henry Mancini. Several tongue-in-cheek pieces followed: one about the computer age of music and how if a composer wasn't careful the machines could control him, and another about a fictional German composer named Friedrich 'Fritz' Kreisel which was illustrated with a picture of Fagen with a centre parting dressed up 1920s style.

Fagen was by this time living with Marcelle Clements who later also wrote for *Première*. Clements went on to write a novel entitled *Rock Me* which was published by Simon and Schuster in 1988 and which described the misfortunes of a rock musician with a drug problem who retreats to Hawaii to recuperate. The similarity to Walter

Becker's predicament was uncanny, but Clements ensured she was on firm ground by making the main protagonist of her story a female.

Around the same time Fagen was composing music for a friend in New York. Jane Aaron was an animator whose brother, Peter, had been at Bard College with Fagen and Becker back in the Sixties. In 1985 and 1986 Aaron made two short films, sponsored by the New York Council for Arts, called *Travelling Light* and *Set In Motion*. Both films featured patterns of light moving around a house (her husband featured in the latter film) and also as the title suggests the set itself shifted to Fagen's electronic music. For Fagen it was just a light-hearted pastime with no pressure which might help his "serious" writer's block.

Fagen went into an eight-track recording studio with Aaron to work on the music and played keyboards while responding to the visual images on the videotape. Even though the animation was only two minutes long, Fagen conducted several sessions and constantly rejected material. Jane Aaron was amazed at his dedication to the project: just when she thought it was great and he couldn't improve on the soundtrack, he would add something else or come up with something even better.

Fagen composed a third piece of music in 1989 to another Aaron animation entitled *This Time Around* which Aaron said was "pretty wild". In 1986 Fagen composed an instrumental composition, 'Shades', for the title track of a Yellowjackets album on MCA Records.

After China Crisis in 1985 Walter Becker was interested in producing an even more mellow band, Norwegian duo Fra Lippo Lippi, named after a Robert Browning poem. Working with his old buddy Roger Nichols again, the album 'Light And Shade' was recorded in Los Angeles and was released on the Virgin label in 1987.

In 1987 when China Crisis's record company were looking for someone to produce their follow up to 'Flaunt The Imperfection', several names were tossed into the hat, but the band didn't want to use someone who would go straight for drum machines and samples. After about six weeks waiting for answers, Eddie Lundon said that the least they could do was let Becker hear their demos and ask his opinion.

Becker again loved the songs and the arrangements and was really keen to do the album. Virgin wanted him to return to England to record the album, but Becker didn't want to come back because that would involve a long separation from his girlfriend and baby.

Becker and Nichols had decided on digital recording and suggested a compromise of working in Los Angeles, but Becker was able to negotiate such a low rate for a Maui studio – a three month block booking at George Benson's studio, Lahaina Sound – that when Virgin saw the projected figures they agreed to China Crisis being accommodated in a rented condo on the paradise isle. They worked twelve six-day weeks in Maui and often before each recording session began at around one or two o'clock, Roger Nichols took them down to the beach and taught them to scuba dive. They all qualified as divers whilst recording the album.

Becker was much more relaxed recording 'Diary Of A Hollow Horse' on his home territory than he had been on 'Flaunt The Imperfection'. Also, he knew the Liverpool lads really well by now and they were all comfortable with each other. The album featured some very tasty Becker guitar work. He came up with a lovely solo on 'Sweet Charity In Adoration' which Roger Nichols thought should go on the record, but Becker remained unconvinced and he got Tim "Weekend Knobjob" Weston (who had been an assistant engineer on 'Countdown To Ecstasy') to replace it. Becker also intended to include brass parts on the album, but the arranger couldn't make it and he took this as a sign from God that there was not meant to be brass on the album. Nichols called Jim Horn, with whom he had worked on John Denver records, and they settled for keyboard brass parts. Becker was also credited with being responsible for starting the song 'Stranger By Nature.'

At that point Becker was more concerned with his leisure time and didn't want to go full tilt back into music. Nonetheless, he still liked to get away from Maui for a month or two just to work on short term projects. In contrast, Fagen loathed surfing and swimming and hadn't particularly enjoyed any of his visits to Maui. So when Fagen showed up on the island with his girlfriend he brought chests full of books and records with him because they considered Maui to be a desert island and they had to bring their own culture with them.

Much to Becker and Nichols' disgust, when China Crisis returned to the UK, Virgin didn't think there was an obvious hit single on the album and hired Mike Thorne to do some work on three songs, including what was to become the first single 'Red Letter Day'. Becker and Nichols' stuff was 24-track Sony digital mixes, but Thorne transferred the tracks to analogue and did more overdubs. The single bombed anyway and despite its lush and clear sound, the album singularly failed to show any success.

Six years after the concert itself in Oregon, The Hoops McCann album came out. "I like their 'Green Earrings' and 'Black Cow'," said Fagen, "and I thought 'Babylon Sisters' was really good. What they heard in the structure and chords were things I never thought of. Also, the things they do with harmonics and solos compensate for hearing it without lyrics, which is an equal component in the original recordings.

"A few years before Woody Herman had done an album, with Chick Corea's tunes on one side and ours on the other. And it had mixed results. The more adventurous arrangements were pretty good, but the less adventurous were not so great. But Joe Roccisano took the originals as a starting point and did something different with them. Our things weren't jazz. There wasn't much improvisation and it was too rigidly constructed. But it's a great side effect of our success that it got a lot of people to listen to jazz who ordinarily had no contact with it. People have told me they started listening to jazz after listening to our records, which is nice."

Once again, Fagen and Daniel Lazerus worked on a mix of 'Black Cow' for the album but after spending some time on it and loving the sound of it, they discovered that they had been given the wrong master tape. It was eventually remixed using the correct master tape by Al Schmitt.

In November 1988 Fagen told David Browne in *The Daily News* that he had six tunes finished – two co-written with Walter Becker – and would soon begin recording his follow up to 'The Nightfly'. "When we get back together, we feel very funny," Fagen said. "It was fun to work for a while but... there's something sad about it. We did come up with two songs, but I think that both of us felt at the end that, well, that was another time.

"I have a problem writing songs. Some people may have noticed. I have to be in control. The collaborator has to know that I'll have the final say. I have a very queer idea about what's acceptable."

Fagen was at his lowest ebb when he was interviewed by Stephen Williams at the Brighton Grill on Manhattan's Upper East Side. Finally laying Steely Dan to rest, he told Williams that he found the group's records... "unpleasant to listen to. I wish it wasn't, but the older it is, the more unpleasant. Although 'Gaucho' does reflect its time in an honest way, it's never dishonest. Just sometimes, it seems no good."

Fagen said that they had reunited two years ago, not with the idea of re-forming Steely Dan, but simply... "to see what would happen. We wrote two pretty good songs and then totally just stopped. I might include one or both of them on my album, and Walter will somehow be involved in the production, but not in the performance."

Fagen was asked to compose the soundtrack for *Bright Lights, Big City*, the new Michael J. Fox film by Mark Rosenberg, the co-producer who was also his cousin. Fagen had often mentioned his cynicism about movie music being sublimated to the director's whim, but on this occasion, since he had enjoyed Jay McInerney's novel and felt attracted to a new experience, he agreed to give it a try.

Rosenberg wanted executive music producer Joel Sill to make Fagen feel comfortable with the project. Sill confessed he had never met Fagen but they became acquainted over the phone and his job was to create a framework where Fagen could work at ease. "After he did a couple cues, it was like second nature to him," he said.

Fagen recorded a one verse and one chorus version of Jimmy Reed's 'Bright Lights, Big City' which was eventually dropped from the soundtrack album. Sill said it was... "more of a cue than a record, so we left it off."

Both Sill and Rosenberg had once worked for Warner Bros so it was natural for them to approach the label about releasing the soundtrack album. In addition to this Fagen was contracted to Warner Bros. Toward the end of negotiations, Warner Bros offered them a Prince song, 'Good Love'. The staff at the label had extremely high expectations for the album, anticipating another 'Dirty Dancing'. "It's a great sampling of contemporary music. Basically it's a dance album, but I think it will appeal to a broad demographic base," Sill said. The record company staff began jokingly referring to it as 'Bright Lights, Big Singles.' United Artists were running ads for the film that included just music, which boded well for the album, too.

After the film's release, Fagen said he was not encouraged by it. "I don't think I'd do another," he told friends. He co-wrote the score with Rob Mounsey but told him he couldn't face writing Diane Wiest's death scene – it was simply too traumatic for him.

Fagen co-wrote with Timothy Meher the lyrics to 'Century's End', the song that closed the film and featured a typically Fagen-like stabbing horn arrangement. It was released as a four-track CD single that also featured 'Shanghai Confidential', 'The Goodbye Look' and 'The Nightfly'. The single went absolutely nowhere. A video was made by Fagen's friend, Jane Aaron, but Fagen was conspicuous by his absence once again. Just to keep it in the family, Jane Aaron's brother Peter took the photograph which was used on the cover of the CD single.

'Shanghai Confidential' with its whistling synths and jungle sounds had originally been called 'The Squash Lesson' and had been composed for a dance troupe. Steve Khan played guitar on the cut, but when he heard the final mix he was very disappointed. "That wasn't the sound we had when I left the studio. When a Telecaster gets placed that far back in the mix it thins out," he said.

Of all people, Mel Torme covered two Fagen songs, 'Walk Between Raindrops' and 'The Goodbye Look' on his 1988 album 'Reunion' with the Marty Paich Dek-tette. Fagen wasn't surprised. "He's always looking for new songs to sing and I guess while checking out material he discovered my tunes," he said. "I think they were done really well."

In December 1988 Fagen made an extremely rare TV appearance playing piano behind Patti Austin on a show called *Sunday Night* which was introduced by Jools Holland and David Sanborn. Each week the show was given over to a different personality. This particular week was producer Tommy Lipuma's idea and the band included Hiram Bullock, Omar Hakim, Marcus Miller and Fagen playing keyboards on three or four songs before they closed the show with Patti Austin singing a version of Fagen's 'IGY'.

Afterwards Fagen said his appearance was purely an experiment. "I really like having a certain amount of privacy. I'm very nervous about going on television, 'cause television is what makes you famous. I did it actually to see how nervous I'd be on television. I wasn't that bad." However, when his turn came to be introduced, Fagen looked distinctly uncomfortable.

Meanwhile, hard on the heels of his China Crisis production, Walter Becker produced Rickie Lee Jones's 1989 album, 'Flying Cowboys'. "It was a real tough school year," he said. "One thing I've learned is that everybody works in a different way and has a different atmosphere that they like to create for themselves. Rickie is as spontaneous as she can be with everything that she does – which is exciting to see when things work. For somebody who has the job of trying to plan things out, it keeps you guessing. But it was a delightful experience for me."

Becker played synthesizer on 'Satellites', bass on the title song and was even given a co-writing credit on the opening tune of the album, 'The Horses'. There was a vivid contrast between Jones' stark records and the polished sheen of Steely Dan's music, and Becker admitted that this had bothered her beforehand. "That was something we talked about from the outset. The Steely Dan stuff that I used to be involved with, we tried to make as slick as we possibly could, because some of the other elements were so subversive that they needed to be sugarcoated or disguised. And Rickie, of course, is quite different from that. The presentation is very honest and open and straightforward."

Although the partnership had cautious beginnings, it worked out very well in the end. Rickie Lee Jones admitted that she was somewhat fearful of working with Becker as her producer and described Steely Dan records as "boy music". She was intimidated by Steely Dan's unsmiling publicity shots and thought Becker was probably just an unpleasant person. She was also worried that Becker would encourage her to adopt the well documented Steely Dan approach of take after take. She wanted simplicity and a "starkness of presentation" but once she had spoken to Becker about the approach to the record, she realized that he had rethought his methods and was prepared to work to her *modus operandi.*

Becker said that the resulting album, 'Flying Cowboys', contained songs that were barely more than cleaned up original guitar and voice demos which she had recorded herself at home. Becker felt that those demos contained such spirit and creative spark that it was virtually impossible to better them. The song 'Rodeo Girl' was Jones' demo and 'Ghost Train' was also her demo, with a few added sampled overdubs.

ഏ

Fagen, meanwhile, was taking his first very tentative steps on the road to what he termed "a new career". Fagen's then girlfriend, Libby Titus (who had once been married to Levon Helm from The Band), was producing some low key jazz and cabaret shows in and around New York and one night in 1989, after he had attended as a spectator a couple of times, she persuaded Fagen to join Dr John and Carly Simon on stage at a small but fashionable restaurant/club on the Upper East Side of New York called Elaine's. They sang 'Such A Night', a hit for Johnnie Ray before Elvis Presley took the song into the US charts in 1964. Fagen enjoyed the experience and Dr John was delighted, too. He told *Rolling Stone* that Fagen was... " a hero of mine. When he jams he's something else."

Fagen evidently had fun doing the show at Elaine's and he began working on an idea of presenting an evening of great Sixties' soul songs – and some personal favourites. Fagen was a fan of songwriters Bert Berns and Jerry Ragavoy and he decided to call the event 'New York Soul'. Fagen was on a crusade. "Those guys and the records they made with Solomon Burke and Garnett Mimms were responsible for a New York soul sound that was never really recognised," he told his radio audience with the kind of enthusiasm he'd never have been able to muster for anything associated with Steely Dan.

The shows were booked in for September 1989 at the Lone Star Roadhouse on 52nd St., and the week before Fagen went on Pat St John's lunchtime WNEW-FM programme to promote them. The two-show evening was completely sold out long before the date and was produced by Libby Titus. The buzz was out on the streets of New York – Donald Fagen was about to break his fifteen year absence from the stage.

Berns and Ragavoy were responsible for writing some classic soul songs in the Sixties, often under pseudonyms such as Norman Meade and Norman Russell. Their catalogue included such classics as 'Time Is On My Side', 'Twist And Shout', 'Piece Of My Heart' and 'Everybody Needs Somebody To Love', some of which were written together and some separately. They were also producers, but their partnership was curtailed when Bert Berns died of a heart attack on New Year's Eve 1967. But Ragavoy turned out to attend the tribute and thank Fagen for his efforts.

Fagen had called Paul Griffin and, working together at Fagen's apartment, they wrote between thirty and forty arrangements of soul and rhythm and blues standards for the succession of gigs which were planned.

Fagen, who emceed the shows, credited Libby Titus with badgering him into getting back on stage. The band consisted of Jerry Jermott on bass, George Naha on guitar, drummer Joe Ascione and Paul Griffin (also the musical director) and Dr John on keyboards. The horn section consisted of David 'Fathead' Newman, Alan Rubin and Lou Marini and vocals were shared between Phoebe Snow, Jeff Young, Jeveeta Steele (from the Gospel at Colonus), singer, harmonica and violin player Mindy Jostyn, and Griffin. Dr John sang 'Cry To Me' and 'Look At Granny Run Run'.

Fagen took to the stage carrying a strange little instrument called a melodica, a toy instrument that was a cross between an oversized harmonica and a small piano. "I'd been looking around for a solo instrument I could play where I could be mobile, so for a while I was playing one of those keyboards you strap around your neck. It was all right, [but] I wanted something that sounded more natural," he said.

The show was introduced by Pat St John and the set opened with a loose version of 'Time Is On My Side'. Other songs included 'Stop!', 'Piece Of My Heart', 'Twist And Shout', 'Cry Baby' and a rousing version of 'Everybody Needs Somebody To Love' by Paul Griffin. The choice of material ensured the gigs were rapturously received, but it was Fagen's presence which drove the crowd wild. As the show progressed, some members of the audience became agitated, yelling and screaming for a variety of Steely Dan songs but Fagen steadfastly refused to perform any of his own material, let alone sing any. His irritation at the incessant demands for Steely Dan songs was apparent and he was obliged to tell the audience that it had been advertised as a soul show and they should not expect anything else. The show closed with a surprise appearance by the Brigati Brothers from The Rascals, who were joined by everyone on the stage for a version of 'Good Lovin'.

After the commotion at the September show Fagen made it quite clear that there was no prospect of a Steely Dan reunion. In November he told *New York* magazine: "Nobody should expect us to do a reunion concert. It would be ridiculous. It used to be, if I heard 'Rikki Don't Lose That Number' I would walk out of a restaurant. Say you were 41 and they put a picture of you from 1972, blown up, on a Broadway stage. There was a narrative of what you thought, how you acted. You'd remember how strange a time it was. Out of the context of time, it seems funny. Or tragic." However, he did concede that Becker may play at one of the forthcoming Lone Star shows.

The September shows proved to be such a success that in November 1989 Fagen returned to the Lone Star for a 'Thanksgiving Soul Party', but by this time musical director Paul Griffin had mysteriously departed. Very soon the only remaining member of the original New York Soul Band would be the Night Tripper himself, Dr John.

This time Fagen publicised the event with an interview with KROQ in New York and stressed several times that it was not a Steely Dan concert and that he was undecided as to whether he would be singing or not. More significantly, during this interview he announced that... "there *is* no more Steely Dan". Speaking as if he was never a part of the ensemble in the first place, Fagen said emphatically, "They're gone". He added that his solo album would be out in 1990 and that he talked to Becker frequently on the 'phone and they were considering other projects for potential production work.

With the soul shows Fagen had tested the water and regained confidence as far as his singing was concerned. "I think for my psychological profile it's a good idea that I sing. I owe it to people who want to hear me sing. On the other hand, I'd like to hear what I sound like."

At the Thanksgiving Soul party Fagen *did* indeed sing, but he again avoided Steely Dan material and chose instead a version of Kenny Gamble and Leon Huff's 'Drowning In The Sea of Love', a Top Twenty US hit for Joe Simon in early 1972.

Amid all the talk about a second Fagen solo album, Becker gave interviews in which he admitted that his appetite for recording an album of his own had been whetted. "Well, maybe [there'll be a Walter Becker solo album]. If Walter Becker could sing a little better, there probably would have been one already. I'm beginning to realise that I don't have the luxury of sitting around wishing I was a better singer than I am, so I'm thinking about doing something. Either I have to accommodate myself to the equipment I have or find better equipment. But I'd like there to be a Walter Becker record now, which I never really thought about before. I think working with Rickie has influenced me. I see how much fun she had doing this and I want to do it too." Becker was honest enough to admit that he had no preconceived notions about how his album would sound and admitted that he wouldn't know until the record was finished. Surprisingly, for such a publicity shy and modest man, who wasn't one to dwell on trivialities, interviewers noted that Becker had press clippings tacked up on his LA office wall and he even admitted that he liked to see his name in print.

On April 4, 1990, the New York Rock and Soul Revue moved into the big time with a concert at the Beacon Theater on Manhattan's West Side. By now the line up had been expanded to feature Fagen, his old Steely Dan buddy Michael McDonald, Patti Austin and Phoebe Snow backed by Jeff Young and his band Curious George, an R&B outfit featuring Sam Butler on rhythm guitar and Drew Zingg on lead. The format for the show was a round robin with everyone on stage all the time. As well as the soul tunes such as 'Shaky Ground', 'Smoke Gets In Your Eyes', 'Soothe Me' and 'At Last', each performer also sang some of their best known work. Michael McDonald sang 'Minute By Minute', Phoebe Snow did 'Poetry Man' and Fagen opened the show with 'Black Friday' and 'IGY' and closed it with 'Pretzel Logic'. Fagen introduced the song as "'Pretzel Logic'... it's a funny name, but it's the blues". Just as they had done on the 1974 Steely Dan tour, Fagen and McDonald shared vocals, with McDonald singing the lines "I stepped up on the platform/The man gave me the news."

Performing Steely Dan material had its drawbacks. It was not going to be easy to persuade the audience that he wasn't there to sing solely Steely Dan tunes. "I guess some people think I owe it to fans to do Steely Dan songs. What I really owe to them is to be honest about what I want to do and to show some evolution. And occasionally take some old things and rework them. But as far as owing anybody a nostalgia show, I don't feel that's my responsibility.

"When we first started doing the songwriter oriented shows, there was a section of the audience that was obviously enraged that I wasn't doing my own material, so rather than make a big deal about it, or be snobbish about it, I started doing a couple of songs. And it turned out to be oddly enough, not a bad mix. Since I grew up with that sort of music, and it was an influence on me, it all flowed together pretty well. In a way it's a tribute to the producers and writers and singers who first invented this music. I hope there's some spirit there that the singers are really connected to the songs. To me (the key element is) just a love of the music, and a desire to get together and play without any sequencers or anything that encumbers live playing."

Throughout May and June 1990 Fagen made various unannounced appearances at New York clubs, the most regular being Tuesday nights at Hades with Jimmy Vivino's Little Big Band. The Little Big Band was a ten-piece band which included some of the best musicians and singers available in New York: Jeff Young on organ and vocals, Catherine Russell on vocals, Vivino himself on vocals, Harvey Brooks (a veteran of Electric Flag and sessions with Bob Dylan, The Doors and Jimi Hendrix) on bass, and three or four horn players, including Vivino's brother Jerry. The band were in it for love since there was certainly no money to be made for an unknown ten-piece outfit playing New York clubs. The Little Big Band opened at Hades to a tiny audience and Jeff Young suggested to Fagen that as they were playing only a couple blocks from his apartment he might like to take a stroll over to the club and check them out.

The gigs were poorly attended and one night Vivino noticed Fagen sitting by himself at a table in the corner. They met up, talked, and one night Fagen joined them on stage to play organ on a couple songs. Vivino had no idea when Fagen would show up, but his visits became gradually more regular, though he didn't sing, and eventually he and Vivino began discussing potential soul and rhythm and blues cover versions and incorporating them into The Little Big Band's set.

Fagen showed no signs of nervousness at these Tuesday night get togethers with the Little Big Band at Hades, even though a barely adequate fifteen minutes' rehearsal was set aside for each song and Fagen showed up for only the second of two days' rehearsal, anyway. Often, on the day of the gig, there would be a frantic scramble as the musicians called each other on the telephone to find out which songs were on the set list and whether they knew their parts. As Fagen became more comfortable with the band, he participated more fully and started singing, initially soul covers and eventually the occasional Steely Dan chestnut.

In May, when Becker was staying in New York, they both showed up at Hades and jammed with the Little Big Band – Becker played guitar alongside Jimmy Vivino, and Fagen shared vocals with Phoebe Snow on '634-5789' and 'In The Midnight Hour', but no Steely Dan material was aired. Fagen's choice of which songs he would sing depended on whether or not he was comfortable with the lyrics. On one occasion a month later, ever mindful of his long performing hiatus (and with a sense of humour about it) Fagen changed the 'Black Friday' lyric "Gonna let the world pass by me" to "Gonna let the years pass by me."

❧

Fagen had decided to produce his second solo album himself, but just before he was about to begin recording he suddenly got cold feet about the prospect of going into a studio without his former partner. Becker was duly installed as producer of the record. The sessions began on his long-awaited follow-up to 'The Nightfly' in May 1990 at the Hit Factory on West 54th St. Both parties were at pains to stress beforehand that it was not a Steely Dan album. Roger Nichols was still busy finishing another project and Fagen really was eager to get under way – he couldn't wait any longer so he hired another engineer, Tony Volante, to start work on the sessions. In his regular article in *EQ* magazine Nichols joked that that was Fagen's first mistake.

Becker refused to name any specific studio musicians involved with the project and described Fagen's recent material as having a soulful flavour with "somewhat greater harmonic and lyrical complexity [than traditional R&B]. It's been delightful. I always have a great time working with Donald. We enjoy each other's company, and over the years we've developed our own little corner of the marketplace where we set up our tent. Even if we haven't been together or talked a lot, we immediately have a rapport and fall right back into a routine."

Fagen continued with his occasional live appearances between recording. The sessions were divided between New York – where they worked on rhythm guitars, drums, horn parts, background vocals and anything that required a pool of musicians – and Becker's home studio in Maui where they recorded Becker's bass, guitar solos and Fagen's keyboard playing and vocals. They quickly fell into a pattern: work for between four and six weeks in New York, take a month off, then work for a similar period in Maui. Their days, weeks and months of endless touring was definitely a thing of the past now.

In typical jocular manner Becker explained why he preferred producing to the hard slog of writing and recording. "All the hard work is really done, and you just book into some swank recording studio, find a comfortable chair, order some food and start recording."

Fagen had made models of each tune in his home studio and came into the studio with a sequence of the tune consisting of drum samples, DX bass and DX-7 rhythm parts. These were to be used as a strict guide to the live musicians. Despite this, Fagen had an aversion to hearing drum machines and sampling on actual records. "I'm insulted when I hear something and I know that for the drum track and maybe a lot of the other instruments, someone just pushed a button and that's what I'm hearing. I feel really manipulated by it." And yet on his album Becker, Fagen and Nichols spent weeks (possibly months) just moving drum sounds around on a track, seeking absolutely perfect time.

In one of his *EQ* pieces Roger Nichols attempted to outline the remarkable precision which Fagen requires for a drum track on his songs. Fagen and Nichols dealt in milliseconds and might spend a month trying to create the perfect drum track by means of editing and piecing together bits of live drums played by Chris Parker. It prompted several letters of disbelief as to how Fagen could be that picky. In fact, in the same amount of time that it took to record drums and piano on two tunes for Fagen, Nichols and Becker had recorded ten hours of music on eleven jazz albums for Triloka and the new-age Windham Hill Records and half of those records were already in the stores. Mixing was also a veritable cakewalk compared to Fagen's schedule: their rate was closer to ten tunes a day instead of ten days per tune. When he wasn't working on Fagen's album, Becker produced several jazz albums for Triloka and Windham Hill with Roger Nichols at the controls. The artists included Leeann Ledgerwood, Andy Laverne, Jeff Beal, Bob Sheppard and Jeremy Steig.

Becker explained the care and attention which went into Fagen's tracks. "One track at a time kind of procedure, stretched out in time, where every track is very finely honed to fit with what's already there, and then each successive layer has the same level of scrutiny and so on. With the things we've been doing with the jazz artists, basically everybody's playing at the once and we're going more for the overall quality of the performance, the main artists' solos probably a primary concern, so if there are little glitches here and there or flaws, that's part of it.

"My approach to these things is that, when you're working for a very condensed period of time in a studio, there's only so much room for a producer to add his two cents to what's going on. For the most part, I just try to facilitate what the artists want to do. It's really their time up at bat, and Roger is really helpful in that way, too."

By a strange coincidence, within a month of Becker and Fagen resuming their working partnership, original Steely Dan drummer Jim Hodder was found dead in the swimming pool at his Point Arena, California, home. Hodder had drowned while his blood alcohol level was more than three times the legal limit for driving in California. After being found by a friend on a Monday afternoon, Hodder was put on a life support machine but was pronounced dead very early on Tuesday morning at the Ukiah Medical Center.

One stormy evening at Hades in October 1990, Fagen jammed with the Little Big Band and former Jimi Hendrix Experience bass player Noel Redding and Paul (*Late Night With David Letterman*) Shaffer. While Redding and Shaffer sat at the front before taking the stage, Fagen jokingly asked for some lighter fluid to set his melodica on fire and launched into 'Purple Haze'. Shaffer took over lead vocals and Fagen played his "burning" melodica.

The same month Fagen headlined at the Long Island Evian Music Festival in Southampton, playing with most of the musicians from the Beacon show and Curious George. Bill Withers was also due to appear, but was forced to cancel at the last minute. They played several classic soul songs including 'Knock On Wood', Sam Cooke's 'Soothe Me' and Sam and Dave's 'You Got Me Hummin', and 'Piece of My Heart' before Fagen sang 'Black Friday', 'Pretzel Logic' and 'Chain Lightning'. The surprise of the evening was the inclusion of 'Home At Last', which he sang live for the first time ever. Fagen even harked back to the halcyon days of Jerome Aniton by introducing himself as Stevie Dan.

Fagen's semi-regular appearance at Hades had increased the size of the audience to a dangerous level so it was unfortunate that once he'd become comfortable with the place, the New York Fire Department should take it on themselves to close the place down. Due to insufficient fire exits, the music licence they issued permitted only three people on the stage at any one time. When the Little Big Band played this limit was exceeded by at least four fold.

After Hades was closed, Vivino took his band to a comedy club called Catch A Rising Star on the Upper East Side which was looking to add music to a schedule that normally comprised up and coming comics. It quickly became obvious that Rising Star wasn't going to work out so Vivino hit the road again and moved to The China Club on 75th and Broadway where eventually Fagen would première a live version of 'Green Flower Street'.

In November, 1990, Walter Becker called Chris Parker who had been on the road with Bob Dylan solidly for eight months. They flew him out to Maui, put him up in a house and each morning picked him up in Walter Becker's truck while listening to Sonny Rollins on the way to the studio. It was a completely different vibe to working in New York – considerably more relaxed, due to the studio being miles from anywhere and only the three of them plus Roger Nichols present.They spent ten days working just on drum sounds and drum tracks at Becker's studio – Hyperbolic Sound – and Parker enjoyed the experience immensely. Becker's studio was housed in two separate buildings with the musicians visible to Becker, Fagen and Nichols in the control room via a video link.

He was in Maui for Thanksgiving Day and as usual they worked all day, but when Parker suggested they go out to dinner together, Becker said, "I'll give you Thanksgiving Day" and offered him some Oscar Mayer smoked turkey sandwiches.

At the Hit Factory Chris Parker played his own drums, but on Maui, Becker and Fagen had a Gretsch kit already set up in the studio provided by Paul Marzetti. Parker played on 'Tomorrow's Girls' but the song was still in its infancy and had a different groove – "a Sly Stone kinda groove" according to Parker – and Fagen had not yet come up with the intro to the song as it finally appeared. They were also uncertain as to who should play bass and it became a running joke that whoever was finally chosen had to have a weird name – Lincoln Schleifer, Zev Katz or Teaker Barfield. Just about the only person not mentioned was Walter Becker himself and Chris Parker said he would have played differently had he known that Becker was going to end up playing all the basslines on the album.

Parker said that Becker and Fagen wanted his drum heads as tight as they could possibly go. For the song 'On The Dunes' Becker came into the studio and fixed some mutes to Parker's drums. The drum break in 'On The Dunes' was not planned, but Parker was really into the tune and just kept playing. They didn't ask him to stop so he continued, assuming that they must like what he was doing. In fact, Parker reckons the take that made the record is one on which Fagen played live Rhodes in the control room, while he played drums separately in the studio. They also altered the drum sounds on the tracks he played on after he had left, making them much crisper and drier from the way they had sounded before.

In March 1991 Fagen took the New York Rock and Soul Revue back to the Beacon Theater and both the Friday and Saturday night shows were recorded for a live album. The line-up now included Michael McDonald, Phoebe Snow, Boz Scaggs and 67-year-old Charles Brown. For the subsequent live album most of the performances were taken from the Saturday night performance and the sequencing was juggled around.

The show opened with Fagen and Jeff Young and The Youngsters performing an instrumental version of 'Madison Time', quickly followed by Michael McDonald and Phoebe Snow's rousing version of Eddie Floyd's Stax standard 'Knock On Wood'. From there each performer stepped up to the microphone intermittently, with Fagen singing 'Home At Last', 'Black Friday', 'Chain Lightning' and 'Pretzel Logic'. Michael McDonald did his own 'Minute by Minute' and 'Little Darling' and Jackie Wilson's vocally challenging 'Lonely Teardrops'; Phoebe Snow covered The Temptations' 'Shakey Ground' and Etta James' 'At Last'; Boz Scaggs sang Joe Simon's 'Drowning In A Sea of Love'; Eddie and David Brigati of The Rascals sang 'Groovin'' and Charles Brown played 'Quicksand', 'Joyce's Boogie' and 'Driftin' Blues', a song he wrote when he was just twelve years old. The full cast joined together on The Rascals' 'People Got To Be Free' before Fagen and Mike McDonald encored with 'Pretzel Logic'. In Fagen's liner notes for the album, he wrote that at Steely Dan shows back in the Seventies the audience reaction to McDonald's singing made him wonder what he was doing up front, but his favourite part of those shows, he added, was when McDonald sang the line about the shoes. A true to the original live version of 'Pretzel Logic' was released as a single, all to no avail.

Becker was due back in New York in May 1991 to continue work on Fagen's album which they hoped to finish by September. In the spring of that year Fagen and Gary Katz's own studio, which they had decided to call River Sound, because of its views over the East River and the Triboro bridge, had opened. It was designed by Frank Comitali and fitted with the old console from Motown's Hitsville Studios in Los Angeles. The studio manager, Todd Alan, warned Fagen that it was a difficult time to be in the studio business, but Fagen said they had only one room to fill and was confident that the project would be a success. "The studio is built for music," he said. "No-one's going to make any videos here or commercials." Fagen left the choice of equipment to Wayne Yurgelun, Gary Katz and Roger Nichols.

On May 9, 1991, Fagen appeared at the Bottom Line in a show entitled 'Five Songwriters Sitting Around Singing'. In an intimate setting, Fagen played piano and was joined by Al Kooper (Korg M1), Dan Penn (acoustic guitar), Spooner Oldham (keyboards) and Gary Nicholson (acoustic guitar). The show was introduced by Vin Scelsa of WXRQ-FM who interviewed the songwriters in turn about their songs. Each writer was also asked to select a couple of their favourites and explore the ways in which they came up with the music and lyrics. Fagen selected 'Black Friday' and 'Green Flower Street' and wound up his segment with 'Home At Last', for which Jimmy Vivino joined the band on acoustic guitar.

Fagen told the audience he played the piano like "a giant guitar with a few notes thrown in" and acknowledged that "a lot of the Steely Dan attitude was Walter's".

Towards the end of the show, each songwriter was asked to perform a song which they wished they'd written and Fagen didn't hesitate in choosing Bacharach and David's 'In The Land Of Make Believe.'

In July 1991 Fagen and the Little Big Band played a concert at the Bearsville Theater in Woodstock, which acted as a showcase for various members of the band to demonstrate their talents before their peers in the upstate New York music community. The week before the show Fagen and Vivino's band played a dress rehearsal at The China Club and Fagen introduced another two "new" songs into the set, 'Josie' and 'Green Earrings'. They also rehearsed 'Sign In Stranger' and 'Deacon Blues' but due to the restrictions on rehearsal time, they were never perfected. "Maybe we're trying to be a little too ambitious," Fagen commented.

By the time the Woodstock gig came around, however, they had managed to fit in some more rehearsal time on 'Deacon Blues' and the song was premièred there. Evidently Fagen hadn't found time to relearn the lyrics, since they were taped to his piano. During the Saturday night encore, the band was joined on stage by Cyndi Lauper and two members of The Hooters.

October 1991 saw the release of yet another Steely Dan compilation, the compact disc 'Gold Expanded Edition' which once again included the rip-roaring live version of 'Bodhisattva' once again a remixed version of 'Century's End', and two songs making their first appearance on CD, 'True Companion' and 'Here At The Western World'.

Fagen spent the entire month of February 1992 in Maui working on his album. But one wonders what progress was made in such a small amount of time. Even Roger Nichols was expressing doubts. In *EQ* he wrote that the level of acceptance that had been set for the project was so high that it involved tempos having decimal points, microseconds replaced milliseconds and a typical Fagen comment on the groove of a track was: "It felt pretty good on that beat right there." Nichols joked about going to his stationery store to buy a calendar planner but found to his dismay that they didn't manufacture "The Rest Of Your Life At A Glance" which he thought would be needed before the album was finished.

Becker was also preparing to embark upon his own solo album with Fagen as producer. Fagen told *Rolling Stone*: "I've heard some stuff that was just great. He's a totally original person, and the songs really express his personality. It's a kind of pop music, but very funny. It's really smart and witty, and I think it will do very well."

In a *Musician* interview in June 1991, Becker said "I'm kind of tired of the record making methods I'm typically known for. It takes too long. I'm into more of the immediate gratification of capturing everybody in the room playing together. You know, the fear is that something is not gonna work, or one of the musicians is not going to be up to snuff or something, but that hasn't happened yet. It's organic and fun. The nice thing about working this way is by the time you've finished something you're not sick of it; you haven't heard it thousands and thousands of times."

Asked if his singing was the primary obstruction to a solo album, Becker replied:

"And laziness and sloth and lethargy, considerations like that. But I am trying to write with that in mind now, and finally realised I might as well just do it. I have some instrumentals, some songs that are pretty firmly rooted in the disco/jazz/spacefunk/ Muzak vein. Hopefully at some point in the next six months or year I'll have enough tunes and an idea about how to go about doing it."

The live album of the Beacon Theater show was released in November 1991. Fagen's versions of 'Black Friday' and 'Home At Last' didn't even make the record, but that was primarily due to time limitation. Fagen and Elliot Scheiner rejigged the order of the songs to make it flow better and it charted briefly in the US Top 200.

Libby Titus was again promoting shows at the Lone Star Roadhouse under the banner 'New York Nights' in which a diverse group of jazz, blues and rock performers guested with the Little Big Band and Fagen to play their music in a casual and low key setting. Among the artists who appeared were Dion DiMucci, Curtis Stigers, Bob Dorough, Annie Ross, Gary Busey and Little Jimmy Scott.

For the October 23 show it was strongly rumoured that both Fagen and Becker would be there. A queue started forming in the late afternoon fully five hours before the show was due to start. Fagen opened the show with 'Green Earrings' and though Becker's guitar wasn't on stage, the atmosphere was still electric. Roger Nichols was spotted in the club and as Fagen swung into 'Deacon Blues' Becker was seen in the upstairs balcony area. Rick Danko was guesting with the band. Jimmy Vivino took the microphone and asked Becker to come up and play. The crowd went crazy, but Becker shook his head and hid his face beneath his sweater in mock horror. Eventually Becker relented, made his way to the stage and, using one of Vivino's spare guitars, played the solo on 'Josie'. He left the stage only to return later to solo on 'Chain Lightning' and 'Black Friday'.

℘

In January 1992, amid much embarassment, it was revealed that MCA had been using inferior analogue master tapes in the manufacture of all seven Steely Dan studio albums. The original run of CD releases in 1985 was made from the correct digital masters, but subsequent pressings were made from the inferior analogue ones. Roger Nichols said that the analogue tapes were in terrible shape and had poor fidelity due to poor storage. Nichols had transferred them to digital in 1981 in anticipation of the demand for CD reissues.

MCA admitted the error, but vice president Andy McKaie defended the engineers' error by explaining that there were various new formats on trial when Steely Dan had remastered their tapes and the oversized Scotch reels which they had chosen lost out. Consequently, when the engineers came to remaster the second run they could not be bothered to locate the machines and reverted to using the inferior analogue copies again. McKaie also pointed out that MCA had not had a single complaint about the quality of the faulty CDs. He promised that in future they would be remastering the CDs from the correct tapes and reissuing them two at a time beginning in early 1992 with a "digitally remastered" sticker affixed to them. MCA had even provided Mobile Fidelity – who manufactured high quality gold-plated CDs and which sold for twice the price of ordinary CDs – with the wrong tapes. There was really no excuse for such carelessness and Roger Nichols was so outraged that he threatened to quit the music business.

Immediately after the record company fiasco, MCA requested Becker and Fagen to look through their old tapes in search of unreleased material for a box set, but they found nothing which they were entirely happy with and the idea was rapidly shelved. "There was nothing too significant," Becker said. "We used to throw away a lot of things because we didn't think they had it. And don't forget this was at a time when a lot of people thought that if a song had lyrics, it was finished." Although both agreed that they would continue to work together they said Steely Dan was dead; Becker even said that the collaboration would be easier to call under "any other rubric".

Despite Fagen's statement that "The idea of a twenty-five song show frightens me" only a few months earlier, the rumours were confirmed that Fagen and Becker were to participate in a three-week twelve-date tour in August 1992 under the name of the New York Rock and Soul Revue. Chuck Jackson was added to the line up alongside stalwarts Michael McDonald, Phoebe Snow and Boz Scaggs. Rehearsals for the tour took place at SIR Studios in New York from August 4 through August 12.

The tour was basically an extension of the Beacon shows in 1991, with the band comprising sixteen pieces. Harvey Brooks had replaced Lincoln Schleifer on bass, Leroy Clouden replaced Denny McDermott on drums and Chuck Jackson had replaced Charles Brown. The set list was expanded to three hours and almost thirty songs: 'Green Earrings', 'Josie', 'Deacon Blues' and 'My Old School' had now been added to the Beacon show set list. But Donald Fagen admitted submitting to pressure: "There was a large vocal minority in the audience that was very insistent about hearing some of those Steely Dan tunes. I was very reluctant to start singing those tunes, but I realised that if I wanted to be involved in the thing, I'd have to make a compromise. After a while I started to enjoy singing them and reinterpreting them." Then Fagen added a warning to that vocal minority for the upcoming gigs: "If they keep making trouble after that, we'll just have them executed." The tour opened at the Riverport Amphitheater in Michael McDonald's home town, St Louis, on August 14 and ended in Detroit on August 30.

The format was the same with each artist performing a mixture of their own material and/or classic soul covers. After publicly expressing his doubts about his vocal abilities, Walter Becker sang an adequate version of Paul Butterfield's 'Mary, Mary'. Fagen prefaced the song with the wry comment, "The Monkees recorded this, but we'll do it anyway."

The tour proved to be extremely popular – not all the shows in the midwest were sold out, but most of the east coast shows were. The opportunity for a lot of younger Steely Dan fans to witness these Becker and Fagen songs live for the first time was too tempting to pass up. Each one was received rapturously, but the emotional high point each night came when a gutwrenching 'Deacon Blues' – which featured a violin solo from Mindy Jostyn – was followed by the hearty and uplifting 'My Old School'.

Steely Dan had fans in very high places. During the 1992 US election campaign Democrat Bill Clinton used music from the Seventies in his rallies across the country. The principal song featured was Fleetwod Mac's 'Don't Stop', but second in line was Steely Dan's 'Reelin' In The Years'. Clinton played the song immediately before 'America The Beautiful' at his Arkansas victory speech.

While Becker and Fagen were in the midst of rehearsals for the Rock and Soul Revue tour, drummer Jeff Porcaro died of a heart attack in Los Angeles as a result of accidentally inhaling pesticide with which he was spraying roses in his garden. Porcaro was not just a widely admired drummer but an enormously likeable man. Gary Katz acted as one of the pall-bearers at the funeral and four songs by Porcaro's two favourite artists were played during the service: Steely Dan's 'Home At last', 'Deacon Blues' and 'Third World Man' (none of which Porcaro played on) and Jimi Hendrix's 'The Wind Cries Mary'. Eulogies were spoken by Gary Katz and Jim Keltner, and Katz read from a letter from Becker and Fagen describing the sense of fun he always inspired in the studio.

A tribute concert was held for Porcaro at the Universal Amphitheater in Los Angeles in December 1992 with the proceeds to be given to a trust fund for his three children. Fagen appeared along with Don Henley, Michael McDonald, David Crosby and Eddie Van Halen. Backed by Toto (with Simon Phillips on drums) each performer sang a couple of their best known compositions. Fagen chose 'Chain Lightning' and 'Josie' and Denny Dias, who had introduced Porcaro to Becker and Fagen and was a very good friend of the drummer's, played guitar. Boz Scaggs played 'Lowdown' and 'Lido Shuffle', Don Henley performed 'Dirty Laundry' and 'You Better Hang Up', Michael McDonald did 'I Keep Forgettin'' and 'Takin' It To The Streets' with David Crosby singing background vocals. George Harrison joined in the big finale when everyone sang a grandstand version of 'With A Little Help From My Friends'.

In 1992 Fagen had a song featured in a film written by David Mamet based on his play *Glengarry Glen Ross*, which dealt with greedy real estate agents. Fagen wrote a song especially for Lou Marini of The Joe Roccisano Orchestra entitled 'Blue Lou'.

With Becker recording his material much faster than Fagen and projected release dates of April 1993 for Fagen's album and midsummer for Becker's, there were strong rumours that they would combine for a Steely Dan tour to promote their respective solo albums and play some of their old favourites. Within months Fagen went from vehemently denying any possibility of a reunion tour to conceding that perhaps it *could* happen.

This time the rumours became reality. Becker and Fagen would blow the dust off Steely Dan and take her on the road again after a mind-numbing nineteen years.

❧

C'mon Snakehips

'Kamakiriad', Donald Fagen's long-awaited follow-up to 'The Nightfly', was finally released in May 1993, fully ten and a half years later. It was the first Steely Dan or Fagen album on which Gary Katz had no direct production involvement – primarily because Fagen was able to record detailed demos in his home studio and Katz was therefore "automated out of a job". Instead, it was produced by Walter Becker who Fagen felt was best suited to assess his vocal performances and was as familiar as anybody with his working methods.

"It's just more fun to work with somebody you know so well," he said. "We crack each other up. We've known each other for twenty-five years now, so we almost talk in code at this point. Walter's got a very personal style and he knows exactly what I'm looking for. He has a very stylised way of playing the guitar which is very swingy and laid back, the kind of thing I like and he takes some weird chances. He was more than a producer really, he was a collaborator as far as some of the music went. Especially in playing."

Becker and Fagen tried out a number of session players, but eventually Fagen decided that since Becker was on the spot and cheaper than any other session players, he should try a few of the songs himself. Becker did and it went so well that they never bothered to hire another bass player or a lead guitarist.

Becker, Fagen and Nichols actually spent three years on and off and almost a million dollars recording the album. Like 'The Nightfly', it was a concept album (although Fagen was still somewhat hesitant to use that term) and one which paralleled the literal journey in the Kamakiri with Fagen's torrid psychological journey through an extreme case of writer's block and various other personal problems, notably the break-up of his long relationship with writer and ex-Bard student, Marcelle Clements.

Fagen was very hopeful about the likelihood of 'Kamakiriad's' success. "I'm optimistic. Things are shaping up nicely for the Nineties. Well, better than the Eighties anyhow." He explained his choice of title by saying that he looked in a Japanese dictionary and discovered the word "kamakiri" which meant praying mantis and which he thought was a great name for his protagonist's mythical, steam-powered, custom-tooled car. The environmentally sound Kamakiri also had a hydroponic farm in the back and a direct link with a Teleologic Routing Satellite acronymically called Tripstar. Fagen had no fixed image of how the car looked, but he imagined it to be a medium-sized car, probably with large tyres and a bubble, covering the garden. He also decided that the car would not move at speeds greater than forty miles an hour.

By setting the scene in the near future Fagen was able to take a detached view of the story and steer away from sentimentality. It also enabled him to invent certain gadgets and instruments which facilitated the advancement of the story past difficult points, but he admitted that he didn't want to "do a hard sci-fi thing".

"I haven't kept up with it (science fiction) that much lately though I have read a few of the William Gibson books, which I find are like the Alfred Bester stuff I used to read. I always liked the idea of total freedom that science fiction allows as regards plotting and characters, and the way you can come up with ideas that have no way of being executed now. I thought it was a good premise to build a story on, because I didn't want it to refer to anything that's happening now, even though in a way it's probably more about the present than the future."

Fagen wrote all the songs on the piano and then arranged them using a sequencer. Once he had the basic structure, he put down his keyboard parts, but almost all the sequenced and electronic parts were replaced by live musicians later.

Fagen was continually asked to explain his long absence. "Well, the Eighties weren't very inspiring for a start. More to the point I had used up all I knew on 'The Nightfly' and I had to live another ten years to write a new album. Basically, I was just trying to get a life, having been a workaholic ever since I was in college. I'd never been able to figure out what to do with myself when I wasn't writing or recording, and it was time to learn. You know, getting into relationships… getting out of relationships. I even practised the piano a little." As well as practising the piano Fagen took some one-to-one lessons in music theory, and singing lessons to strengthen his voice.

The continuing questions about his activities in the meantime soon wearied him, though, and he began to start cracking the jokes. He told one interviewer that he had been working in a shoe store on Madison Avenue and said that when he was recognised on New York streets and asked about the release date of his new album he bounced the question straight back, "I dunno, where's *your* record?" Fagen even had the audacity to jokingly blame Steely Dan fans the world over for his eleven-year hiatus, since the continuing and steady sales of their albums enabled him to maintain an affluent lifestyle throughout his dry years. On another occasion he said sardonically that he suffered from the same problem as Prince – being too prolific.

Fagen explained that he gained the energy to begin writing in earnest for the album in 1988. Playing local gigs around New York and working with musicians he admired enthused him, but he said: "My songs are still basically inspired by music I listened to as a kid." Some of the songs came to Fagen in sequence, but they weren't written in sequence. 'On The Dunes' was in fact written in 1983, long before Fagen had conceived the project as a whole. He also mentioned several times that there would be a couple of tunes which he and Becker had written together on the album, but he wound up using only one collaboration – the song 'Snowbound' – while the other one might turn up on Becker's own album.

'Kamakiriad' opens with a song which was originally entitled 'The Trip', but which Fagen renamed 'Trans-Island Skyway'. It tells how the main character picks up his multinationally constructed Kamakiri and embarks on the first stage of a hazardous and random journey through such places as Five Zoos, Cape Sincere, Lake Nostalgia, Laughing Pines, Key Plaintain, Good Time Flats and finally Flytown where he is faced with a decision as to whether to abandon the journey or press on regardless. Soon after departing, he happens across an accident and picks up an attractive female survivor whose presence more than compensates for the dangers ahead.

Fagen described 'Countermoon' as being "a moon that makes people fall out of love". It features his only solo on the record and was based on a sax sample; it was also the first time that Fagen had played a keyboard solo based on a sample. Six months after the release of the album Fagen realised that some snare drum fills which had been intended to be included in the mix had been mixed so low as to be inaudible. He called Roger Nichols and requested him to insert the appropriate fills into the song. But Fagen said that apart from the missing fills, the mix was perfect, so he didn't want to go into the studio and remix the whole song. Nichols obliged and subsequent pressings of 'Kamakiriad' were issued with Chris Parker's drum fills up where they could be heard.

'Springtime' is the name of the most popular amusement park on the Funway, which is like a sci-fi Disneyland. The narrator decides to stop and have his brain scanned and some old romances replayed to him in a virtual reality theatre. The first verse introduces the park and its attractions, then each successive verse replays one of his lusty encounters and their attendant memories: Connie Lee's car, listening to Coltrane with Mad Mona and partying at the Smokehouse in the Sand. Fagen's creative sense of humour was still intact and he demonstrated this by using an old Steely Dan trick – putting music with an inappropriate mood beneath the lyric. He said that nostalgia was a trap everyone fell into sometimes and nostalgia prevented people moving forward.

'Snowbound' was the first new Fagen/Becker collaboration to be released for almost thirteen years, even though it had been written in 1985 during one of their early attempts to revive their songwriting partnership. In subsequent years frequent writing sessions followed, during which they discovered that they *did* still have what it took to compose together despite the radical divergence in their lifestyles and the five thousand miles between them.

Fagen cited a lyric from 'Snowbound' as one of his favourites on the album: "We sail our icecats on the frozen river/Some loser fires off a flare/Amen/For seven seconds it's like Christmas Day/And then it's dark again."

While he was working on 'Kamakiriad', Fagen realised that 'Snowbound' could fit nicely into the album's theme. The song covers an episode where the Kamakiri pilot is stuck in a frozen city which suffers with terrible weather most of the time. Due to the climatic conditions, the inhabitants have little to do except party all night and sleep all day. He is inexorably drawn into this lifestyle for a while before he manages to escape the city's decadent clutches and continue his journey.

The first single to be taken from the album was 'Tomorrow's Girls', undoubtedly the most accessible and commercial song on the record. With a cracking guitar solo by Becker, 'Tomorrow's Girls' again reflected Fagen's sci-fi leanings insofar as the narrator wakes up one morning to discover his female partner has been replaced by an alien lookalike. "I've put the song into a B-movie context, where aliens are replacing yesterday's girls with pseudo-women. Fagen said he thought that in many ways the album was about loss, and the loss in this case was waking up to a partner from whom the narrator has been drifting apart for some time. Fagen had himself been through a traumatic break-up and the song could be his comment on the termination of his relationship with Marcelle Clements.

The CD single also included Fagen's previously unreleased demo version of 'Confide In Me' and the bonus track called 'Shanghai Confidential'. 'Confide In Me' featured Drew Zingg on guitar, Lincoln Schleifer on bass, Denny McDermott on drums and Mindy Jostyn on harmonica and background vocals. A token video was made for 'Tomorrow's Girls' featuring Rick Moranis as the nerdy husband whose wife becomes alienised and Fagen also appeared wearing sunglasses, intermittently lip-synching to the song. Despite airings of the video on MTV, the song failed to chart to any degree.

Fagen married his girlfriend Libby Titus at City Hall in New York in April 1993, and held a party at the Lone Star Roadhouse to celebrate. He had given his new wife a co-writing credit for helping with the lyrics on 'Florida Room' and dedicated the album to the memory of his former girlfriend, Dorothy 'Dotty' White, who had since died of breast cancer.

Fagen confessed that at one point he was going to link all the tunes on the album in some musical way, but decided against it because he feared it would become pretentious. He did decide he needed a musical transition from 'Tomorrow's Girls' into 'Florida Room' and wrote a horn arrangement to achieve that.

'On The Dunes' had been intended to be part of one of Fagen's abortive follow-up attempts to 'The Nightfly'. As with 'Snowbound', although the song had been written years before the concept for 'Kamakiriad' took shape, Fagen knew he would comfortably be able to slot the song into the story somewhere. This song breathes space, warmth and contentment, yet despite its romantic setting the lyrics tell a completely different story of an affair's termination leading to despair and suicide. Fagen was originally also going to write a horn chart for 'On The Dunes', but had acquired a Roland FP-8 and instead used synth strings on the tune.

'Teahouse On The Tracks' is the name of a club which the narrator encounters along the way when he is exhausted and has to decide whether to continue or call it a day. After a particularly inspiring night's dancing at the club, he is rejuvenated and finds the necessary energy to press on. Fagen admitted that it was an old idea: "Dance away the heartache". The trombone solo was played by Birch Johnson.

With 'Kamakiriad' Fagen played his own demo to the musicians and then asked them to play *exactly* the groove that was on the tape. Almost all the sequenced drums were replaced by live drummers. Despite the sophistication of drum machines Fagen had done an about turn and now didn't like the "mechanical thing". He argued that "the difference between having a groove and not having a groove can be a tenth of a millisecond or less. That's how detailed a live drummer's rhythmic sensibility can get. It would be very hard to duplicate that with a machine."

Fagen didn't much like modern dance music and wanted to pay tribute to what he considered classic dance material. "It's a little more aggressive than anything I've done before. Dance music to me is still the soul of the Sixties and the funk of the Seventies, and that's kind of what I wanted to capture on the record – funk based on sixteenth notes rather than eighth notes, everything from Sly to Earth Wind And Fire. I was writing the album when we were putting the Rock and Soul Revue together, and that whole experience had a major impact on the songs."

Fagen told Giles Smith in *The Independent* that during the recording of 'Kamakiriad' his voice occasionally caused the microphone to distort the sound. "My engineer, Roger Nichols, says sometimes there's what sounds like an electronic distortion triggered by my voice, that must have to do with some sort of harmonic quality. We've never been able to figure out what it is. It only happens under certain notes. My voice freaks out the microphone."

This was the first time that Fagen had written the horn charts without outside assistance and he was wary of taking on the task alone. Previously he'd always had Rob Mounsey or Tom Scott there to advise him. The horn arrangements were the last thing Fagen did after the vocal was done and he could see where each one sat. He admitted that his arranging techniques were basically just to fill the holes – just as any big band arranger would do. He gave himself a pat on the back for his work when he said that at a listening party for the album the horn players had a great time, because where usually horn sections were put back in the mix, on 'Kamakiriad' they were way up front and they could really hear themselves.

When he was asked about the lack of synthesizers on the album Fagen said that their lack of stretch tuning caused him anxiety. "Records that mainly use synthesizers aren't in tune and listening to them makes it feel like my head is in a vice," he said. "A new Grammy category should be introduced for a record being most in tune. If it was, I'm confident I would win it!"

Fagen told Robert Doerschuk in *Keyboard* that he was losing his interest in melody and was getting more into rhythm. He said things used to bother him if they didn't have a nice melody, "but now I don't care much about it."

After the long list of guitar players who graced Steely Dan albums, Fagen displayed a rare sense of economy on 'Kamakiriad'. Apart from Walter Becker, the only guitarist he used was Georg Wadenius. He did his sessions over a period of many months but had no idea that he was the only rhythm guitarist playing on the record.

Three drummers are credited on the album: Leroy Clouden, Chris Parker and Denny McDermott, but it was strongly rumoured that Buddy Williams had played on some of the sessions in New York. Parker played four songs; Clouden played three and McDermott played only on the most Steely Dan-like tune on the album, 'Snowbound'.

Fagen admitted that during his "writer's block", the pressure to create had been more internal than external. He was often confronted with the shattering fear that he had lost his songwriting skills for good. He was a big fan of Burt Bacharach and Hal David, but Fagen knew what had happened to the former: "He had this couple of years of incredible inspiration. That's what most artists have, just a couple of years. You're very lucky if you have them and very lucky if you can maintain some standards. There's only a few people, great artists, who work until they die: Stravinsky or Vladimir Nabokov..."

Fagen warned his record company that... "there was no way I could be sure of meeting any particular deadlines" but despite this he formed a good relationship with Mo Ostin, the chairman of Warner Bros Records, having regular discussions with him about the scheduling of his album. Fagen said that often when he called the record company the secretary didn't even recognise his name and he would be required to spell it out for her.

He also said that the projected release of his album became a running joke between Ostin and himself. Fagen would eagerly tell Ostin about his latest idea and Ostin would schedule the album, only later to be told once again that Fagen had thought better of it and the album was removed from the list.

'Kamakiriad' was mixed in February 1993 at River Sound by Roger Nichols. The first problem they had was that the board had only 40 inputs and they had 48 plus tracks full of instruments to mix. They hired some extra equipment from Neve and Nichols mixed the album to CD-R (recordable CD).

Fagen admitted that he knew the album was finally ready for release when he liked every last part of all the tunes – nothing in any of them rubbed him the wrong way. He said, "I just try to write a solid song and sort of hope that it gets over." But he did admit on one occasion that he could still be working on the material some three months after its release.

Fagen seemed to be blaming his parents and the American lifestyles in the Fifties for his thirtysomething creative problems. He explained how he had been "an extreme idealist" in everything he did and this eventually led to his having to seek proper psychological help. He eventually came to realise that while he could seek perfection in his music, he could not expect perfection in his personal life. He drew parallels between his journey through his own maze of difficulties and the problems faced by the album's narrator: "Most people start out rather optimistic about their life. They fall in love, they idealise their partner, and it doesn't work out so well. The main character on the album goes through a series of losses ending 'On The Dunes' where he is totally abandoned and despondent, even suicidal. Then, he experiences a sort of resurrection through music. It's salvation through art in a sense." Fagen spoke about his fondness for sci-fi and his penchant for writers such as Alfred Bester, Philip K Dick, William Gibson, but said his favourite was Frederik Pohl. "I've always liked science fiction because you can comment on the present in an advanced way. You can deal with cultural or social issues of today by using the setting of tomorrow."

As for William Gibson, the admiration was mutual because his novels are littered with obscure references to Steely Dan lyrics. "Kids today probably think of Steely Dan as the ultimate musos," said Gibson. "Whereas their albums were easily the most subversive records made in the '70s. I always wonder what Donald Fagen must think when he stumbles on a bar I called The Gentleman Loser!" As well as that, in a later novel, *Count Zero*, the location was called Barrytown, in *Mona Lisa Overdrive* Gibson included a character called Becker and he dedicated another of his novels to a "major dude, my friend."

Since the average length of song on 'Kamakiriad' was well over twice the usual pop single, Fagen knew that he would have to edit them down for the singles market, but he was willing to do that. He said he viewed singles as merely advertisements for the album.

The second single from the album was 'Trans-Island Skyway' and it was backed by some teasing previously unissued material: another Fagen demo of 'Big Noise, New York' and the live version of 'Home At Last' from the New York Rock and Soul Revue show at the Beacon Theater in March 1991. As with 'Tomorrow's Girls' the single went nowhere.

Fagen described his hero in 'Kamakiriad' as "kind of a fuck-up, but with excellent intentions." He contended that the album "completes some inherent trilogy", with 'The Nightfly' being the past, the Steely Dan records about the present as it unfolded and this album being about the future. "In Steely Dan we were very arrogant kids and when life starts to kick you around, you have to swallow your pride. See, there was a real family feeling about the Rock and Soul Revue that I'd never experienced before, and certainly not in Steely Dan. In a way, people from my generation have had to create new families, since their own families have so often failed to satisfy the needs that a family historically provided."

Fagen claimed that he couldn't even recognise himself as the person who wrote and recorded those early Steely Dan records, but he wasn't repudiating their cynicism and aloofness. "No, because it wasn't like we were promoting or endorsing that cynical attitude. We were just reflecting the Zeitgeist, talking about the way the world seemed to us in the Seventies. But by the end, when we were making 'Gaucho' I think both Walter and I were down and depressed, and both of us really had to make changes." In Fagen's words Becker's idyllic Hawaiian lifestyle "is very amusing to me, and to him as well."

"I was part of a generation that believes you can reinvent yourself at will; start from scratch and detach yourself from a past that had bad faith in it and lots of values that weren't valuable. I really did try to invent myself according to the spirit of the times. And one of the things you learn as you get older is that there's no escape. I don't know what it was inventing but whatever it was, it wasn't what my parents expected of me. That was my addiction. The Fifties were so repressed they were a recipe for insanity."

Fagen described 'Kamakiriad' as a science fiction allegory of his Eighties experiences but hoped it wasn't as dull as *Pilgrim's Progress*. "But yes, it's a journey of loss. I like the sci-fi idea because it divorces you from the present. It lends itself to a mythic, heroic plot, gives the story a magical quality. Plus you imagine all kinds of marvellous technologies.

"I've grown more suspicious of romance as I've grown older. When Walter Becker and I were first working together in the late Sixties, we were jazz fans, but the vocabulary of jazz had already been co-opted for commercial purposes. Our idea was to use that already corrupted vocabulary, with its romantic connotations, and combine it with anti-romantic lyrics.

"I think it's different from 'Nightfly' in a number of ways. It's more aggressive as far as the rhythms go. I write in a certain style, which I don't know how much I could depart from – it's the natural way I play the piano and derive the harmonies. I'm not interested in any kind of radical departure, unless it comes naturally, otherwise it would just be pretentious. But I think it's a much more mature album."

Fagen's Seventies workaholism had even extended to trying to persuade engineers to work on Christmas Day, because he was bored if he wasn't working. "I think a lot of it had to do with not wanting to address certain things I had to address personally, and working gave me the chance not to do any kind of self-examination. I'm a very introspective person as it is, so I like the action of always working, it's a kind of therapy in itself. I'm basically someone who has to fight nervousness and depression. I've experienced numb periods in my life, for sure. I'm an emotional person and I think that for that reason maybe I'm a little guarded. I feel a lot happier now, but I still keep my therapist busy." He even admitted that during one of his worst periods of block, he considered going back to college or university to learn to do something entirely different.

The single biggest factor in unblocking Fagen's muse was the resumption of his collaboration with Walter Becker. After several songwriting sessions together Fagen felt he was beginning to find some creative spark again. "Nobody can make transitions from chord to chord like Walter. I think Walter and I have an idea of groove that goes back to the Thirties and Forties – very laid back and [it] sounds almost like the whole thing is going to crash every bar. It has this kind of falling over feeling about it that gives it a lot of forward motion. And a lot of guys don't play like that now, don't play naturally laid back."

Fagen's musical policy, he said, was a combination of picking the best from the past and the present; past music such as Thirties swing and Fifties bebop which had humanity combined with current technology which enabled him to achieve the effects that a modern recording studio offered.

Despite having made a video for 'Tomorrow's Girls', Fagen wasn't keen on making videos for the songs on 'Kamakiriad'. " 'Kamakiriad' is meant to be listened to without associated visual imagery like videos," he said. "See, I used to love radio and records, and what was great about them was they made the listener an active participant. You could summon up your own images. Videos just make the listener a passive spectator."

ℰ∕೧

After the enjoyable low pressure experience of the Rock and Soul Revue in 1992, a Becker/Fagen summer tour on which they would perform old Steely Dan material as well as tunes from their respective solo albums was definitely on the cards. Although he'd apparently laid Steely Dan to rest during a radio interview a couple years earlier, Fagen now relented and said, "I'm afraid there'll be pressure for us to call it a Steely Dan tour. I don't know whether we can get out of it. If people think they're going to make more money calling it Steely Dan rather than the Don and Walter show, I don't really care that much."

During the spring of 1993 in interviews to promote 'Kamakiriad', Fagen began talking about a Steely Dan tour that summer. He was still uncomfortable with using the name Steely Dan, but manager Craig Fruin assured him it would make more money if they *did* call it Steely Dan. Fruin also reminded them that nowadays – if you were rich enough – it was possible to undertake a tour without the practical problems and discomfort which had soured them on the touring treadmill in 1973 and, to a lesser extent, 1974. The New York Rock and Soul Revue had been a relaxed affair and the response to the Steely Dan material they played was overwhelming. "It made up for some of the love we never got as kids," said Becker. "There were moments when the level of pandemonium during the intro to 'Deacon Blues' became frightening."

There were no actual auditions for the Nineties look Steely Dan. Becker and Fagen joked that they had left it too late to think about hiring musicians and wound up having to hire whoever happened to be free for the summer. The line up of the band eventually settled on ex-Weather Report drummer Peter Erskine, jazz pianist Warren Bernhardt, bassist Tom Barney and Rock and Soul Revue guitarist Drew "Larry Carlton Junior" Zingg, who was also the musical director. Michael McDonald was asked, but he had just released an album of his own and had prior commitments; Pat Metheny was also asked but declined saying that three guitar players would be one too many.

Fagen promised that the band would be rearranging some Steely Dan tunes if only to make them more interesting to play, but when they came to rearrange some of them – they cited 'Babylon Sisters' as an example – "it was difficult to know what to do with it". Their criteria for selecting the material was simple: if they didn't enjoy playing any one tune, they dropped it from the set. Fagen confessed to being "allergic" to 'Do It Again'. "I despise that song," he said, adding that he found 'Rikki Don't Lose That Number' very boring, too. Their attempts to rearrange these songs and "get something fresh happening" weren't successful so both were omitted from their potential set list. The only song which actually ended up being extensively rearranged was 'Reelin' In The Years' with saxophones replacing the guitar-driven original's pace, but it still didn't have the spark of the 1972 version.

Fagen warned people not to expect too much spectacle wise. "We both started as jazz fans and our idea of a good show is a bunch of guys in cheap suits, with their backs turned to the audience." But Fagen was the focal point of the evening, usually dressed in a dark suit and shades, moving between a grand piano, a synthesizer perched on top of the piano or standing at the mike to sing with an ungainly portable synth strapped over his shoulder. Becker was more informal, usually in jeans and a black shirt and looking suitably indifferent to all that was going on around him. "We're counting on people still responding to a good rhythm section, a live band and lyrics that are about a number of different things," said Fagen. Fagen even told *USA Today* that he had tried to get Becker to sing a duet with him, but failed.

Fagen met with Becker in Hawaii before Steely Dan started rehearsals for the 1993 US tour and they proceeded to plough through their songs for interesting live ideas and Becker even confessed to going out and buying all their back catalogue CDs so that they could learn the chord changes from some of the older tunes. "That was a toughie because all the songbooks, of course, have all the wrong chords in them," he said. Even more surprisingly Fagen later admitted that during a gig, he would "lay out on a couple, because I keep forgetting what the chords are."

The rehearsals were conducted in July at SIR Studios in New York. Initially, Warren Bernhardt, Drew Zingg, Peter Erskine and Tom Barney worked for three days learning the charts and running through the suggested set list even before Becker and Fagen arrived. The next week the horn section arrived until by the third week all the assembled musicians were running the complete show down. They soon realised that the intended show would be far too long and had to take some difficult decisions in order to shorten it to a manageable length. Becker and Fagen then took the band to the Auburn Arena in Detroit for three nights to rehearse the entire show replete with lights, sound and full stage.

The tour kicked off the following month at The Palace, Auburn Hills, Michigan and wound across America for six weeks, twenty-seven cities and thirty-two gigs closing at the Richfield Coliseum in Cleveland in late September. It was, according to *Performance Magazine*, one of the three hottest tours of the summer along with Peter Gabriel and Van Halen. Steely Dan sold out the Greek Theatre in seventy-five minutes – the fastest Los Angeles sell out since Paul McCartney sold out the Forum in 1989. Then the Madison Square Garden and the Chicago shows allegedly sold out in forty minutes and half an hour respectively. Steely Dan played to some 415,000 people and grossed about $12 million in ticket sales. Merchandising stands did very brisk business too, selling the much sought after Steely Dan T-shirts, Kamakiriad and Aja T-shirts, official tour logo T-shirts and even ones which borrowed a lyric from 'Deacon Blues' – "Sue Me If I Play Too Long" – printed on the back.

The 1993 set opened with a favourite tactic of Becker and Fagen's – an overture of 'The Royal Scam'/'Peg'/'Aja', during which time neither of them was on the stage. Towards the end of the overture, they would come out, shake hands and the band would launch into 'Green Earrings'. "We've always wanted to have an overture, to tell you the truth," Becker said, "in fact, at one time we had kind of an overture and we were bullied out of it by the audience. It went on the beginning of 'Do It Again' but [it] received such an unenthusiastic, soggy welcome that it didn't really go over, so we took this opportunity." Fagen was considerably more bullish about their recent effort: "When we hear the overture, we start to fill up with blood." The overture was changed after three gigs when Fagen suggested that they should dispense with 'Peg' and introduce 'Bad Sneakers' as the middle leg of the trio.

The set was made up of a combination of classic Steely Dan songs, Fagen solo material from both 'The Nightfly' and 'Kamakiriad' and a few audacious previews of some Becker solo material slated for his own album. Becker and Fagen were still juggling the set list early on in the tour and 'Springtime' was dropped after the Madison Square Garden gig, then mostly due to the audience response, Becker's 'Girlfriend', 'Our Lawn' and 'Cringemaker' were also consigned to the sidelines.

Becker himself came to calling the mass exodus "the procession to the concession" and later agreed when a critic suggested that the Midwest dates hadn't turned out too good: "Show business isn't really in my blood anyway. I'm looking forward to getting back to working on my car." But Fagen didn't find it as amusing as his partner, remarking that although a large proportion of the audience took the opportunity to "go get some steamed clams – that was their loss."

Another problem raised its head after a couple of dates. Becker and Fagen became dismayed about the lacklustre audience reaction and Roger Nichols wrote in his regular *EQ* column that they considered abandoning the tour right there and then. It turned out that they couldn't hear the audience because their in-ear monitors blocked out the sound of the audience. Thenceforth Nichols set up two shotgun mikes on either side of the stage aiming out at the audience and mixed them into Becker and Fagen's ear monitors. They could then hear the excitement being directed their way and the tour and indeed the principals' enthusiasm was back on course again.

During the encores at the Saratoga Performing Arts Center Becker's son Kawai joined them on stage to sing along with 'My Old School' and 'FM' and Fagen dedicated the final two tunes to Jeff Porcaro who had contributed so much to so many Steely Dan albums over the years and who had tragically died in 1990.

For old times' sake, Becker and Fagen invited Denny "Stereo Mixmaster General" Dias to join them on stage at the Greek Theater. Denny relived his guitar spotlight for 'Bodhisattva', and jammed along with 'Countermoon' and 'Teahouse On The Tracks'. Later on in the tour their erstwhile Rock and Soul Revue buddy, Boz Scaggs made a guest appearance in San Francisco at the Shoreline Amphitheatre.

Gary Kamiya of the *San Francisco Examiner* was convinced by Becker and Fagen's assertions that they were not trying to cash in on baby boomers' vague memories and reckoned they were back at the top of their form. However, in the *San Francisco Chronicle*, Joel Selvin was unjustly critical – surprisingly not of Becker's singing but of his guitar work – arguing that he "brought little to the party other than a smattering of brittle guitar solos which stood in the shadow of the powerful Zingg."

The tour, however, was a resounding success; in fact, after they resolved the early teething problems, it proved to be so successful and enjoyable that Becker and Fagen would be back for yet more next year.

∾

The third single to be lifted in vain from 'Kamakiriad' was the Becker and Fagen composition, 'Snowbound'. The CD single featured an interesting couple of rarities in support of the edited version of 'Snowbound': sparse bass, drums and vocal mixes 'Snowbound' and 'Trans-Island Skyway' with assorted grunts, groans and vocal experimentation from Fagen. A video with a mixture of stop motion animation with live actors' faces was made to support the single; each character was represented by a face with a vehicle for a body and two spanners instead of arms. It was set in a futuristic, frozen city where everything was mechanized and Fagen was portrayed as an all-seeing dictator who sat in a corkscrew cockpit towering over the rest of the city, ensuring all his flat cap-wearing, oppressed workers were pulling their weight. As soon as he spotted someone slacking or falling asleep on the job, Fagen zapped him with a lightning bolt. The video was made at C. J. S. Studios in Phoenix by a Frenchman named Michel Gondry and was inspired by Fritz Lang's 1926 futuristic epic *Metropolis*. In the end, one of the workers drives up the tyrant's tower and after a brief spanner-waving struggle, Fagen is thrown over the edge.

As with 'Tomorrow's Girls' and 'Trans-Island Skyway', the single didn't sell, but the lack of a hit single didn't affect sales of the album which officially hit gold status and was rapidly heading towards a platinum award for a million copies sold at the turn of the year. 'Kamakiriad' has already outsold 'The Nightfly' – even after eleven years 'The Nightfly' has still to attain platinum status – a testament to the power of the live concert.

In December 1993 MCA released 'Citizen Steely Dan 1972–1980', the long-awaited

Steely Dan CD box set of four CDs that comprised every track they'd ever released, but disappointingly only featured one previously unreleased song, a 1971 demo version of 'Everyone's Gone To The Movies' that was tacked on to the end of the set almost as an afterthought. Although they claimed to have listened to many of their old tapes for potential unreleased material for possible inclusion in the set, they reckoned they couldn't find any interesting tunes that they liked. The 1971 demo was recorded at one of Steely Dan's very first sessions and included Flo and Eddie on background vocals. Becker and Fagen apparently included this to verify Flo and Eddie's claims to having "worked with Steely Dan in the old days".

Neither 'Dallas' nor 'Sail The Waterway' – both of which have still yet to be released on CD – were included, while 'Here At The Western World', 'FM' and the old chestnut live version of 'Bodhisattva' – all of which have had at least a couple of outings on various Steely Dan/Donald Fagen CD releases – appeared yet again.

In an open letter to MCA vice president Andy McKaie which was reprinted in the accompanying booklet, Becker and Fagen reckoned that as far as outtakes, rarities and alternative versions went their "shelves were pretty much empty". But there is very good reason to believe that they were being economical with the truth: a couple of years earlier Fagen admitted in a *Q* interview that there were "ten to twenty things" which were then under consideration for inclusion in the box set. A much more realistic appraisal of the situation is that Becker and Fagen are too perfectionist and plain embarrassed to allow any of their discarded material to be released into their fans' grabbing hands.

Many of the badges, buttons, ticket stubs and picture sleeve singles which Becker and Fagen admitted help to make the set a "fun package" had been supplied by Pete Fogel of *Metal Leg*, the Steely Dan fanzine. The sleeve notes were basically a reprint of an article written by Chris Willman and published in the *Los Angeles Times* during Steely Dan's 1993 tour, but once again this was the way Becker and Fagen wanted it.

Much of the disappointment at the lack of outtakes and rarities and the sequencing of the 'Movies' demo can be attributed to Becker and Fagen themselves. Although they are no longer signed to MCA, they are in the enviable position of being able to control everything the label releases, including the contents of the box set. A clause written into their contract back in the late Seventies prevents MCA from issuing anything new by Steely Dan without their consent, so for once the record company is not to blame.

Nevertheless, it was still an extremely frustrating episode. The band's biggest hits and most popular tunes have already been repackaged many times in different guises and the box set was just another example. The sales will surely reflect that; there can't be too many Steely Dan fans who would be prepared to spend forty-plus pounds or sixty-plus dollars for one new version of an already released song plus a booklet.

The first project to be completed in 1994 was an album of children's music which Walter Becker worked on with Windham Hill recording artist John Beasley. The music was composed as the soundtrack for an episode of the *American Heroes And Legends* TV show on Showtime called *Mose The Fireman*. Released on Rabbit Ears Records on March 1, the show was narrated by Michael Keaton and dealt with the exploits of a Gotham Fireman.

☙

Walter Becker went back to Hawaii to work on his forthcoming solo album and Donald Fagen broke the habit of a lifetime to personally accept *Q* magazine's 'Inspiration' Award. Presenting the trophy, Ricky Ross of Deacon Blue said: "He's made a unique contribution to popular music, co-founding one of the most influential and creative bands in the world. A lot of people think I named my band after him, but the truth is he actually wrote 'Rikki Don't Lose That Number' about me…" A dapper Fagen, dressed in a blue suit, white shirt and thin red tie, mumbled his thanks and looked suitably embarrassed.

The *Q* award was highly appropriate. In the eight years of Steely Dan's initial existence Walter Becker and Donald Fagen created some of the finest popular music since The Beatles. They consistently turned out one gem after another and can now rightfully be ranked alongside the greatest popular songwriters of all time.

It was somewhat unfortunate that Walter Becker wasn't there to share in the plaudits, but far from signalling a recognition of a past career, the *Q* award was, in fact, just another small step along Becker and Fagen's comeback trail. But, as ever, Becker and Fagen were in no great hurry. The real comeback would take another five years.

☙

CHAPTER XIII

Sizzling Like An Isotope

In April 1994 Becker and Fagen took their All New Fresh for (1994) Steely Dan Orchestra (it was the same line-up as the '93 US tour) to Japan for gigs in Osaka, Nagoya, Tokyo and Fukuoka. It was their first time playing in the land of the rising sun and they had retained virtually the same set list as the 1993 US tour; the only exceptions being that 'Tomorrows Girls' and 'Countermoon' had been excised from shows due to time constraints and 'Parkers Band' replaced 'Bad Sneakers' in the overture. Donald Fagen was given to announcing that they were very proud of their band and as the duo had often admitted their passion for all things Oriental, in the concert programme Becker and Fagen wrote that "the Japanese people have long come to admire the icy and sophisticated stylings identified with the group Steely Dan" and in return praised the strength and wisdom of the heroic Japanese people.

The Japanese audiences upheld Becker and Fagen's high opinion of them by bestowing their full level of attentive reverence on the band; short and scattered bursts of polite applause interspersed each song and dried up immediately Fagen spoke or an introduction began. There was very little whooping and hollering. Rod Stewart and Jackson Browne were also touring at this time and members of their backing bands made sure that they caught at least one of the Dan shows, though by all accounts they were not nearly as reserved in their appreciation as their Japanese hosts.

Whilst rehearsing in New York Fagen mentioned that they needed what he called some "travelling music" to start the second half of the show and he liked 'Tuzz's Shadow' from a Warren Bernhardt solo album entitled 'Reflections'. Fagen played it for Becker and they asked Bernhardt if he would be interested in writing an arrangement of the song for two tenors and an alto to accompany people back to their seats after their refreshments etc. Bernhardt obliged and a barometer of the knowledge and musicality of their band could be gleaned from the fact that occasionally at the soundcheck, Fagen would launch unannounced into 'Confirmation' by Charlie Parker or 'Solar' by Miles Davis and the rest of the band were able to effortlessly come in on time and jam along with them.

Subsequently a couple of bootleg CDs – 'An Evening With Steely Dan' and 'At The Bay Area' (the latter was on Rikki Records!) – appeared of the Japanese shows with a few intriguing misspellings, the best being 'Box Of Rears' ('Book Of Liars'). Overall, the shows were fairly low key and unremarkable, with the band seeming to find it difficult to get motivated by the naturally withdrawn disposition of the Japanese people, which could have been misinterpreted as an apparent lack of enthusiasm.

During this tour, Fagen took to doing a corny little rap in the middle of 'Hey Nineteen' which few of the audience could have understood in which he and his female counterpart had in their possession a bottle and sleeping bag to keep out the cold but he could not remember what the drink was and which was the cue for the girls to come in with the line about the "Cuervo Gold".

During high summer, Becker and Fagen reconvened their band back in rehearsal for a week and a half, learning twenty-five to thirty songs for their forthcoming jaunt. As ever, they had rung a couple of changes from the 1993 line-up just to keep everyone on their toes and what came to be known as the Citizen Steely Dan Orchestra now had Dennis Chambers replacing Peter Erskine on drums and Swedish guitarist and ex-Blood Sweat & Tears man Georg Wadenius replacing 1993's lead guitarist Drew Zingg. But Erskine and Zingg need not have felt aggrieved at their exclusion this time around, because Becker and Fagen simply wanted to experiment and explore their compositions with some different musicians. As one musician reasoned, what film director uses the same cast for each of his/her movies? As it turned out, Zingg was rapidly snapped up by ex-Rock and Soul Revuer Boz Scaggs, who was about to tour to promote his critically acclaimed 'Some Change' album. The ex-Parliament-Funkadelic drummer had been the original choice for the previous year's tour but had other commitments at the time.

The previous year's overture had now been remodelled to 'The Royal Scam'/ 'Parker's Band'/'The Fez' and had been shifted toward the end of the first half of the show. Rather inevitably, after the general critical enthusiasm of the previous year, having Steely Dan back playing a very similar live show again so soon was too much and one critic likened it to having a long lost relative back after the initial reunion telling the same stories all over again. Another frequent criticism was the lack of showmanship and the soulless nature of the performance; and in *Entertainment Today*, Marc Weingarten called it "the most predictable oldies show to come down the pike since the Eagles Monsters of Schlock" review, labelling Becker and Fagen as "just not compelling enough performers."

It's true that Steely Dan's musical intricacies are much better suited to a recording studio and theirs is not the sort of anthemic music which necessarily translates well to a large venue, but the musicians' quality just about carried them through; Dennis Chambers excelled on 'Bodhisattva', 'Sign In Stranger' boasted a sinuous, vibe-laden introduction and some new lyrics, and though the spunky rearranged 'Reelin' In The Years' could never match the original version it came close. Georg Wadenius also had the impossible task of trying to live up to Larry Carlton's perfect 1976 execution, but made a Herculean effort nonetheless.

When he was back on his avocado farm on Maui, a typical day for Walter Becker was to wake up, have a cup of tea, take his kids to school, go to his studio which was a forty-five minute drive away from his house and try to write some material for three or four hours, have another beverage and then go to the beach. This languorous and leisurely lifestyle was the antithesis of Becker's earlier routines which had been centred wholly around his creative output, though he would never claim to be quite as driven as his partner had been.

In September 1994 the result of those labours was released – his first solo album entitled 'Eleven Tracks Of Whack' on Irving Azoff's Giant label – just as Steely Dan were wrapping up their second successive summer tour of the US. Having observed the way some of his production clients had enjoyed making their albums, Becker originally intended to make an instrumental album. As time went on he wrestled more and more with the problem and even considered hiring in a singer. Eventually he decided that if the public weren't ready for his voice yet, then to hell with it.

Becker had started work on the album in between stints working on 'Kamakiriad', but found that his concept had drifted as he wrote more songs. As with Fagen's 'The Nightfly' in 1982, the album was mainly autobiographical, based on his own experiences and immediate environs in Hawaii, but he was able to add the inevitable twists to many of the tunes by introducing various imaginary lowlifes and exotic characters such as the ones which used to populate Steely Dan songs. As for the music, Becker explained: "My original concept involved a very stripped down sound with strong emphasis on melody and bass line and not too much in the way of chording."

Becker had written a number of songs with friend and session guitarist Dean Parks, but only 'Cringemaker' made it onto the final list. He also experimented by recording all the tracks with The Lost Tribe whose eponymous début album Becker had produced in 1993. Becker sent the band his tracks and they were able to familiarise themselves with the material prior to going to Maui. They spent a month recording at Hyperbolic Sound with Becker singing live as he was trying to get a real band sound and Becker's intention was to go with all the tracks, but eventually he decided that only three of the "live" songs would make the final album. Becker then decided to use his own sequenced demos for the rest of the tracks as he felt that they contained the real heart of each composition. He later confessed that he felt he was only partially successful in achieving his intended goal. At one stage, Becker had twenty-five or thirty songs on tape and by the time Fagen arrived Becker was grappling with all these songs and bits and pieces of tracks and, with his uncluttered and objective outlook, Fagen was able to help Becker whittle the surfeit down to manageable proportions and get his partner back on track. Becker said that by this time he was going around in circles and driving himself nuts.

Describing his composing talents with typical blunt amusement, Becker said, "Songwriting is a place for me to do some lashing out in a mild sort of way." His partner was frequently asked about Becker's composing skills and contrasted their respective solo writing styles thus: "It's obvious that a lot of Walter's things are more the type of things a guitar player would write – more derived from folk music and folk rock, although he also had a jazz background... like I did."

The album's back cover featured a photograph of a shattered windscreen and a pool of blood with a baseball bat lying across it, which perhaps gave a clue as to much of the quirky subject matter of the songs. Becker also put a definition of the word "whack" on to the album sleeve as a first crude attempt which he said "somehow seemed appropriate". The album actually contained twelve songs and on that subject Becker explained, "Just a joke really. Think of it as a clerical error in your favour." (The Japanese pressing contained an extra song again entitled 'Medical Science' which contains the great line "Wherein the angel tangos with the infidel" and whose main characters wind up as yet more drug-induced casualties in its second verse.) Becker and Fagen have always enjoyed these word puzzles (the cryptic "Donald and Walter are well aware that Aida is not joking with you" episode from 'The Royal Scam' period was another) and he exploited this deliberate clerical error to its full extent, challenging interviewers and journalists to try and crack it. The former puzzle was eventually revealed to be nothing more than eleven tracks of whack and then an unashamed sentimental paean to his young son.

Giant issued a four-song sampler in advance of 'Eleven Tracks Of Whack' to try and raise awareness of its existence. Product manager Connie Young said, "We wanna make sure the music is out there since they'll be on tour. The best visibility we can get with Walter is to have him out there on tour with Steely Dan."

Once he had got used to the idea of singing, Becker enjoyed it, but he was careful to lower expectations whenever the occasion arose and as with his live performances, critics were divided by Becker's efforts. Brad Bradley in *Goldmine* wrote that "his vocals are surprisingly good, though not as resonant as Fagen. He hits every note on the money and often injects a smirky lilt to his songs." However, Tom Moon in *Musician* called it "a jagged-edged saw, a born irritant. A voice that stubbornly refuses to stay within the confines of a given pitch" and John Bungey in *Mojo* was wholeheartedly disappointed with the album full stop: "The dull funk of 'Hard Up Case' and 'Girlfriend' is feeble fare from the man who helped create 'Aja' and 'The Royal Scam'."

However, 'Eleven Tracks Of Whack' opens with two of the most melodic songs on the album. Sporting the same title as a Willie Dixon song as recorded by Howlin' Wolf, Becker opined that 'Down In The Bottom' was originally going to be called 'The Dopest Cut'. He really liked the title but eventually decided that the word "dopest" didn't look that good written down. This drum machine stompalong is the story of a friend of Becker's who was involved in a relationship with a girl but "withheld a part of himself in a really obnoxious way."

'Junkie Girl' is surely a homage to his one-time girlfriend, "nurse" and "security" Karen Stanley. And what a homage. Becker seems to be articulating the thought that in 1980 he would have wanted to die with her – then going on to celebrate the fact that he had come through his own distasteful situation intact and was now able to enjoy his idyllic and organic lifestyle in the Hawaiian sunshine. Becker's anger and sorrow is palpable as he sings: "No foolin'/It's a fucked-up world" – a wonderful song in terms of both structure and theme.

'Surf And/Or Die' was based on a real event when a young and healthy acquaintance of Becker's was killed in a tragic hang-gliding accident. At the memorial service for him a group of Tibetan monks from the Dorma Center in Paia where Becker lived spoke very movingly about life and death and their outlook on life after death. The Buddhist input made the tragedy easier to endure. Becker initially wrote a poem about it and this eventually became the basis for the lyrics to the song. Later Becker's then wife Elinor invited the monks to his recording studio to bless it and Becker realised that their chants were in the same key as the song he had written and that the rhythms also suited. He utilised the chanting intermittently throughout the song. Driven by Ben Perowsky's drumming, this song without a chorus wraps itself around you like a hungry python.

'Cringemaker' features a Mustang Sally-type groove and features a guitar solo which Becker admitted "was based on an old Chess record where a guy finds a good note on his guitar and just wails away on it from beginning to end." Slim Harpo's 'I'm A King Bee' is the most likely suspect and indeed Becker even mutters "Buzz awhile" over the guitar break at the end. But Becker mocked his own guitar playing, saying that "It's like how they say people with Alzheimer's disease make new friends every day."

'Book Of Liars' had been performed in the 1993 tour and provides a welcome change of pace. It's an effervescent song which tells of a girl who can't speak at all but for lapsing into untruths. Lucky Henry features a couple of really nice guitar solos: the first rawboned but all-too-brief one is by Dean Parks and the second whirlwind effort is by Adam Rogers. 'Hard Up Case' could hardly be more aptly titled – the malevolent intro almost rivals 'Don't Take Me Alive' for the sheer personification of evil. After the wallowing self-pity of 'This Moody Bastard', the album winds down towards its close, with traces of Becker's mordant sense of humour on display, with 'Hat Too Flat' seemingly about extra-terrestrial job hunting.

Obviously never a man to wear his emotions on his sleeve, of 'Little Kawai', Becker said: "It's hard for a person like me to incorporate in a work of art a genuine expression of fondness for somebody without reservation, so I figured it would be a good exercise to see if I had the courage to do this. Kawai was delighted. It kind of confirmed what he had suspected about himself all along. That he is, in fact, a star. That song became so popular in the family and within the group of people that knew my songs, I figured if I put that song on the album I would get brownie points forever." The album failed to chart in the UK and the US.

Steely Dan's first ever official live album, 'Alive In America', was released in 1995 and was a single CD representation of the 1993 and 1994 US tours. Most of the chosen performances had been selected from the 1994 band with a heavy bias towards the Detroit show of August 27 which provided four of the eleven songs. Roger Nichols had been on hand with a Sony 48-track digital recorder and had taped all the 1993 and 1994 shows and he and Donald Fagen ploughed through all the tapes and using digital edits and cross fades gave the impression that it all happened on one night. However, that night wasn't a particularly glorious one by Steely Dan's very high standards, and the album was a grave disappointment. The performances were sterile and as Steely Dan went into the recording studio later to do "some fixing-up", one hesitates to imagine what it would have sounded like without said fix-ups. Even during the band introductions and between-song patter Becker and Fagen sounded like they were merely reading a script and going through some very boring motions. However, there was at least one lighter moment: in his sleeve notes for the album, under the heading "My most unforgettable moment of the tour" Cornelius Bumpus illustrated how the set introductions gave the horn players a chance to inject some humour into the last show of the tour. At every show, Becker had been saying that there were "no trumpets, no trombones, no kazoos, just saxophones," so for the Cleveland show the horn players got hold of some trombones in advance and stood there behind Becker, awaiting his usual intro while holding their trombones. It was also a testament to the wonderful camaraderie which existed between the players on both the '93 and '94 tours.

Considering their shows had been running at two and a half hours plus, the 'Alive In America' CD ran to a very paltry hour. The live version of 'Josie' was nowhere near as funky as the recorded one, 'Green Earrings' had no fewer than five solos; on 'Kid Charlemagne' Fagen's phrasing seemed rushed and his voice tremulous and 'Third World Man' boasted about as much emotion as a rusty nail. Even the cover image didn't inspire much in the way of confidence: it was an extensively retouched patchwork of some old Forties Universal *Mummy* movies, hence the reason for no credit on the sleeve notes, as Universal guard the copyright of their movies ferociously. The album reached only number 62 in the UK and spent just a single week on the chart.

In 1994 Becker had quipped that "we're just bluffing" when asked the inevitable question about the likelihood of another Steely Dan studio album, but in an interview in *The Independent* newspaper with Giles Smith a year or so later Fagen and Becker were hinting at the possibility of just such an album, saying: "We have a list of very amusing titles, but that's about it. We also have tapes of discarded songs going back to the Seventies." Becker: "Maybe when we get around to trying to write new songs, those old songs will look very attractive."

After their year off, Becker and Fagen were willing to give the live circuit yet another battering. Having adopted the custom of titling their tours, they called the 1996 venture Steely Dan's Art Crimes, and the band this time featured another three débutants: Ricky Lawson on drums, Wayne Krantz on lead guitar and John Beasley on piano. The tour began in Charleston, South Carolina on July 5 and wound its way through the USA ending at The Gorge in Washington on August 17. They also made a quick hop across to Europe for gigs in Rotterdam, Hamburg, Frankfurt, Brussels, London, Birmingham, Glasgow and Dublin and a month later headed back to Japan for another whistle-stop tour there.

Interestingly, Becker and Fagen previewed three new songs on the tour, and Fagen usually made a point of announcing that "we're still working on that". These were a very punchy, horn-driven 'Jack Of Speed' with Walter Becker on lead vocals, the satirical but jubilant 'Wet Side Story' and 'Cash Only Island', although the latter was dropped early on during the dates, perhaps indicating its eventual fate in the studio. The most interesting revelation which would later emerge in a *JamMusic* interview with John Sakamoto was that Becker and Fagen had discussed performing 'The Second Arrangement' on their various summer jaunts, but had decided against it. They traded vocals on 'Everyone's Gone To The Movies', lead guitarist Krantz is obviously a fantastic player, but was a little too ostentatious to complement Steely Dan, and as excellent a drummer as Ricky Lawson is, two drum solos in the first four songs ('Do It Again' and 'Josie') was stretching even the Dansters' musical hipness to the limit.

Very few people saw Steely Dan perform live on their only previous visit to the UK in May 1974 as this tour was cancelled after only three dates, so the expectation of Becker and Fagen returning to these shores after twenty-two long years was positively tangible. Steely Dan were received ecstatically by the fans, but the critics proved much, much harder to please. Kevin Courtney in *The Times,* reviewing the Dublin gig at The Point, was almost blasphemous in his damnation: "They seemed as dated as a pair of old boots," he wrote. David Cheal in *The Telegraph* echoed one or two of the US critics when he wrote that it was "a show lacking in emotional impact and depth."

Oddly enough, Becker and Fagen have been quite heavily sampled since De La Soul began the trend with their delightful, good-natured 'Eye Know' (featuring a sample from 'Peg') in 1989. In 1996 Super Furry Animals wanted to use an altogether less good-natured sample, the line "You know they don't give a fuck about anyone else" from 'Show Biz Kids' in their tribute – "The Man Don't Give A Fuck" – to ex-Cardiff City footballer and rebel Robin Friday. This was the man "who made George Best look like a lightweight" and who was pictured on the cover giving his trademark post-goal scoring V-sign to the camera. Initially, Becker and Fagen refused permission which meant that the group were all set to go into the studio to record a replacement song as the line was repeated over fifty times throughout and without it there *was* no song. But after another approach from Creation in which they stressed the great reaction the track was receiving, Steely Dan relented and permitted its use. "It's the best thing we've ever recorded" lead singer Gruff said. His confidence was well placed as the song peaked at number 22 in December 1996 in the UK.

A few years later Becker and Fagen were involved in a sampling controversy when two New York rap artists called Lord Tariq and Peter Gunz sampled the hook from 'Black Cow' without Becker and Fagen's permission on their song 'Deja Vu (Uptown Baby)'. This episode blew up into full scale hostilities with Tariq and Gunz accusing Becker and Fagen of having no respect for hip hop music and indeed challenging them to appear live on MTV playing the song while they rapped over the top of it. Fagen later charged them with piracy. Having overlooked the need to ask for permission to use the sample, Becker and Fagen then demanded $105,000 for it (the industry standard was around $30,000) and consequently Tariq and Gunz bemoaned the fact that they didn't make a dime off the record, although it was a number one in the R'n'B charts and how the whole tawdry episode had "turned me off to them."

Steely Dan were nominated for the Rock'n'Roll Hall of Fame in 1998, but failed to make it which provided Becker and Fagen with endless ammunition to snipe at the institution. On their official website Becker and Fagen joked that they had asked for $380,000 to play at the event and although they would be prepared to let former members of the band (namely Jeff Baxter) participate, they would require him/them to be presented with the award off camera or backstage! Becker and Fagen were again nominated in 2000, but once again the selection panel passed them by. They will surely make it in future years, but Becker and Fagen's sarcasm and attitude may continue to jeopardize their chances. What do they care anyway?

After the debacle surrounding various poor quality reissues of Steely Dan CDs, in November 1998 MCA began once again reissuing them in pairs in chronological order, this time with all the original artwork, all the lyrics to the songs and with additional new liner notes by Becker and Fagen themselves. These CDs will now surely be *the* definitive copies (unless, of course, they reissue them again with previously unreleased songs, outtakes and alternative versions). Remastered by Roger Nichols, the sound quality was somewhat better and Becker and Fagen took it upon themselves to disseminate some useful background details (both real and light-hearted) about the albums and about their personal circumstances at the time. However, the trend did not continue and the notes for 'The Royal Scam' and 'Aja' were most disappointing, with most of the latter being comprised of a fictitious conference call whereby ex-ABC President Steve Diener and Michael Phalen are being lambasted by Becker and Fagen and absolutely nothing about the recording of the album.

Also in 1998 between sessions for the new Steely Dan album 'Two Against Nature', Donald Fagen made a guest appearance, playing acoustic piano on a song called 'Sweet Love' (not the Anita Baker classic, although Ricky Lawson did play on it) and co-written with Phil Collins and Nathan East, on Lawson's début solo album 'First Things First'. Upcoming Louisiana singer/songwriter Sean Holt sang lead vocals on the track.

In order to take a break from the sessions for 'Two Against Nature', the 1999 Independence Day weekend found Becker and Fagen in a bar up near Woodstock, New York playing with a blues band led by former Band drummer Levon Helm. Fagen took to the stage and did his versions of a couple of Dylan songs – the old chestnut 'Down In The Cove' and a dirty bluesy version of 'Meet Me In The Morning' from 'Blood On The Tracks'.

The latter part of 1999 eventually saw the showing of Isis Productions *Classic Albums* series, including among others Bob Marley's 'Catch A Fire', The Who's 'Who's Next', U2's 'The Joshua Tree' and Steely Dan's 'Aja'. It was produced by Nick de Grunwald and was made by Martin Smith who travelled to the US and spoke to many of the essential players as well as Becker and Fagen themselves. Becker and Fagen were interviewed sitting at the recording console listening to each song and airing previously unheard snippets, including a couple of the failed guitar solos for the infamous 'Peg'. Also aired was Jim Keltner's unusual percussion – a garbage can lid on 'Josie', a minor gem which is lost in the mix of the album version. The dearth of footage of check-shirted Becker and aviator-shaded 'Aja'-period Fagen meant that a reunion of some of the main players – Chuck Rainey, Bernard Purdie, Paul Griffin – together with Becker and Fagen and Jon Herington was held at River Sound in New York where they played 'Josie', 'Peg' and 'Deacon Blues' to provide Smith with some much-needed footage of the Dan in action. This was mixed with film of the Dan from live concerts and constituted a very interesting fifty minutes which was expanded to sixty minutes with the inclusion of an additional River Sound performance in the Eagle Rock Entertainment video.

The term long-awaited has often been used in rock circles for an album, but surely few have been more eagerly awaited than Steely Dan's 'Two Against Nature'. Becker and Fagen took the inspiration for their album title from an obscure nineteenth-century comic French novel by Joris-Karl Huysmans, which had originally been translated as *Against the Grain* but which has now been revised to *Against Nature*. After several lengthy delays, 'Gaucho' hit the stores in November 1980; also after a couple of postponed release dates, 'Two Against Nature' finally saw daylight on February 29, 2000 – the same day as Oasis's 'Standing On The Shoulder Of Giants'. Becker and Fagen waited fully nineteen years between Steely Dan tours and they eventually succeeded in spinning out their recording hiatus to a similar length of time.

In an online interview with John Sakamoto, Becker and Fagen said they began writing it in 1997 and then spent five days a week, eight hours a day over the course of the next two years in the studio. As in their Seventies heyday, they recorded all the tunes with countless combinations of players. During this time, they cut fifteen or sixteen songs and have a considerable amount of material in the can, including the two songs which were previewed on the 1996 tour, 'Wet Side Story' and 'Cash Only Island'. When current Steely Dan favourite Ricky Lawson wasn't able to make the sessions, Becker and Fagen, who trust Tom Barney's judgement unreservedly, asked him if he could recommend anyone. He suggested Maze's Michael White, keyboardist Ted Baker and new lead guitarist Jon Herington, as well as respected session player Vinnie Colaiuta. At the start of the project, recording took place at Becker's Hyperbolic Sound in Maui, after that much of the tracking was done at Clinton Studios with overdubs being recorded at Fagen's own River Sound on the Upper East Side.

Becker and Fagen's official website had been pretty static throughout 1999 and had been easily outshone by some of the fan-based sites, but in readiness for the release of 'Two Against Nature', they improved their site with competitions, news, sound clips in advance of the album release and are now updating much more often and offering some tasty exclusives by way of compensation.

'Two Against Nature' opens with a song called 'Gaslighting Abbie' – which sets the tone for the rest of the album. This breezy tale is the story of a ménàge à trois and the difficulty the furtive lovers are experiencing in disposing of the unwanted party. Tom Barney and Ricky Lawson drive the thing along like an express train while Becker's guitar noodles spatter over their granite foundation. Becker and Fagen explained that they had apprised the verb "to gaslight" from the 1944 Charles Boyer, Ingrid Bergman film of the same name in which a Victorian schizophrenic tries to drive his wife insane and which had become an accepted New York slang term for such an evil aspiration.

'What A Shame About Me' is a fine song about a classic underachiever and substance abuser encountering a much more successful former colleague and lover and has already been selected as a focus track. The song is very reminiscent of 'Springtime' from 'Kamakiriad' and Becker does a great job with both guitar and bass. Fagen said that Becker was playing so well that they just kept recording and never got around to hiring in the highly paid studio players to which they usually resorted. The title song is percussive and almost more lyrically obtuse than 'Your Gold Teeth' and contains references to voodoo (a subject they have tackled in the past). Walter Becker told Barney Hoskyns in *The Guardian*: "It's about the songwriters invocation of their own powers to overcome the natural and supernatural forces arrayed against them. They're offering to help their audience prevail in the face of all sorts of mysterious and frightening beings." It was selected as the title track because of their perception that in their middle age they are indeed fighting the passage of time both creatively and physically.

The snappy 'Janie Runaway' finds a nubile Tampa teenager relocating to Gramercy Park to become the darling of the New York set. Rather amazingly the song was rejected by an important US radio station as a possible single because it features a saxophone solo – the station in question adding that they only play songs with guitar solos! In a *Mojo* interview, Donald Fagen joked that you could write a song about "fucking your grand-mother [and they would play it] as long as it featured a guitar solo". 'Almost Gothic' is a fine melodic song about a girl of remarkable contradictions with a doleful Michael Leonhart trumpet solo and has already become a favourite among fans. 'Jack Of Speed' has undergone change of tempo and key compared to the 1996 live version and Fagen now takes the lead vocal; it contains the essence of a really great song, but Becker and Fagen appear to have held back on it and restrained themselves and the players. 'Cousin Dupree' is a rather interesting and commercial rumination on the pros and cons of would-be familial sexual relations, but still contains the funniest line on the album: "I pretended to be readin' the National Probe/As I was watchin' her wax her skis." A Steely Dan album wouldn't be a Steely Dan album if Becker and Fagen didn't sit out at least one track and this time it is the detached but lovely mood piece 'Negative Girl', which was recorded live on the second take. She could almost be the twin sister of the heroine in 'Almost Gothic' – Vinnie Colaiuta's drumming is great and the ninth and last song is a classic Steely Dan title – West of Hollywood which Becker said contained "a Heart of Darkness thing going on there." Clocking in at eight and a half minutes, the last four minutes are basically composed of Chris Potter blowing his brains out over countless modulations, almost as Pete Christlieb did on 'Deacon Blues'. Fragments of the song can be traced back to one of Becker and Fagen's 1980s reunion songwriting stints of what was originally a reggae-style tune which they had not yet set to lyrics, but then they realised that the snippets could fit with their idea for West of Hollywood.

Fagen told *Mojo* magazine that the album was "crisp and self-reflexive like our earlier work, but more sophisticated. I'm not really interested in radical departures." However, they did discuss the possibility of pursuing just such a radical departure, indeed they set out with exactly that in mind, but eventually elected to stick with their tried and tested methods. Known as they are for their countless requests for rerun after rerun of studio performances, Fagen admitted to asking one engineer to execute him if he dared to ask for one more variation.

In a classic case of understatement Fagen said, "We don't think of ourselves as being perfectionists. To us, it's more like desperately trying to have it sound more or less OK."

Steely Dan have plans to go on the road again in the summer of 2000; rehearsals will begin in New York at the end of April. The intention is to begin in May in Japan, coming back to the US in June and then winding up in Europe. The rhythm section will consist of Tom Barney on bass, Jon Herington on lead guitar, Ricky Lawson on drums and Ted Baker on keyboards.

This summer will also see the release of a Bobby and Peter Farrelly film featuring Steely Dan covers. Called *Me, Myself And Irene* and starring Jim Carrey, this comedy is the story of a Rhode Island State Trooper who has a multiple personality each of whom fall in love with the same girl. At this time the list includes Wilco doing 'Any Major Dude', The Brian Setzer Orchestra on 'Bodhisattva', Leon Redbone doing 'Chain Lightning' and Ben Folds Five covering 'Barrytown'.

Becker and Fagen have undertaken more promotion for this album than ever before and on January 28 and 29 Steely Dan played a tight live set of eighteen songs at Sony Studios in New York for PBS, a satellite station which is to be broadcast on March 1, 2000. They played five songs from the new album and, of course, included some of the old favourites such as 'Deacon Blues' ,'FM', 'Peg', 'Kid Charlemagne' and 'Aja'. Fagen introduced the three girl backing singers as the bare midriff section. The band were especially tight and the set went down extremely well with the limited numbers lucky enough to be in the audience.

A few days later they recorded 'Storytellers' for VH-1 whereby a group plays some of their songs and then answers questions about them in a question and answer session with the audience. Steely Dan played nine songs in total, but only the two focus tracks from 'Two Against Nature' were included: 'Cousin Dupree' and 'What A Shame About Me'.

"We don't really fit into any of the slots that we know about," Becker confessed. "But we never have, so we're just hoping that whatever carried us through before will again." On that score, Becker and Fagen need have absolutely no doubts, because Steely Dan can justifiably be proud of their sublime back catalogue and even more proud of their comeback album. 'Two Against Nature' proves unequivocally that despite the prolonged interruption in their career and even though both men have cracked fifty, by God, they can still do it: prodigious melodies, engaging lyrics, peerless musicianship, hang-your-coat-up-on-the-grooves and pristine production. Steely Dan was never dead and clearly the music will never die either.

∽

Discography

SINGLES

Dallas/ Sail the Waterway
Probe PRO 562 June 1972

Do It Again/ Fire in the Hole
Probe PRO 577 January 1973

Reelin' in the Years/ Only A Fool Would Say That
Probe PRO 587 April 1973

Show Biz Kids/ Razor Boy
Probe PRO 602 August 1973

My Old School/ Pearl of the Quarter
Probe PRO 606 November 1973

Rikki Don't Lose That Number/ Any Major Dude Will Tell You
Probe PRO 622 May 1974

Pretzel Logic/ Through With Buzz
ABC 4019 August 1974

Black Friday/ Throw Back the Little Ones
ABC 4058 June 1975

Do It Again/ Fire in the Hole (reissue)
ABC 4075 September 1975

Kid Charlemagne/ Green Earrings
ABC 4124 May 1976

Haitian Divorce/ Sign in Stranger
ABC 4152 November 1976
(not released as a single in the US)

Do It Again/ Haitian Divorce/ Dallas/ Sail the Waterway
ABC ABE 12003 (Plus Fours 12″ picture sleeves) January 1978

Peg/ I Got the News
ABC 4207 March 1978

Deacon Blues/ Home at Last
ABC 4217 (Also released in 12″ format) June 1978

FM (No Static At All)/ Reprise
MCA 374 July 1978

Rikki Don't Lose That Number/ Any Major Dude Will Tell You
ABC 4241 (Reissue with picture sleeve) October 1978

Hey Nineteen/ Bodhisattva
MCA 659 November 1980

Babylon Sisters/ Time Out Of Mind
MCA 680 March 1981

FM (No Static At All)/ Reprise
MCA 786 (Reissue with picture sleeve) July 1982

FM (No Static At All)/ East St Louis Toodle-Oo
MCA MCAT 786 (12″ picture sleeve) July 1982

Do It Again/ Rikki Don't Lose That Number
Old Gold OG 9321 April 1983

Reelin' in the Years/ Rikki Don't Lose That Number/ Do It Again/ Haitian Divorce
MCA MCAT 852 (12″ picture sleeve) 1983

Reelin' in the Years/ Rikki Don't Lose That Number
MCA MSAM November 1985

Rikki Don't Lose That Number/ Do It Again
MCA 1214 October 1987

Reelin' in the Years (live)/ Peg (live)
Giant Steely 01 1995

Reelin' in the Years/ Third World Man/ Peg/ Kid Charlemagne
PRO-CD 7706 1995

Cousin Dupree (radio edit)/ (album version)
Giant PRO-CD 4265 February 2000

What A Shame About Me (radio edit)/ (album version)
PRO-CD 4267 February 2000

Jack of Speed (radio edit/album version)
PRO-CD 9690

US SINGLES DISCOGRAPHY, ONLY WHERE DIFFERENT FROM ABOVE:

Bad Sneakers/ Chain Lightning
ABC 12128 August 1975

The Fez/ Sign in Stranger
ABC 12222 October 1976

Josie/ Black Cow
ABC 12404 August 1978

PROMOS

Countdown To Ecstasy
Three song 7" jukebox EP with picture cover
My Old School/ Pearl of the Quarter/ King of the World
ABC PRO 779

Pretzel Logic Quadrophonic four song 7" with picture cover
With A Gun/ Rikki Don't Lose That Number/ Barrytown/ Pretzel Logic
ABC PRO 40015

ALBUMS

Can't Buy A Thrill
Do It Again/ Dirty Work/ Kings/ Midnite Cruiser/ Only A Fool Would Say That/ Reelin'
in the Years/ Fire in the Hole/ Brooklyn (Owes the Charmer Under Me)/ Change of the
Guard/ Turn That Heartbeat Over Again
Probe SPB 1062 January 1973
Reissued as ABC ABCL 5034 October 1974

Countdown To Ecstasy
Bodhisattva/ Razor Boy/ The Boston Rag/ Your Gold Teeth/ Show Biz Kids/ My Old
School/ Pearl of the Quarter/ King of the World
Probe SPB 1079 July 1973

Pretzel Logic
Rikki Don't Lose That Number/ Night By Night/ Any Major Dude Will Tell
You/ Barrytown/ East St Louis Toodle-Oo/ Parker's Band/ Through With Buzz/ Pretzel
Logic/ With A Gun/ Charlie Freak/ Monkey in Your Soul
Probe SPBA 6282 March 1974
Reissued as ABC ABCL 5045 October 1974

Katy Lied
Black Friday/ Bad Sneakers/ Rose Darling/ Daddy Don't Live in That New York City
No More/ Doctor Wu/ Everyone's Gone to the Movies/ Chain Lightning/ Your Gold
Teeth II/ Any World That I'm Welcome To/ Throw Back the Little Ones
ABC ABCL 5094 April 1975

The Royal Scam
Kid Charlemagne/ The Caves of Altamira/ Don't Take Me Alive/ Sign in Stranger/ The
Fez/ Green Earrings/ Haitian Divorce/ Everything You Did/ The Royal Scam
ABC ABCL 5161 May 1976

Aja
Black Cow/ Aja/ Deacon Blues/ Peg/ Home at Last/ I Got the News/ Josie
ABC ABCL 5225 September 1977

You Gotta Walk It Like You Talk It (Or You'll Lose That Beat)
You Gotta Walk It Like You Talk It/ Flotsam and Jetsam/ War and Peace/ Roll Back The
Meaning/ You Gotta Walk It Like You Talk It (reprise)/ Dog Eat Dog/ Red Giant, White
Dwarf/ If It Rains
Spark SRLP 124 March 1978
Originally released in 1970 on Spark SPA-02 then reissued in 1971 on Visa 7005.

Greatest Hits
Do It Again/ Reelin' in the Years/ My Old School/ Bodhisattva/ Show Biz Kids/ East St
Louis Toodle-Oo/ Rikki Don't Lose That Number/ Pretzel Logic/ Any Major Dude Will
Tell You/ Here at the Western World/ Black Friday/ Bad Sneakers/ Doctor Wu/ Haitian
Divorce/ Kid Charlemagne/ The Fez/ Peg/ Josie
ABC ABCD 616 November 1978

Gaucho
Babylon Sisters/ Hey Nineteen/ Glamour Profession/ Gaucho/ Time Out of Mind/ My
Rival/ Third World Man
MCA MCF 3090 November 1980

Gold
Hey Nineteen/ Green Earrings/ Deacon Blues/ Chain Lightning/ FM (No Static At All)/
Black Cow/ King of the World/ Babylon Sisters
MCA MCF 3145 June 1982

Reelin' In The Years (The Very Best of Steely Dan)
Do It Again/ Reelin' in the Years/ My Old School/ Bodhisattva/ Show Biz Kids/ Rikki
Don't Lose That Number/ Pretzel Logic/ Black Friday/ Bad Sneakers/ Doctor Wu/
Haitian Divorce/ Kid Charlemagne/ The Fez/ Peg/ Josie/ Deacon Blues/ Hey Nineteen/
Babylon Sisters
MCA DANTV 1 October 1985

Sun Mountain
Berry Town(sic)/ Android Warehouse/ More to Come/ Sun Mountain/ Ida Lee/ Any
World/ Stone Piano/ Caves of Altamira/ A Horse in Town/ Roaring of the Lamb/
Parker's Band/ Oh, Wow It's You/ You Go Where I Go/ This Seat's Been Taken/ A Little
With Sugar/ Take It Out On Me
Showcase SHLP 128 April 1986

Berry Town
Ida Lee/ Any World/ You Go Where I Go/ This Seat's Been Taken/ Berry Town/ Android
Warehouse/ More to Come/ Sun Mountain/ A Little With Sugar/ Take It Out On Me/
Stone Piano/ Roaring of the Lamb/ Parker's Band/ Oh, Wow It's You
Bellaphon 230.07.065 May 1986

Stone Piano
Android Warehouse/ A Horse in Town/ More to Come/ Parker's Band/ Ida Lee/ Stone
Piano/ Any World/ Take It Out On Me/ This Seat's Been Taken/ Barrytown
Thunderbolt THBL 054 April 1988

CDs

A Decade Of Steely Dan
FM/ Black Friday/ Babylon Sisters/ Deacon Blues/ Bodhisattva/ Hey Nineteen/ Do It
Again/ Peg/ Rikki Don't Lose That Number/ Reelin' in the Years/ East St Louis
Toodle-Oo/ Kid Charlemagne/ My Old School/ Bad Sneakers.
MCA DIDX August 1985

Sun Mountain
You Go Where I Go/ A Little With Sugar/ Roaring of the Lamb/ Charlie Freak/ Sun Mountain/ Oh Wow It's You/ Undecided/ Any Major Dude Will Tell You/ Caves Of Altmira (sic)/ Any World That I'm Welcome Too (sic)/ More to Come/ Parker's Band/ Barrytown/ Brain Tap Shuffle/ Brooklyn/ Mock Turtle Song/ Yellow Peril
Thunderbolt CDTB 139 1992
Note: Track seven was listed as Undecided but in fact was Caves Of Altamira; track nine was also Caves Of Altamira.

Do It Again The Very Best Of Steely Dan
Telstar TCD 2297 September 1987
Rikki Don't Lose That Number/ Reelin' in the Years/ Kid Charlemagne/ Doctor Wu/ FM/ My Old School/ The Fez/ Do It Again/ Pretzel Logic/ Any Major Dude/ Black Friday/ Show Biz Kids/ Peg/ Haitian Divorce

A succession of other demo albums/ CDs of dubious origins were released in the late Eighties and early Nineties mostly originating in the EEC, all basically comprising the same nucleus of songs:

Old Regime – May 1988
Becker And Fagen – The Collection – June 1988
Steely Dan Featuring Walter Becker and Donald Fagen
You Go Where I Go
Becker and Fagen Founders of Steely Dan – 1989
The Roaring Of The Lamb – 1993

Gold – (Expanded Edition)
Hey Nineteen/ Green Earrings/ Deacon Blues/ Chain Lightning/ FM/ Black Cow/ King of the World/ Babylon Sisters/ Here at the Western World/ Century's End/ True Companion (Donald Fagen)/ Bodhisattva (live)
MCA MCD 10387 November 1991

Remastered – The Best of Steely Dan
Reelin' in the Years/ Rikki Don't Lose That Number/ Peg/ FM/ Hey Nineteen/ Deacon Blues/ Black Friday/ Bodhisattva/ Do It Again/ Haitian Divorce/ My Old School/ Midnite Cruiser/ Babylon Sisters/ Kid Charlemagne/ Dirty Work/ Josie
MCA MCD 10967 November 1993

Citizen Steely Dan 1972–1980

Do It Again/ Dirty Work/ Kings/ Midnite Cruiser/ Only A Fool Would Say That/ Reelin' in the Years/ Fire in the Hole/ Brooklyn (Owes the Charmer Under Me)/ Change of the Guard/ Turn That Heartbeat Over Again/ Bodhisattva/ Razor Boy/ The Boston Rag/ Your Gold Teeth/ Show Biz Kids/ My Old School/ King of the World/ Pearl of the Quarter/ Rikki Don't Lose That Number/ Night By Night/ Any Major Dude Will Tell You/ Barrytown/ East St Louis Toodle-Oo/ Parker's Band/ Through With Buzz/ Pretzel Logic/ With A Gun/ Charlie Freak/ Monkey in Your Soul/ Bodhisattva (live)/ Black Friday/ Bad Sneakers/ Rose Darling/ Daddy Don't Live in That New York City No More/ Doctor Wu/ Everyone's Gone to The Movies/ Chain Lightning/ Your Gold Teeth II/ Any World That I'm Welcome To/ Throw Back The Little Ones/ Kid Charlemagne/ The Caves Of Altamira/ Don't Take Me Alive/ Sign In Stranger/ The Fez/ Green Earrings/ Haitian Divorce/ Everything You Did/ The Royal Scam/ Here at the Western World/ Black Cow/ Aja/ Peg/ Deacon Blues/ Home at Last/ I Got the News/ Josie/ FM/ Babylon Sisters/ Hey Nineteen/ Glamour Profession/ Gaucho/ Time Out of Mind/ My Rival/ Third World Man/ Everyone's Gone to the Movies (demo)
MCAD4 10981 (4 CD boxed set) December 1993

Alive in America

Babylon Sisters/ Green Earrings/ Bodhisattva/ Reelin' in the years/ Josie/ Book of Liars/ Peg/ Third World Man/ Kid Charlemagne/ Sing In Stranger/ Aja
Giant 74321 25691 2 October 1995

Two Against Nature

Gaslighting Abbie/ What A Shame About Me/ Two Against Nature/ Janie Runaway/ Almost Gothic/ Jack Of Speed/ Cousin Dupree/ Negative Girl/ West Of Hollywood
Giant 74321 62190 2 February 2000

BOOTLEG ALBUMS

Rotoscope Down Pleasantly Retired (A Peak Behind The Curtain)
The 1973 American Tour

The Boston Rag/ Do It Again/ Any Major Dude Will Tell You/ King of the World/ Rikki Don't Lose That Number/ Pretzel Logic/ Untitled Instrumental/ Reelin' in the Years/ Mobile Heart (sic)/ Bodhisattva
The Amazing Kornyfone label TAKRL 1924

Bent Over Backwards – Katy Lied "Outtakes"

Daddy Don't Live in That New York City No More/ Chain Lightnin'/ Black Friday/ Rose Darling/ Throw Back the Little Ones/ Doctor Wu/ Your Gold Teeth II/ Do It Again/ Reelin' in the Years
Unmitigated Audacity Records·SD 7000

BOOTLEG CDs

Reelin' Through The Years (Living Legend Records LLRCD 100) and **This All Too Mobile Home** (Scorpio SD-91-02-02) recorded live at the Record Plant March 20, 1974, same track listing:
Bodhisattva/ The Boston Rag/ Do It Again/ Any Major Dude Will Tell You/ King of the World/ Rikki Don't Lose That Number/ Pretzel Logic/ Instrumental/ Reelin' in the Years/ This All Too Mobile Home (sic)

Steely Dan Live (Oh Boy Records 1-9074) first eight tracks as above.

An Evening With Steely Dan Live In Nagoya, Apr 16 1994
Steel 1 SD001/ 2

At The Bay Area Live At Tokyo NK Hall, Apr 17 1994
(Overture) Green Earrings/ Bodhisattva/ IGY/ Josie/ Hey 19/ Book of Liars/ Chain Lightning/ Green Flower Street/ Home at Last/ Black Friday/ Tuzz's Shadow/ Deacon Blues/ Babylon Sisters/ Reelin' in the Years/ Fall of '92/ Peg/ Third World Man/ Teahouse on the Tracks/ My Old School
Rikki Records

Doing It Live-Live In St Louis Missouri, Sept 1 1993
KTS 519/ 20

The Steely Dan Orchestra Live In Columbia Maryland, Aug 8 1993
Home Records HR 5956/ 7

Doing It Again Live In New York, Aug 24 1993
The Royal Scam/ Bad Sneakers/ Aja (Overture) Green Earrings/ Boshisattva/ IGY (listed as Deacon Blues)/ Josie/ Hey 19/ Book of Liars/ Chain Lightning/ Green Flower Street (listed as IGY) / Home at Last/ Black Friday/ Tuzz's Shadow Deacon Blues (listed as Mobile Heart)/ Tomorrow's Girls/ Babylon Sisters/ Reelin' in the Years/ Fall of '92/ Peg/ Third World Man/ Countermoon (listed as Kamakiriad)/ My Old School/ FM
Front Row Front 38

The Summer Of 1993 Live At Saratoga Performing Arts Center
Gold Standard GS 96007

Steely Dan Manassas Virginia July 21, 1996
Do It Again/ Bad Sneakers/ Everyone's Gone to the Movies/ Josie/ Jack Of Speed/ FM/ Hey 19/ Green Earrings/ Any Major Dude/ Green Flower Street/ Rikki Don't Lose That Number/ Peg/ East St Louis Toodle-oo/ Glamour Profession/ My Waterloo/ Wet Side Story/ Midnite Cruiser/ Black Cow/ Home at Last/ Kid Charlemagne/ IGY/ My Old School
Midnight Beat Records MB CD 102

(NB: The track listing on many bootlegs is much the same and often unreliable with wrong song titles listed on the sleeve.)

Donald Fagen

ALBUMS / CDs

The Nightfly
I.G.Y. (What A Beautiful World)/ Green Flower Street/ Ruby Baby/ Maxine/ New Frontier/ The Nightfly/ The Goodbye Look/ Walk Between Raindrops
Warner Bros 92-3696-2 October 1982

Kamakiriad
Trans-Island Skyway/ Countermoon/ Springtime/ Snowbound/ Tomorrow's Girls/ Florida
Room/ On the Dunes/ Teahouse on the Tracks
Reprise 9362-45230-2 May 1993

SINGLES

IGY/ Walk Between Raindrops
Warner Bros W 9900 November 1982

New Frontier/ Maxine
Warner Bros W 9792 January 1983

New Frontier/ Maxine/ The Goodbye Look
Warner Bros W 9792T (12″ picture sleeve) January 1983

Ruby Baby/ Walk Between Raindrops
Warner Bros W 9674 (picture sleeve) April 1983

Century's End/ Shanghai Confidential
Warner Bros W 7972 April 1988

CD SINGLES

Century's End/ Shanghai Confidential/ The Nightfly/ The Goodbye Look
Warner Bros W April 1988

Tomorrow's Girls (edit)/ Confide In Me/ Shanghai Confidential
Reprise W0180CDX June 1993

Trans-Island Skyway/ Big Noise, New York (demo)/ Home at Last (live)
Reprise W0196CD September 1993

Snowbound/ Snowbound and Trans-Island Skyway (bass, drums and vocals only mixes)
Reprise W0216CD November 1993

Walter Becker

Eleven Tracks of Whack
Down in the Bottom/ Junkie Girl/ Surf and/or Die/ Book of Liars/ Lucky Henry/ Hard Up Case/ Cringemaker/ Girlfriend/ My Waterloo/ This Moody Bastard/ Hat Too Flat/ Little Kawai
Giant 9 24579-2 September 1994

Book of Liars/ Hard Up Case/ Fall of '92
Giant PRO-CD7353-R (sampler)

Down at (sic) the Bottom/ Junkie Girl/ Lucky Henry/ Surf and/or Die
PRO-CD 7132 (sampler) 1994

Becker And Fagen Involvement Discography

1969 Terence Boylan – **Alias Boona**. Becker plays bass and guitar/Fagen plays piano and organ.

1969 Jay and The Americans – **Sands Of Time**. Strings and horns arranged by "... you know who you are, thanks."

1970 Jay and The Americans – **Wax Museum**.

1970 Jay and The Americans – **Capture The Moment**. String and horn arrangements on four songs.

1970 The Original Soundtrack – **You've Gotta Walk It Like You Talk It Or You'll Lose That Beat**. All songs by Becker/Fagen. Bass and guitars: Becker/all keyboards: Fagen.

1970 Barbra Streisand – **Barbra Joan Streisand**. Features a Becker/Fagen composition, I Mean to Shine, and Fagen plays organ on their song.

1972 Navasota – **Rootin'**. With a Becker/Fagen song, Canyon Ladies/Fagen plays piano on a few songs/Becker and Fagen arranged horns and/or strings on three songs.

1973 John Kay – **My Sportin' Life**. With a Becker/Fagen tune Giles Of The River.

1973 Thomas Jefferson Kaye – **Thomas Jefferson Kaye**. Becker plays bass on two songs and Fagen sings background vocals.

1974 Thomas Jefferson Kaye – **First Grade**. Featuring two Becker/Fagen songs, American Lovers and Jones. Fagen plays piano on Northern California, while Becker plays bass on both Becker/Fagen songs.

1977 Terence Boylan – **Terence Boylan**. Fagen plays piano on Don't Hang Up Those Dancin' Shoes and Shame.

1977 Poco – **Indian Summer**. Fagen plays keyboards on the title track and Win Or Lose.

1978 Marc Jordan – **Mannequin**. Fagen plays piano on unspecified tracks.

1978 Pete Christlieb/Warne Marsh Quintet – **Apogee**. Produced by Becker/Fagen and featuring a composition called Rapunzel based on Bacharach/David's In the Land Of Make Believe.

1979 Dr Strut – **Dr Strut**. With an instrumental Becker/Fagen song called Canadian Star.

1980 Far Cry – **The More Things Change**. Fagen sings background vocals on three tracks.

1981 Rickie Lee Jones – **Pirates**. Fagen plays synth on the title song.

1981 Various Artists – **Heavy Metal Soundtrack**. Featuring a Fagen composition called True Companion.

1982 Eye To Eye – **Eye To Eye**. Fagen plays a synth solo on On The Mend.

1983 Eye To Eye – **Shakespeare Stole My Baby**. Fagen plays synth on Jabberwokky.

1983 **King of Comedy Soundtrack**. Fagen song called The Finer Things by David Sanborn.

1984 **Thelonious Monk Tribute – That's The Way I Feel Now**. Fagen and Steve Khan cover Monk's Reflections.

1984 **The Gospel at Colonus**. Produced by Bob Telson, Gary Katz, Fagen, and Daniel Lazerus.

1984 Greg Phillinganes – **Pulse**. With a Donald Fagen song, Lazy Nina.

1986 Rosie Vela – **Zazu**. Fagen played synth on seven songs/Becker played guitar on a couple of songs and synth on Tonto.

1986 Yellowjackets – **Shades**. Fagen wrote the title song.

1988 **Bright Lights, Big City Soundtrack**. Fagen wrote the film score with Rob Mounsey. A single was released called Century's End, co-written with Timothy Meher.

1990 William Burroughs – **Dead City Radio**. A New Standard by Which To Measure Infamy co-written by Fagen and Burroughs.

1991 Manhattan Transfer – **The Offbeat of Avenues**. With a Fagen composition called Confide in Me.

1991 New York Rock And Soul Revue – **Live At The Beacon Theater**.

1992 Glengarry Glen Ross soundtrack. Blue Lou written by Fagen and performed by The Joe Roccisano Orchestra.

1992 Jennifer Warnes – **The Hunter**. Featuring a Fagen/Marcelle Clements composition, Big Noise, New York.

[In addition to the above Becker and Fagen are rumoured to have arranged singles by Ersel Hickey ('Self Made Man') and Maximum Security ('Same Song') during the late Sixties/early Seventies]

Walter Becker Productions

1985 China Crisis – **Flaunt The Imperfection**. Becker also played synth and percussion. Virgin.

1987 Fra Lippo Lippi – **Light and Shade**. Becker played on unspecified instruments. Virgin.

1989 China Crisis – **Diary of a Hollow Horse**. Eight songs produced by Becker. Virgin.

1989 Rickie Lee Jones – **Flying Cowboys**. The Horses co-written by Jones and Becker/Becker played synth on Satellites and bass on title song. Geffen.

1990 Michael Franks – **Blue Pacific**. Becker produced three songs. Reprise.

1991 Bob Sheppard – **Tell Tale Signs**. Windham Hill Jazz.

1991 Andy Laverne – **Pleasureseekers**. Triloka.

1991 Leanne Ledgerwood – **You Wish**. Triloka.

1991 Jeff Beal – **Objects In The Mirror**. Triloka.

1991 Bob Bangerter – **Looking on the Bright Side**. Produced by Bob Bangerter and George Tavy/co-produced by Walter Becker and Tom Hall/mixed by Becker. DSM.

1992 Jeremy Steig – **Jigsaw**. Triloka.

1992 Dave Kikoski – **Persistent Dreams**. Triloka.

1993 Lost Tribe – **Lost Tribe**. Windham Hill Jazz.

1993 Andy Laverne – **Double Standards**. Triloka.

1993 John Beasley – **Cauldron**. Windham Hill Jazz.

1993 John Beasley – **A Change of Heart**. Windham Hill Jazz.

Index

A Little With Sugar, 20
A&M, 176
A&R Studios, New York, 99, 122
Aaron, Jane, 178, 181
Aaron, Peter, 178, 181
ABC, 147
ABC Dunhill, 36–7, 42–4
ABC Recording Studios, Los Angeles, 85, 96, 98
Abell, David Music, 86
Adler, Lou, 37
Aida, 107, 209
Ain't Too Proud To Beg, 13
Ain't That Peculiar, 82
Aja (album), 56, 114–132, 134, 142, 145, 149, 153, 166, 177, 202–3, 210, 214, 216
Aja (song), 22, 120–1, 134
Alan, Todd, 189
Alexander Hall, 15
Alias Boona, 14–5
Alice Through The Looking Glass, 24
Alive In America, 211
Almost Gothic, 215–6
Altamira Cave, 105
Amazing Kornyphone record label, 73
America The Beautiful, 193
American Heroes And Legends, 206
An Evening With Steely Dan, 207
Android Warehouse, 20, 22, 25
Angel Stadium, 44
Angels, The, 62, 63
Aniton, Jerome, 81
Any Major Dude Will Tell You, 62, 71, 75, 216
Any World That I'm Welcome To, 89
Anyway You Want It, 29

Apogee, 131–2
Appletree Theatre, 13
Armstrong, Louis, 21
Arrows, 171
Ascione, Joe, 183
Asylum Records, 128–9
At Last, 184, 189
At The Bay Area, 207
Auburn Arena, 203
Austin Patti, 181, 184
Automated Sound Studios, New York, 133, 141, 155, 166
Avalon, Frankie, 8
Avco Embassy, 34
Avery Fisher Hall, 75
Azoff, Irving, 129, 130, 208

Babylon Sisters, 141–3, 145, 156–8, 179, 202
Bach, 59
Bacharach/David, 34, 198
Bacharach, Burt, 131
Bad Rock Group, 12
Bad Sneakers, 86, 89, 92, 96, 114, 203, 207
Baker, Anita, 214
Baker, Ted, 215–6
Balboa Stadium, 56
Balsam, Jerry, 30
Band The, 14, 32, 62, 206
Baner, Billy, 21
Bard College, 4, 9–15, 32, 42, 59, 194
Bard drug bust, 15
Barfield, Teaker, 188
Barney, Tom, 202, 215–6
Barnstorm, 43
Barri, Steve, 37, 39, 40–1, 45–6

Barry, Jeff, 25
Barrytown, 64, 72, 87, 199, 202, 216
Basie, Count, 59
Baxter, Jeff, 35, 40–1, 43, 45, 50–51, 53,
    55, 58–60, 63–64, 66, 69–72, 74–5,
    77–8, 80, 82, 94, 213
Bay of Pigs, 165
Bayside, 58
Beach Boys, The, 53
Beacon Theatre, 184, 187, 189, 191–2, 199
Bead Game, The, 34, 41
Beal, Jeff, 187
Beasley, John, 206, 212
Beatles, The, 8, 16, 176, 205, 206
Becker/Fagen: as staff writers, 37–42;
    at Bard College, 9–13;
    attitude to punk rock, 122–3;
    Becker/Fagen reunited, 175;
    Becker on Aja success, 123;
    Becker moves to Hawaii, 172;
    Becker breaks leg, 142;
    Becker drug problems, 138;
    contract with MCA, 147–8;
    cover versions of Dan songs, 151–2;
    early Steely Dan gigs, 53–56;
    early years, 7–11;
    Fagen applying to Bob Dylan, 154;
    Fagen denying Steely Dan, 183–4;
    Fagen on reading sci-fi, 194–5;
    Fagen writing for *Premiere*, 177;
    Fagen work routine, 172;
    hiring of Irving Azoff, 129;
    in Brooklyn, 17;
    marketing of Aja, 130;
    patronage of Root Boy Slim, 133;
    playing on albums, 142;
    post Aja tour, 127–8;
    relationship with Dias/Thomas, 21–5;
    relationship with Kenny Vance, 19–20,
        25–30;
    relationship with Larry Carlton, 103;
    relationship with Terence Boylan,
        13–15;
    relationship with ABC Records, 124;
    relationship with Roger Nichols, 44–45;
    relationship with Bernard Purdie,
        100–102;
    relationship with Garry Sherman,
        99–100;
    relationship with Elliott Scheiner,
        98–99;
    return to New York, 133;
    split, 155;
    sued by Keith Jarrett, 144;
    uneasy relationship, 136;
    unfamiliarity with musicians, 138–9
Becker, Elinor, 210
Becker, Wendy, 11
Beckett, Samuel, 29
Being And Time, 67
Bell Harbour, 30
Belmondo, Jean-Paul, 22
Belonging, 144
Ben Folds Five, 216
Benay, Ben, 58
Bennett, Crusher, 155
Berberian, Cathy, 59
Berg, Deborah, 169, 171
Berghofer, Chuck, 158
Bergman, Ingrid, 215
Berklee, 10
Bernhardt, Warren, 202, 207
Berns, Bert, 182–3
Berry, Chuck, 7–8, 13, 160
Best, George, 213
Bester, Alfred, 195, 199
Beverly Boulevard, 39
Bickhart, Jim, 88
Big Nardo And The Eighth Grade, 42
Big Noise, New York, 172, 199
Bigard, Barney, 70
Billboard 61, 122, 126

Binky Jones, and The Americans, 18
Birtha, 151
Biscayne Bay, 151
Black Cow, 115, 119, 125, 157, 179, 213
Black Friday, 5, 32, 88, 92–3, 184, 186–187, 189, 191, 203
Black, Jay, 18–9, 27–9, 35, 47
Black Oak Arkansas, 53, 82
Black Sabbath, 155
Blaine, Hal, 68, 89
Blakes Hotel, 79
Blakey, Art, 29
Bland, Bobby, 115
Blatt, David, 18
Bley, Carla, 171
Blithewood, 13
Blood On The Tracks, 214
Blood Sweat & Tears, 208
Blue, Lou, 193
Blue Note, 90
Bodhisattva, 4, 59, 62, 77, 81, 152, 153, 190, 202–5, 208, 216
Bogota, 151
Bonfa, Luis, 165
Boogie 'Til You Puke, 133
Book Of Liars, 207, 211
Borscht Belt, 7
Boston Rag, The, 58–9, 62, 73, 78, 82
Bottom Line, 189
Boulez, Pierre, 66
Bowie, David, 51
Boyer, Charles, 215
Boylan, John, 15
Boylan, Terence, 13–5, 128–9
Bradley, Brad, 210
Brain Tap Shuffle, 18, 24, 25, 169
Bramley, Peter, 32
Brands Hatch, 61
Brandy, 55
Bread, 51

Brecht, Bertolt, 29
Breskin, David, 143–4
Brigati Brothers, 183, 189
Bright Lights, Big City, 180
Brighton Grill, 180
Brill Building, 18–9, 29, 31, 169
Brooklyn (Owes The Charmer Under Me), 18, 46, 50, 62, 77–8
Brooks, Harvey, 185, 192
Brown, Charles, 189, 192
Brown, James, 21
Browne, David, 178
Browne, Jackson, 207
Browning, Robert, 178
Bucky, 62–3
Buffalo Broadside, 13
Buffett, Jimmy, 121
Bugs Bunny, 124
Bullock, Hiram, 137, 181
Bumpus, Cornelius, 211
Bungey, John, 210
Burke, Solomon, 182
Burroughs, William, 4, 9, 12, 42–3, 66–7, 70, 89
Bus Driver Is A Fruitcake, 15
Bush, George, 203
Butler, Sam, 184
Butterfield, Paul, 192
Bye Bye Dallas, 45
Byrds, The, 65
Byrne, David, 171

California, Randy, 11
Canadian Star, 133
Can't Buy A Thrill, 4, 43, 45, 48, 51–3, 62, 64, 72, 147, 158
Canyon Ladies, 41
Captain Midnight, 115
Capture The Moment, 98
Cara, Mia, 18, 27
Caraeff, Ed 73, 109

Carlton, Larry, 44, 92–3, 99, 102–3, 106, 118, 120–1, 145, 166, 203, 208
Carpenter, Karen & Richard, 44
Carrey, Jim, 216
Carson, Johnny, 131
Cash Only Island, 212, 215
Cassidy, Ed, 11
Catch A Fire, 214
Catch A Rising Star, 188
Cavaliere, Felix, 88
Caves Of Altamira, The, 19, 105, 110, 151
Century's End, 180, 190
Chain Lightning, 5, 88, 92, 95–6, 187, 191, 193, 216
Chambers, Dennis, 205, 208
Champ, 82
Change Of The Guard, 40, 50
Charlie Freak, 18–20, 29, 64, 106
Cheal, David, 212
Cher, 90
Cherokee Sound, Chatsworth, 67–8
Chest Fever, 32
Chick, Donald, Walter & Woodrow, 131
China Club, 188, 190
China Crisis, 173–5, 178–9, 181
Chong, Rae Dawn, 109
Chorane, Eddie, 19
Christlieb, Pete, 121, 128, 130–1, 216
Cinema Malibu, 33
Cinema Village, 33
Citizen Steely Dan, 204–5
City Mug, 35
CJS Studios, 205
Clapton, Eric, 68, 107
Clark, Petula, 15
Clarke, Steve, 107, 110, 126
Clash, The, 122
Clement, Marcelle, 172, 177, 194, 196
Clinton, Bill, 193
Clinton Studios, 215
Clooney, Rosemary, 11

Cloud Nine Productions, 34
Clouden, Leroy, 192, 198
Cohen, Joel, 53, 74, 76, 79, 83–4, 129
Colaiuta, Vinnie, 215–6
Cold Sweat, 21, 23
Collins, Dennis, 41
Collins, Phil, 214
Coltrane, John, 66, 82, 90, 126, 142, 152, 196
Columbia Records, 150
Columbia Studios, New York, 34
Come A Little Bit Closer, 18, 27
Come Back Baby, 29, 33
Comitali, Frank, 189
Confide In Me, 197
Confirmation, 207
Congress Of Vienna, 110
Contemporary Leaders, 160
Contemporary Records, 86
Continental Baths, 30
Cooke, Sam, 34, 187
Corbijn, Anton, 132
Corea, Chick, 131, 179
Corlett, Elaine, 124
Corso, Gregory, 12, 29
Count Zero, 199
Countdown To Ecstasy, 53–63, 64, 72, 74, 78, 91, 133, 179
Countdown To Love, 192
Countermoon, 196, 203, 204, 207
Court And Spark, 88
Courtney, Kevin, 212
Cousin Dupree, 216–7
Craven, Wes, 33
Creation, 213
Creatore, Luigi, 34
Creem, 74, 126
Cringemaker, 203, 209–10
Criteria Studios, Miami, 133
Cromelin, Richard, 74, 82, 91, 95, 107, 115

Crosby, David, 193
Crosby, Stills, Nash & Young, 51
Cross, Christopher, 90
Crusaders, The, 68, 92
Cry Baby, 183
Cry To Me, 183
Cucumber Studios, 167
Cunningham, Billy, 30–1
Curiosity Killed The Cat, 177
Curious George, 184, 187
Curzon Hotel, 79

D.O.A., 167
Da Nang, 93
Daddy Don't Live In That New York City
    No More, 32, 92
Daily Mirror, 175
Daily News, 33, 179
Daisy, 30
Dallas, 45, 61, 125, 129, 204, 205
Daly, Garry, 174
Damned, The, 122
Dancing In The Street, 13
Danko, Rick, 191
Darin, Bobby, 34, 37
Davenport, Darius, 14
David, Hal, 131, 190
Davis, Miles, 8, 82, 115, 122, 160, 174,
    207
Davlin Studios, Los Angeles, 99
Dawn, 61
Dawson Sound, 65, 75
Dawson, Stuart 'Dinky', 65–6, 75–6,
    78–9, 101
DBX debacle, 96–97
De La Soul, 213
Deacon Blue, 177, 206
Deacon Blues, 121–2, 125, 131, 153,
    190–3, 201, 203, 214, 216
Decade Of Steely Dan, 176
Dee, Kiki, 76, 80

Deja Vu (Uptown Baby), 213
Demian, 21–4, 35
Denver, John, 179
Deodato, 151–2
Derek And The Dominos, 68
Derringer, Rick, 60–1, 63, 92, 95, 143,
    169
Destiny, 98
Destocki, Bob, 155
Diamond, Neil, 18, 27
Diary Of A Hollow Horse, 178
Dias, Denny, 20–21, 23–4, 31–32, 35, 38,
    40–1, 45, 49, 51–2, 55–60, 64–5,
    68–9, 71, 74, 77–80, 83–4, 89, 92,
    104, 106, 111, 121, 127, 129, 193,
    203, 204
Dick, Philip K., 199
Diener, Steve, 123, 214
Dion, 159, 191
Dire Straits, 135
Dirty Dancing, 180
Dirty Laundry, 193
Dirty Work, 39, 46, 48, 54, 62, 77–8,
    151–2
Discepolo, John, 23–4, 31, 33–4
Disneyland, 196
Do It Again, 47–9, 52–3, 56, 60, 73, 75,
    77, 91, 96, 106, 129, 151, 158,
    202–3, 212
Dodgson, Charles, 24
Doerschuk, Robert, 198
Dog Day Afternoon, 106
Dog Eat Dog, 31
Doherty, Denny, 45
Dolphy, Eric, 90
Domino, Fats, 160
Donna, Lee, 131
Don't Hang Up Those Dancing Shoes,
    129
Don't Let Me In, 33
Don't Stop, 192

Don't Take Me Alive, 4, 102, 105–6, 142, 211
Doobie Brothers, The, 83, 94, 109
Doors, The, 185
Dorfman, Stanley, 75
Dorma Center, 210
Dorough, Bob, 191
Dorsey, Tommy, 7
Down In The Bottom, 210
Down In The Cove, 214
Downbeat, 74, 88, 154
Downey, Robert, 30, 33
Dr Buzzard's Original Savannah Band, 144
Dr John, 171, 182–3
Dr Strut, 133
Dr Wu, 66, 86, 88, 91, 114, 121, 165
Dragonara Hotel, Leeds, 79
Drifters, The, 27, 159, 166
Driftin' Blues, 189
Drowning In A Sea Of Love, 184, 189
Duke Ellington, 4, 59, 64, 70, 90, 115, 139, 151, 164
Dylan, Bob, 13–5, 18, 66, 104, 154, 185, 188

Eagle Rock Entertainment, 214
Eagles, The, 54, 108, 109, 129–30, 155, 208
Earl Mallory, 31
Early Years, The, 169
Earth Wind & Fire, 154, 197
East, Nathan, 214
East St Louis Toodle-Oo, 5, 64, 70
Ego, The Making Of A Musical, 18
Elaine's, 182
Electric Black Man, 34
Electric Flag, 184
Electric Light Orchestra, 75
Eleven Tracks Of Whack, 208
Eliot, T. S., 67
Ellwood Avenue, 22, 24

Entertainment Today, 208
Epiphone, 10
EQ, 186, 190, 203
Ericsson, Eric, 35
Erskine, Peter, 202, 205, 208
Evans, Bill, 29, 115
Evans, Richard, 135
Everybody Needs Somebody To Love, 182–3
Everyone's Gone To The Movies, 92, 204, 205, 212,
Everything You Did, 108–9
Evidence, 171
Exodus, 8
Eye Know, 213
Eye To Eye, 161, 169–70, 176

Fabriani, Tristan, 47
Faces, The, 48
Fagen, Don, Jazz Trio, 12
Fagen, Elinor, 7
Fagen, Joseph 'Jerry', 7
Fagen, Susan, 7
Faith, Percy, 77
Fall Of '92, 203
Fame, 129
Famular, John, 60
Fantasy, 90
Farrelly, Peter & Bobby, 216
Fear And Loathing, 67
Felder, Don, 155
Felder, Wilton, 92–3
Feldman, Victor, 63, 67, 99, 112, 121, 128, 140, 157–8
Feliciano, Jose, 151
Fellestrio, 31
Fenelly, Michael, 57
Ferlinghetti, 12
Ferrante & Teicher, 8
Fez, The, 104, 208
Fields, Carter, 31–2

Fields, Venetta, 63
Finah Mynah From China, 22
Findley, Chuck, 157
Finer Things, The, 169
Finfer, David, 30
Fire In The Hole, 49
First Things First, 214
Flack, Roberta, 68
Flaunt The Imperfection, 174–5, 178
Fleetwood Mac, 65, 123, 130, 171, 192
Flo And Eddie, 41, 204–5
Florida Room, 197
Flotsam And Jetsam, 32
Flying Cowboys, 181–2
FM, 130–2, 203–5, 216
Focus, 53
Fogel, Pete, 205
Fogelberg, Dan, 129
Fools Paradise, 176
Footprints On The Moon, 29
Ford, Gerald, 93
Ford, Robben, 118
Forman & Clark, 44
Forum LA, 203
Four Seasons, The, 27
Four Tops, The, 21, 119
Fra Lippo Lippi, 178
Franklin, Aretha, 68
Frey, Glenn, 109, 130
Fricke, David, 150
Friday, Robin, 213
Froelich, Gene, 148, 153
Front Line Management, 129, 148, 152, 155
Fruin, Craig, 201
Fugs, The, 35
Fujii, Hideki, 130
Funny Girl, 34

Gabriel, Peter, 203
Gadd, Steve, 120, 128, 134, 137

Gadson, James, 166
Gambino, 28
Gamble & Huff, 184
Ganse, Charlie, 109
Garbarek, Jan, 144
Garland, Red, 8
Garsszva, Jerry, 163
Gary, Kannon, 33
Gaslight, 215
Gaslighting Abbie, 215
Gaucho (album), 4, 56, 95, 98, 101, 116, 133–156, 163, 166, 168, 170–1, 200, 214
Gaucho (song), 122, 140–1, 144
Gaye, Marvin, 24, 82, 119
Gee Officer Krupke, 16
Geffen, David, 128
Geils, J. Band, 48
Gelder, Rudy van, 122
Ghost Train, 182
Gibson, Les Paul, 11
Gibson, William, 195, 199
Gift Of Freedom, 174
Gilberto, Astrud, 165
Giles Of The River, 45
Gillespie, Dizzy, 125
Gillett, Charlie, 159
Girlfriend, 203, 210
Glamour Profession, 141, 143–4, 151, 158
Glass Bead Game, The, 39, 62, 139
Glengarry Glen Ross, 193
Go West, 177
Godfather, The, 43
Going To Chicago Blues, 59
Gold, 155, 158, 190
Goldberg, Marshall, 65
Goldmine, 210
Gondry, Michel, 205
Good Love, 180
Good Lovin', 183

Goodbye Look, The, 162, 165, 180–1
Gordon, Jim, 67–8, 70, 72, 88, 128
Gorman, Klaus, 132
Gospel At Colonus, The, 171, 183
Gottlieb, Stan, 31
Grand Funk Railroad, 155
Granola, Gloria, 62
Grapevine, The, 21
Grass Roots, 37–9, 44
Grateful Dead, The, 39, 62, 139
Graydon, Jay, 118
Greatest Hits, 4, 132, 158
Greek Theatre, 203
Green Earrings, 104, 106, 121, 131, 157,
   179, 190–2, 202–3, 212
Green Flower Street, 164, 167, 188–9
Greene, Ed, 137, 166
Griffin, Paul, 104, 106, 119, 129, 183,
   214
Grolnick, Don, 95, 117, 137, 155
Groovin', 189
Gruff, 213
Grunwald, Nick de, 214
Guardian, The, 215
Guerin, John, 88
Guess Who, The, 43, 53
Guitar, 172
Gullywater, 89
Gunz, Peter, 213

Hades, 185, 187–8
Haitian Divorce, 91, 100, 106–7, 129, 158
Hakim, Omar, 181
Halen, Eddie van, 193
Hamilton, James, 159
Hamilton, Joe Frank & Reynolds, 44, 150
Hampton, Hawes, Quintet, 129
Hampton, Lionel, 19
Hang On Sloopy, 95
Hard Up Case, 210–1
Hardin, Tim, 15

Harley Street, 80
Harris, Bob, 75
Harrison, George, 68, 193
Harvey, Peter, 80
Haslip, Jimmy, 172
Hat Too Flat, 211
Hathaway, Donny, 68
Have You Seen Her?, 82
Hayes, Tubby, 82
Heart Of Darkness, 216
Heartbreak Of Psoriasis, 133
Heartbreak Souvenir, 136, 158
Heatwave, 27
Heavy Metal, 155
Heider, Wally, 131
Heidigger, Martin, 66, 67
Hellbound Train, 54
Helm, Levon, 182, 214
Hendrix, Jimi, 13, 185, 187, 193
Henley, Don, 109, 130, 193
Here At The Western World, 126, 132,
   190, 204–5
Herington, Jon, 214–6
Herman, Woody, 131, 179
Hesse, Hermann, 10, 21, 34
Hey Nineteen, 81, 144–5, 150, 172, 207
Heyward, Nick, 177
Hi Fidelity, 126, 148–9,
Hi Mom, 33
Hicksville, 20–2, 24, 40
Highway 61 Revisited, 47
History Of The CIA, 132
Hit Factory, New York, 14, 186, 188
Hitler, Adolf, 92
Hitsville, 189
Hodder, Jim, 34, 40, 41, 45–6, 50, 62,
   64, 66, 68–9, 73–5, 77–80, 82, 94,
   187
Hold On, I'm Comin', 21
Holder, Mitch, 157
Holland, Jools, 181

Holland Dozier Holland, 206
Holly, Buddy, 8
Hollywood Palladium, 53
Holt, Sean, 214
Holy Modal Rounders, 35
Home At Last, 101, 120, 121, 187, 189,
    191, 193, 199, 203
Hooker, John Lee, 43
Hoops, McCann, 158, 179
Hooters, 190
Hoover, Linda, 34–5
Horn, Jim, 179
Horses, The, 181
Hoskyns, Barney, 215
Hotel California, 109
Humphrey, Paul, 119, 157
Hunter, The, 172
Hutchinson, Bobby, 157
Huysmans, Joris-Karl, 214
Hyperbolic Sound, Maui, 5, 188, 209,
    215

I Can't Function, 22, 29, 33, 169
I Can't Write Home About You, 148
I Got The News, 120–1, 123, 131
I Keep Forgettin', 193
I Mean To Shine, 34–5
I Shot The Sheriff, 107
I'm A King Bee, 210
I'm Old Fashioned, 131
Ida, Lee, 32
If It Rains, 31–2
IGY, 159, 161–2, 164, 166, 181, 184
Illegal Records, 133
Image Bank, 132
In A Station, 35
In Concert, 76
In The Land Of Make Believe, 131, 190
In The Midnight Hour, 185
Independent The, 198, 212
Interlude, 175

Irma la Douce, 47
Isis Productions, 214
It Takes A Lot To Laugh, It Takes A Train
    To Cry, 47

Jabberwokky, 170
Jack Of Speed, 212, 215
Jackson, Anthony, 136, 138, 140
Jackson, Chuck, 192
Jackson, Joe, 171
Jackson, Rudy, 70
Jacobs, Jim, 66
Jagger & Richard, 206
Jake And The Family Jewels, 46
Jamerson, James, 103
James, Etta, 189
James Gang, The, 43, 53, 79
Janie, Runaway, 215
Jankel, Annabel, 167
Jarrett, Keith, 144
JATA Enterprises, 18
Jay And The Americans, 18, 20, 23, 27–8,
    33–4, 47, 50, 63, 98
Jazz Junction, 8
JER Releasing, 30
Joel, Billy, 162
John, Elton, 53, 55–6
John, Pat St, 182–3
John, Sakamoto, 212, 214
Johnson, Birch, 197
Johnson, Gazza, 175
Johnson, Jimmy, 14
Jones (song), 35
Jones, Rickie Lee, 181, 184
Jones, Royce, 57, 62–3, 77–9, 82
Jordan, Steve, 155
Joshua Tree, The, 214
Josie, 115, 117, 120, 125, 153, 190–3,
    211–2, 214
Jostyn, Mindy, 197
Joyce's Boogie, 189

Junkie Girl, 210
Just Like Tom Thumbs Blues, 13

Kama Sutra, 5, 34
Kamakiriad, 194–206
Kamiya, Gary, 204
Kane Gang, The, 177
Kane, Walter, 142
Katy Lied, 51, 66, 70, 85–97, 99–101,
    108, 114, 127–8, 136, 168
Katz, Gary, 6, 33, 35, 37, 39, 41–2, 44–7,
    49–51, 54–5, 57–58, 61, 63, 67–8,
    73–5, 80, 84, 89–90, 96–9, 102, 104,
    106, 110, 112, 115, 117–9, 121, 123,
    125, 127, 129, 133–7, 140, 142–3,
    145–6, 148–9, 155, 157, 160–2, 164,
    167–172, 174–6, 189, 193–4
Katz, Zev, 188
Kaufman, Howard, 155
Kawai, 204
Kay, John, 45
Kaye, Phil, 44
Kaye, Thomas Jefferson, 63
Kaylan, Howard, 41
KBCA, Los Angeles, 90
Keaton, Michael, 206
Keltner, Jim, 68, 88, 125, 128, 169, 193
Kennedy, Center, 81
Kennedy, John F., 93, 160, 164
Kent, Nick, 92
Kern, Jerome, 131
Kerouac, Jack, 9, 12
Kessel, Barney, 120
Keyboard, 198
Khan Steve, 128, 140, 143, 145, 155, 171,
    181
Khrushchev, 164
Kick Horns, 175
Kid Charlemagne, 4, 99, 103–4, 131, 212
Kind Of Blue, 174
King Of Comedy, 169

King, B.B., 11, 43
King, Carole, 34, 40
King, Clydie, 63
King Of The World, 57–8, 73, 77, 174
King, Zalman, 30, 32
Kings, 50
Kings County Carnival, The, 29–30
Kingsmen, The, 12
Kinks, The, 48, 53, 65, 79, 165
Klein, Robert, 150
Kline, Reamer, 16
KMET, 73
Knock On Wood, 187, 189
Knopfler, Mark, 135, 139
Kooper, Al, 189
Koppel, Ted, 162
Koppleman & Rubin, 15
Korvette, E.J., 8
KPFK, Los Angeles, 31–2, 115
Krantz, Wayne, 212
Kriesel, Friedrich, 177
KROQ, 183
Krueger, Freddy, 33
Kubernik, Harvey, 97, 115
Kudo III, 53
Kulee Baba, 148
Kupersmith, Marty, 27, 31, 169, 172

L'Europe Hotel, 132
LA Forum, 85
LA Free Press, 48
LA Times, 95, 205
Ladd, Jim, 64, 119
Lahaina Sound, Maui, 178
Lambert, Ed, 37, 40–1
Landisberg, Steve, 30
Landy, Elliott, 14
Lang, Fritz, 205
Lankersham Blvd, 99
LaPalm, Dick, 42, 57, 131, 157
Lasker, Jay, 37, 39, 40, 43, 45–6, 60

Lauper, Cyndi, 190
Laverne, Andy, 187
Lawson, Ricky, 212, 214–6
Layla, 68
Lazerus, Daniel, 161, 164, 166, 168, 170–2, 179
Lazy Nina, 172
Leary, Timothy, 104
Leather Canary, 12
Led Zeppelin, 122
Ledgerwood Leanne, 187
Lee, Will, 137, 139, 155, 164
Leiber & Stoller, 18, 34, 66, 159
Leiber, Jerry, 29
Lennon & McCartney, 206
Lennon, John, 68, 133
Leon, Mark, 23
Leone, Sergio, 49
Leonhart, Michael, 215
Let George Do It, 18, 24–5, 169
Let's Lock The Door, 27
Levine, Joseph, 34
Levy, Morris, 35
Lewis, Jerry Lee, 8
Lewis, Jimmy, 54, 76
Liddy, Gordon, 15
Lido Shuffle, 193
Lifschutz, Richie, 17–8
Lift Me Up, 171
Light And Shade, 178
Like A Rolling Stone, 13
Lincoln Center, 75
Linn, Roger, 139
Lipuma, Tommy, 181
Little Big Band, 184, 187–91
Little Darlin', 189
Little, Kawai, 211
Little Richard, 13
Loche, Federico, 30
Locke, Peter, 30–2
Lone Star Roadhouse, 182–3, 197

Long As You Know You're Living Yours, 144
Long Island, Evian Music Festival, 187
Long Way Down, 34
Look At Granny Run Run, 183
Looking Glass, 55
Lord, Tariq, 213
Lost Tribe, The, 209
Love Will Make It Right, 170
Love You Live, 114
Lovelle, Herb, 14–5, 100
Lovin' Spoonful, 15
Lowdown, 193
Lubow, Arthur, 43
Lucille, 13
Lucky, Henry, 211
Lundon, Eddie, 174–5, 178
Lurie, Elliott, 55

Mack, Charles, 19
Madison Square Garden, 203
Madison Time, 189
Magic Smile, 176
Magna-tism, 131
Magnaplaners, 70
Mahavishnu Orchestra, 65
Mahler, Gus, 47
Mailer, Norman, 30
Mamas And Papas, 37, 45
Mamet, David, 193
Man Don't Give A Fuck, The, 213
Mancini, Henry, 9, 177
Mandel, Johnny, 130
Manhattan Transfer, 154
Manilow, Barry, 30
Mann, Herbie, 151–2
Manson, Charles, 29, 104
Mantovani, 122
Marge, George, 142
Marini, Lou, 183, 193
Marley, Bob, 107, 214

Marotta, Rick, 98, 100, 102, 117, 119, 172
Marshall, Julian, 169, 171
Martha And The Vandellas, 13, 27
Mary Mary 192
Marzetti, Paul, 188
Matthews, Shirley, 63
Max's Kansas City, 48
Maxine, 166, 168
Mayer, Oscar, 188
Maze, 215
Mazzi, John, 33
McCartney, Paul, 95, 203
McCoys, The, 95
McCracken, Hugh, 89, 92, 95, 144, 171
McDermott, Denny, 192, 197–8
McDonald, Ian, 73, 80
McDonald, Michael, 75, 77–9, 89, 112, 119, 184, 189, 192–3, 202
McDonald, Ross, 165
McInerney, Jay, 180
McKaie, Andy, 191, 205
McKenna, Kristine, 149, 150
McNamara, Dennis, 106
McNeil, Paul, 35
McPike, Gary, 54, 76, 79
Me Myself & Irene, 216
Meade, Norman, 182
Media Sound Studios, New York, 170–1
Medical Science, 209
Medow, Evan, 41
Meet Me In The Morning, 214
Megashine City, 54, 78
Meher, Tim, 180
Melody Maker, 45, 62, 73, 77, 92, 108, 113, 115, 126, 135, 149–50
Mendelsohn, John, 92
Mercer, Johnny, 131
Mercury, Eric, 34
Metal Leg, 205
Metheny, Pat, 202

Metropolis, 205
Michelangelo, 135
Midnight Special, 56
Midnite Cruiser, 40, 50
Miley, Bubber, 70
Milland, Ray, 58
Miller, Marcus, 181
Miller, Mitch, 150
Miller, Steve, 80
Mimms, Garnett, 182
Mingus, Charles, 8–9, 29, 88, 90, 1??
Minute By Minute, 184, 189
Mister Micawber, 17
Mitchell, Joni, 88
Mobile Home, 73, 77–8, 80
Mock Turtle Song, The, 18, 24
Modern Drummer, 88, 102, 125
Modern Music Studios, 62
Mojo, 210, 216
Mona Lisa Overdrive, 199
Monk, Thelonious, 8, 50, 152, 155, 160–1, 171
Monkees, The, 192
Monkey In Your Soul, 72
Moon, Keith, 111
Moon, Tom, 210
Moranis, Rick, 197
More Than A Feeling, 132
More To Come, 20
Morongell, Mike, 165
Morricone, Ennio, 177
Morrison, Van, 14, 24, 104, 109
Morton, Rocky, 167
Mose The Fireman, 206
Mothers (Frank Zappa And The), 80
Motortown, 177
Motown, 125, 133
Mounsey, Rob, 135, 137–8, 140, 169, 180, 198
Mount Hood Jazz Festival, Oregon, 157
Mr Fantasy, 10

Mr Lyle, 29
Mr Sam, 89
Mt Belzoni, 164
Murdoch, Rupert, 177
Museum of Rock Art, 110
Music For Big Pink, 32
Music Gig, 114
Musician, 134, 143, 149, 190, 210
Mustang Sally, 210
My Boyfriend's Back, 62
My Old School, 59, 61, 77, 192, 203–4
My Rival, 143
My Sportin' Life, 45
Myddle Class, 46

NAACP, 12
Nabokov, Vladimir, 29, 198
Naha, George, 183
Naked Lunch, The, 4, 9, 42–3, 67, 70
Nanton, Tricky Sam, 70
Napoleon, 71, 80
Napoleonic Museum, 110
Narziss & Goldmund, 10
Nashville Skyline, 14
Navasota, 41–2
Negative Girl, 216
New Frontier, 159, 164, 167
New Musical Express, 73, 76–7, 80, 82,
    92, 94, 107, 110, 112–13, 126,
    149
New Times, 43
New York club gigs, 184–9
New York Magazine, 183
New York Nights, 191
New York Post, 33
New York Rock & Soul Revue, 5, 95, 184,
    189, 192, 197, 199–202, 208
New York Times, The, 8, 149–50, 155
Newman, David 'Fathead', 183
Newport Jazz, 7
Newsweek, 112

Nichols, Roger, 44–6, 57, 60, 63, 69–72,
    86, 96–7, 99, 101, 110, 122–3, 130,
    136–7, 143, 145–6, 152, 154,
    161–3, 167, 171–2, 178–9, 186–91,
    194, 196–7, 198–9, 203, 204, 211,
    213
Nicholson, Gary, 189
Nicks, Stevie, 155
Nico, 13
Night By Night, 68, 72, 75
Night Owl, The, 13
Nightbird And Co, 50
Nightfly, The, 5, 7, 66, 92, 157–168, 169,
    174, 179–80, 186, 194–5, 197, 200,
    203–5, 209
Nightmare On Elm Street, 33
96 Tears, 22
Nugent, Ted, 67
Number, One, 29–30
Nylon Curtain, The, 162

O'Connell, Helen, 7
Oasis, 214
Odo, Vinnie, 24
Odyssey, 62
Oh Green Dolphin Street, 164
Oh Wow, It's You, 20
Old Grey Whistle Test, The, 75
Old Regime, 24, 169
Oldham, Spooner, 189
Omartian, Michael, 67–70, 72, 85–6,
    88–91, 93, 120–1, 132, 165, 174
On The Dunes, 188, 195, 197, 199
On The Mend, 169
One Ticket To LA, 29
Only A Fool Would Say That, 50–1
Oor, 132
Original Soundtrack, The, 31
Osbourne, Ozzy, 67
Ostin, Mo, 198–9
Our, Lawn, 203

Pacino, Al, 106
Page, Jimmy, 50
Paich, David, 93
Paich, Marty Dektette, 181
Palace Theatre, Manchester, 76,
    79–80
Palma, Brian de, 33
Palmer, David, 46, 48, 54–7, 60, 62–3,
    68, 78
Palmer, Robert, 131, 143, 155
Panic In The Year Zero, 58
Papua, 174
Pareles, Jon, 134
Park Lane Hotel, 149
Parker, Charlie, 11, 14, 29, 82, 89–90,
    115, 125, 131, 145, 207
Parker, Chris, 196, 198,
Parker's Band, 18, 20, 22, 29, 64, 68, 73,
    207–8
Parkgate Studio, Sussex, 174
Parks, Dean, 67, 70, 91–2, 106, 128, 169,
    209, 211
Parliament-Funkadelic, 208
Patton, Charley, 172
Pearl Of The Quarter, 58, 61
Peel, John, 61
Peer Southern, 19, 31
Peg, 116–9, 122–3, 125, 153, 203, 213–4,
    216
Penn, Dan, 189
People Go To Be Free, 189
Peretti, Hugo, 34
Performance Magazine, 203
Perkins, Barney, 99
Perowsky, Ben, 210
Perry, Richard, 29, 34, 172
Peter, Camezzind, 10
Peter Gunn, 9
Phalen, Michael, 214
Phillinganes, Greg, 164–5, 172
Phillips, Simon, 193

Piece Of My Heart, 182–3, 187
Pilgrim's Progress, The, 200
Pillow, 14
Pink Floyd, 122
Planet Records, 172
Poetry Man, 184
Pohl, Frederik, 199
Pomus, Doc, 27
Porcaro, Jeff, 66–8, 73, 75, 77–81, 88–9,
    100, 105, 112, 117, 140, 164, 166,
    169, 170, 172, 193, 204
Porcaro, Joe, 68
Porky, 62–3
Potter, Chris, 216
Premiere, 9, 177
Preminger, Otto, 8
President Street Pete, 50
Presley, Elvis, 8, 182
Pretzel Logic (song), 56, 69,
Pretzel Logic, 64–84, 86, 88, 92, 108,
    136, 158, 184, 187, 189
Pretzel, Paul, 82
Prince, 180, 195
Probe Records, 45, 80
Procol Harum, 51
Producers Workshop, Los Angeles, 117,
    133
Proud To Be Your Slave, 40
Pryor, Richard, 30, 33
Pulse, 172
Purdie, Bernard, 69, 98–102, 104, 106,
    112, 117, 136, 214
Purple Haze, 187
Putney Swope, 33

Q, 204, 205
Quaid, Dennis, 167
Quantum, 44
? And The Mysterians, 22
Quicksand, 189
Quinlan, Lawrence, 15

Rabbit Ears Records, 206

Radio Free Steely Dan, 115

Radio Luxembourg, 61, 80

Rafferty, Gerry, 55

Ragavoy, Jerry, 14, 182–3

Rain King, 128

Rainbow Theatre, 76, 79–80

Rainey, Chuck, 14, 67–8, 88, 99, 102–3, 105, 112, 117, 119–20, 128, 157–8, 164, 167, 169, 214

Randall, Elliott, 50, 92, 106, 169

Ransohoff, Richard, 17, 36

Rapunzel, 131

Rascals, The, 98, 183, 189

Ray, Johnnie, 182

Reach Out, I'll be There, 21

Record Mirror, 76, 80

Record Plant, Los Angeles, 73

Recording Engineer & Producer, 162

Records And Recording, 62

Red Giant Music, 38

Red Giant, White Dwarf, 32

Red Hook, 32

Red Letter Day, 179

Red Roosters, 11

Redbone, Leon, 216

Redding, Noel, 187

Redding, Otis, 21

Reed, Jimmy, 180

Reed, Lou, 65

Reelin' And Rockin', 7

Reelin' In The Years, 50, 51, 56, 77, 80, 96, 128, 151, 158, 193, 202, 208

Reflections (Thelonious Monk song), 171

Reflections (Warren Bernhardt song), 207

Reunion, 181

Rich, Buddy, 23

Richardson, Jerome, 49, 157

Richfield Coliseum, 202

Richmond, Dannie, 9, 88

Rikki Don't Lose That Number, 67, 71–2, 75, 77, 81, 92, 128, 144, 151, 158, 183, 202, 206

Ritenour Lee, 128

River Sound, New York, 189, 199, 214–5

Roachford, 177

Roaring Of The Lamb, 19–20, 34

Roberts, Ken, 28

Robertson, Keith , 76

Robertson, Robbie, 32, 169

Roccisano, Joe, 131, 157, 179, 193

Rock Me, 177

Rodeo Girl, 182

Rodgers & Hart, 157

Roe, Tommy, 37–8

Rogers, Adam, 211

Rogers, Kenny, 44

Roll Back The Meaning, 31

Rolling Stone (magazine), 51, 62, 67, 74, 84, 92, 132, 142, 167, 182, 190

Rolling Stones, The, 8, 114, 130

Rollins, Sonny, 8, 82, 90, 152, 160, 188

Ronk, Dave van, 12

Ronstadt, Linda, 83, 123

Room 335, 118

Root Boy Slim, 133

Rootin', 41–2

Rose Darling, 89, 91–2

Rose, Howard, 76

Rosenberg, Mark, 180

Ross, Annie, 191

Ross, Diana, 125, 170

Ross, Ricky, 206

Rotoscope Down, 73

Roulette Records, 35

Royal Scam, The (album), 98–113, 114–6, 121, 123, 126, 132, 143, 202–3, 208–10, 214

Royal Scam, The (song), 107–8

Rubenstein, Raenne, 73

Rubin, Alan, 183

Rubinstein, Jerry, 124, 166
Ruby Baby, 66, 159, 161, 165–6, 174
Rumours, 123
Rundgren, Todd, 171
Russell, Catherine, 185
Russell, Norman, 182
Ryan, Meg, 167

634–5789, 185
Sachs, Annexe, 15
Sail The Waterway, 45, 129, 205
Saints, The, 21
Sam And Dave, 21, 187
San Francisco Examiner, 204
Sanborn, David, 169, 181
Sanders, Zack, 155
Sands Of Time, 29
Santa Monica Civic, 62, 81, 83, 85, 110
Satellites, 181
Scaggs, Boz, 129, 189, 192–3, 203, 204, 208
Scelsa, Vin, 189
Scheiner, Elliott, 69, 98–100, 106, 116, 122, 132, 137, 140, 143, 146, 155, 172, 197
Schleifer, Lincoln, 188, 192, 197
Schlitz, 51–2
Schmit, Tim, 130
Schmitt, Al, 117, 157, 179
Schroeder, Aaron, 29
Schuman, Mort, 27
Scoppa, Bud, 74
Scorsese, Martin, 169
Scott, Little Jimmy, 191
Scott, Tom, 119, 198
Scrapple From The Apple, 125
Second Arrangement, The, 137–8, 145, 148, 212
Selvin, Joel, 204
Set In Motion, 178
Setzer, Brian Orchestra, The, 216

Sex Pistols, The, 122
Shades, 178
Shaffer, Paul, 187
Shakespeare Stole My Baby, 170
Shakey Ground, 184, 189
Shangai Breakdown, 122
Shanghai Confidential, 180–1, 197
Shapiro, Michael, 84
Shapiro, Susan, 114
She Cried, 18
Sheppard, Bob, 187
Sherman, Garry, 99
Shirelles, The, 27
Shoreline Amphitheater, 204
Shorter, Wayne, 120, 128
Show Biz Kids, 57, 60–1, 64, 77, 213
Shuffling Up Your Downs, 19, 29–30
Siddhartha, 10
Sigma Sound, New York, 133
Sign In Stranger, 100, 106, 157, 190, 208
Signorelli, Jimmy, 21
Sill, Joel, 180
Silver, Horace, 72, 144
Simmons, Sylvie, 123
Simon & Schuster, 177
Simon, Carly, 68
Simon, Joe, 184, 189
Simon, Paul, 95, 133
Simple, Dreams, 123
Sims, Sylvia, 7
Siner, Bob, 153
SIR Studios, New York, 202
Slade, 53, 62, 82
Slim Harpo, 210
Slyde, Hyde, 157
Smith, Giles, 198, 212
Smith, Martin, 214
Smoke Gets In Your Eyes, 184
Snow, Phoebe, 183–5, 189, 192
Snowbound, 195–8, 204
Snyder, 29

Solar, 207

Soledad On My Mind, 43

Solitary Man, 27

Some Change, 208

Song For My Father, 72, 144

Sonny & Cher, 68

Sony Studios, 216

Soothe Me, 184, 187

Sopwith Camel, 62, 82

Soul Ram, 4, 22, 29, 42

Soule, Jenny, 62

Sounds, 51, 61, 124

Soundstream, 146

Soundworks, New York, 133, 137, 143,
    155, 159, 164, 167, 170, 172

Speak Low, 144

Spector, Phil, 13

Spielberg, Steven, 161

Spirit, 11, 51

Sportsman's Lodge, 43

Springfield, Dusty, 89

Springtime, 196, 215

Squash Lesson, 181

Stage Deli, 137

Stand By The Seawall, 22, 121–2

Stanhope Hotel, New York, 133

Standing On The Shoulder Of Giants,
    214

Stanley, Karen, 138, 210

Starkweather, Charlie, 29

Stealers Wheel, 55

Steele, Alison, 51

Steele, Jeveeta, 183

Steeleye Span, 51

Steely Dan influence on UK 80s bands,
    177

Steely Dan Orchestra, 6

Steig Jeremy, 187

Steppenwolf, 45

Stereo Review, 62, 74

Stewart, Rod, 207

Stigers, Curtis, 191

Stills, Stephen, 51

Stoller, Mike, 29

Stone Piano, 14, 18

Stone, Sly, 28, 188, 197

Stoner, Rob, 153

Stop!, 183

Storytellers, 217

Stranger By Nature, 179

Stravinksy, 198

Streisand, Barbra, 34

Struttin', 133

Stuck In The Middle With You, 55

Studio 54, 24, 166

Subterranean Homesick Blues, 14, 15

Such A Night, 182

Sumlin, Hubert, 143

Sunday And Me, 18

Sunday Night, 181

Super Furry Animals, 213

Supremes, The, 68

Surf and/or Die, 210

Surreal, 29

Sutherland, Sam, 148–9

Swedish Schnapps, 29

Sweet Charity In Adoration, 179

Sweet Love, 214

Symphony, Sid, 8

10cc, 109

Take A Dip With Dinah, 29

Take It Out On Me, 20

Take My Money, 54, 78

Takin' It To The Streets, 193

Talk Radio, 158

Teahouse On The Tracks, 197, 204

Telegraph, The, 212

Tell It To The Fat Man, 19, 30

Tell Me A Lie, 39

Telson, Bob, 171

Temptations, The, 13

Tequila, 82
Thanksgiving Soul Party, 183–4
That's The Way I Feel Now, 171
The Gentleman Loser, 199
Theme From A Summer Place, 77
There Goes My Baby, 27
Third World Man, 137, 145, 153, 166,
    193, 203, 212
This Magic Moment, 18, 27
This Moody Bastard, 211
This Time Around, 178
Thomas, Keith, 21–5, 28, 35–6
Thompson, Hunter, 67
Thorne, Mike, 179
Three Dog Night, 37, 39, 46, 53
Through With Buzz, 64, 71, 84, 92
Throw Back The Little Ones, 91–2
Thundering Herd, 131
Time Is On My Side, 182–3
Time Out of Mind, 81, 135, 141, 143,
    153
Times, The, 212
Titus, Libby, 5, 182–3, 191, 197
Toccata And Fugue, 59
Tommy, 18
Tomorrows Girls, 188, 196, 199, 201,
    205, 207
Tonight Show, 20, 121, 131,
Tonto, 175, 193
Too Sick to Reggae, 133
Torme, Mel, 181
Torres, Liz , 30
Toto, 140
Traffic, 10, 68
Trans Island Skyway, 195, 199, 204–5
Trans Texas Airlines, 33
Travelling Light, 178
Traynor, John 'Jay', 18
Triloka, 187
Trip, The, 195
Tripstar, 194

True Companion, 155, 158, 169, 190
Turn My Friend Away, 35
Turn That Heartbeat Over Again, 50
Turner, Mary, 159
Turner, Pete, 132
Turtles, The, 41
Tuzz's, Shadow, 207
Twelfth Street Productions, 41
Twist And Shout, 182–3
Two Against Nature (album), 207–217
Two Against Nature (song), 215
Tyler Steve, 115

U2, 214
UK gigs, 76–80
Ukiah Medical Center, 187
Ultimate Spinach, 35
Undecided, 25
Under The Ice House, 48
United Artists, 30
Uriah Heep, 53, 82
US 1974 gigs, 80–84
USA Today, 202

Valentine, Penny, 51
Valley Sound, 59
Van Halen, 203
Van Ness, Chris, 48
Vance, Kenny, 18–22, 25, 27–38, 46, 105,
    169, 172
Variety, 33, 48
Vela, Rosie, 175–6
Velvet Underground, 13
Village Recorder, Los Angeles, 41–2, 46,
    50, 57, 59, 67, 70, 85, 115, 118, 131,
    137, 158, 162, 165, 175
Village Vanguard, 9
Village Voice, 20–1
Virgin, 178–9
Visa Records, 32
Visions Of Johanna, 66

Vivino, Jerry, 185
Vivino, Jimmy, 185, 188–91
Volante, Tony, 186
Volman, Mark, 41

WABC-FM, Los Angeles, 153
Wadenius, Georg, 198, 208
Wakeman, Rick, 68
Walk Between Raindrops, 140, 161, 164, 168, 181
Walls, Rich, 126
Walsh, Ed, 155
Walsh, Joe, 43
War And Peace, 32
Ward Manor, 13, 16
Warner Bros, 97, 114, 124–5, 129, 133, 147
Warnes, Jennifer, 172
Warren, Wallace, 56, 60, 121
Warwick, Dionne, 131
Was Not Was, 171
Watergate, 15
Watts, Ernie, 157
Watts, Michael, 108, 113
Weather Report, 202
Weill, Kurt, 29, 144
Weingarten, Marc, 208
Welch, Chris, 77
Welcome, 34
Wendel, 101, 139, 152, 161, 166, 172
Were You Blind That Day?, 122, 145
West Of Hollywood, 216
West Side Story, 16, 23, 212, 215
Weston, Tim, 133, 179
Westwood, 167
What A Shame About Me, 215, 217
Whisky A Go Go, 54
White, Dorothy, 15, 17, 31, 60, 86, 197
White, Michael, 215
White, Trash, 95

Whitney Museum, New York, 159
Who Got the Credit?, 14–5
Who's Next, 214
Who, The, 214
Wiest, Diane, 180
Wilco, 216
Williams, Buddy, 198
Williams, Joe, 59
Williams, Stephen, 180
Williams, Tony, 120
Willman, Chris, 204
Willner, Hal, 171
Wilson, 8
Wilson, Danny, 177
Wind Cries Mary, 193
Windham Hill, 187, 205
Wingate Music, 38
Wings, 95
Winter, Edgar, 95
Winwood, Steve, 24
With A Gun, 72, 106
With A Little Help From My Friends, 193
Withers, Bill, 187
WLIR-FM, 89, 106
WNEW-FM , 182
Wolf, Howlin', 11, 143, 172, 210
Wolfe, Randy, 11
Wolfe, Tom, 67
Wolverine, 59
Wonder, Stevie, 125, 162
Wood, Herb, 125
Woodford, David, 133
Woods, Phil, 86, 91, 165
Working With Fire And Steel, 174
WXRQ-FM, 189

Yamaguchi, Saeko, 130
Yamaha, 127
Yellow Peril, 22, 29
Yes, 82, 122

Yongue, Lonnie, 9–10, 17, 58
You Better Hang Up, 193
You Got Me Hummin', 187
You Gotta Walk it Like You Talk It, 30,
    32–3, 130
You Really Got Me, 165
Young, Connie, 210
Young Jeff, 183–5, 189
Your Gold Teeth, 59–60, 91, 215
Your Gold Teeth II, 73, 86, 88, 91–2

Yurgelun Wayne, 163, 189

Zappa, Frank, 12, 33, 44, 75
Zazu, 176
Zingg, Drew, 184, 197, 202–3, 205,
    208
Zoo World, 83
Zoom, 137
Zox, 109
ZZ Top, 42

10/07 (41783)